PENGUIN

THE POEM OF THE KILLING OF MEGHNAD

Michael Madhusudan Dutt (1824-1873) was born in the Jessore district of Bengal. His Persian-educated father, a pleader in Calcutta's law-courts, brought his family to the city, and Madhusudan was sent to Hindu College to acquire an English education. In 1843 he converted to Christianity, and moved to Bishop's College, where he studied Latin and Greek. In 1848 he moved to Madras, where he worked as a teacher and journalist, and married an Anglo-Indian woman. He left her and their four children for Amelia Henrietta White, the daughter of an English colleague at the school where he taught. She joined him in Calcutta in 1858, and lived with him thereafter, bringing up three children by him.

Madhusudan initially had ambitions as a poet in English, but on returning in 1856 to Calcutta embarked on his career as a dramatist and poet in Bengali, earning his living as an Interpreter and Clerk in the Police Court. After a legal battle to secure his inheritance, he sailed to England in 1862, to read for the Bar at Gray's Inn. The financial arrangements he had made to pay for this went wrong, and he moved his family to Versailles. He was saved from destitution by Ishwarchandra Vidyasagar.

On returning to Calcutta again in 1867, Madhusudan found it difficult to practise as a barrister. Extravagance and alcoholism overcame him, and he died three days after Henrietta. They were buried in Lower Circular Road Cemetery. A bust of Madhusudan was installed there in the 1950s.

William Radice has pursued a double career as a poet and as a scholar and translator of Bengali. Well known for his translations of the poems and stories of Tagore, he has also published nine books of his own poems. He has been a lecturer in Bengali at SOAS, University of London since 1988. His literary work in recent years has included opera libretti, and his many books include *Myths and Legends of India*, *Teach Yourself Bengali* and *A Hundred Letters from England*. His work on Madhusudan began in the 1980s with his Oxford D.Phil thesis.

The Poem of the Killing of Meghnād

(*Meghnādbadh kābya*)

Michael Madhusudan Dutt

Translated with an Introduction and Notes
by
William Radice

PENGUIN BOOKS
An imprint of Penguin Random House

PENGUIN BOOKS

USA | Canada | UK | Ireland | Australia
New Zealand | India | South Africa | China

Penguin Books is part of the Penguin Random House group of companies
whose addresses can be found at global.penguinrandomhouse.com

Published by Penguin Random House India Pvt. Ltd
4th Floor, Capital Tower 1, MG Road,
Gurugram 122 002, Haryana, India

Penguin Random House India

First published in Penguin Books India 2010

10 9 8 7 6 5 4 3 2

ISBN 9780143414131

Typeset in Sabon by Eleven Arts, New Delhi
Printed at Repro India Limited

www.penguin.co.in

to
R. K. DasGupta
Tapan Raychaudhuri
Ghulam Murshid
and
to all young people worldwide
tomrā sakale tribhuban-jayī raṇe
(*MBK* VII.229–30)

CONTENTS

MADHUSUDAN'S EMBLEM

from Dinanath Sanyal (ed.), *Meghnād-badh kābya*
(S. C. Sanyal & Co., Kolkata, 1917)

INTRODUCTION

nil parvum aut humili modo,
    nil mortale loquar.
    ('I shall utter nothing
insignificant, lowly or not immortal')

Horace, *Odes* III.25.17–18,

tr. W. G. Shepherd (Penguin, 1983), p. 158

In this view, identification with the lost person is not just another way of postponing the realization of loss; it is the necessary condition without which grief cannot end and a new identity be developed. The object is never truly given up; it is made into a part of the self.

Colin Murray Parkes, *Bereavement: Studies of Grief in Adult Life*

(third edition, Penguin, 1998), p. 103

Gora said, 'Can you follow what I am saying? That which I sought day and night to become but could not, today I have indeed become that. Today I am Bharatiya. Within me there is no conflict between communities, whether Hindu or Muslim or Krishtan. Today all the castes of Bharat are my caste, whatever everybody eats is my food . . .'

Rabindranath Tagore, *Gora*

(tr. Sujit Mukherjee, Sahitya Akademi, New Delhi, 1997), p. 475

In Nagendranath Som's *Madhusmṛti* (1916)—which along with Yogindranath Basu's *Māikel Madhusūdan Datter jībancarit* (1893) remains a primary source for all scholars and translators of Michael Madhusudan Dutt—there is a photo of a very curious document. Written in Madhusudan's rather clumsy Bengali handwriting (his English handwriting was much better) is his sonnet on Dante, which in 1865 he sent to King Victor Emmanuel II of Italy, in response to a call for poems to honour the sixth centenary of Dante's birth. Madhusudan sent his sonnet with an accompanying French translation, and an elegantly humble letter in English:

Versailles—France
12 Rue des Chantiers 12
5th May 1865

Sir,

A poor rhymer who does not dare give himself the name of a poet, born on the shores of the Ganges and a passionate admirer of the father of Italian poetry, takes the liberty of presenting at the feet of Your Majesty along with this letter, a Bengali sonnet, a little oriental flower which he wishes to join to the garland to be wreathed in Italy, for decorating the tomb of the illustrious Dante.

Of your Majesty, The very humble Servant,
Michael Madhusudan Datta[1]

It was curious enough that a Bengali poet in the 1860s should be writing a sonnet on Dante and sending it from

[1]Ghulam Murshid (ed.), *The Heart of a Rebel Poet: Letters of Michael Madhusudan Dutt* (Oxford University Press, New Delhi, 2004), p. 248.

Versailles with a flawless French translation he had done himself.[2] But even more curious was the specially printed notepaper on which the sonnet was written, with an elaborate border, and at the bottom left-hand corner a mysterious heraldic emblem. Presumably designed by Madhusudan himself, the emblem consisted of a shield with a cross of St. George, surmounted by an elephant, lion, sun and *śatadal* (lotus), and a Sanskrit scroll underneath with the inscription: *śarīraṃ vā pātayeyaṃ kāryaṃ vā sādhayeyam* ('I would rather die than fail to achieve what I have set out to do'). What did this emblem mean? It had already been reproduced on the covers of most of the early editions of Madhusudan's works, though it was omitted from later editions, and to this day has not been noticed much by Madhusudan's critics and biographers. Nagendranath Som quotes a personal letter in which Dinanath Sanyal (editor of Madhusudan's masterpiece, *Meghnādbadh kābya*) attributes the omission to lack of understanding of its meaning, and gives his own interpretation.[3] The Sanskrit inscription is illuminated by the emblem above, for 'anyone who has read Madhusudan's poetry and plays will know that they are a literary fusion of east and west', and the emblem expresses that fusion. The elephant is India, the lion is Europe, the sun symbolizes Madhusudan's own personality and creative genius, and the *śatadal* is the work, the *kārya* that he was determined to complete even if it killed him.[4]

[2]For more about this sonnet, see my article, 'Michael Madhusudan Dutt (1824–1873): A Bengali Poet with Italian Connections', in Debraj Bhattacharya (ed.), *Of Matters Modern: The Experience of Modernity in Colonial and Post-colonial South Asia* (Seagull Books, Kolkata, 2008), pp. 149–72.

[3]Nagendranath Som, *Madhusmṛti* (Kolkata, 1920; second edition, 1954), p. 298.

[4]Dinanath Sanyal reproduced the emblem as the frontispiece to his

Has any poet, in any language, ever left behind a more succinct and diagrammatic indication of how he wished his works to be read? Ever since my first encounter with it, I have been convinced that the emblem is the key, and a rounded description and assessment of Madhusudan's achievement—especially in *Meghnādbadh kābya* itself—must make full use of it. But because the emblem is a fusion, with the lion and the elephant reaching out to touch both the sun and the lotus with their front legs, any attempt rigidly to separate one element from the others is doomed to failure. The three main sections that follow, though headed with the three productive elements of the emblem, will therefore return repeatedly to four main themes: Romanticism, Tragedy, Humour and Mind. Even those will often blend into each other, like the colours of a prism. But our subject, after all, is a poet, and poetry can only be grasped as a many-sided whole, elusive of reductionist analysis.

The Sun: Madhusudan's life, personality and genius

Defining Romanticism in a sentence is impossible, yet most of us can recognize it when we see it. In Madhusudan we can readily find the familiar ingredients of Romanticism: egotism, passionate love, idealization of women, worship of Nature, patriotism. It is not even necessary to go to his poems and plays to find it, as Madhusudan the romantic leaps out from the pages of his extraordinary English letters. I myself first encountered him through his letters,

---

pioneering and still indispensable edition of *Meghnādbadh kābya* (Kolkata, 1917). It had presumably been re-engraved for this purpose, with the title and author of the poem added above and below. The frontispiece to the present translation is taken from there.

and I can picture myself now, standing in 1974 between the shelves of the SOAS Library, transfixed by Kshetra Gupta's edition of them (1963). The notes to the letters were in Bengali—with their wealth of contemporary and literary allusions they need copious notes—but with the publication in 2004 of Ghulam Murshid's meticulous edition in English they have now become fully accessible to all.[5] As an epic and dramatic poet, Madhusudan was usually not directly self-revelatory in his writing, but in his letters he was under no such constraint. One can pick out sentences almost at random, and immediately feel that one is in the same room as him, so audacious, bumptious, ardent and compelling is his voice. Ranging from his student days in Kolkata, his eight years in Madras 1848–56, his brief period of literary success in Kolkata in the early 1960s, his five years in Europe 1862–7, and his final years of alcoholic decline, the letters are the main source for his biographers, and it is possible to tell the story of his life—as Murshid has done in his edition—through his letters alone:

> 25 November 1842, to Gourdas Basak
> I am reading Tom Moore's Life of my favourite Byron—a splendid book upon my word! Oh! How I should like to see you write my 'Life' if I happen to be a great poet—which I am almost sure I shall be, if I can go to England.

[5]Murshid's edition of the letters (see fn. 1 above) stemmed from his ground-breaking biography of Madhusudan in Bengali: *Āśār chalane bhuli: Māikel-jībanī* (Ananda Publishers, Kolkata, 1995; rev. 1999), which appeared in an abridged form as *Lured by Hope: A Biography of Michael Madhusudan Dutt*, translated by Gopa Majumdar (Oxford University Press, New Delhi, 2003). The three books together are an outstanding contribution to the understanding and dissemination of Madhusudan's achievement.

19 March 1849, to Gourdas Basak
The 'Captive'[6] is nearly ready—I am going to dedicate it to George Norton Esqr. the Advocate General of the Presidency and a great encourager of Literature. I wrote to him for his permission to dedicate the Poem to him and sent the whole of the 1st and part of the 2nd Cantos for his perusal. You have no idea what a kind and flattering reply I got from him. He says he will consider it an honour to have a work 'exhibiting such great powers and promise' dedicated to him. I have great hopes of his patronage. I wonder how the Calcutta critics will receive me.

?Mid-July 1858, to Gourdas Basak
Do not let me frighten you with my *audacity.* I have been showing the second Act,[7] already complete, to several persons totally ignorant of English, and I do assure you, upon my word, that they have spoken of it in terms so high that, at times, I feel disposed to question their sincerity and yet I have no reason to believe that those men would flatter me.

?1 or 2 September 1860, to Rajnarayan Basu
I never like to conceal anything from you, so that you must not think me vain if I say that in my heart I begin to believe that this Meghanad is growing up to be a splendid Poem! I fancy the versification *more Melodious* and *Virgilian* and the language easy and soft.

?15 January 1861, to Rajnarayan Basu
The poem is rising into splendid popularity. Some

[6] *The Captive Ladie*, a narrative poem in two cantos published in Madras in 1849.

[7] Of his first Bengali play, *Śarmiṣṭā* (1859).

> say it is better than Milton—but that is all bosh—nothing can be better than Milton; many say it licks Kalidasa; I have no objection to that. I don't think it impossible to equal Virgil, Kalidas and Tasso. Though glorious, still they are mortal poets; Milton is divine.
>
> ?Beginning of February 1862, to Rajnarayan Basu
> But I suppose, my poetical career is drawing to a close. I am making arrangements to go to England to study for the Bar and must bid adieu to the Muse! . . . No more Modhu the *kabi* [poet], old fellow, but Michael M. S. Dutt Esquire of the Inner Temple Barrister-at-Law!! Ha!! Ha!! Isn't that grand? But I hope I shan't be disappointed.[8]

Self-consciousness probably begins with name-consciousness, and Madhusudan had that in abundance, not only in his longing for fame and literary immortality but in his awareness of the rich possibilities that his names gave him for puns and games with identity. To his friends he was 'Modhu', which carries in Sanskrit and Bengali the meanings 'sweet, delicious, charming, pleasant' and also Spring, honey, nectar and wine. In the words of his Hindu College contemporary Bholanath Chanda:

> Modhu fully justified his name—he was all *madhu*, all that endeared one to another. No gall or acrimony in him—he was never on stilts, and always in slippers. The smile was ever on his face. He seemed to be under inspiration for twenty-four hours. Not merely was he liked by all with whom he came across, but regarded with friendship and affection. His best

[8]Murshid 2004, pp. 29, 65, 107, 144, 157 and 178.

> friend wished only that he had known a little more of the art of making money. Necessity obliged him to take to the law, in which he was out of his element.[9]

Madhusudan puns very charmingly on 'Madhu' in several places in his works, notably at the end of the invocation with which he starts his masterpiece, *Meghnādbadh kābya*;[10] and in his *Brajāṅganā kābya* (1861), his pseudo-Vaishnava lyrics about Radha's love for Krishna, he cheerfully exploits not only the fact that 'Madhusudan' or 'Sri-Madhusudan' is a name for Krishna, the 'slayer (*sūdhana*) of the demon Madhu', but also the convention that lyrics or *padas* of this kind should end with a *bhaṇitā*, a line in which the poet gives his own name. But his complex, hybrid identity also embraced the 'Michael' that he took on after his Christian baptism in 1843, and his letter before his departure for England, quoted above, revels—with more than a touch of irony—in English initials and in anglicized 'Dutt' for his *padabi* or family name 'Datta'.[11]

Passion, ebullience and enthusiasm in a poet and a man are not everyone's cup of tea, and no less a poet than Rabindranath Tagore never really warmed to his unsettling predecessor, as we shall see later in this Introduction. But for many, and especially for the opposite sex, they can be highly attractive, and the story of Madhusudan is the story of his loves: his love for women—and their love for him—

[9]Yogindranath Basu, *Māikel Madhusūdan Datter jībancarit* (Kolkata, 1893, reprint ed. Sukhamay Mukhopadhyay, Kolkata, 1978), Appendix, p. 34.

[10]See Notes, p. 5.

[11]He will probably always be known in English as 'Dutt' as well 'Datta', as he himself fluctuated between the two. In this book I have followed Ghulam Murshid in calling him 'Dutt', but in several of my articles as well as in my Oxford D.Phil thesis (1986) I called him 'Datta'.

as well as his love for poetry, Bengali, other languages, his native village of Sagardari in the Jessore district of present-day Bangladesh, grand mountains, the sea, and the many poets, places and heroes both western and eastern that he eulogized in the 102 sonnets which he wrote during his sojourn in Europe.[12] The two photos of Madhusudan that have survived, though doctored and touched up through a process of repeated reproduction, still convey his virility and charisma, the energy and pluck that drove him to be first with so many things—first to write Bengali blank verse, first Bengali to court and win not just one Englishwoman but two, first Bengali to sport Victorian 'mutton-chop' whiskers. His tone of voice, whether in English or Bengali, was something new in India—an irrepressible enthusiasm that had never been heard before.[13] Unfortunately, however, romantic ecstasy and ardour are difficult to sustain: 'As high as we have mounted in delight/ In our dejection do we sink so low', as Wordsworth famously put it,[14] and Madhusudan's life-story provides classic instances of this.

His childhood and adolescence were happy. The village of his birth and the Kapotaksha river that flowed past it were recalled with poignant nostalgia in a sonnet written twenty years later at a much less happy time:

Always, O river, you return to my mind.
Always I think of you in this isolation;

[12]See my article 'What Sort of Sonnets did Michael Madhusudan Dutt Write?', in Bhuiyan Iqbal (ed.), *Samāj o saṃskṛti: Anisujjāmāner sammāne prabandha-sambhār* [Festschrift for Anisuzzaman] (Mowla Brothers, Dhaka, 2007), pp. 409–23.

[13]I have written about the novelty of this in an article in German: 'Michael Madhusudan Datta und sein Euthusiasmus' (Beiträge des Südasien-Instituts, Humboldt-Universität zu Berlin, Heft 7, 1994), pp. 141–56.

[14]'Resolution and Independence', ll. 24–5.

Always I imagine I am soothing my ears
With your murmur (like the phantom music that people
Hear in dreams). I have seen many rivers
In many lands, but which can satisfy
This thirst for love that I feel?
You are like a stream of milk flowing from the breast
Of my birthplace. Shall I ever see you again?
Till the end of time, you will give your
Water to the sea, like a subject paying taxes to his king.
This is my prayer, that you will sing in the ears
Of the people of Bengal, friend, the name (as of a friend)
Of one who in exile sinks now in love for you
As he takes your name in Bengali verse.[15]

Several siblings died in infancy, so he became the pampered only child of a mother, Janhabi Devi, who seems to have had enough education to foster in him a love of the classics of medieval Bengali literature, and a father, Rajnarayan Datta, who knew Persian well and did well in his career, first as a clerk in a law court in Jessore, and later as a pleader in the 'Sudder' Diwani Court in Calcutta, under the Moghul-established system that the British still operated.[16] Within three years of his arrival in Calcutta, Raj Narayan had progressed to a large house in the Kidderpore suburb of Calcutta, and his wife and son joined him there in 1831.

[15] *Caturdaśpadī kabitābalī*, No. 34. My translation.

[16] In 1772 the East India Company took over the civil justice system and moved the two main courts of appeal—the Sadr Diwani Adalat for civil cases, and the Sadr Nizamat Adalat for criminal cases—from Murshidabad to Calcutta. In 1773 Lord North's Regulating Act established the Calcutta Supreme Court. In 1790 the Company took over the criminal justice system, and in 1797 Parliament gave it full legislative powers. Persian remained the language of the courts until 1837.

As a beneficiary of the new economic opportunities provided by the growing city of Calcutta, Rajnarayan, like other members of the rising Bengali elite, could see that the future lay with English, and Madhusudan was sent first to the Junior Section and then the Senior Section of Hindu College, founded in 1817 by a group of progressive Bengalis and Englishmen, and by now the unrivalled centre of English education in Bengal. Madhusudan flourished there, and certainly had the brains to become as high in social status and successful in his career as other products of the college, who had collectively come to be known as 'Young Bengal'. But on 9 February 1843, in the Old Mission Church in Calcutta, he was baptized by Archdeacon Thomas Dealtry, a socially cataclysmic step that may in time—as we shall see—have made him the poet he later became, but which also set in motion events that were personally tragic.

Imbued with Western notions of love and courtship that he had acquired through his education at Hindu College, Madhusudan converted mainly, it seems, to evade a traditional marriage to a child-bride that his parents wished to arrange. It led to an irrevocable rift not only with his family but with the whole of educated Hindu society. Despite their assiduous efforts over several decades, Christian missionaries in Bengal never achieved conversion on a large scale. The conversion of the child of a well-to-do family was particularly scandalous, and Madhusudan's Christian mentors had to incarcerate him in Fort William before the baptismal service, and place an armed guard round the church too.

Although Madhusudan was now unmarriageable in Hindu society, and could no longer perform the *śrāddha* ceremonies that a Hindu father needs after death from his son (which is why his father took on three more wives—all before Jahnabi's death in 1851—in a vain attempt to father a new heir), Rajnarayan continued to try to do his best by him, which must have made the situation all the more agonizing. He paid for Madhusudan's education to be continued at Bishop's College, Calcutta's Anglican seminary (Christians were not allowed at Hindu College), and also allowed him to make secret visits to his home from time to time, when Rajnarayan 'would entertain his apostate son with his former affection, but did not dare keep him in the house for fear of scandal.'[17] But relations seem to have broken down completely in 1847, when the monthly allowance from his father was suddenly stopped.

This forced him into his first period of exile from Bengal: his years in Madras, 1848–56. We now know from Ghulam Murshid's researches that Madhusudan had thought, on becoming a student at Bishop's College, of becoming a missionary, and was later in correspondence with the Bishop of Madras about this.[18] But a job that the Bishop offered him in 1846 was not to his liking, and letters from Alfred Street, a professor at the College, indicate that doubts arose about his religious commitment. So his move to Madras was a desperate step in the dark: he left Calcutta 'half-mad with vexation and anxiety',[19] penniless after having sold his books to pay for his passage. Establishing a livelihood for himself there, first as 'a poor "usher" in a poor school—viz. the Madras Male Asylum for the children of Europeans and their descendants',[20] and later as Second Tutor in the High School Department of the so-called

[17]Yogindranath Basu, p. 100.
[18]See Murshid 2004, p. 12–13 and 2003 [*Lured by Hope*], pp. 64–5.
[19]Letter to Gour, 14 February 1849; Mushid 2004, p. 62.
[20]Letter to Gour, 19 March 1849; Murshid 2004, p. 65.

'Madras University';[21] making himself acceptable in Madras's British and Eurasian social circles; and finding outlets for his poetry and journalism in English; all this took much effort, with doubtless many humiliations and setbacks along the way. But as with the sudden loss of his future at Hindu College, so with the life he made for himself in Madras: it could have prospered, had it not been for the second major trauma of his life.

On 31 July 1848 Madhusudan married Rebecca Thompson, daughter of an English gunner in the horse artillery brigade and his Indo-British wife.[22] Nothing is known about her as person, but he must have married her for love, confirming to Gour on 20 December 1855 upon hearing the shocking news of his father's death: 'Yes, dearest Gour, I have a fine English wife and four children.' But when he returned to Calcutta on 2 February 1856, to begin the arduous process of establishing himself yet again (and to start a protracted legal battle to secure his inheritance from grasping relatives who regarded him as an outcaste), the woman who joined him there two-and-a-half years later was not Rebecca but was Amelia Henrietta Sophia White, daughter of a colleague at the Madras University. She lived with him for the rest of his life, and brought up three children by him, but he was never

[21]Not the Madras University that exists today, which was formally constituted in 1857.

[22]Her identity has been established by Ghulam Murshid, from his study of baptismal records. On the marriage certificate, she falsely gave as her father Dugald McTavish, the Indigo Superintendant of Cuddapah, which led to confusion in Madhusudan's biographical record. He himself exaggerated his own background, describing himself as 'the only son of an advocate of the Calcutta Supreme Court'. In fact Rajnarayan was one of 400 or so pleaders attached to various courts in Calcutta. See Murshid 2004, p. 50.

able to marry her, for his marriage to Rebecca remained undissolved until her death in 1892.

Gauging whether Madhusudan was happier with Henrietta than he was with Rebecca is impossible, despite Gour's sentimental assertion in his memoir of the poet: 'He was as happy in her company as possible in this world and she was as faithful as Savitri herself.'[23] But it is inconceivable that he did not have severe and life-long pangs of regret and sorrow at the loss of his wife and children because of an impetuous adulterous affair, for this it seems to have been. When he left Rebecca—or she threw him out—their eldest daughter was only eight years old and their youngest son a baby of one year and ten months (he died three months later). He never referred to the tragedy in any surviving letter, and it appears he never had any contact with his wife and children again.

But his grief at their loss surfaced in his poetry, indirectly in great passages of *bilāp* ('lament') in *Meghnādbadh kābya*, and more directly in his famous autobiographical poem, *Ātma-bilāp* (1861), which is given in translation on pp. cxv–cxvi of this book.

Constructive, fulfilling achievement, and then tragic loss: the same pattern was repeated for a third time, when, after achieving fame and acclaim in his true vocation as a Bengali poet and dramatist, and having finally secured his patrimony, Madhusudan sailed for England on 9 June 1862. His plan was to read for the Bar at Gray's Inn, and return to Calcutta as yet another 'first'—Bengal's first London-trained barrister. He did qualify, and did return, but only after four-and-a-half years of acute financial insecurity, with feelings of loneliness and exile even greater

[23]Yogindranath Basu, Appendix, p. 19.

than he had endured in Madras. His plans for a regular income from the mortgage of his property went disastrously wrong, he had to appeal to the great Bengali educationist and philanthropist Ishwarchandra Vidyasagar for financial support, and the home he tried to set up for Henrietta and their children in Versailles became a nightmare of poverty and worry. The story of all this can be read in great detail in his collected letters, so sensitively edited and annotated by Ghulam Murshid.

Much less well documented is the final phase of Madhusudan's life, the most tragic of all. His attempts to practise as a barrister were largely unsuccessful: he was up against not only the hostility of the English judges—suspicious, no doubt, of his moral reputation and unconventional reputation as a poet—but also his own reckless extravagance and excessive drinking. He and Henrietta were forced to leave the grand house they had set up and furnished 'in French style' in Loudon Street, spent a year in humble lodgings in the Entally-Beniapukur area, and finally finished up in lodgings attached to the Uttarpara Public Library on the banks of the Hooghly north of Calcutta. Henrietta died on 26 June 1873, and Madhusudan three days later. His ever loyal friend Gourdas Basak has given us a memorable evocation of their pitiful end:

> I shall never forget the heart-rending sight I witnessed on the last occasion on which I visited Modhu in the rooms of the Uttarparah Public Library, where he was staying for a change. He was in bed, gasping under the excruciating effects of his disease, blood oozing from his mouth, his wife lying in high fever on the floor. Seeing me enter the room, Modhu sat

> up a little and burst into tears. The pitiable condition of his wife had unmanned him, he heeded not his own pangs and suffering; 'affliction in battalions' were the words he uttered. I knelt down to feel her pulse and temple; she pointed with her finger towards her husband, heaved a deep sigh and sobbed out in a low voice. 'Look to him, tend him, leave me alone. I care not to die.'[24]

This is a perfect picture of the tragic destiny that Wordsworth, in two more lines from the poem I quoted earlier, implies is inevitable for a romantic poet:

> We Poets in our youth begin in gladness;
> But thereof comes in the end despondency and
> madness.[25]

But more true to character, perhaps, is a story told by another of Madhusudan's friends, Manmohan Ghosh, who arrived once before mid-day to find Madhusudan already drinking neat spirits. He expressed his horror, and Madhusudan agreed it was suicidal, but commented it was better than cutting one's throat ('This is a process equally sure, but less painful.')[26]

This anecdote is convincing because of its humour. All the Hindu College friends whose reminiscences of the poet were collected by Yogindranath Basu in an Appendix to his biography recall his qualities of charm, wit and humour—a warmth and openness that struck Bhudeb Mukhopadhyay the very first time he met him:

[24]Yogindranath Basu, Appendix, pp. 20–1.
[25]'Resolution and Independence', ll. 48–9.
[26]Nagendranath Som, p. 388, and Yogindranath Basu, p. 474.

> While all this conversation was going on between me and Ramchandra Babu [teacher of Bengali at Hindu College], I noticed that one of the boys in the class had his eyes fixed on me with particular intensity. Though dark in colour, the boy was of handsome appearance, with a vigorous physique, a broad brow, and eyes that were large and very bright. He had a very intelligent and determined look about him. His keen gaze continued to fall on me at intervals during the rest of the day's classes, and when school was over he came straight up to me and asked, '*Bhāi*, what is your name, where do you live' and so on. So charmed was I by his pleasant way of speaking and courtesy, that one by one I answered all his questions.[27]

Gourdas Basak also singles out the eyes:

> He, like Krishna of old, was dark in complexion, but handsome in features, with eyes beaming with expression. His sparkling wit and brilliant repartee were to him the flute, as it were, with which he charmed and enthralled. It was the poetry of his soul, the music in the fibres of his composition, that made everyone gravitate towards him. The magic of his conversation, the sweetness of his manners, acted like electricity upon those who associated with him. When he was in your presence, you could never open your mouth; you would only hear him talk, laugh and break your sides with laughter. He was a universal favourite. Once met he was always and ever afterwards, 'Hail fellow, well met.'[28]

[27]Yogindranath Basu, Appendix, p. 22.
[28]Ibid., p. 19.

There was humour in his games with clothes and perfumes and hairstyles, and concomitant with his famous extravagance ('Look at my beautiful hairstyle—I payed a whole *mohur* for it')[29] was a spontaneous generosity (Bhudeb Mukhopadhyay recalls how when his impecunious Brahmin Pandit father became unable to afford the five rupees a month college fee, Madhu immediately offered to pay it).[30] The extravagance and generosity were ultimately to become self-destructive, as did his love of food, drink and tobacco, but his attractiveness of personality survived throughout his life. He seemed incapable of bearing grudges. Gour recalls how on his return from Europe, the 'scurvy treatment' that his traitorous agent Digambar Mitra had dealt him while he was away, 'would, in any other case, have led not only to open rupture but to a mortal severance, but Madhu forgave and forgot, as if nothing had occurred.'[31]

Madhusudan could be very deliberately witty and humorous in his writings, but that is true of many writers (such as Tagore) who in other places are earnest, melancholy, spiritual or solemn. What is so striking is a quality of wit and gaiety that runs through all his writing, whether in Bengali or English, and however tragic or sublime his theme. Always with Madhusudan, *Le style est l'homme.* This will already have been sensed from the extracts I have quoted from his letters. His love of exclamation marks is fundamental, so much so that in the translation of *Meghnādbadh kābya* that follows this Introduction I have

[29]Another famous anecdote, recalled by Yogindranath Basu, pp. 53–4, and quoted by many other writers. *Mohurs*—gold coins of the Moghul era—still circulated and were even struck by the East India Company till the 1840s.

[30]Yogindranath Basu, Appendix, p. 23.

[31]Ibid, pp. 19–20.

preserved every single one.[32] But examine almost any piece of writing by him, and you will find linguistic games going on that are characteristic not only of him but also the entire subversive, eclectic, ambivalent, hybrid culture of the nineteenth century Bengal Renaissance. It was a culture formed by an elite, a 'babu' class who acquired through English education a knowledge of Western ideas, manners and literature; who developed Bengali as a vehicle for modern literary and social expression, but who also mastered English; who moulded their growing nationalist identity out of diverse elements in the Hindu, Sanskrit, medieval, Persian or Moghul past, but with more than a dash of the Western detachment from indigenous traditions that their British rulers had.

Here is Madhusudan writing to Gour at midnight on 27 November 1843 at a moment of severe personal crisis: the conflict with his parents over their choice of bride for him. The detachment from traditional marriage customs is expressed not only in the sheer fact he is writing in English but in the wit and flamboyance of all the direct and concealed quotations from writers with a very different attitude to love, courtship and marriage:

> It is the hour for writing love-letters since all around, now, is love-inspiring. But alas! The heart that 'Melancholy marks for her own' imparts its own morbid hues to all around it; and how can I, the most wretched being, on whom yon 'refulgent lamp

[32] I have written elsewhere about Madhusudan's use of the exclamation marks as a token of the differences between him and Tagore. See 'Confession Versus the Exclamation Mark: Why Rabindranath Tagore did Not Like the Poetry of Michael Madhusudan Dutt', *Temenos Academy Review* 8, London, 2005, pp. 167–83.

> of night' now shines, write love-letters or gay letters? You don't know the weight of my afflictions. I wish (Oh! I really wish) that somebody would hang me! At the expiration of three months from hence I am to be married; dreadful thought! It harrows up my blood and makes my hair stand like quills on the fretful porcupine! My betrothed is the daughter of a rich zemindar;—poor girl! What a deal of misery is in store for her in ever-inexorable womb of Futurity! You know my desire for leaving this country is too firmly rooted to be removed. The sun may forget to rise, but I cannot remove it from my heart. Depend on it—in the course of a year or two more—I must either be in England or cease 'to be' at all;—*one of these must be done*! You are my friend, Gour! I disclose these secrets to you, without the slightest fear of their ever seeing the light: *You are a gentleman.*[33]

'Melancholy marks for her own' is (almost) from Gray's 'Elegy Written in a Country Churchyard'; 'refulgent lamp of night' is from Pope's translation of the *Iliad* (Book VIII, l.687); 'It harrows up my blood' etc. is from *Hamlet* Act I Scene 4; and 'to be' is also of course from the most famous speech in *Hamlet*. A young Bengali writing to a fellow-Bengali in the 1840s in this way assumes a shared and very special educational background, and really everything Madhusudan wrote requires a special range of literary and linguistic knowledge for its appreciation—a range that it is very hard for any one reader to possess. Not for nothing did *Tilottamāsambhab kābya* ('The Poem of the Origin of Tilottamā', 1860; a poem in four books that is a kind of

[33]Murshid 2004, pp. 32–3.

trial run for *Meghnādbadh kābya*) bear on its title-page the epigraphs: 'Neque te ut miretur turba labores, contentus paucis lectoribus' from Horace, and 'Fit audience find—tho' few' from Milton.[34]

Tilottamāsambhab kābya is about the threat posed by the demons Sunda and Upasunda, who have driven Indra and the other gods out of heaven. They are only defeated after Visvakarma, the supreme architect of the universe, fashions a perfectly beautiful woman, who is called Tilottamā because she is made *til til laiya*—'bit by bit', i.e. her separate parts are made out of all the most beautiful things in Nature. Sunda and Upasunda both fall for her, fight over her and kill each other, so that their gods are then able to rout the demon-army and repossess heaven. The witty and sensuous description in Book IV of Madhusudan's poem of Visvakarma putting Tilottomā together from 'things inanimate, animate and spiritual—anything he recalled'[35] can be taken as an allegory of Madhusudan's own poetic craftsmanship. It is a style that can create the highest poetic effects, but can also be applied to out-and-out farce and humour. In 1860, during rehearsals for Madhusudan's first play *Śarmiṣṭā*, the brothers Raja Ishwarchandra Singh and Raja Pratapchandra Singh, who had commissioned the play and were mounting it with no expense spared at their newly-formed Belgachia Theatre, wrote to Madhusudan raising the idea of 'some domestic farces . . . just to show the public that we can act the sublime and ridiculous both at the same time and with the same

[34]'Do not work for the crowd to admire you, [be] content with a few readers.' Horace, *Satires*, I.10, ll. 73–4. The Milton quotation is from *Paradise Lost*, VII.31.

[35]*sthābar, jaṅgam, bhūt yata . . . yāhāre smarilā* (*Tilottamāsambhab kābya*, III.571–2).

actors.'[36] The two farces that Madhusudan quickly wrote, *Ekei ki bale sabhyatā* ('Is this called civilization?') and *Buṛa sāliker ghāṛe rõ* ('A ruff on the neck of an old myna-bird') proved to be rather too near the bone, the first being a satire on the debating-clubs and 'learned societies' of the babus who would be its likely audience, and the second being an assault on Hindu orthodox hypocrisy. They were published by the Rajas, and rehearsals commenced, but then had to be called off, with the first play not performed till 1865 and the second not at all in Madhusudan's lifetime. In *Ekei ki bale sabhyatā*, Madhusudan's linguistic eclecticism makes hilarious use of English itself. The effect is not really translatable, but by putting the English words in inverted commas one can convey something of its flavour. The setting of the play is a meeting of the *Jñānataraṅgiṇī Sabhā* ('Wave of Knowledge Society'). In this brief extract, two of its members, Naba and Kali, have arrived late:

Enter Naba and Kali.

All: (*rising to their feet*) 'Hip, hip, hooray!'

Kali: (*drunkenly*) 'Hooray, hooray.'

Naba: Sit down, friends, everyone sit down. (*They all sit.*) Friends, you must 'excuse' us for being late—we were held up by some work we had to do.

Sibu: (*drunkenly*) 'That's a lie.'

Naba: (*angrily*) 'What?' Are you calling me a 'liar'? Do you want me to 'shoot' you?

Chaitan: (*forcing Naba to sit down*) Oh leave it, leave it—why quarrel over such a 'trifling' matter?

[36]Letter quoted by Nagendranath Som, p. 101.

Naba: 'Trifling?' To call me a 'liar'—is that 'trifling'? Why didn't he speak to me in Bengali? Why didn't he call me a *mithyābādī*? No *śālā*[37] would get angry at that. But 'liar'—that's intolerable.[38]

In a sense, when reading Madhusudan in whatever genre or language, one has to be able to read many of the words in inverted commas, with a flexible and good-humoured awareness of the special, parodic nuance and association they would have had for Madhusudan himself.

Wit requires intellect. We should never forget that the wittiest of Shakespeare's tragic heroes is also the cleverest, and that he went 'to school in Wittenberg'.[39] All Madhusudan's coevals attest to his intellect as well as his charm and humour, and their recollections contain memorable anecdotes of his intellectual powers. These included mathematical ability. By the time he had reached the top class at Hindu College, he had lost all interest in mathematics, and would read novels or poetry during lessons on the subject. But in a college debate on whether Shakespeare or Newton was the greater genius, he had argued that 'Shakespeare could, if he had wanted, have become Newton, but Newton could never have become Shakespeare however hard he tried'—and it seems since then he had been waiting for an opportunity to prove his point. The opportunity came when Mr Rees, their maths

[37]'Scoundrel', though the word actually means 'brother-in-law'.

[38]A longer extract, and more on the nineteenth century babu ambience, can be found in my article, 'The Humour of Calcutta', in Christina Oesterheld and Claus Peter Zoller (ed.), *Of Clowns and Gods, Brahmans and Babus: Humour in South Asian Literature* (Manohar, New Delhi, 1999), pp. 102–17.

[39]*Hamlet* I.2.113.

teacher, gave them a problem that even the brightest students were unable to solve. Madhusudan's friend Bhudeb Mukhopadhyay noticed that Madhu was busily working on the problem. He pointed this out to Rees, who invited him to complete his calculations on the blackboard. This he did with great ease and elegance. On returning to his desk, he nudged Bhudeb and said, 'Do you see now how Shakespeare could have become Newton if he wanted? But now I'm finished with mathematics.'[40]

Finished with mathematics, maybe, but not with 'numbers' in the sense of metrics. As a poet, his love of hyperbole, exclamation marks and emotional excess would all be froth and bombast if it did not have a rock-solid backbone of formal discipline and control. His early English poems can rightly be dismissed as juvenilia, yet even in those one can see him mastering his craft, handling English rhyme and metrics deftly (never easy if one's mother tongue is not English) and even engaging in formal experiments such as 'Evening in Saturn: a Sonnet in Blank-verse dedicated to a pigmy' (?1841), with a characteristic preface in prose:

> Reader! who ever publishes a sonnet with a preface? I hear, or fancy that I hear, you say, '*none*'! Well! I publish. I am an enemy to what men call 'custom'. But be that as it is, I publish my sonnet with a preface; I have to teach the world something new. Don't get offended. Behold! I have written a *Sonnet in Blank-verse*. What a rare experiment! believe me, reader, the Muse appeared not to resent this 'breach of etiquette' towards her. O Joy! O Glory! O Happiness!

[40]Yogindranath Basu, pp. 37–9.

> that I have done successfully what none dared do before me! Excuse this short outbreak of impassioned exclamation. I have laid my scene in the planet Saturn, because I despise everything earthly.[41]

That a romantic exuberance could be successfully combined with technical brilliance had been richly demonstrated by Madhusudan's early literary hero Lord Byron; but the interest in blank verse here is a foreshadowing of the status he later gave it as a badge of real greatness and intellect in a poet. As the ever-to-be renowned inventor of blank verse in Bengali, he first took the plunge in response to a wager. Raja Jyotindramohan Tagore, one of the founders of Belgachia Theatre, recalls in his reminiscences how during a rehearsal Madhusudan had suddenly remarked that 'no real improvement in the Bengali drama could be expected until blank verse were introduced in it.' Jyotindramohan expressed extreme skepticism that blank verse would be possible in Bengali (in the medieval Bengali tradition, poetry is always rhymed). He accepted Madhusudan's argument that what had been possible in Sanskrit ought to be possible in Bengali, but he felt that 'as yet the Bengali seems to be a weakling though born of a healthy and robust mother'. Madhusudan immediately leapt to the challenge:

> 'Write me down as an ass,' said he laughingly, 'if I am not able to convince you of the error within a short time.' Then looking sharply at me he added 'and what if I succeed in proving to you that the Bengali is quite capable of the blank verse form of

[41]Kshetra Gupta (ed.), *Madhusūdan racanābalī* (Sahitya Samsad, Kolkata, revised edition, 1974), p. 450.

> poetry?' 'Why then,' I replied, 'I shall willingly stand all the expenses of printing and publishing any poem which you may write in blank verse.' 'Done' said he, clapping his hands, 'you shall get a few stanzas from me within three or four days', and as a matter of fact within three or four days the first canto of *Tilottamāsambhab kābya* was sent to me.[42]

Madhusudan's blank verse, like Shakespeare and Milton's blank verse, is not based on a rigid count of syllables. Indeed, defining the syllable count in each line of blank verse that he wrote is not a simple matter, as in Bengali the short 'a'—the vowel that in the Bengali script is inherent in a consonant—is frequently not pronounced. In Sanskrit, the inherent vowel is always pronounced except where a special sign (*virāma*) indicates that it should be dropped. In modern South Asian languages, the inherent vowel can be frequently dropped, especially at the end of words, though Bengali differs from Hindi in that if a word ends in a 'conjunct' (two consonants combined), the inherent vowel *is* pronounced (thus 'Swami Vivekananda', whereas in Hindi he would be called 'Vivekanand'). The celebrated opening lines of *Meghnādbadh kābya* show that in each line there are 14 *mātrās* (as defined by the letters of the Bengali script), but not necessarily 14 syllables, though readers have some choice and flexibility as to which to put in, just as readers of French poetry have flexibility in the pronunciation of the 'silent e' in words such as *tante* or *frère*:

> sammukh(a) samare paṛi, bīr(a)-cūṛāmaṇi
> in open combat having fallen, the crest-jewel of heroes

[42]Yogindranath Basu, Appendix, p. 30.

bīr(a)bāhu, cali yabe gelā yam(a)pure
Virbāhu, when he went to Yama's city

akāle, kaha, he debī amṛt(a)bhāṣiṇī,
untimely, say, O ambrosia-speaking goddess,

kon(a)[43] bīr(a)bare bari senāpati-pade,
which hero of heroes having appointed as general

pāṭhāilā raṇe punaḥ rakṣaḥkul(a)nidhi
did (he) send once more into battle the fount of the Raksha race

rāghabāri?
Rāvan (the enemy, *ari*, of the descendant of King Raghu, i.e. of Rām)

Analysing Madhusudan's blank verse in full is a hugely complicated business, as so many factors come into play, including the 'holding' of double or conjunct consonants in Bengali (as in *sammukh*, the very first word of the poem) to produce a syncopated effect, the way some vowels are longer than others, the way in which some syllables in Bengali words are stressed more than others, and the way the meaning of a phrase or sentence will also impose stress on particular words. But Madhusudan's own, very explicit comments in his letters indicate that for him the primary energy of his blank verse lay in the phrasing and pausing. Whereas in medieval Bengali *payār*, the commonest metre, fourteen syllables to the line, rhymed in couplets, the caesuras are fixed, coming after the eighth syllable and at the end of the line, in Madhusudan's blank verse there is

[43]With this word Madhusudan puts in the *virāma* sign, indicating that it has to be *kon* (which?) not *kona/kono* (some, any), and also making it absolutely clear that in his kind of blank verse some *mātrās* are silent.

constant *enjambement* (running on of lines) and perpetual flexibility of caesura. In letters to Rajnarayan Basu, he wrote:

> If your friends know English, let them read the *Paradise Lost*, and they will find how the verse in which the Bengali poetaster writes is constructed . . . Let your friends guide their voices by the pause (as in English blank verse) and they will soon swear that this is the noblest measure in the Language.[44]
>
> So many fellows have, of late, been at me to explain to them the structure of the new verse, that I have been obliged to think on the subject, and the result is that I find that the *yati* [caesura] instead of being confined to the 8th syllable, naturally comes in after the 2nd, 3rd, 4th, 6th, 7th, 8th, 10th, 11th and 12th.[45]

Moreoever, it is clear from other comments that for Madhusudan, successful blank verse was a measure of *intellectual* power in a poet. To Keshabchandra Gangopadhyay he wrote:

> I need scarcely tell *you* that the Blank verse is the *best* suited for Poetry in every language. A *true* poet will always succeed best in Blank verse as a bad one in Rhyme. The grace and beauty of the former's thoughts will claim attention, as the melody of the latter will conceal the poverty of his mind. Besides, a truly noble mind will always wither away under restraint, of whatever description that restraint may

[44]Murshid 2004, p. 128.
[45]Ibid., p. 145.

be. In China, they confine the feet of their woman in iron-shoes. What is the result? Lameness![46]

His sentiments here echo those of the English poet who replaced Byron as his foremost literary hero, John Milton, who in his preface to *Paradise Lost* cast similar aspersions on rhyme. Madhusudan returns to the point (and the same foot-binding image) in one of his sonnets, which though written in rhyme is firmly against rhyme (he would himself have seen the joke of this):

I consider him cruel, O language,
He who formerly would fetter you
In chains of rhyme! What pain it causes you
When you wear these shackles on your soft feet—
When I think of this my heart burns with anger!
Tell me, O lady, was there no true wealth of feeling
In the storehouse of his mind, that he had
To deck you in such ugly ornaments, to deceive you
With bogus love? What is the point of daubing
The petals of the lotus with colour?
The moon is bright in the sky from its own beauty!
What is the point of purifying the waters of the Ganges
With *mantras*? What is the point of pouring perfume
Over the scent of the *pārijāt*-flower?
Poetry is naturally beautiful by the power
Of its own nature—why put its feet
In iron fetters like the women of China?[47]

[46]Ibid., pp. 114–15.

[47]*Caturdaśpadī kabitābalī*, No. 97. My translation. *pad* (foot, or metrical foot) can be punned on in Bengali just as it can in English. The *pārijāt* is the never-fading flower of heaven. (See Notes to *MBK* II.439.)

Madhusudan the man and poet had a strong mind as well as strong feelings, and he valued in literature and people what he called 'Mind'. In a letter to his friend Rajnarayan Basu—who was a member of the Brahmo Samaj, the 'Hindu church' that had such an impact on social and religious reform in nineteenth century Bengal, his comments on religion are teasing, but his praise for the sermons Rajnarayan had sent him is genuine:

> Many thanks for your kind letter and the volume of sermons, for such, I suppose, I must call them. O! Rev'd. Sir, I have read several of them and like them very much. Rajendra[lal Mitra] once told me, you are a good Bengali writer; your book confirms his opinion. The style is free from all those vices that disgrace the Bengali of the present day, and what is more, it shows that very *unfashionable* thing, *mind*! If I felt more interest in religious matters than, I am sorry to say, I do, this book would be my constant companion. But you know I am 'smitten with the love of sacred song'.[48]

[48]Murshid 2004, p. 130. The quotation (with 'smit' altered to 'smitten') is from Milton's 'Light', l. 29. Madhusudan's use of the word 'mind' here may have the heritage of Derozio, Young Bengal, and the Scottish Enlightenment behind it (see below, p. xliii). Derozio was educated at the Durromtollah Academy, whose founder and Principal, the Scotsman David Drummond, introduced him to the writings of David Hume, Dugald Stewart and Thomas Reid, many of which deal with the human mind and understanding. In a letter to *The Weekly Examiner* of 15 August 1840, after Derozio's death, Drummond wrote: 'Mr Derozio was devoutly attached to that glorious study, the Science of the Human Mind . . .' See *Derozio, Poet of India: The Definitive Edition*, edited, and with an Introduction, by Rosinka Chaudhuri (Oxford University Press, New Delhi, 2008), Introduction, p. lvi. Madhusudan entered the Senior Department of Hindu College in 1841, a decade after Derozio's dismissal and death, but Derozio's radical legacy lived on, despite official attempts to suppress it and render it 'unfashionable'.

We need, in the sections of this Introduction that follow, to explore how Madhusudan's works, and especially his masterpiece *Meghnādbadh kābya,* were an expression of his own mind, of the mind of the Bengal Renaissance itself, and even of the wider Indian modernity that has, to a large degree, emerged from that era. The combination of feeling and intellect, of dynamic forward movement but also balance and symmetry, that was central to his blank verse, and thus to the opening lines of his epic quoted above, was an engine of something much bigger. To understand what this was, we need to move beyond the sun of his own genius to the other elements in his carefully designed heraldic emblem. They were much larger than he alone could be.

The Lion of Europe

A writer's early works will generally be more obviously indebted to cultural influences than the works of his maturity. In Madhusudan's case this is transparently so, because his early works were actually written in English. It is tempting to make a clear divide between the English juvenilia (1841–55) and his Bengali poems and plays (1858–73), and to ally this with a shift from Romanticism to Classicism. A famous letter to Gour, written in Madras on 18 August 1849, after Madhusudan had been stung by some discouraging comments on *The Captive Ladie* by J. E. D. Bethune, Chairman of the Education Council in Calcutta, indicates a long and arduous preparation for this shift:

> Perhaps you do not know that I devote several hours daily to Tamil. My life is more busy than that of a school boy. Here is my routine: 6–8 Hebrew, 8–12 School, 12–2 Greek, 2–5 Telegu and Sanskrit, 5–7

> Latin, 7–10 English. Am I not preparing for the great object of embellishing the tongue of my fathers?[49]

A later letter, to Rajnarayan Basu in July 1860, confirms how Madhusudan had moved on in his taste in poetry:

> Rungolal[50] says, he never received your letter. He is very proud of your approbation; of course, I have not told him what you and I think of his prose. He is a very touchy fellow, more so than a sensible poet should be. He is writing another tale about Rajputana. Byron, Moore and Scott form the highest Heaven of poetry in his estimation. I wish he would travel further. He would then find what 'hills peep o'er hills'—what 'Alps on Alps arise!'[51] As for me, I never read any poetry except that of Valmiki, Homer, Vyasa, Virgil, Kalidasa, Dante (in translation), Tasso (Do) and Milton. These *kabigurus* [master-poets] ought to make a fellow a first rate poet if Nature has been gracious to him.[52]

[49]Murshid 2004, p. 78. Gour had given Bethune the book, and he replied on 20 July 1849 with 'the same advice I have already given to several of his countrymen, that he might employ his time to better advantage than in writing English poetry. As an occasional exercise and proof of his proficiency in the language, such specimens may be allowed. But he could render far greater service to his country and have a better chance of achieving a lasting reputation for himself, if he will employ the taste and talents, which he has cultivated by the study of English, in improving the standard and adding to the stock of the poems in his own language, if poetry at all events he must write.' (Yogindranath Basu, p. 125)

[50]Rangalal Bandyopadhyay (1827–1887), a poet associated with the introduction of European-style romanticism into Bengali poetry.

[51]Alexander Pope, *Essay on Criticism* II.32.

[52]Murshid 2004, pp. 128–9.

But if we go a bit more deeply not only into Madhusudan's own poetic development but also into trends and changes in English (and European) Romanticism, we find it is not at all easy to define a radical shift or break.

There is no doubt that the poetic ambience of Hindu College in its first two decades was heavily and directly influenced by 'the first generation' of English and Scots romantic poets—Thomas Moore, Walter Scott, William Rogers, Thomas Campbell, Robert Burns and the early Byron. It was fostered by members of the British community in Calcutta who wrote and published English poems—by Henry Meredith Parker and Emma Roberts, and above all by the Eurasian Henry Louis Vivian Derozio (1809–1931), famous as a charismatic young teacher whose radical and reformist ideas inspired the generation of students who became known as 'Young Bengal', and who thus became too hot for the college authorities to handle. Forced to resign from the College before his tragically early death, he has remained a legendary figure in Bengal, forever associated with secular, liberal and progressive strands in the Bengal Renaissance. Educated at the Durromtollah Academy, a school run by the Scotsman David Drummond, he imbibed the ideals of the Scottish Enlightenment, which were also those of the French Revolution, and his teaching at Hindu College extended way beyond English literature and history to Locke, Hume, Reid, Dugald Stewart and even Tom Paine's notorious *Rights of Man*. He was also a talented poet, and under his influence his pupils started to write English poetry too. In 1830 Kasiprasad Ghosh published *The Shair and Other Poems*, announcing himself in the Preface as 'the first Hindu who has ventured to publish a volume of

English poems . . . having received his education at the Anglo-Indian College of Calcutta, in English only, among the other languages of Europe which are taught along with it as essential for the acquirement of the recondite learning of the West.'

Madhusudan's earliest English poems, written while he was at Hindu College, can certainly be read as a chip off Derozio's block. His sonnet 'Written at the Hindu College' which begins

> Oh! How my heart exulteth while I see
> These future flow'rs, to deck my country's brow,
> Thus kindly nurtured in this nursery!

Is almost a paraphrase of Derozio's own 'Sonnet to the Students at the Hindu College':

> Expanding, like the petals of young flowers;
> I watch the gentle opening of your minds,
> And the sweet loosening of the spell that binds
> Your intellectual energies and powers,
> That stretch (like young birds in soft summer hours)
> Their wings to try their strength . . .[53]

But when Madhusudan joined the College, Derozio had been dead for ten years, and the charismatic Principal and teacher of English literature who inspired him there,

[53]*Derozio, Poet of India* (see fn. 48 above), pp. 314–5. This book and Rosinka Chaudhuri's earlier study, *Gentlemen Poets in Colonial Bengal: Emergent Nationalism and the Orientalist Project* (Seagull Books, Kolkata, 2002) give us detailed and sympathetic access to the poetic achievements of the Derozians and their successors, and confirm their central role in the unfolding Bengal Renaissance.

Captain D. L. Richardson (1801–1865) differed from Derozio in some crucial respects. Firstly, he was not a political idealist, or interested in politics at all, and Madhusudan's own lack of interest in politics can be attributed partly to his influence.[54] Secondly, he was a much more thoroughgoing literary man than Derozio. A contemporary of Hazlitt, he had returned to England after a spell in the Indian army, and was set on a literary career, publishing his *Sonnets and Other Poems* in 1825, and starting a journal, *The Weekly Review*, to which Hazlitt contributed. Financial problems forced him to return to Calcutta, and his subsequent writings—prolific and diverse though they were—were published locally, and never

[54]The exception to Madhusudan's apparent indifference to politics might appear to be his supposed translation of Dinabandhu Mitra's famous play about oppressive British indigo-planters, *Nīl-darpaṇ* (1860). But as has been conclusively argued by Tapobijay Ghosh in a Bengali article in a 100th anniversary Madhusudan special issue of *Catuṣkoṇ* (Kolkata, Baisakh 1380 [May 1973]) edited by Shibprasad Chakravarti and Arunkumar Ray, there is no external or internal evidence whatsoever that Madhusudan had anything to do with this translation. The notion that he had emanates from a sentence by Bankimchandra Chatterjee in an introduction he wrote to the collected works of Dinabandhu: 'For doing its English translation Michael Madhusudan Datta was secretly rebuked and humiliated and I have heard that eventually he even had to resign from the job at the supreme court on which his livelihood depended.' This is doubly misleading, because at the time of the electrifying case (1861) against the Rev. James Long that was brought by the indigo planters for his libel in publishing (at the Government's instigation) an English translation of the play, Madhusudan's career as a barrister lay six years ahead, and he was still working in the Police Court as an interpreter and clerk. There is no mention of the translation in Yogindranath Basu's pioneering biography of Madhusudan (1893), but Nagendranath Som in *Madhusmṛti* (1920) picked up the notion of it from Bankim and from Dinabandhu's son Lalitchandra, who wrote in his *Indigo Disturbance in Bengal* (1903) that 'the actual translation was made by the immortal poet of the Meghnadbadh,—Michael Madhusudan Dutt. The translation was hurried through in a single night, and this would account for the many defects in the English rendering of the drama.' But as Ghosh

received any critical attention in England.[55] This made him bitter at times, and his most poignant poems are expressions of nostalgia and exile. Madhusudan's own most famous English lyric, which has traditionally been quoted as a personal expression of the desire to go to England that may have been one of the reasons for his conversion to Christianity, can also be read as an imitation of 'D.L.R.':

I sigh for Albion's distant shore,
Its valleys green, its mountains high;
Tho' friends, relations, I have none
In that far clime, yet, oh! I sigh
To cross the vast Atlantic wave
For glory, or a nameless grave![56]

Thirdly, he seems to have been something of a libertine. Derozio had been accused by his opponents of teaching atheism and influencing students who were 'cutting their way through ham and beef and wading to Liberalism

---

shows in his article, the errors and infelicities would have been quite impossible for Madhusudan to make, and it is highly unlikely that the translation was done 'by a Native' at all. The continuing appearance of the translation in collected editions of Madhusudan's works is really a slander on him, and the situation has not been helped by Geoffrey A. Oddie's statement in *Missionaries, Rebellion and Proto-Nationalism: James Long of Bengal 1814-87* (Curzon, London, 1999) that the translation was done 'by Michael Datta under Long's supervision'. (p.119) In his notes on p. 229 Oddie refers to two letters by Long in support of this, but I am informed by Ghulam Murshid that the first of these letters does not exist and the second makes no mention of Madhusudan.

[55]When I read his three large volumes of collected essays and verse—*Literary Leaves* (1836; expanded edition 1840), *Literary Chit-chat* (1848) and *Literary Recreations* (1852) in the Bodleian Library in Oxford in the 1980s, I found that the pages were still uncut.

[56]Kshetra Gupta (ed.), *Madhusūdan racanābalī*, p. 438.

through tumblers of beer',[57] but in fact he was very high-minded, and his pupils, whatever the indiscretions of their youth, went on to become pillars of education, Brahmoism, teetotalism and even Christianity (one of them, the Rev. Krishnamohan Banerji, was a leading sponsor of Madhusudan's own conversion).[58] Richardson, in contrast, had to be cautioned by Bethune for his irregular way of life (he kept a Bengali mistress) and like Derozio was forced to resign, though he remained in Calcutta for a further fourteen years and taught at various schools. One can well imagine that Madhusudan's own weaknesses of the flesh were fostered in part by Richardson's engaging example.

Fourthly, and most importantly, Richardson through his teaching and his massive and pioneering anthology *Selections from the British Poets*, published in 1840 in two volumes that ran to a total of 1635 pages, led the student Madhusudan way beyond the literary tastes of the Derozio generation. Its Introduction was heady stuff: it set Poetry up as the be-all and end-all, the noblest thing in life, superior to science or religion as an expression of Truth; it excoriates utilitarians, materialists and philistines; it 'exults' in the thought that the minds of generations of young Hindus are to be shaped by the glories of English poetry. And not just English poetry: it includes translations from Homer, Virgil, Dante and many other classical and

[57]Elliot W. Madge, *Henry Derozio: The Eurasian Poet and Reformer* (Calcutta, 1905), p. 7, quoting a writer in the *Oriental Magazine*.

[58]Probably the high-mindedness would not have had such an influence without the high spirits. Derozio's letters to Horace Hayman Wilson, Visitor to Hindu College, denying the charges that had been made against him, are rightly celebrated for their dignity and nobility, but the writings collected by Rosinka Chaudhuri include a poem about Epicurus ('Philosophical Utopia: A Fragment') and an essay in praise of Drunkenness. See *Derozio, Poet of India*, Introduction, pp. xxxix–xlii.

continental poets. It also includes five whole Shakespeare plays, and large chunks of Spenser and Milton. It is full of the enthusiasm for the greatest classics of literature that characterizes the second generation of Romantics: the sentiment that inspired Keats to travel in the 'realms of gold' of Chapman's Homer, the love of Greece that we find in Shelley and the mature Byron, the adoration of Shakespeare that thrilled the romantic poets of France and Germany. When Richardson read out his Introduction to his Hindu College pupils before it was published, Madhusudan is said to have blurted out: 'I wish I had been the author of it'.[59] Its closing address to the reader must have stayed with him, for one senses both its sentiment and its imagery in the end of his invocation to *Meghnādbadh kābya*:

> In this work he has a rich and varied garden of English Poetical Literature spread out before him, and he may wander as he lists from flower to flower, luxuriating in pleasures that are followed by no sickening satiety or vain repentance, and hiving up a store of nectarean wisdom. (Richardson)

> And you come,
> Goddess, honey-making Imagination! Having taken
> honey from the flowery wood of the poet's heart,
> Build a honeycomb from which the people of Gauṛ,
> in joy, will drink nectar for ever. (*MBK* I.29–32)

From Richardson, therefore, Madhusudan acquired a 'mature romanticism'—one that embraced the Classics with romantic enthusiasm. He never lost that ardour: it fed directly through to the Bengali works of his maturity.

[59] Yogindranath Basu, p. 62.

It can also be found in the English poems he wrote in Madras, which were a big advance on his Hindu College lyrics. Because they still await a careful editor, and suffer in collected editions of his works from many misprints and flaws in punctuation, they have been dismissed too readily as a hangover from Hindu College. But they show, in my view, that the scope and aspirations of Richardson's *Selections from the British Poets* had not been in vain. The poems by Keats and the early Tennyson that he included took Madhusudan into new and daring poetic spheres. His unfinished poem *The Upsari*, which is about a divine nymph flying down to earth and encountering near 'a holy fane' (a Kali-temple) a beautiful youth whom she loses but ultimately finds again, sleeping in 'a lonely cot' inside a 'lovely bower/ Bosom'd upon a mound soft rob'd in green', shows the influence of Keats' *Endymion* (1817). A careful reading of Madhusudan's first major Bengali poem, *Tilottamāsambhab kābya*, would also, I believe, reveal in its scenes of metamorphosis, its wondrous spectacles created out of nothing, its luxurious sensuousness of language, the further influence of Keats, and through him, Spenser; and beyond Spenser the world of Greek mythology interpreted by Ovid.

It is not only Romanticism that connects Madhusudan's English poems with his Bengali works. When *The Captive Ladie* was published in Madras in 1849, the volume also included a remarkable poem called *Visions of the Past*, which had earlier been published in four instalments in the *Madras Circulator* under the title *A Vision*. This poem is a kind of dream vision of Paradise, Fall and Redemption. It begins with a description of primeval Man and Woman lying in a Bower of Bliss attended by a Choir of Angels. Then Satan comes along, and all is plunged into darkness, the Angels replaced by Devils. Then comes redemption, 'that fulgent vision bright'. But it seems that Redemption does not restore Paradise—far from it. The bower of beauty is sadly 'changed alas! From primal loveliness'; the 'gentle beings and fair' flee guiltily, and poem ends with the poet waking to the knowledge that only penitence and divine grace will save them:

> I woke—that vision of ethereal ray
> Had melted—and 'twas night again and dark,
> With stars of sickly smile and pallid brow:—
> I look'd tow'rd that fair bow'r and as I look'd
> I saw a sword of flame and fiery gleam
> Wav'd round it by some viewless hand and fierce!
> And on the silent plain that gentle pair—
> Its tenants—wandered in dim solitude.
> They wept—but were those tears which gently flow'd,
> Oh! were they tears which dark despair will wake
> T'embalm the memory of our blasted hopes?
> They wept—but not in dark despair—they wept
> As Guilt—all penitent—when, Mercy! thou
> Dost plead—nor plead in vain—in gentle strains
> To justice stern to win redeeming grace!

Yogindranath Basu said that *A Vision* was the only poem that Madhusudan wrote in which his Christianity is apparent.[60] But is that so? Leaving aside the hymn he wrote for his own baptism, which some might dismiss as being written to order ('Long sunk in superstition's night,/ By sin and Satan driven', etc.),[61] there are at least two explicitly

[60]Yogindranath Basu, p. 114. He also assumed—wrongly, I think—that it was incomplete.

[61]Kshetra Gupta (ed.), *Madhusūdan racanābalī*, p. 467.

Christian sonnets from the last phase of his career, one written for his godson Khrishtadas Sinhạ in 1872, and another that he included in his main book of sonnets. Here is a rhymed translation of the latter that I did in the 1980s:

AFTER-LIFE [*paralok*]

Into the dawn sun's radiant sea of light
The star of morning sinks her smiling fire;
And flowers there are whose swelling buds desire,
And greet with blooming love, approaching Night;
And eager are the streams that rush to reach
Joyous Nirvana at the ocean's feet—
Likewise mortality receives the sweet
Jewel of immortal life (the Scriptures teach)
If we have faith. Ah Faith, to what false gain
Does man forget you, choose the path of sin?
What lures prevail on him to sever
Your golden boat, to let the windswept main
Of the world drag her down? Willing to win
Two paltry days of life, to die forever.[62]

I am not myself in the business of trying to prove that Madhusudan was a believing Christian. He never talked about his inner beliefs, so the argument can never be settled between his lack of regular religious observance and his flippant remarks about religion in his letters on the one hand, and on the other the evidence that Ghulam Murshid has unearthed of his interest in becoming a missionary when he became a student at Bishop's College, or the account that Nagendranath Som gives of his declaration of faith

[62]Included in my D.Phil thesis. See fn. 144 below.

when the Rev. Krishnamohan Banerji came to see him on his deathbed.[63] What I think is undeniable is that his sense of tragedy, whether in *A Vision* or the *Ātma-bilāp* or *Meghnādbadh kābya* itself, is shot through with a very Christian sense of sin. Most Bengali critics, in looking for Western sources for Madhusudan's sense of tragedy, turn to Homer, who undoubtedly played a major role, for *Meghnādbadh kābya* was to a large extent an attempt to make a kind of 'Bengali *Iliad*' out of part of the *Rāmāyaṇa*, as is shown in detail in the Source Notes I have supplied at the end of this book. But we do not find in the *Iliad* a sense of sin. Achilleus is foolish in his wrath, Paris was wrong to abduct Helen and start the Trojan war, but none of Homer's characters can be accurately described as sinful. Rāvan in *Meghnādbadh kābya*, however, is regarded by all the gods—even by his protector Siva—as well as by Rām and his supporters, including Rāvan's brother Vibhishan, as a sinner who has brought about his own downfall through his nefarious abduction of Sitā. The morality of the epic conflates *pāp* (sin) with the Hindu law of *karma*—the fruit of one's actions. Many quotations would confirm this. Here are just three:

> . . . *nij karma-phale,*
> *majāle rākṣas-kule*
>
> ('through the fruits of your own actions you are drowning the Rākshas race')

[63]'I do not care for any man-made church; I don't need anyone's help; I am going to rest in the Lord—he will hide me in His best resting-place. You can bury me where you like—near your house, under a tree in some deserted secluded place . . .' Nagendranath Som, p. 424. Madhusudan was buried, despite opposition from the Bishop of Calcutta, in Lower Circular Road Cemetery, next to Henrietta. See Murshid 2004, p. 284.

Queen Chitrāngadā to her husband Rāvan, *MBK* I. 404–5

pāpe pūrṇa svarṇa-laṅkā!
('golden Lankā is oozing with sin!')
Lakshmi, guardian deity of the Rākshasas, *MBK* I.607

kintu nij karma-phale maje duṣṭamati . . .
. . . hāy, debi, debe ki mānabe,
kothā hena sādhya rodhe prāktaner gati?
('but the wretch is sinking through his own misdeeds . . . Alas, Devi, where in god or man is there power to stop the results of past actions?')
Siva, reluctantly accepting his wife Durgā's arguments, *MBK* II.431, 433–4

Fundamentally, Madhusudan himself seems to have accepted this morality. Despite his famous preference for the Rākshasas ('I despise Ram and his rabble; but the idea of Ravan elevates and kindles my imagination; he was a grand fellow'[64]) and the accusation by Tagore among others that *Meghnādbadh kābya* undermines Rām's righteous and heroic status, a careful reading of the epic will show that the portrayal of Rām, Lakshman and Vibhishan is not unsympathetic or disrespectful. Some of the finest passages of *bilāp* ('lament') are given to Rām,[65] and when Madhusudan wrote despairingly from France it was Rām, not Rāvan whom he quoted.[66]

[64]Letter to Rajnarayan Basu; Murshid 2004, pp. 168–9.
[65]E.g. his grief over the lifeless body of his brother Lakshman, Book VIII.18f.
[66]See Source Notes, p. 355.

Nevertheless, there are countercurrents, an ambivalence about *pāp*, *karma*, and *dharma* too, the Indian term for the principle of righteous action and moral duty. This ambivalence reflects not only the doubts that Madhusudan may have had about his own Christianity, but also the complex position that Christian morality assumed in the Bengal Renaissance as a whole. Whether one is considering social and religious reform movements such as the Brahmo Samaj, or English education even when it aspired to be secular, or new attitudes to women, or puritanical campaigns against drink, or the pieties of Victorian romantic poetry of the sentimental type, it is seldom possible to leave Christianity wholly out of the picture. With the growth of patriotic and nationalist ideas in the later nineteenth century, many of these Christian elements became suspect, and it is not surprising that in Madhusudan's epic, christianized moral values become suspect too. In Book VI of *Meghnādbadh kābya*, the pivotal book in which Rāvan's son Meghnād (Indrajit) is killed by Lakshman, assisted by the goddess Māyā and accompanied by Vibhishan, we find the word *dharma* used in two opposing ways. When Rām prays to Durgā before sending his brother off to carry out the deed, he invokes the *dharma* of piety and conventional morality:

> Do not forget, goddess, this servant of yours!
> The trials I have suffered, mother, in upholding
> *dharma*,
> Are not unknown to your rosy feet. Feed the fruits
> of *dharma*, O beloved of Siva,
> To this wretched petitioner![67]

[67] *MBK* VI.207–11.

But when the defenceless Meghnād sees his uncle Vibhishan supporting Lakshman, he is outraged by his offence against another kind of *dharma*, the *dharma* of the Kshatriya warrior-code that all Rākshasas are obliged to follow:

> The terror of Indra grew furious! Like a thunder-cloud roaring angrily in the sky at night, the hero of heroes said:
> 'You are renowned throughout the world, O brother of the Rākshas king, for following the path of *dharma*.
> By what sense of *dharma*—tell me, I am listening—
> Do you sacrifice utterly kinship, fraternity, lineage?
> The Sāstras say: "If an enemy is virtuous, and a kinsman is without virtue,
> Nevertheless a virtueless kinsman is best—an enemy is always an enemy!" O best of Rākshasas,
> Where have you learnt the evil you are doing?'[68]

Moreover, the manner in which Meghnād is killed by Lakshman, in a temple, where he has come to carry out a *pūjā* to Agni and where he has no way of defending himself, is a shocking departure from the warrior-code and totally at odds with the *Rāmāyaṇa* tradition. It is the most subversive and original feature of Madhusudan's epic, and his chief way of turning Meghnād into a tragic hero. It is particularly shocking because neither Meghnād nor his father Rāvan have any sense that they have done wrong. All their afflictions they attribute to *bidhi* ('Fate'). They have, in fact, a kind of moral innocence, expressed early on by Rāvan in his cry of despair at his son Virbāhu's death:

[68]Ibid. VI.579–88.

ki pāpe hārānu āmi tomā hena dhane?
ki pāp dekhiyā mor, re dāruṇ bidhi,
harili e dhan tui?

('By what sin have I lost such a treasure as you? O harsh Fate, what sin did you see in me to steal this treasure?')
MBK I.86–88

In Book VI the dying Meghnād comes out with precisely the same sentiment:

. . . ki pāpe bidhātā
dilen e tāp dāse, bujhiba kemane?
('How shall I understand why God has dealt this torment to me? What sin have I committed?')
MBK VI. 650–1

Dinanath Sanyal, still unsurpassed as an editor of *Meghnādbadh kābya*, comments here: 'Meghnād too has no conception that the abduction of Sitā by Rāvan is a most serious sin; because stealing other people's wives is not outside the *dharma* of the Rākshasas.'[69] Some will argue that this contradiction between two moralities is inherent in Indian tradition, and there is no need to look to Christian influence to account for it. But the ambivalence and moral uncertainties of Madhusudan's epic go beyond its ideas or characters or plot. They are conveyed too by its tone, and here again, as with Romanticism and Tragedy, one needs to look for continuities between his English and Bengali writing.

[69]Dinanath Sanyal (ed.), *Meghnād-badh kābya* (Kolkata, 1917), p. 410.

In 1854 in Madras Madhusudan published an extraordinary lecture on *The Anglo-Saxon and The Hindu*, which continues to embarrass his Bengali admirers to this day. It ends with the promise of 'a future discourse', but no follow-up lecture has been found and we cannnot be sure he even wrote it. It argues, in about twenty pages of wonderfully florid English prose, full of quotations from or allusions to classical literature both European and Indian, that Hindu Civilization is hopelessly decadent and that 'it is the Mission of the Anglo-Saxon to renovate, to regenerate, to Christianize the Hindu.' It concludes with an ecstatic paean to the English language:

> I acknowledge to you, and I need not blush to do so—that I love the language of the Anglo-Saxon. Yes—I *love* the language,—the glorious language of the Anglo-Saxon! My imagination visions forth before me the language of the Anglo-Saxon in all its radiant beauty; and I feel silenced and abashed . . .[70]

But the lecture doesn't just celebrate English language and literature. It lauds 'the pale-faced stranger from the West' as 'greater—far greater than victorious Baber . . . than sagacious Acbar, than lofty Jehangir! Thc fabric of his power vaster; bayonet-wall which glitters round the citadel of his power, firmer.' Hindu civilization, once glorious, has been ruined by 'centuries of servitude and oppression', and the Hindu is now 'an aged, a decayed race'. Yet all is not lost, for 'with the great Architect of the Universe, nothing is impossible', and God has willed that the Anglo-

[70]Kshetra Gupta (ed.), *Madhusūdan racanābalī*, p. 638.

Saxon should come 'to raise from his grave the Hindu to a brighter, a fairer existence'. The Anglo-Saxon is the successor to the Holy Roman Empire: 'The Anglo-Saxon is the soldier of the Cross—the Crusader . . . After quelling the obstinate antagonism, after crushing the stout resistance of European Paynimrie, this victorious gonfalon of the Cross is now unfurled before the mighty and vast citadel of Braminism and it is the hand of the Anglo-Saxon which must plant it on the embattled towers of that citadel.'[71]

In its ideology and battle-imagery, the lecture is very close to language used by leading missionaries in nineteenth century Calcutta like Alexander Duff, founder in 1830 of the General Assembly's Institution (now Scottish Church College), which became the main rival to Hindu College as a centre of English education. Duff writes in a letter of being called 'to light the battles of the Lord in the land of the enemy'; and in another, 'We shall, with the blessing of God, devote our time and strength to the preparing of a mine, and the setting of a train which shall one day explode and tear up the whole from its lowest depths.'[72] But whereas Duff and his associates were deadly serious, the question one has to ask about Madhusudan's lecture is: did he actually mean it? Are its excesses partly, at least, a joke? Is he writing tongue in cheek?

It's a question one is also often forced to ask about his greatest achievements as a Bengali poet. Take, for example, this passage from Book VIII of *Meghnādbadh kābya*, the book that is the most conspicuously derived from Western influence, for it describes Rām's descent into the underworld of the dead, guided by the goddess Māyā, and has no

[71]Ibid., pp. 624–39.

[72]Gorge Smith, *Life of Alexander Duff* (London, 1879), p. 57, 108.

counterpart in the *Rāmāyaṇa*. As in Virgil's *Aeneid* Book VI and Dante's *Inferno*, the sinners in hell are luridly described. Their punishment is in accordance with the christianized morality of *karma* and *dharma* represented in Madhusudan's epic by 'Ram and his rabble', but as with that notorious phrase itself, how seriously are we meant to respond?

Rām sees a 'troupe of women, of ravishing beauty!', and then soon after sees 'a handsome band of youths', at which—

> Like a bird and its mate when they flit here and there in the sport of love, the amorous women whisked those lusty youths off into the forest—their intentions writ large in their eyes.
>
> Suddenly the forest filled with a howling noise! In horror Rām saw the men and women rolling horribly on the ground, scrabbling and scratching,
> Thumping and kicking each other. They tore at hair and gouged at eyes, slashed at noses and faces with their hard finger-nails.
> A stream of blood soaked the earth. Both groups fought viciously, like Bhim in the kingdom of Virāta,
> Disguised as a woman and fighting ferociously with Kichak. All the henchmen of Death who were there then pounced, quickly drove both groups away with iron clubs.
> In gentle tones, the beautiful Māyā spoke to Rām, the joy of the Raghu clan:
>
> 'In life—listen, my child—
> The men were the servants of Kāma; and the women too. Kāma satisfied their greed unceasingly,
> Sinking *dharma*, alas, in the waters of *adharma*,

Discarding shame; now they are being punished in
this city of Yama! . . .[73]

Set against passages elsewhere in the epic, such as Durgā's seduction of Siva in Book II, or Meghnād and his wife Pramilā waking up in bed together in Book V—let alone his own life-story—it is hard to believe that Madhusudan took this grim punishment for sexual passion seriously. Doubts about his taste and sincerity have indeed puzzled and unsettled his more high-minded critics and editors ever since *Meghnādbadh kābya* was published. On the simile 'Excited horses whinnied,/ Like Siva's shouts of ecstasy when demon-pounding Kāli's lotus-feet press upon his breast!',[74] for example, Dinanath Sanyal comments: 'To compare Siva with horses is not appropriate. Comparing small with great is always inappropriate and should be avoided.'[75] And Madhusudan's Brahmo friend Rajnarayan Basu, in an essay on *Meghnādbadh kābya* that included (like Sanyal in the Introduction to his edition) a section on *doṣas* ('faults'), strongly objected to a line in Book IX, where after a moving description of the grief-stricken Pramilā sitting on her husband's funeral bier we have a delightfully onomatopoeic line evoking ceremonial and martial drums that Rajnarayan felt was far too light and completely out of place:

bāje ḍhāk, bāje ḍhol, kārā kaṛa-kaṛe . . .[76]

Comments like this not only miss the wit and humour of Madhusudan's writing; they also fail to relate his work

[73]*MBK* VIII.461–81.
[74]Ibid., III.110–12.
[75]Dinanath Sanyal, p. 179. See Notes, p. 84.
[76]*MBK* IX.295.

to his personality and to the weirdly bicultural situation in which he found himself. Early on in my work on Madhusudan, in the 1980s, I looked for theoretical writing on humour that might help me to understand him better, and was greatly helped by Arthur Koestler's remarkable and now rather neglected book *The Act of Creation* (1964). Koestler places humour at the heart of creativity: Part One of his book is called 'The Jester' and the subject of his opening chapter is 'The Logic of Laughter'. This is because, in his view, all human creativity derives from our capacity for 'bisociative thinking', our ability to connect previously unconnected frames of reference. Humour does this too, and one of the diagrams[77] that Koestler provides to illustrate his argument might well be adopted here as an alternative to Madhusudan's heraldic emblem:

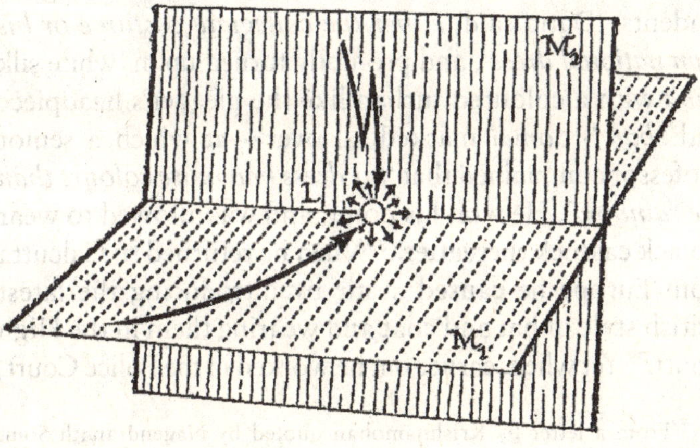

[77]'Figure 2' from Arthur Koestler, *The Act of Creation* (Hutchinson, London, 1964; Pan Books edition, 1970), p. 35.

If for the 'two frames of reference' M1 and M2 we read the Lion of Europe and the Elephant of India, then the vibrating sun of Laughter in the middle can be read as Madhusudan's radiant and witty personality. In everything he wrote, whether in English or Bengali, and in the many anecdotes that are told about his life, we find what Koestler called 'bisociation'. The numerous influences and sources, both Western and Indian that I have explored in my Source Notes to his epic, produce a work, a lotus, a *śatadal* that is positively buzzing with it. In a sense, the whole poem is 'put on', just as Madhusudan delighted in surprising his friends by 'putting on' both Western and Indian clothes.

The biographies and reminiscences of him contain many anecdotes about clothes. The Rev. Krishnamohan Banerji recalls how he clashed with the authorities at Bishop's College over their insistence that he should wear a white cassock instead of the black one worn by the English students. 'Datta said, *either the collegiate costume or his own national dress*', and promptly turned up in 'white silk *kaba* with a coloured turban like the pleader's headpiece and *shawl-roomal* marked all over'—at which a senior professor complained that '*his dress had more colours than the rainbow*'. He won his point, and was allowed to wear a black cassock thereafter.[78] When he returned to Calcutta from Europe he caused a stir by introducing the latest British style of hat and coat and wearing them in the High Court.[79] Yet when, earlier on, he worked in the Police Court,

[78]From a letter by Krishnamohan quoted by Nagendranath Som, p. 44.

[79]By now the legal system had changed to a British model, following reforms initiated by the Governor General Lord William Bentinck, advised by Thomas Babington Macaulay, from 1837 on. See fn. 16 above.

he would often wear the Persianized dress that was associated with aristocrats: 'Once he was about to go out wearing *pugṛī*, *cogā*, *ăckān* and a silk handkerchief when he met an admirer: laughing, Madhusudan said jokingly, "Dinoo, do I not look like the Maharajah of Burdwan!"'[80] And so on.

One can find, if one looks, English sources for aspects of his humour. The exuberance of his letters can be traced to 'Tom Moore's Life of my favourite Byron';[81] the British in Calcutta liked writing and publishing humorous as well as romantic verse; newspapers and journals displayed a typically British capacity for self-mockery; and when the Rajas Ishwarchandra and Pratapchandra Singh abandoned the idea of putting on Madhusudan's Bengali farces, they replaced them with three English farces.[82] But the essential reason why Madhusudan and other nineteenth century Bengalis took to British-style satire, burlesque and humour so readily—in the paintings of the Kalighat School as well as many Bengali books and journals—was precisely because their cultural situation, caught between East and West, constantly negotiating two languages, two sets of manners, two styles of dress, provided such rich, 'bisociative' material for humour.

A writer who, like Madhusudan, has the ability to stand back from his traditions and materials, whether literary, linguistic, or religious, and uses words in inverted commas, as it were, with constantly conscious awareness of their

[80]Nagendranath Som, p. 341.

[81]Letter to Gour, 24 November 1842, Murshid 2004, p. 29.

[82]According to Yogindranath Basu, Appendix, p. 47, the farces were 'Prince for an Hour', 'Power and Principle' and 'Fast Train, High Pressure Express', which were printed in T. H. Lacy's *Acting Edition of Plays*, which ran to many volumes in the 1850s.

cultural associations, needs an independent quality of Mind, and here the intellectual aspects of Madhusudan's achievement come in again.

In July 1861 Madhusudan published his *Brajāṅganā kābya*, a group of lyrics about the love of Rādhā and Krishna deliberately derived in their imagery and emotions from Bengal's Vaishnava tradition. Nagendranath Som tells a delicious story of a visit by a Vaishnava fan of the poems:

> When *Brajāṅganā kābya* was published, a pious Vaishnava living at Nabadvip read it and was so entranced by it that he eagerly set off to Calcutta to meet Madhusudan. He never imagined that the poet might be a Christian. When he got to Calcutta he found Madhusudan's house after a great deal of searching. He went up to the house and looked through the door: a dark-skinned gentleman in saheb's clothes was sitting on a chair and writing at a table. Afraid that he had come to the wrong place, the Vaishnava began to leave in a fluster—but then Madhusudan caught sight of him. Surprised and intrigued he asked in Bengali, 'Who are you looking for?'
>
> Vaishnava: Does Madhusudan live in this house?
> Madhusudan: Why? Do you need him?
> Vaishnava: Sir! I have been greatly impressed by his *Brajāṅganā kābya*. I have come from Nabadvip to Calcutta so that I might see that deeply, pious, virtuous, Vaishnava-paragon. Where is he, sir?
> Madhusudan: (*laughing slightly*) My name is Madhusudan.

> At Madhusudan's reply, the Vaishnava was absolutely astounded. Speechless and stunned he stared at him for a while with unblinking eyes, then blurted out passionately, '*Bābā*! You are a fallen angel!'[83]

The poems are in fact highly innovative in their metre and rhyme schemes, but even if they were a total pastiche of Vaishnava *pada*s of Chaṇḍidās and other medieval Bengali poets the fact that Madhusudan wrote them, with the background that he had and at the time that he did, gives them a totally different flavour. The effect is like that of Pierre Menard's re-creation of *Don Quixote* in Jorge Luis Borges's celebrated story. In the story Borges places a quotation from Cervantes and a quotation from Menard side-by-side. They are verbally identical, but not only are the ideas they express quite different, 'The contrast in style is also vivid. The archaic style of Menard—quite foreign, after all—suffers from a certain affectation. Not so that of his forerunner, who handles with ease the current Spanish of his time.'[84]

It is probably worth keeping Pierre Menard in mind when we consider the numerous classical sources and influences, both Western and Indian, that went into the making of *Meghnādbadh kābya*. A wide and detailed survey of them can be found in the Source Notes at the end of this book, but this needs to carry a caveat: when used by another poet of genius, writing in a different age and context, every source, like the sea-buried father in Ariel's song, 'doth suffer a sea-change/ Into something rich

[83]Nagendranath Som, pp. 195–6. The Vaishnava's last word—*śāpbhraṣṭa*—means 'fallen from heaven as a result of a curse'.

[84]Translated by James E. Irby in Jorge Luis Borges, *Labyrinths: Selected Short Stories and Other Writings* (Penguin, 1970), p. 69.

and strange'.[85] An analogy for Madhusudan's self-confessed use of Homer, Virgil, Dante, Milton and Tasso might be the story of Orpheus in the Underworld as used by the fourteenth century English author of the poem *Sir Orfeo*:

> Orfeo was a king
> In Inglond an heighe lording,
> A stalworth man and hardi bo,
> Large and curteys he was also.
> His fader was comen of King Pluto,
> And his moder of King Iuno . . .[86]

The source may be classical, but effect is quite different from Ovid. It belongs to its time and place, just as Madhusudan's use of his classical sources belongs to his time and place—mid-nineteenth century Calcutta.

Nevertheless, I would say that there are two vital respects in which *Meghnādbadh kābya*—and Madhusudan's other mature poems and plays too—are steeped in Western classical influence. The first is formal and structural. The Bengali critic and university teacher Mahitlal Majumdar put this well:

> It is necessary first to say something about the form of *Meghnādbadh kābya*. The poet himself said about this: 'I think I have constructed the Poem on the most rigid principles, and even a French critic would not find fault with me.'[87] Any literary critic must admit that this is absolutely true. Skill in construction of an

[85]*The Tempest* I. 2.403–4.

[86]Kenneth Sisam (ed.), *Fourteenth Century Verse & Prose* (Oxford, 1921), p. 14.

[87]See Source Notes, p. 337 for a longer quotation from this letter.

> epic or a long poem—unity and grace in the orderly arrangement of all its parts—first appears in our literature in *Meghnādbadh kābya.* As a result of his profound and attentive reading of the great classical poets of Europe, Madhusudan learnt what was not possible to learn from the method and example of his country's epic or narrative poetry. To form the beginning, middle and end of a story round one basic theme, event or character—this way of writing a poem did not exist in our country.[88]

I do not have space here to analyse the structure of *Meghnādbadh kābya* in depth, but I believe that its entire structure can be derived from its magnificent opening invocation (pp. 3–5), with its two long rhetorical questions at the beginning that encompass the entire story of the poem, its obeisance to Bhārati (Sarasvati), its comparison with Vālmiki, its short question 'Who on this planet knows your might?' acting as a central pivot, its three sentences extending the parallel with Vālmiki, its two sentences of further obeisance to Bhārati, and its magnificent call to her and to Kalpanā ('Imagination') to descend and inspire the work that is to follow. In the structure of Book I similar principles of symmetry and onward movement can be found, with the conversation between Vāruni and Muralā at the bottom of the sea acting as a central pivot; and in the epic as a whole the climactic, dastardly killing of Meghnād in Book VI (foreshadowed by *ki kauśale*, 'by what trick?' in the Invocation) being the pivot round which the whole action revolves. The conclusion of the poem, in which the Rākshasas raise a golden *maṭh*—a tomb or shrine—over

[88]Mahital Majumdar, *Kabi Śrī Madhusūdan* (Calcutta, 1947), p. 120.

Meghnād and Pramilā's funeral pyre, takes it into eternity in the same way that the Invocation ends with the hope that the poem will attain immortality.

Madhusudan's main model for the structuring of *Meghnādbadh kābya* was undoubtedly Milton's *Paradise Lost*, for in Milton we have a much greater simplicity of plot and structure than in Homer or Virgil, and far fewer characters. Devices such as the 'analepsis' whereby Sitā in Book IV tells her friend Saramā the story of her abduction by Rāvan can be found in Homer and Virgil, but Milton, who allots Books V-VII to Raphael's account of the Fall of the Angels and the Creation of the Earth, was perhaps the first epic poet to make the recall of earlier events part of his epic architecture, rather than a digression introduced for narrative convenience. In the letter which Mohitlal Majumdar quotes above, Madhusudan expresses some uncertainty about the placing of Book IV, 'since it is scarcely connected with the main progress of the Fable';[89] but in fact his structural instincts were absolutely sound, as the book not only explains the background to Sitā's captivity, it also provides an aesthetically necessary 'calm before the storm', a pause before the relentless build-up in Books V and VI to the killing of Meghnād himself.

Miltonic too is the placing of Meghnād's death—not too near the end of the poem, any more than Milton placed the eating of the forbidden fruit too near the end of *Paradise Lost.* (It comes in Book IX, which out of twelve books is proportionally similar to Book VI out of Madhsuduan's nine.) Instead of the 'argument' that Milton supplies at the beginning of each book, Madhusudan gives titles,

[89]See Source Notes, p. 337.

appended to the end of each *sarga*. These are themselves an indication of his structural control, as they serve as an extremely succinct summary of the whole.

The other respect in which the influence on Madhusudan of Western literature was profound was in his conception of character. When the youthful Rabindranath Tagore published two rather scathing critiques of *Meghnādbadh kābya* in the journal *Bhāratī* in 1877 and 1882, he complained (a) that it was an almost sacrilegious betrayal of Vālmiki's *Rāmāyaṇa*, (b) that it was not a proper epic, as it did not present epic heroes as models of moral excellence, (c) its language was unnatural and artificial, 'gathered from five places' or made 'from opening a dictionary' and (d) it demeaned its male protagonists by making them indulge in displays of effeminate emotion. Of Rāvan's *bilāp* in Book I, Tagore wrote:

> When we read this, we feel that a widowed *woman* is weeping with her head in her hands. Even if an ordinary hero were to weep like this we would shudder, but this is an epic hero, more than a hero, one who has made heaven tremble by his might; his resolution is so strong that though his sons and grandsons and brothers have been killed before his eyes, and wealthy, populous, golden Lanka has become a cremation ground, and even though he is desperately wounded on the battlefield, he still cannot be killed by Rām. What right then has the poet to make him weep like a girl?[90]

[90]*Rabīndra-racanābalī* (Visva-Bharati, Kolkata, 1997), Vol. 29, p. 84. Further material on Tagore's objections to Madhusudan can be found in my article mentioned in fn. 32 above.

Tagore does not seem to have understood that Madhusudan's aim was to match the poets and dramatists of Europe by giving his characters—whether human, demonic or divine—realistically human qualities. In a letter about his play *Kṛṣṇakumārī* (1861) to the actor Keshabchandra Ganguli, he drew a crucial contrast between characters in the Western and Indian traditions:

> . . . I must here tell you, my dear G, what, I dare say, you will allow at least to some extent, viz, that we Asiatics are of a more romantic turn of mind than our European neighbours. Look at the splendid Shakespearean Drama. If you leave out *A Midsummer Night's Dream*, *Romeo and Juliet* and perhaps one or two more, what play would deserve the name of *Romantic*? Romantic in the sense in which Sacoontala is Romantic? In the great European Drama you have the stern realties of life, lofty passion and heroism of sentiment. With us is all softness, all romance. We forget the world of reality and dream of Fairylands.[91]

Realism, mimesis—so central to the entire Western literary tradition even among poets and dramatists who use mythological material—is what Madhusudan aspired to himself. That is why Rāvan weeps so unrestrainedly at the death of his son Virbāhu and later over Meghnād himself. It is the humanly realistic and natural thing to do. In the same way, Milton expresses through all his characters—Adam, Eve, Satan, even God himself—a full gamut of human emotions, just as Homer and Virgil

[91]Murshid 2004, p. 139.

before him had expressed human emotion through their characters too.

It is clear, however, from Madhusudan's comments on Milton in his letters that he found in him a combination of learning and grandeur and technical skill that made him truly great, but not really lovable. He was 'the *toughest* of poets';[92] in a way he was the Lion of Europe itself, to be admired and emulated, yes, but also to be feared and to be regarded as aloof and alien, for was the lion not, in the form of British colonial rule, subjugating the land and the civilization that Madhusudan belonged to and which he loved so much? To Rajnarayan Basu, who had written to him warmly after the publication of the first volume of *Meghnādbadh kābya* in January 1861:

> Your feeling is anything but uncomplimentary. He who is 'beautiful', 'tender' and pathetic, with a dash of 'sublimity' is sure to float down the stream of time in triumph. All readers are sure to unite in loving and adoring him. Look at the Sanscrit Kalidas, the Latin Virgil, the Italian Tasso. I don't think England has a single poet worthy of being named with these; her Milton is a grander being. Like his own Satan, he is full of the loftiest thoughts, but has little or nothing that may be called amiable. He elevates the mind of the readers to a most astonishing height, but he never touches the heart. And what is the consequence? He has a glorious name but few readers. He is Satan himself. We acknowledge him to belong to a far superior order of beings; but we never feel for him. We hear the sound of his ethereal voice with awe and

[92]Letter to Rajnarayan Basu, 24 April 1860. Murshid 2004, p. 117.

> trembling. He is the deep roar of a lion in the silent solitude of the forest.[93]

But Madhusudan the man and the poet was not like that. Time now to move to the qualities that have made his poetry *loved* by his countrymen as well as admired: the qualities that made him a great Bengali and Indian poet, not a '*kālo* [dark-skinned] *sāheb*' who offered them only mimicry and pastiche. For, as he said in a letter to Gour: 'In matters literary, old boy, I am too proud to stand before the world in borrowed clothes. I may borrow a neck-tie, or even a waist coat, but not the whole suit.'[94]

The Elephant of India

When Madhusudan was a student at Hindu College, he won the Gold Medal in a college competition of 1842 for an essay 'On the importance of educating Hindu Females, with reference to the improvement which it may be expected to produce on the education of children, in their early years, and the happiness it would generally confer on domestic life'. Youthful though the essay is, it firmly allies Madhusudan with the efforts of reformers such as Rammohan Roy, Ishwarchandra Vidyasagar, and a number of leading figures in the Brahmo Samaj to promote the education and emancipation of women, to stamp out *satī* (suttee), child marriage and polygamy, and to promote widow remarriage. It is male-oriented in that it calls for female education so that the English-educated members of the *bhadralok* class can have wives more suited to them,

[93]Ibid., p. 171.
[94]Murshid 2004, p. 107.

but that was an attitude that even the most progressive and liberal shared:

> The happiness of a man who has an enlightened partner is quite complete. The very idea of so sweet a possession awakens even in the most prosaic bosoms feelings truly poetical . . . In India, I may say in all the Oriental countries women are looked upon as created merely to contribute to the gratification of the animal appetites of men. This brutal misconception of the design of the Almighty is the source of much misery to the fair sex, because it not only makes them appear as of inferior mental endowments, but no better than a sort of speaking brutes. The people of this country do not know the pleasure of domestic life, and indeed they cannot know, until civilization shows them the way to attain it.[95]

Madhusudan certainly kept faith with these principles, sacrificing his parental home and religion for them, and seeking a modern kind of companionate marriage based on courtship, love and equality, even if with Rebecca his first attempt at that came to grief. Even more striking is the vigour, independence and assertiveness that we find in the female characters in his poems and plays. But are these characters 'Western'? Not at all. Sarmishṭhā and Krishnakumāri in his plays of those names, the women depicted in the eleven 'verse letters' (based on Ovid's *Heroides*) of *Bīrāṅganā kābya* (1862), the women from epic and mythology celebrated in his sonnets, and above all Meghnād's wife Pramilā in *Meghnādbadh kābya* are all Indian. The most famously

[95]Kshetra Gupta (ed.), *Madhusūdan racanābalī*, pp. 622–3.

Westernized poet in nineteenth century Bengal depicted in his literary works—his English poems included—not a single European woman, unless we include the 'fond sweet blue-eyed maid' he fantasized about in the earliest poem of all that has been preserved.[96] He would certainly have seen the subjugation and degradation and illiteracy of women in Indian society at all social levels as a symptom of the general decay of Hindu civilization that he excoriated in his Madras lecture on the Anglo-Saxon and the Hindu. But in looking for models to counteract such attitudes, he mined Indian sources, Islamic as well as Hindu. We have already seen in Madhusudan's biography a pattern of loss and recovery: the loss of his parental family and education at Hindu college followed by recovery at Bishop's College; the loss of notions he may have had of a career in the Anglican Church followed by recovery as a teacher, journalist and married man in Madras; the loss of his position as a poet in English and of his first marriage and children followed by recovery with Henrietta and the start of his Bengali literary career; the loss of his position as a Bengali poet and dramatist when he departed for England followed by his painfully won qualification as a barrister and return to Calcutta where for a brief while he lived in considerable style. The pattern may have been broken by his final stage of defeat and collapse, but it provides an unconscious foundation, I think, for what is going on ideologically in his literary works.

It is tempting to look for covert connections between the women in Madhusudan's plays and poems and the two

[96]Like 'I sigh for Albion's distant shore' (see above, p. xlvi) it is probably best to read the poem entitled 'My fond sweet blue-eyed maid' and dated 28 March 1841 as an imitation of the kind of ditties the British in Calcutta liked to pen, rather than expressing any kind of serious personal longing. See Kshetra Gupta (ed.), *Madhusūdan racanābalī*, pp. 435–6.

women in his own life and his relationship with them. In his play *Śarmiṣṭhā* (1859), King Yayati is torn between his love for his wife Devyāni and Sarmishṭhā, daughter of Sukrāchārya, king of the Asuras. There is bitter enmity between the two women too, starting when Sarmishṭhā threw Devyāni down a well in a quarrel. The play ends happily with Sukrāchārya calling on Devyāni to forgive his daughter, and with Devyāni herself saying to her husband: 'My sweetest lord, two creepers embrace today the same stately tree.'[97] If we read the play as somehow derived from the Rebecca-Henrietta-Madhu triangle, it obviously represents wishful thinking. Much deeper tensions and a more mature exploration of the various ways in which men and women can hurt each other can be found in *Bīrāṅganā kābya*, where the women who write the verse letters to their lovers or spouses seem to alternate between the betrayed or neglected (Sakuntalā, Kekayi, Draupadi) and the traitorous or seductive (Tārā, Surpanakhā, Urvasi)—between what we could call 'Rebecca' and 'Henrietta' types if we actually knew more about their personalities. The contrast between two types of woman is also very marked in *Meghnādbadh kābya*, with Sitā's plaintive passivity emphasized in order to make Pramilā's Amazon-like forcefulness all the more erotic and glamorous.

But the important thing about all these female characters, wherever they may lie on the active/ passive, seductive/ betrayed, Henrietta/ Rebecca scale, is they stand up for themselves, and they do so from a strong sense of honour, their own honour and the honour of their family or lineage. In *Kṛṣṇakumārī nāṭak* (1861), Madhusudan's finest play,

[97]Madhusudan's own translation in his English version of the play, *Sermista* (1859).

a tragedy on a Shakespearean scale though with many elements from the Sanskrit dramatic tradition, rivalry between Jagatsinha, king of Jaypur, and Mānsinha, king of Marabar, for the hand of Krishnakumāri, daughter of King Bhimsen of Udaypur, threatens to lead to total war and the destruction of Udaypur. Through an elaborate series of intrigues, King Bhimsen is persuaded that the only way out is to have Krishnakumāri killed. The King goes mad with the agony of this, and his brother Balendrasinha, engaged by the king to carry out the deed, shrinks back at the last minute and reveals the plot—at which Krishnakumāri forgives him, then kills herself, arguing that 'She who dies to benefit another or to preserve the honour of her lineage (*kulmān*) will be remembered for ever.'[98] It is from the same kind of motive that Pramilā joins her dead husband Meghnād on his funeral pyre at the end of *Meghnādbadh kābya*. As an actual and iniquitous social practice, *satī* would have appalled Madhusudan, and he would certainly have regarded Rammohan Roy's campaign against it, culminating in Lord William Bentinck's outlawing of it in 1829, as a major step forward on the path of social and religious reform. Yet like his European contemporary Richard Wagner, ending *Tristan und Isolde* (1865) and *Götterdämmerung* (1876) with Isolde's *Liebestod* and Brunnhilde's self-immolation, he could not resist the image of Meghnād and Pramilā being swept up to heaven in 'a chariot of fire' as the only fitting apotheosis for their love.

Through his female characters, Madhusudan was, it seems to me, engaging in an act of cultural recovery—compensation for the loss of power and self-esteem that women in India had suffered through the purdah-system

[98]*Kṛṣṇakumārī nāṭak*, Act V Scene 3.

and the cult of the 'perfect wife'.[99] It wasn't difficult for him to find characters from India's heritage to counteract such notions, because the epics and myths of India are full of dynamic and powerful female characters, the Brahmanical traditions of Bengal gave pride of place to the worship of Durgā and Kāli as expressions of Siva's creative energy or *śakti*, and the folk traditions of Bengal were full of powerful mother-goddesses too. In *Kṛṣṇakumārī nāṭak*, the scheming Madanikā—whose manipulations bring about the catastrophic rivalry between the two suitors—says in an Iago-like soliloquy:

> Ha! Those who despise women as stupid don't realize that women are born into a powerful lineage [*strīloker śaktikule janma*]! The Siva who can destroy the universe in a trice is easily kept under the feet of Bhagavati [Kāli]. Ah! Ah! Who has the intelligence to match the intelligence of women?[100]

And in his play *Māyā-kānan* (1872, written after his return from Europe), a citizen who is discussing the course of events with two others comments:

> It will have to be admitted that in all ages women are at the root of men's ruin! . . . If Draupadi had not been insulted, the terrible battle of Kurukshetra might not have happened . . . And King Rāvan destroyed his own race because of his lust for Sitā.[101]

[99]See Julia Leslie, *The Perfect Wife: The Orthodox Hindu Woman according to the* Strīdharmapaddhati *of Tryambakayajvan* (Oxford University Press, New Delhi, 1989).

[100]*Kṛṣṇakumārī nāṭak*, Act II Scene 3.

[101]*Māyā-kānan*, Act IV Scene 3.

So women can use their power for good or ill, but power they most certainly have—or did have in the world of epic and myth that Madhusudan explored in his works.

A focus on women, and on passion and intensity in the relations between men and women, is a quality in literature that we often describe with that capacious and flexible term 'romantic'. Madhusudan's interest in romantic heroines may indeed have been influenced by his early exposure to Western literature, and he may have gone on to portray Sarmishṭhā, Pramilā, Krishnakumāri and the women in *Bīrāṅganā kābya* because of his acquaintance with Helen, Andromache, Hera, Juliet, Portia, Cleopatra or Eve. But Indian sources gave him all that he needed for the exploration of the *rasas* or emotions that classical Indian aesthetic theory defined as being central to the effect of all the arts. His series of sonnets written in Europe include four on the *rasas* of *karuṇa* (pathos), *vīra* (valour), *śṛṅgāra* (eros) and *raudra* (wrath). The one which he depicts as being 'the queen of *rasas*' and the essence of poetry itself is *karuṇa*:

I saw a graceful woman by a stream,
Grave and sorrowful as the autumn moon
When it fears eclipse. All alone she sat;
Her face was wet with softly-flowing tears.
One by one they slid from her eyes like pearls,
Fell on the surface of the stream, and there,
Floating, turned into full-bloomed lotus flowers—
Golden lotus, moist with nectar for bees
To suck, rich with scent for the breeze to waft.
Bemused, I looked around uneasily.
The land was empty; a divine voice spoke:

'That stream is poetry; that woman's name
Is Pathos, queen of *rasas*. Blessed is he
Who can, through meditation, conquer her.'[102]

This a very Indian poem, and all the emotions of pathos, grief, despair, sorrow, anguish etc. that we find in *Meghnādbadh kābya* can be traced to Indian sources as well as Western ones, as my Source Notes show. But what of tragedy as a genre? Of Madhusudan's introduction of tragedy into Bengali literature not only with *Kṛṣṇakumārī nāṭak* but *Meghnādbadh kābya* itself? Was there an Indian source for that?

In his Introduction to his translation of the *Bhagavad-gītā*, Juan Mascaró eloquently states the standard view:

> Sanskrit literature is a great literature. We have the great songs of the Vedas, the splendour of the *Upanishads*, the glory of the *Bhagavad Gita*, the vastness of the *Mahabharata*, the tenderness and heroism found in the *Ramayana*, the wisdom of the fables and stories of India, the scientific philosophy of the Sankhya, the psychological philosophy of Yoga, the poetical philosophy of Vedanta, the laws of Manu, the grammar of Panini and other scientific writings, the lyrical poetry and drama culminating in the great poetry and dramas of Kalidasa.
>
> There are, however, two great branches of literature not found in Sanskrit. There is no history and there is no tragedy: there is no Herodotus or

[102]*Caturdaśpadī kabitābalī*, No. 48. This and my translation of the other three sonnets can be found in my book *Beauty, Be My Brahman: Indian Poems* (Writers Workshop, Kolkata, 2004), pp. 89–91.

> Thucydides; and there is no Aeschylus or Sophocles or Euripides.
>
> Sanskrit literature is, on the whole, a romantic literature interwoven with idealism and practical wisdom, and with a passionate longing for spiritual vision . . . .[103]

Similarly, Lee Siegel, in his seminal study of the Comic Tradition in India, writes:

> The Western theatrical curtain is decorated with the comic and the tragic masks. Under the influence of Greek forms and Aristotelian theory, Western drama is characterized by a division into comedy and tragedy. The tension between these binary forms invigorates and perpetuates each, and comedy has been largely understood in its relationship to tragedy, its polar opposite. But the Western categories fail in the Indian context. In Western terms there is no tragedy in India. There are no plays which begin in joy and culminate in sorrowful defeat, no stories of glory in grief and disaster, no conclusions to arouse pity and fear, and no catharsis of those emotions. Rather, there are heroic or romantic melodramas in which one particular aesthetic mood dominates and in which others may play a part. In terms of Western categories there is only comedy in India—the plays inevitably end happily—'life goes on.'[104]

[103]*The Bhagavad* Gita, translated from the Sanskrit with an Introduction by Juan Mascaró (Penguin Books, 1962), Introduction, pp. 9–10.

[104]Lee Siegel, *Laughing Matters: Comic Tradition in India* (The University of Chicago Press, 1987), p. 8.

In terms of genre, this is true, and Sanskrit theoreticians such as Bharata, the legendary author of the *Nāṭyaśāstra* (treatise on the theatrical arts), have no place for tragedy. But I think it is possible to find an Indian basis for Madhusudan's conception of tragedy that may not be rooted in Sanskrit aesthetics but which is certainly related to his place and time, as a Bengali writing in Calcutta in the 1860s.

In order to find this, we need probe beneath the surface of his great poem, understand what it may be saying at a symbolic or allegorical level, even if such meanings were not consciously in the mind of its author. It is one of the key characteristics of a literary 'classic' that it should contain many layers of meaning, so that each generation of readers will find new things in it. The greatest classics are often the most contradictory, paradoxical or ambiguous, precisely because they are so many-layered. As the critic Frank Kermode put it in an article in 1996: 'Broadly speaking . . . any book that is kept modern by continuous and varied interpretation . . . is entitled to be called a classic. Such a work will present different aspects at different periods . . . Either by its own inherent virtue or because of the labours of many interpreters, the classic must display a capacity to be indefinitely plural.'[105]

Meghnādbadh kābya was published in two volumes in January and April 1861. That was very soon after the suppression by the British of the 'Indian Mutiny' of 1857 and the assumption by the British Crown in 1858 of total rule and authority over India. Madhusudan never comments on political affairs in his letters (see above, p. xlv), so we have no record of his views on this watershed in Indo-

[105]*The Guardian*, 23 February 1996. Kermode was writing about his own book, *The Classic* (1975).

British relations. He may well have shared the view common among the Bengali elite at the time that the Mutiny was a threat to law and stability which the British had a right to suppress. But feelings of racial or social humiliation were certainly not alien to him, and were all the more keen because he was outwardly so anglicized. Winning full acceptance in British social circles was as hard for him in Madras in the 1850s as it was when he returned to Calcutta as a barrister in 1867. He moved his family to Versailles when he was reading for the Bar at Gray's Inn, partly perhaps because he found less racism there. On 26 October 1864 he wrote in an upbeat mood to Gour:

> This is unquestionably the best quarter of the globe. I have better dinners for a few Francs than the Rajah of Burdwan ever dreams of! . . . Come here and you will soon forget that you spring from a degraded and subject race. Here you are the master of your masters! The man that stands behind my chair when I dine, would look down upon the best of our princes in India. The girl that pulls off my muddy boots on a wet day, would scorn to touch our richest Rajah in India. Every one, whether high or low, will treat you as a man and not a 'damned nigger.' But this is Europe, my boy, and not India.[106]

I believe that some of these tensions and humiliations can be found in *Meghnādbadh kābya* as soon as we begin to see that Rāvan, Meghnād and the Rākshasas are presented as 'insiders', whereas 'Ram and his rabble' are the outsiders, the invaders, the violators of 'golden Lankā'

[106]Murshid 2004, p. 223.

in all her pride and glory. The shift from the reformers of the first half of the nineteenth century in Bengal to the nationalists of the second, which occurred largely as a result of the Mutiny and the change from East India Company rule to full imperialism, has been described as an antithesis between xenophilia and xenophobia.[107] Madhusudan, in his personality and in his writing, is on the cusp: xenophilia was there aplenty, as we have seen, but xenophobia, 'fear of the stranger', was there too.

I have developed this argument in detail in an article,[108] and can only sketch it here. I have already indicated above (p. lii) that the morality of *pāp* and *karmaphal* that Rām and his supporters represent, and which is accepted by the gods and even (to some extent) by Madhusudan himself, can be linked to Christianity, even if it had Indian roots. One can carry this argument further by associating the Rākshasas closely with Hinduism. The epic shows them to be—at crucial points such as the anointing of Meghnād by Rāvan at the end of Book I, or the devotions of Meghnād's mother Queen Mandodari in the Siva-temple in Book V, or Meghnād's funeral rites in Book IX—devout Hindus, with a Saivite emphasis derived largely from the medieval Bengali *Rāmāyaṇ* of Krittibās. Rām, Sugriv *et al.* are also Hindus; we see Rām performing a *pūjā* to Durgā in Book II;[109] and Lakshman, instructed by the Goddess of

[107]See David Kopf, *The Brahmo Samaj and the Shaping of the Modern Indian Mind* (Archives Publishers, New Delhi, 1988), pp. 129–30.

[108]'Xenophilia and Xenophobia: Michael Madhusudan Datta's *Meghnād-badh kābya*, in Rupert Snell and I. M. P. Raeside (ed.), *Classics of Modern South Asian Literature* (Harrassowitz Verlag, Wiesbaden, 1998), pp. 143–169. Broadly speaking, the Bengali Hindu elite initially welcomed East India Company rule and the new commercial and educational opportunities it brought them, because it offered an escape from earlier domination by Muslim rulers.

[109]*MBK* II.225f.

Dreams as engaged by Māyā, goes to the temple of Chaṇḍi in Book V. But in a crucial variation of the *Rāmāyaṇa* story that is at the heart of his tragic vision, Madhusudan has Meghnād killed by Lakshman in Book VI in an utterly sacrilegious way. Meghnād has gone to the Nikumbhilā grove to perform the *pūjā* to the fire-god Agni that will make him invincible in battle. (This invincibility derives from a boon that Brahmā gave him in order to gain Indra's release when Meghnād defeated him in battle—an aspect of the story that *is* in the *Rāmāyaṇa* tradition, but which is assumed, never explicitly stated in Madhusudan's epic.[110]) He is defenceless and alone, and resorts to throwing his *pūjā*-vessels at Lakshman in a vain attempt to ward him off. Because Lakshman and Vibhishan are enabled by Māyā to enter Lankā invisibly, Meghnād dies because of a trick, a *kauśal*. That is why Madhusudan asks, 'By what trick [*ki kauśale*] did the enjoyer of Urmilā destroy Meghnād . . .?' in his opening Invocation.

The British conquest and rule of India was also a trick, involving extraordinary feats of deception, skullduggery and illusion from beginning to end. In *Meghnādbadh kābya*, Rām is described as *māyābī*, invincible through sorcery, which is another inversion of the *Rāmāyaṇa*, for there it is the Rākshasas who are *māyābī*, not Rām.[111] In Tagore's great story about the Indian Mutiny, *Durāśā* ('False Hope', 1898), a Muslim ruler called Golamkader Khan who declines to join the rebellion says of the British: 'Those damned English can do the impossible . . . The

[110]It is surprising that he didn't find a way of bringing it in explicitly, as it explains why it is so important for Lakshman to kill Meghnād before he completes the *pūjā*. See Notes, p. 3 and Source Notes, pp. 306–8.

[111]See Source Notes, p. 349, 354.

people of Hindusthan can never match them. I'm not going to stake this fort of mine on so slender a chance . . .'[112]

Is it far-fetched to suggest that some of these same ideas may have been lurking in Madhusudan's mind, at an unconscious level, when he decided to write a version of the *Yuddhākāṇḍa* of the *Rāmāyaṇa* that would turn the Rākshasas into tragic heroes?

As with his female heroines, his male heroes too are an act of recovery, for loss, for defeat, for dastardly humiliation. In Meghnād's death we have the 'glory in grief and disaster' that Lee Siegel rightly says was absent from Indian literature previously. But its power in the context of *Meghnādbadh kābya* as a whole is not an import from the West: it is an act of defiance and resistance to the West, an assertion of patriotism that can, I believe, be read as containing the seeds of post-1857 Indian nationalism and the eventual expulsion of the British from South Asia.

Heroic tragedy is one form of defiance; another is humour. The richly humorous literature and art of nineteenth and twentieth century Calcutta—from Madhusudan's two farces or his contemporary Kaliprasanna Sinha's *Hutom pyā̃cār naksā* ('Sketches by a Barn Owl') (1862–4)[113] to the satirical cartoons of Gaganendranath Tagore (1867–1938), the nonsense verse of Sukumar Ray (1889–1923) and the incomparable stories of 'Parashuram' (Rajshekhar Basu, 1880–1960)[114]—may have wittily and sometimes savagely

[112]Rabindranath Tagore, *Selected Short Stories*, translated by William Radice (Penguin Books, rev. edn. 1994), p. 221.

[113]Available now in English as *The Observant Owl: Hootum's Vignettes of Nineteenth-century Calcutta*, tr. Swarup Roy, foreword by Partha Chatterjee (Black Kite, Permanent Black, Ranikhet and New Delhi, 2008).

[114]A selection of them is available now in English: Parashuram (Rajshekhar Bose), *Selected Stories*, tr. Sukanta Chaudhuri and Palash Baran

mocked the culture of the English-educated Bengali babu, but it was itself produced by that class and was an assertion of its distinct identity. Participants in learned societies, debating-clubs or informal *āḍḍā* (groups of friends meeting to discuss and gossip about topics of mutual interest) delighted in their special jargon and lingo, in the fluidity of the borders between Bengali and English, in their inaccessibility to those—especially the British—who did not share their linguistic, cultural and educational accomplishments. Their cultural self-assertion could be in English—as in Madhusudan's letters or early poems, or in the humorous writings of Shoshee Chunder Dutt (1824–1886),[115] —or in Bengali, or a mixture of the two; but its combined effect, not only in Bengal but all over the subcontinent, was ultimately to make India too big, too dynamic, too rebellious for the British to continue to rule.

The very special style of Bengali that Madhusudan developed for *Meghnādbadh kābya* and his other mature works was in some ways a blind alley. Subsequent Bengali writers have found it easy to parody, but very hard to build on, though the blank verse and sonnet-form that he

Pal, Introduction by Sukanta Chaudhuri (Penguin Books India, New Delhi, 2006). I explore this tradition in the article mentioned in fn. 38 above. See also Parimal Ghosh's article 'Critique of the Bhadralok and the Bhadralok critic' in Debraj Bhattacharya (ed.), *Of Matters Modern* (see fn. 2 above).

[115]Shoshee Chunder Dutt, *Selections from 'BENGALIANA'*, edited by Alex Tickell (Nottingham Trent University: Trent Editions, 2005), has rescued this somewhat forgotten member of a highly educated extended family—not related to Madhusudan—which also produced the poet Toru Dutt. He and several cousins were educated at Hindu College, and were described by Captain D. L Richardson as 'the Rambagan nest of singing birds'. Shoshee's story 'Shunkur: A Tale of the Indian Mutiny of 1857', which contains a shocking rape by two English soldiers on the run of the married daughter of a village woman who gives them refuge, shows that the Mutiny certainly did impinge deeply on the minds of the Bengali *bhadralok*.

introduced have certainly become part of every Bengali poet's repertoire. His style is 'funny' in both senses of the word: constantly witty and playful ('funny ha-ha') but also 'funny-peculiar'. This can be attributed partly to his youthful neglect of Bengali, of which there are several famous admissions in his letters, such as his request to Gour from Madras that he should write to his father 'to say that I have got a daughter. I do not know how to do the thing in Bengali.'[116] His shift from English to Bengali as his poetic medium was an act of deliberate and artificial reclamation. Stylistic oddness reached an extreme in his last work, an unfinished prose version of the *Iliad* which he called *Hekṭar-badh* ('The Killing of Hector', 1871). It was criticized by his biographer Yogindranath Basu for being 'ungrammatical, full of coarseness, and because it is from beginning to end influenced by Western modes it is impossible for readers who do not know English to understand'.[117] A later biographer and critic, Sureshchandra Maitra, was more sympathetic, praising him for devising a *dhrupadī* ('solemn, majestic') prose style that was non-Sanskritic. He finds creative innovation, not incompetence in its strange compounds based on Greek epithets and its complex sentence structures that may even have been influenced by the German.[118] (Madhusudan's letters from Versailles indicate that he studied German while he was there, as well as French and Italian.)

Madhusudan's linguistic debt or otherwise to the Sanskrit tradition lies beyond this Introduction and beyond my competence too. In his letters he can appear cavalier about

[116]Mushid 2004, p. 78.

[117]Yogindranath Basu, p. 470.

[118]Sureshchandra Maitra, *Māikel Madhusūdan Datta: jīban o sāhitya* (Calcutta, 1975), p. 252f.

Sanskrit,[119] but Vyāsa, Vālmiki and Kālidāsa became firm members of the small band of poets he really read and admired.[120] Moreover, if there was any precedent at all for his mastery of pause and phrasing, it has to be found, I think, in the highly Sanskritized Bengali prose that was developed by Ishwarchandra Vidyasagar in his prose adaptation of *Śakuntalā* (1854) and in the massive Bengali translation of the *Mahābhārata* that was started by Vidyasagar but completed magnificently by Kaliprasanna Sinha and published—contemporaneously with *Meghnādbadh kābya*—in 1859–66. Vidyasagar was credited by Rabindranath Tagore among others for introducing Western-style punctuation into Bengali. This was not strictly true, for punctuation had been used before him by the Bengali pandits employed by the British at Fort William College, by Rammohan Roy, and by Debendranath Tagore and Akshaykumar Datta in the Brahmo magazine the *Tattvabodhinī Patrikā*.[121] But what is shown by the emergence of Madhusudan's blank verse style from the rhythmic, punctuated, yet Sanskritic prose of Vidyasagar and Kaliprasanna is that Bengali could be big: it could have the sinuous flexibility that modern phrasing and punctuation allowed, but it could connect too with India's great classical language and become its equal.[122]

[119]See, for example, his comment on the name 'Vāruni', quoted in my Notes to *MBK* I.443, p. 25.

[120]See his letter to Rajnarayan Basu, quoted above, p. xlii.

[121]This was established by Sisirkumar Das in his London Ph.D thesis (1963) on early Bengali prose. See my article, 'Iswarchandra Vidyasagar, Śakuntalā, and the Liberation of Bengali', in Manik Mukhopadhyay (ed.), *The Golden Book of Vidyasagar: A Commemorative Volume* (All Bengal Vidyasagar Death Centenary Committee, Calcutta, 1993), pp. 193–99.

[122]It was Kaliprasanna who organized a reception on 15 February 1861, described by Madhusudan in a letter to Rajnarayan: 'You will be pleased to

In his exuberant letter to Keshabchandra Gangopadhyay about his invention of blank verse (see above, p. xxxviii), Madhusudan went on to say:

> Take my word of it, that Blank verse will do splendidly in Bengali and that in the course of time, like the modern Europeans, we too shall equal, if not surpass, our classic writers. What we want at present are men of zeal, of diligence, of energy, of enthusiasm, of liberal views to give our language a jolly lift. If we have no 'genius' among ourselves, let us prepare the way for future ones. Have you heard of Sackville—Lord Buckhurst, born in 1527? This nobleman's play, called 'Gorboduc', first introduced to Englishmen the form of verse in which William Shakespeare wrote. My motto is, 'Fire away, my boys!' The namby-Pamby-Wallahs—the imitators of Bharat Chunder—*our* Pope, who has—
> 'Made Poetry a mere mechanical art,
> And every warbler has his tune by heart!'
> may frown or laugh at us, but I say—'Be hanged' to them![123]

One can say that Madhusudan is talking about Bengali here, not about other South Asian languages or about the

hear that not very long ago the *Bidyotsâhinī Sabhā* and the President Kali Prasanna Singh of Jorasanko, presented me with a splendid silver claret jug. There was a great meeting and an address in Bengali. Probably you have read both address and reply in the vernacular papers. Fancy! I was expected to speechify in Bengali!' (Murshid 2004, p. 160)

[123]Murshid 2004, p. 115. The quotation is from William Cowper's *Table Talk*. 'Bharat Chunder' is Bharatchandra Ray (1712–1760), the leading poet of eighteenth century Bengal.

subcontinent as a whole, but actually whenever he is in this exaltedly optimistic and patriotic mood he seems to reach beyond Bengal itself. In a letter to Rajnarayan he writes: 'What a vast field does our country now present for literary enterprise! I wish to God, I had time. Poetry, the Drama, Criticism, Romance—a man would leave a name behind him "above all Greek, above all Roman fame".'[124] This vagueness about region or country may have been inevitable at a time when the nation state of India was still a long way in the future, and with much of the subcontinent still under the rule of native princes; but it also reflects the cosmopolitan character of Calcutta, which to this day is both a Bengali cultural centre and also a melting pot for people from all over South Asia. In *Buṛa sāliker ghāṛe rõ*, the second of his two farces, Bhaktaprasad Babu, a lecherous old Vaishnava zamindar who lives outside Calcutta, has a son who is studying at Hindu College. Bhakta asks his friend Ananda Babu about how his son is getting on:

Enter Ananda Babu.

Bhakta: Who's this? Ananda? Come in, dear chap, come in. When did you get back?

Ananda: (*doing* praṇām *and then sitting down*) I got back last night, thank you.

Bhakta: What's the news then, tell me.

Ananda: All the news is good. I haven't been home for ages, so I've taken a few months' holiday.

Bhakta: Quite right too. Have you been seeing my son Ambika?

[124]Ibid., p. 122. The quotation is from Pope's *Epistles*, I.2.26.

Ananda:	Why, I see Ambika nearly every day in Calcutta.
Bhakta:	How so? Don't you live at Pathureghat?
Ananda:	I used to live there, yes, but now I've moved to Kidderpore.
Bhakta:	How are Ambika's studies going?
Ananda:	My dear Sir, there's scarcely another student at Hindu College as 'clever' as he.
Bhakta:	As what as he, babu?
Ananda:	'Clever'—I mean to say bright, intelligent.
Bhakta:	Ha ha, so that's one of your English words is it! They sound awful to me. If you said *jahīn* or *cālāk* I would understand you. Very well, Ananda, you're an excellent fellow: tell me then, Ambika hasn't learnt any *adharmācaraṇ* [bad behaviour] has he?
Ananda:	Please, what is *adharmācaraṇ*?
Bhakta:	It's being rude to Brahmins, neglecting to bathe in Ganges water, all this Christian carrying-on, such as—
Ananda:	I wouldn't know about any of those things.
Bhakta:	I daresay Ambikaprasad could never show disrespect for religion: he's my son, isn't he? God! You are the truth! Well now, I've heard that everything's getting mixed up in Calcutta. Kaysthas, Brahmins, lower castes, merchants, Saivites, weavers, Muslim weavers, oilmen, is it true that they all live together and eat together? Is this so, dear chap?
Ananda:	That would be a way of putting it.

Bhakta: How ghastly! Hinduism has completely lost its dignity! What has it got left? Kali's strength grows from day to day.[125]

The mixed-up nature of Kolkata makes it (still) a funny place, funny-ha-ha as well as funny-peculiar, but the mixing brings us to some final, more serious reflections on the wider aspects of Madhusudan's achievement, and the significance that it has today, as we approach the 150th anniversary of the publication of *Meghnādbadh kābya*.

It may seem something of a paradox that despite all the inspiration and material he derived from the literature of the past, first from Romanticism, then from the Classics of both Europe and India, Madhusudan has always been rightly regarded as a pioneer of modernity, a key figure in the Bengal Renaissance, 'the cognitive revolution' from which 'the modern Indian mind' has emerged.[126] Modernity and its definition has been a major theme in the fields of postcolonial and 'Subaltern' studies that have been developed over the last few decades, notably by Bengali scholars such as Partha Chatterjee, Ranajit Guha, Dipesh Chakraborty, Sumit Sarkar, Ashis Nandy and Gayatri Spivak, and which have had an immense international impact. The notion of 'one' modernity that developed first in the West, and then was introduced into India and other parts of the world through the activities of colonizers

[125]For the Kali-yuga, see Notes, p. 104, 188.

[126]I take the term 'cognitive revolution' from Subrata Dasgupta's book *The Bengal Renaissance: Identity and Creativity from Rammohun Roy to Rabindranath Tagore* (Permanent Black, New Delhi, 2007). The book is an interesting application of the principles of 'cognitive science' to change and creativity in Bengal Renaissance, and contains an insightful account of Madhusudan's life and work (pp. 89–102).

working alongside a 'progressive' native elite, has been hotly contested. The lives of non-elite, subaltern classes have been rightly brought into the picture, and a conception of rival modernities—'Western' and 'colonial'—or multiple modernities has become quite widespread. Yet a recent collection of essays edited by Debraj Bhattacharya indicates the beginnings of a shift back to a more unified notion of modernity, one in which distinctions between West and East and colonizer and the (formerly) colonized are becoming increasingly meaningless.[127] A universal modernity of this sort—even though there will be an infinite number of variations and gradations within it—suits our twenty-first century world of air travel, email, mobile phones, the internet, migration, multiculturalism and the ongoing shift of economic and demographic power from Europe and America to China and India. It is also, I believe, a world in which the outlook and achievements of a figure like Madhusudan have a natural place.

Madhusudan was not just 'modern' because he adopted an extremely non-traditional lifestyle, dress or mode of speaking. He was modern because he wrote an epic poem in which the contradictions and tensions and anxieties of universal modernity are prophetically and vividly expressed.

On the one hand *Meghnādbadh kābya* is about loss. If I am right in reading the slaughter of Meghnād, the humiliation and defeat of the Rākshasas, and the implied destruction of Lankā as an—albeit unconscious—expression of grief at the loss of the 'old India', brought about by 'outsiders' whose morality of sin and retribution owes a

[127]*Of Matters Modern*. See fn. 2 above. The editor's Introduction to the volume is a succinct and convincing expression of this shift.

lot to Christian influence, then the epic stands as a howl of anguish at much from the past that is inevitably being damaged and lost from our globalized world. This is why the death of Meghnād, so brilliantly built up to by the preceding books, is so devastating:

> In the blink of an eye, the mighty armed one picked
> up the *koṣā* vessel and hurled it at Lakshman,
> roaring terribly.
> The hero fell to the ground with the force of the
> impact, like a mighty tree crashing down in a
> storm! His divine weapons clattered,
> And the temple rocked, as if from a huge earthquake!
> A stream of blood flowed.
> Meghnād instantly seized the divine sword—but he
> could not lift it. He pulled at the bow—
> It remained in Lakshman's hand. He angrily grasped
> the shield, but his efforts were useless.
> As vainly as an elephant wrapping his trunk round
> an outcrop of rock and trying to pull it, that
> greatest of heroes dragged at the quiver.[128]

The dying hero is like the Elephant of India herself, the old India, many of whose beauties and traditions are now being damaged or lost.

But the glory of that image makes *Meghnādbadh kābya* also a poem about recovery. Precisely as an act of compensation for loss, the epic projects an image of the power and glory of the past, even at the moment of its tragic defeat. As Madhusudan put it in a letter to Rajnarayan on 15 May 1860:

[128] *MBK* VI.502–15.

> I am going on with *Meghanad* by fits and starts. Perhaps the poem will be finished by the end of the year. I am glad you like the opening lines. I must tell you, my dear fellow, that though as a jolly Christian youth I don't care a pin's head for Hinduism, I love the grand mythology of our ancestors. It is full of poetry. A fellow with an inventive head can manufacture the most beautiful things out of it.[129]

Inspired by this love, identifying with what has been lost, Madhusudan peels away the pieties that the *Rāmāyaṇa* has acquired over the centuries and restores, through the vigour and glory of the Rākshasas and their older, less religious conception of *dharma*, something that may be closer in spirit to Vālmiki's original work. 'It is worth stressing that, far from being a Vaiṣṇava epic, Vālmīki's Rāmāyaṇa is no religious epic at all', writes John Brockington in his authoritative study,[130] and there are quite a few other points that he makes which indicate that, subversive though *Meghnādbadh kābya* was of the 'brahmanized' or 'Hinduized' *Rāmāyaṇa*, it was not fundamentally a departure from India's oldest epic traditions.[131]

[129]Murshid 2004, p. 122.

[130]J. L. Brockington, *Righteous Rāma: The Evolution of an Epic* (Oxford University Press, Oxford, 1984), p. 13.

[131]'Thus, far from being the demons of later mythology, the Rākṣasas in the Rāmāyaṇa are mainly depicted as not merely human but also cultured.' (p. 204) 'In its early stages at least, the Rāmāyaṇa is a martial epic with a kṣatriya background, and Rāma is its noble hero. As Jacobi put it, he is "durchaus Mensch", "thoroughly human".' (p. 218) 'With the subsequent brahmanization of the work and consequent shift in emphasis of dharma from "tradition, social duty" to "righteousness, religious duty" comes the desire to assign divine status to Rāma, at first usually expressed through comparison with Indra.' (p. 221) 'The ethical polarization already apparent

But is 'the grand mythology of our ancestors' as reclaimed by a mid-nineteenth century Bengali poet likely to be as it was for those ancestors? I earlier mentioned (p. lxix) the harsh critiques of *Meghnādbadh kābya* that Rabindranath Tagore wrote when he was a very young man. It is unfair, really, to dwell on them, as he later modified his views, and in his *Jībansmṛti* ('Reminiscences', 1917), dismissed his *Bhāratī* articles as youthful bravado. Much more respectful comments on Madhusudan's achievement can be found in his essays on metrics,[132] and in several literary essays too. He even—an ultimate act of atonement—did translations of an extract from *Meghnādbadh kābya* and two sonnets.[133] Especially

---

in the developments of the second stage [of its evolution] . . . leads naturally to a stress on Rāma's activity on behalf of dharma and his defeat of evil in the form of Rāvaṇa. This receives its fullest development . . . in the Uttarakāṇḍa, where Rāvaṇa's genealogy and past exploits are so presented as to turn him into an adversary of the gods . . .' (p. 325). Even the account Brockington gives of the language of the epic as it once was—'basically a clear-cut and cohesive language, which appears to be independent of, though possibly a little later than, the language described by Pāṇini and thus to form, together with the older parts of the Mahābhārata, a genuinely separate epic Sanskrit' (pp. 45–6)—is evocative of Madhusudan's 'clear-cut and cohesive' Bengali epic style.

[132]Collected in *Chanda* (Visvabharati, Calcutta, 1936). See especially the essays *Chander prakṛti*, *Bāṅglā śabda o chandan* and *Chander artha*.

[133]These translations are not at all well known. Written in a notebook of translations that he started in February 1915, they remained unpublished until they appeared in the journal *Rabīndra bīkṣā* No. 29, 7 August 1996 (Rabindra Bhavana, Santiniketan). Tagore's choice of texts is interesting. The passage from *Meghnādbadh kābya* is from Book IV, the 'straightest' book of the epic in that it presents Sitā's story with no real departure from the *Rāmāyaṇa* tradition. The sonnets are *Paricay* (No.13), a paean to 'the land that is mine' and *Kabibar Alfred Tennyson* (No. 84). The prose translations are lyrical and eloquent, but slightly sanitized, with exclamation marks and some rhetorical flourishes removed. The choice suggests to me that Tagore was happy with Madhusudan when he was enthusing about either the East or the West, but less happy when he mixed up the two.

interesting are his comments in his essay *Sāhityasṛṣṭi* ('Literary Creation', 1907). Comparing the *Rāmāyaṇa* to the mighty Ganges, he sees the various versions of it through the ages as its tributaries, feeding into it through a natural process of growth that goes beyond the input of particular poets. *Meghnādbadh kābya* has arisen because of 'the impact of new ideas from Europe': the change it embodies 'harbours a revolt . . . . Ravana and Indrajit are greater in this poem than Rama and Lakshmana . . . . [The poet] found joy in the fearsome play of instinctual power.' This power (*śakti*) Tagore associates with 'the might of Europe . . . in this modern age, a new-strung chord of the *Ramayana* narrative is inwardly attuning itself to the hymn praising such power—could this have been brought about by an individual's whim?'[134]

This may seem at odds with the link that I have made between the Rākshasas and India, with 'Ram and his rabble' standing for the outsiders, the invaders, and thus, in a way, for 'the might of Europe'. But on reflection, I find Tagore's perceptions—as they almost invariably are—to be correct. Given the time at which he was writing, and with his own tendency always to think in terms of East/West binaries, it is not wrong to find in Madhusudan's glorification of the Rākshasas the same *śakti* that was driving the Renaissance itself, and whose energies came to a large extent from the West.

Today, our situation is very different, and it seems as inadequate to describe that *śakti* as 'Western' as it does to describe the mental and physical energy that is fuelling the massive and rapid economic growth of India and China as

[134]Translation by Swapan Chakravorty in Sukanta Chaudhuri (ed.), *Rabindranath Tagore: Selected Writings on Literature and Language* (Oxford University Press, New Delhi, 2001), pp. 162–3.

'Western'. Yet at the same time, many technological, industrial and managerial features of that growth developed in the West before they spread East. And Madhusudan's detachment—'as a jolly Christian youth'—from the very traditions that he uses places him in a position not so different from the poets, composers, film directors or painters of today who, wherever they may come from, are happy to use whatever cultural, religious or mythological traditions may serve their creative purpose, be those traditions European, American, Asian, Australasian or African.

For all his difficulty and complexity, his appeal in his lifetime to a very small elite, Madhusudan is a poet whom any modern person can love. In Bengal, divided as it is between West Bengal and Bangladesh, this already seems to be the case. Whereas Tagore can seem *bideśi* (foreign) to some Bangladeshis, Madhusudan does not. He may use Sanskrit and Hindu materials, but not in a way that excludes anyone. He was as open to Islamic traditions as he was to Hindu and Christian. His English writings in Madras included *Rizia: Empress of Inde*: 'a dramatic poem' in three acts (1849), taken from a Persian source: Muhammad Casim Gerishta's *The History of Hindostan*, translated by Alexander Dow in 1768. A letter to the actor Keshabchandra Ganguli in September 1860 indicates that Madhusudan remained very attached to the subject, and would have written a Bengali play based on it if his potential audience had been less prejudiced.[135]

His works contain no political statement, no explicit call for inter-cultural or inter-religious unity, but they

[135] 'After this we must look to 'Rizia'—I hope that will be a drama after your own heart! The prejudice against Moslem names must be given up.' Murshid 2004, p. 150.

nevertheless—formed as they are from such a potpourri of traditions and influences—match what Gora (son, though he has grown up without knowing it, of an Irish father and a 'memsahib' mother[136]) discovers at the end of Tagore's great novel: that 'Bharat' is something that goes beyond race or caste or religion or the nation states into which South Asia is divided today.

I find him, therefore, though his greatest work was a tragic epic and his life had tragic elements too, always uplifting, exciting and rejuvenating as a poet. In his *Ātma-bilāp* he wrote about being 'dazed by the tricks of hope', but the effect of his poetry is always hopeful. If I was to choose one word to sum him up, it would be YOUTH. Even when he became middle-aged and ill, he retained an indelible buoyancy, an irrepressible optimism and exuberance.[137] Perhaps this was, above all, what made him and his majestic successor Rabindranath Tagore so different from each other. Tagore was a greater poet than Madhusudan, and there was no limit to his range. It certainly included energy and zest, even when he became

[136]See *Gora*, chapters 6 and 75. By having Anandamoyi, Gora's adoptive mother, refer to Gora's natural mother as *sei mem* ('that mem[sahib]'), Tagore indicates that she wasn't Indian, but she could have been Eurasian perhaps—a likely background for the wife of a British soldier in India, and similar to the parentage of Madhusudan's wife Rebecca. Up to 1857 wages for British soldiers were so low that they could not usually afford to bring wives from Britain.

[137]Madhusudan was not exactly a member of Derozio's 'Young Bengal' group (see above, p. xliv). He was of a slightly later generation, became cut off from any group in Calcutta by his Christian conversion, and satirized Young Bengal mercilessly in his farce, *Ekei ki bale sabhyatā*. He also lacked their political and philosophic radicalism. But as a poet he described himself as 'a tremendous literary rebel' (Murshid 2004, p. 130), and to that extent the rebellious, subversive Young Bengal heritage was alive in him. See also fn. 48 above.

old. But Tagore, unlike Madhusudan, was old even when he was young. He had a tendency to melancholy, and a deep-seated wisdom and compassion that Madhusudan lacked. Madhusudan absorbed notions of sin and retribution from Christianity, but not mercy—Tagore had much more of that.[138] Maybe the note of comedy that runs through Madhusudan precluded compassion. Not for him the famous question asked by the Buddha: 'How can there be mirth or laughter when the world is on fire?'[139]

Time now to savour the *śatadal*, to enter the exuberant, extravagant, flamboyant, virile, youthful, rebellious, subversive world of *Meghnādbadh kābya* itself, spattered with its umpteen exclamation marks. It will have to be a 'virtual world', as what follows is an English translation, not the real thing. So first, some words on that.

About this translation

I am personally sceptical about the theory of the transmigration of souls, but I do believe that the transmigration of the soul of a literary work, through translation, is possible. In a lecture I gave in Chittagong, Bangladesh in 2003, on 'The significance of Michael Madhusudan Dutt and his epic',[140] I said that a translation of *Meghnādbadh kābya* needed to do justice to its language,

[138]In several essays, Tagore pays tribute to the spirit of *duḥkha* (sorrow), *śebā* (service) and *manuṣyatva* (humanity) that he felt were at the heart of Christianity. See Pulinbihari Sen (ed.), *Khṛṣṭa* (Visva-Bharati, Calcutta, 1959).

[139]*Dhammapada* 146. Quoted by Lee Siegel, p. 4 (see fn. 104 above). On p. 19 of his book Siegel writes: 'Compassion as the Buddha demonstrates, knows no laughter. Comedy demands a suspension of mercy. The laughter which is tinged with sympathy is melancholy.'

[140]*IIC Quarterly* 30.1, summer 2003, pp. 73–88.

its subject, its tone and its structure. Those categories will also be useful here.

Although the translation should be clear and polished and accessible in English, the reader should feel that he or she is gaining a new kind of linguistic experience. Even to Bengalis, Madhusudan's Bengali can seem odd; I don't mind, therefore, if the English I have used sometimes seems odd too.

To make the subject matter of the poem accessible to all, a considerable amount of information needs to be given. Hence the detailed annotation I have supplied, with allusions, myths, deities etc. explained at the bottom of each page, and additional notes on Madhusudan's use of sources and influences supplied at the end.

Meghnādbadh kābya includes a gamut of emotions from the angry and heroic, or the sensuous and erotic, to the despairing and pathetic. All the *rasas* are there, and a translation will fail if it cannot convey them. At same time there is an overall tone, a unique voice, which the reader needs to hear. Every line of Madhusudan—as with any great poet—is unmistakably his. The reader should hear that voice, and if the translation is read aloud it should ring out even more strongly.

The tight structure of the epic, so formidable an indication of the power of Madhusudan's mind, is, I believe, closely linked to the way in which his blank verse works, with its mastery of phrasing, pause and *enjambement*.[141] In rendering it into English poetry, I have therefore adopted a simple form based on three phrases per line, a phrase being defined by a punctuation mark. This means that the lines vary greatly in length, from the short to the very long.

[141]See above, p. xxxvif. and lxvif.

My translation therefore looks quite different on the page from the original text, as Madhusudan's 14-*mātrā* lines have an evenness of length. But I know no better way of conveying the pace, energy and music of his verse. The discipline of the form lies in the need always to end a paragraph at the end of a line, as in the blank verse of Milton and Madhusudan himself.

The numbers in the text correspond to the lines at which paragraphs begin in the Bengali original. They will enable readers of Bengali to find particular lines quite quickly. I.1, I.33 etc. in the Notes, Source Notes and Introduction refer to paragraphs, not lines.

My translation is the fourth that has been done. The first (not at all well known) was done by Rajendranath Sen and published in Benares in 1926. It is in fluent English blank verse, and the translator deserves more credit for his achievement than he has ever received.[142] Another translation, by Shyamal Bandyopadhyay, was published by Tomsi Publications in Calcutta in 1986. It is described on the title page as 'translated into English Blank Verse', but in fact it is in free verse: the lines do not follow any metrical or rhythmic pattern. Then, in 2004, Clinton B. Seely's translation appeared, published by Oxford University Press in New York and titled: *The Slaying of Meghanada: A Ramayana from Colonial Bengal*. This book was a major step forward in the interpretation and dissemination of *Meghnādbadh kābya* to non-Bengali readers, and I must admit that when it arrived on my desk—when I was still only about half way through my own translation—I was

[142]So far I as I know, there is only one extant copy, in the British Library. Professor Clinton B. Seely drew my attention to it while I was working on my D.Phil thesis, and I included an extract from it in an Appendix to the thesis.

strongly tempted to give up. Professor Seely urged me not to, saying in a very generous inscription in the copy he sent me that he warmly welcomed my translation as a companion piece to his book. His view—and I agree with him—is that a great poem like *Meghnādbadh kābya* deserves many translations. I am sure that mine will not be last.

I count myself lucky that Professor Seely's translation came out before I had completed mine, because I have been able to use his work as a control. We have translated the poem entirely independently of each other, but in revising and polishing my draft I have checked my translation carefully against his, sometimes disagreeing with his version, but often learning from it too. Every translator of a work—such as Homer's *Iliad*—for which a succession of translations is available is wise to do the same.

Professor Seely's method of translating Madhusudan's blank verse is quite different from mine, as he writes an English line based on a count of fourteen syllables (ending each paragraph at the end of a line). We thus, in the four translations that have been done, have four different methods: blank verse, free verse, syllabic verse and phrasal verse, and critics can if they wish compare and weigh up the advantages and disadvantages of each.

I have also benefited from Professor Seely's Glossary and Notes, as well his Introduction and articles, and I am equally indebted to the others who have written on Madhusudan or edited or annotated his works. My Source Notes, especially, aim to bring together the accumulated work that has been done, as well as adding observations of my own. Again, any presenter of a major literary work is wise to make full use of the work of other scholars.

A word on transliteration. It is not an easy matter. Bengali is spelt in a way that derives from its Sanskrit origins, but pronunciation has diverged from Sanskrit. As in other modern South Asian languages, the short 'a' or 'inherent' vowel is frequently dropped in pronunciation—'Rām' rather than 'Rāma', 'Meghnād' rather than 'Meghanāda' etc. All three sibilants ('ś' as in *Śiva*, 'ṣ' as in *Viṣṇu* and 's' as in *Sītā*) are pronounced 'sh' in Bengali, except sometimes when combined with other consonants. The inherent vowel 'a' in Bengali is pronounced as an open or closed 'o'—so *Kṛṣṇa* is pronounced 'Krishno'. The dilemma is whether to transliterate names in *Meghnādbadh kābya* as they would be in Sanskrit (which is what Professor Seely does, using the standard system of diacritical marks), or render them in a way that is closer to Bengali pronunciation. If one goes the whole hog, then one ends up with spellings that can be bizarre and confusing for readers who know those names from more standard spellings. So I decided against 'Shib' for *Śiva* or 'Rabon' for *Rāvaṇa*, etc. At the same time, I felt that to retain all the inherent vowels would upset the rhythm of my lines, which may be different from Madhusudan's Bengali rhythm but is always, I hope, influenced by it. Once one starts dropping inherent vowels, one is already diverging from how the names are spelt. So I decided to compromise too on the use of diacritical marks. I have retained only those that I consider to be crucial for pronunciation. The distinction between 'ā' and 'a' is vital, and needs to preserved by the reader, even if he does not pronounce 'a' as 'o' in the Bengali fashion. The sounds 'ṭ' and 'ḍ'—defined as 'retroflex', with the tongue pointing up to the alveolar ridge behind the teeth, as opposed to 'dental' 't' and 'd' which are made by pressing the tongue against the upper teeth—also need to be distinguished, so I have retained those signs, but not 'ṇ', which is not different in pronunciation from 'n'. I have not used 'ī' or 'ū', because these are not distinguished in Bengali pronunciation from 'i' and 'u'. Of course none of this will indicate pronunciation fully. I have in the end decided to use 's' for the first of the two sibilants above, and 'sh' only for the third (thus 'Siva' rather than 'Shiva'); and I have used 'ch' for 'c', though it should be an unaspirated sound—as in English 'tea<u>ch</u>' rather than the aspirated sound we tend to make when it comes at the beginning of a word such as 'change'. I have retained the Sanskrit distinction between 'b' and 'v', even though they have become one letter—'b'—in Bengali. Some inherent vowels have been left in, even when they are not pronounced in Bengali. This is sometimes for reasons of sound, sometimes because I have added an English plural 's' (thus 'Rākshas' in the singular but 'Rākshasas' in the plural), and sometimes because to drop the inherent vowel from well-known names like 'Siva' and 'Kāma' would be confusing. My partial use of diacritics may annoy some Sanskritists. But I feel that in the twenty-first century we need a new approach to transliteration in some circumstances, and if they do complain I can always quote Madhusudan's own 'intention to throw off the fetters forged for us by a servile admiration of everything Sanskrit'.[143]

For all *italicized* words, phrases and book titles I have used the normal Sanskritic system of diacritical marks, though sometimes I have dropped the inherent 'a' if the language is Bengali, not Sanskrit.

Finally a word on how this translation came about in the first place. It stems, in many respects, from a failure to

[143]Murshid 2004, p. 107.

complete my Oxford D.Phil thesis. I completed it so far as the degree was concerned,[144] but it wasn't the full three part study I had originally planned. Following, as in the Introduction above, Madhusudan's heraldic emblem, my aim was to consider the Sun of his genius, the Lion of Europe and the Elephant of India. I only managed the first two. I didn't feel competent at the time to tackle the Elephant, and I was occupied with looking after my young daughters while working on my Tagore translations and other literary tasks.

I also knew that there were gaps in Madhusudan's biographical record which at the time I did not feel able to fill, and I found there were problems in writing about a poet and an epic poem which was not (apart from Rajendranath Sen's 1926 translation) accessible to the non-Bengali reader through a complete English translation. As the years after I submitted my thesis went by, my knowledge gradually increased, and Ghulam Murshid's researches were published, so completion of the third part of the thesis became more feasible, but I still held back, feeling that a full translation of the epic was a higher priority. This I have now done, adding an Introduction that combines the Elephant with the Sun and the Lion, and incorporating into my Notes and Source Notes many details that were unexplored in my thesis.

Many people have helped and encouraged me with my work on Madhusudan, especially the three to whom this book is dedicated. Dr R. K DasGupta lent me his personal collection of Madhusudan's English letters—which has since been used by Ghulam Murshid in preparing his

[144]Charles William Radice, 'Tremendous Literary Rebel: The Life and Works of Michael Madhusūdan Datta (1924–73)', D.Phil in the Faculty of Oriental Studies, University of Oxford, Trinity Term, 1986.

definitive edition of the letters. I shocked my hosts in Calcutta by carrying the priceless file from South to North Calcutta on a crowded bus, though Dr DasGupta—always the soul of scholarly calm and courtesy—had been happy to put it into my hands with the words, 'I know you will look after them.' Professor Tapan Raychaudhuri supervised my D.Phil thesis. Since then he has gently asked me from time to time, 'When are you going to publish your thesis?' I still can't answer that question, but I hope he will regard this book as better than nothing. Dr Ghulam Murshid, whose work as Madhusudan's biographer and editor, has been of such vital importance, has been a friend and supporter for many years. We have sat at many A Level and GCSE Bengali exam meetings together, but have frequently during coffee breaks ended up talking about Madhusudan. All three have my heartfelt thanks. I would also like to mention with equal gratitude: my teacher at SOAS Dr Tarapada Mukherji, Sureshchandra Maitra and Shubhasekhar Mukhopadhyay (all of whom are no more), France Bhattacharya, Sukanta Chaudhuri, Anuradha Chaudhuri, Professor J. C. Wright, Renate Söhnen-Thieme, Hanne-Ruth Thompson, Christopher Gibbons, Alexander Riddiford, Projit Mukharji, Elizabeth Radice, Katharine Radice, Uma Das Gupta and, once again, Clinton B. Seely, my friend and fellow-devotee of Madhusudan, not rival.

Northumberland, 2008

CHRONOLOGY

1824	January 25	Madhusudan born at Sagardari in Jessore District.
1837		Enters the Junior Department of Hindu College.
1841		Enters the Senior Department of Hindu College; English poems published in student magazines.
1843		Baptized in the Old Mission Church.
1844		Enters Bishop's College.
1848		Goes to Madras: works as a teacher at the Madras Orphan Asylum; marries Rebecca Thompson McTavish.
1849		*The Captive Ladie* published; journalism for various Madras papers.
	November	Becomes editor of the *Eurasian*.
1850	October	Becomes editor of the *Hindu Chronicle*; death of his mother; secret visit to Calcutta and meeting with his father.
1852	March	Appointed Second Tutor in the High School, at the time called Madras University.
1854		*The Anglo-Saxon and The Hindu* published.
1855		Engaged as editor of the Madras *Spectator*, a daily paper.
1855	January 16	His father dies.
	December	Separates from Rebecca and his four children.

1856	January	Amelia Henrietta Sophia White starts to live with him as his wife.
	February	Returns to Calcutta.
	April?	Madhusudan employed as Interpreter in the Police Court; lives at Kishorichand Mitra's garden-house at Dum-Dum.
1857	February	Promoted to Judicial Clerk at the Police Court.
1858		Translates into English Ramnarayan Tarkaratna's Bengali translation of Sriharsha's Sanskrit play *Ratnābalī* for the Paikpara Rajas; starts to write *Śarmiṣṭhā*.
	July	*Ratnābalī* performed at the Belgachia Theatre, with Madhusudan's translation at hand for the English spectators.
1859	January	*Śarmiṣṭhā* published by Jyotindramohan Tagore and the Paikpara Rajas.
	September	*Śarmiṣṭhā* performed at the Belgachia Theatre.
		First child with Henrietta born.
1860	January	His two farces are published by the same patrons.
	February	Litigation to recover his paternal inheritance is partially successful.
	April	*Padmābatī* published.
	May	*Tilottamāsambhab kābya* published.
1861	January	1st volume of *Meghnādbadh kābya* published.
	February 15	He is presented with a silver claret-jug by Kaliprasanna Sinha's Bidyotsahini Sabha.
	July	*Brajāṅganā kābya* published.

	August	2nd volume of *Meghnādbadh kābya* published.
		Kṛṣṇakumārī nāṭak published.
	October	Recovers ancestral property at Kidderpore after litigation; signs tenancy agreements for his other properties so as to provide income for his spell in Europe.
1862	January	*Bīrāṅganā kābya* published.
	March-April	Sells his property at Kidderpore; appointed editor of the *Hindu Patriot*, but quickly resigns.
	June 9	Sails for England, leaving Henrietta and their two children behind.
	August	Admitted to read for the Bar at Gray's Inn.
1863	May	Henrietta and the children arrive in England, after failure of financial arrangements in Calcutta.
	July?	Madhusudan moves them to Versailles.
1864	June	Writes to Ishwarchandra Vidyasagar, appealing for financial help.
	August	Vidyasagar starts to send money.
1865		Madhusudan sends his sonnet on Dante to the King of Italy.
		Returns to England to resume his studies at Gray's Inn.
1866	January	Professor Theodore Goldstücker offers Madhusudan an (unpaid) lectureship at University College London.
	August	*Caturdaśpadī kabitābalī* (sonnets) published in Calcutta.

	November 17	Madhusudan qualifies as a Barrister.
1867	January	Leaving Henrietta and the children at Versailles, he returns to Calcutta.
	February	Applies to practise as a Barrister at the High Court; at first objections are raised.
	May	Allowed to practise, after Vidyasagar and others campaign in his support; lives extravagantly at Spence's Hotel.
1868	January	Forced to sell remaining property to pay debts.
1869	May	Henrietta and the children arrive in Calcutta; Madhusudan rents a grand house in Loudon Street.
1870	June	Abandons his practice and accepts post of Examiner of the Privy Council Records of the High Court.
1871	September	*Hekṭar-badh* published.
1872		Moves to cheaper lodgings; appointed as legal advisor to the Raja of Panchakot, but quickly resigns; health declining fast.
	September	Tries to practise at the High Court again, but his health is too bad.
1873	February?	Writes *Māyā-kānan* for the new Bengal Theatre.
	April	Lives for a while on the second floor of Jaykrishna Mukherji's Library at Uttarpara.
	June	Henrietta very ill; they return to Calcutta.

		Madhusudan admitted to the Calcutta General Hospital.
	June 26	Henrietta dies.
	June 29	Madhusudan dies.
	June 30	Buried next to Henrietta at Lower Circular Road Cemetery.
	August 16	The Bengal Theatre opens with *Māyā-kānan* for its first performance.
1888	December 1	Madhusudan's grave is marked by a headstone installed by public subscription.

MADHUSUDAN'S *ĀTMA-BILĀP*

Dazed by the tricks of hope, what, I wonder,
  What fruits have I gained?
The stream of life flows to the sea of death;
  How can we turn it back?
Each day we grow older, each day we grow weaker—
  But does hope slacken its addictive grip? What a trial it is!

Oh my frenzied mind! When will night end?
  When will you awake?
In the garden of your life, the bright bloom of youth,
  How long will it last?
Can a water-drop quiver forever on a petal?
  Who does not know that a bubble always collapses on itself?

What is the joy of one who is joyous only in his nightly dream?
  He wakes weeping!
Momentary flashes of lightning only increase the darkness,
  Blinding the wayfarer!
Mirages in the desert destroy a life with thirst—
  The deceits of false hope are like these three deceptions.

You long to shackle your feet with the chains of love:
  What fruits have you gained?
Yearning for fire's bright flame, you flutter down
  Into death's snare:

Lured like an insect, alas, you rush blithely,
    Seeing not, hearing not, and now your heart aches.

Is anything left of your vain search for wealth
    To satisfy avarice?
Your hands are scratched on the thorny stem
    Of the lotus you try to pick.
The snake merely bites you when you try to steal its jewel!
    How shall your mind forget that fiery poison?

To whom shall I speak of the years you have wasted
    In pursuit of fame?
Just as the flower's sweet scent attracts the blind worm
    Who hurries to cut it off—
So envy's poison tooth bites you continually!
    What profit have you gained, forgoing food,
    forgoing sleep?

The fisherman troubles to dive into deep water
    To bring up pearls—
But you have thrown your years worth a hundred
    times more
    Into the sea of death, you sinner!
Who will give you back your lost jewel, O foolish mind,
    Dazed, alas, by all the magic tricks of hope![1]

[1]My translation; it was done originally for my 1986 Oxford D.Phil thesis, and was published in 'Confession Versus the Exclamation Mark: Why Rabindranath Tagore did Not Like the Poetry of Michael Madhusudan Dutt', *Temenos Academy Review* 8, London, 2005, pp. 167–83.

THE ARGUMENT

[*as supply'd from beyond the grave by* Mr. Alexander Pope]

Book I

The fable begins with King Rāvan *of* Lankā *dismay'd at the slaughter of his son* Virbāhu *by the armies of* Rām. *On viewing the field of battle from the rampart of his palace, and rebuk'd by his queen* Chitrāngadā, *mother of* Virbāhu, *he calls his* Rākshasas *to arms; whereupon the sea-goddess* Vāruni *is alarm'd. She sends her friend* Muralā *to the throne of* Lakshmi, *the guardian deity of* Lankā. *The two observe the muster of the* Rākshasas; Lakshmi *then hastens to* Meghnād *in his pleasure-garden, disguis'd as his nurse. Arous'd to defiance by her report, he flies in his winged chariot to* Rāvan, *who kisses, blesses and anoints him as the hope of the* Rākshas *race.*

Book II

Night falls; the scene is in the court of Indra, *King of the gods, enthron'd with his consort* Sachi. Lakshmi *arrives, to supplicate for the safety of* Rām. Indra, *who before has been worsted by* Meghnād *(who thereby is graced with the epithet* 'Indrajit'*), agrees to petition* Siva. *With* Sachi, *he flies in his chariot to Mount* Kailās. *Queen* Durgā *agrees to awaken her husband from his trance, and is help'd by the arrows of* Kāma. *Ravish'd with her charms and persuaded of* Rāvan's *sin,* Siva *has* Kāma *sent to* Indra, *to command him to take counsel from* Māyā. *She furnishes* Indra *with* *the weapons that will kill* Meghnād, *which* Chitrarath, *the charioteer of* Indra, *conveys to* Rām *in his camp.*

Book III

Pramilā *in her garden pines for her husband* Meghnād, *confiding in her companion* Vāsanti. *Resolv'd to find him in* Lankā, *she calls up her army of* Dānavis, *and leads 'em to the western gate. Her prodigious envoy* Nrimunḍamālini *demands of* Rām *their passage to the city; who admitting defeat at the beauty of* Pramilā *and her army, allows 'em to proceed. They enter, and* Pramilā *is joyously re-united with her husband. As night falls,* Lakshman, *brother of* Rām, *inspects with* Vibhishan *(brother of* Rāvan, *but no longer of his party) the besieging army, while* Durgā *in heaven marvels to her maid* Vijayā *at* Pramilā*'s splendour.*

Book IV

In the forest of Asoka, *the imprison'd* Sitā *recounts to the kindly* Saramā *(wife of* Vibhishan*) her cruel capture by* Rāvan, *when she was happily dwelling in rustick exile with* Rām *and his brother* Lakshman. *Her dream when swooning while* Rāvan *fought* Jaṭāyu *is avow'd by* Saramā *to be true:* Lankā *is indeed surrounded, and* Rāvan *will be slain.*

Book V

Sleepless in his heavenly palace, Indra *is still perturb'd by the danger threaten'd by* Meghnād. *How will* Lakshman *withstand him?* Sachi *attempts but fails to dispel his fear.* Māyā *appears; she persuades* Indra *she will bring about* Meghnād*'s slaughter by a trick. Cheer'd,* Indra *swears he will himself join battel with* Rāvan *if* Meghnād *is slain.* Māyā *sends the goddess of dreams to* Lakshman*'s pillow.*

In the shape of his mother, she charges him to worship Chaṇḍi *in her temple by a lake. He goes, resisting on the way various lures and dangers. Arriv'd, he hears from the image of* Chaṇḍi *the voice of* Māyā *herself. She promises her protection if bearing* Indra*'s weapons and companion'd by* Vibhishan, *he surprizes* Meghnād *during his worship of* Agni. *The scene alters to the amorous awaking of* Meghnād *and* Pramilā *in their bower of blisse. They are borne in a palanquin to his mother* Mandodari, *who tearfully and fearfully prays for his victory in battel. He leaves, but is follow'd and stopp'd by* Pramilā, *who with plaintive foreboding finally bids him farewell.*

Book VI

Notwithstanding Rām*'s despair and dread,* Lakshman *and* Vibhishan *set out for* Lankā, *to the grove of* Nikumbhilā, *where* Meghnād *must perform the worship of* Agni *that will make him invincible. Dawn breaks;* Māyā *shields them with a mist as they pass thro' the gates. Amaz'd by the riches of the city, they reach the grove, where the unarm'd* Meghnād *is completing his worship.* Lakshman *ignobly insults then attacks him;* Meghnād, *weaponless, stands combate by hurling the vessels of his ritual.* Lakshman *is for a space brought low, but he rallies, and vilely slaughters the valiant* Meghnād. Vibhishan *grieves;* Lakshman *comforts him, blaming on Fate the champion's grisly end. They return to* Rām, *who with his army of* Rāghavas *hails their triumph.*

Book VII

Bathing the while, Pramilā *detects fateful signs. Urged by her companion* Vāsanti, *she hastens to the city, whence wailing is heard. On* Kailās, Siva *sorrows at* Meghnād's *death; he determines on his favourite worshipper* Rāvan's *revenge on* Lakshman, *and* Durgā, *satisfy'd at* Meghnād's *end, does not gainsay him. Siva sends his warrior* Virbhadra *to tell* Rāvan *of the tragick death of his son and to fill him with the fire of his own wrath. This done,* Ravān *leaps from agony to fury, orders the grieving* Mandodari *back to her chamber, calls out his armies, and charges into battel. The slaughter multiplies apace;* Indra's *army of Deities joins in;* Vishnu *too, alerted by* Earth, *lends the fire-stealing power of his great bird-vehicle* Garuḍa; *but naught can stay* Rāvan *from felling* Lakshman *with a deadly and prodigious missile. Sham'd, the divine armies fly back to heaven.*

Book VIII

Night falls; battlefield fires burn; Rām *laments over the body of* Lakshman. *To* Durgā, *grieving at* Rām's *grief,* Siva *promises* Māyā's *assistance once again. She will take* Rām *to* Yama's *realm of torments and ghosts, where his father* Dasarath *will tell him how* Lakshman *can be brought back to life.* Māyā *is called and instructed; she hastens to* Rām, *and leads him down a tunnel to the nether world. They cross by a magick bridge the river* Vaitarani, *pass on thro' manifold scenes of horror and punishment, till at length they reach the field of heroes where* Dasarath's *spirit dwells. Tearfully greeting his son, he describes the* Gandhamādan *mountain where grows the herb that will revive* Lakshman. Rām *reaches for his father's feet, but they are too ghostly to be touch'd. He hastens back to his camp, conducted by* Māyā.

Book IX

Day dawns; Rāvan *hears with surprize cheers from the armies of* Rām. *His minister* Sāran *tells him that (who can say how?) a herb from* Gandhamādan *has brought* Lakshman *back to life. Still blind to the sin of his theft of* Sitā, *the despairing* Rāvan *attributes his reversals to Fate. He sends* Sāran *to* Rām *with a plea for a truce of seven days, so that obsequies for* Meghnād *can be fitly perform'd. This being granted by the noble* Rām, *the body of* Meghnād *is convey'd in a solemn procession to the sea-shore, with* Pramilā *seated beside him. In the forest of* Asoka, *the tender heart of* Sitā *is stirred by the plight of* Pramilā *as describ'd by* Saramā. Rām *sends his general* Angad *to the scene of the funeral pile with a thousand charioteers, to do honours to their fallen enemy. The pile is lit;* Pramilā *ascends it, resolv'd to burn with her husband.* Rāvan *laments piteously before his dead son.* Siva *on Mount* Kailās *grieves for* Rāvan. *He sends* Agni, *who transports in his chariot* Meghnād *and* Pramilā *to heaven, while the gods rain flowers. The* Rākshasas *build a golden memorial; then retire to* Lankā, *where seven days and nights of mourning bring the epic to a close.*

BOOK I

§1
When Virbāhu, crest-jewel of heroes, fell in open combat,
And went on his untimely way to Yama's city, say, O
ambrosia-speaking goddess,
Which hero of heroes did Rāghav's enemy, the fount of
the Raksha race, appoint to the post of general,
And send once more into battle? By what trick did the enjoyer
of Urmilā destroy Meghnād, the Rākshasas' hope,
Invincible in the world, the vanquisher of Indra, making
Indra free of fear?

§1

Virbāhu 'valiant-armed'; recently killed son of Rāvan and Chitrāngadā. He is a character in Krittibās's medieval Bengali version of the *Rāmāyaṇ* but not Vālmiki's *Rāmāyaṇa*. See Source Notes, p. 308.

Yama's city *yamapurī*; the underworld realm of the god of death, vividly described in Book VIII of *MBK*, in which Rām, guided by Māyā, descends into the underworld to meet his dead father, Dasarath.

Rāghav's enemy i.e. Rāvan, the enemy of Rām, who is frequently called Rāghav ('descendant of Raghu') in *MBK*.

Raksha in compounds (as here, *rakṣaḥkulanidhi*, 'the fount of the Raksha race'), M often uses *rakṣaḥ* instead of *rākṣas* as an adjective or noun for the demon inhabitants of Lankā. I have retained this variation for its sound-effect, dropping the final 'ḥ' as it is not pronounced in Bengali and is often not written either.

By what trick *ki kauśale?* This foreshadows the dastardly killing of the unarmed Meghnād by Lakshman in Book VI, following his and Vibhishan's deceitful entry into Lankā, guided by Māyā.

enjoyer of Urmilā i.e. Lakshman, Rām's younger brother, husband of Urmilā, who is Sitā's younger sister.

Invincible in the world, the vanquisher of Indra Rāvan and Mandodari's son Meghnād is celebrated for his victory over Indra, king of the gods. When he defeated him, he brought him to Lankā, bound as a captive. The other gods, led by Brahmā, pleaded for his release, and in return for releasing him Meghnād secured a boon (see below, §751, and Source Notes, p. 306–8), namely, that if he performed a *pūjā* to the fire-god Agni before going into battle he would be invincible. This is why in Book VI Meghnād has to be killed by a *kauśal*, a trick.

I adore your lotus-feet, base-minded as I am; I call you again,
White-armed Bhārati! In the same way, mother,
That you came and sat on the tongue of Vālmiki (as on
 a lotus-seat) when,
With the sharpest of arrows, in the deep forest, the
 huntsman pierced the heron when the heron was with
 its mate,
Come, chaste one, and do kindness to your servant!
Who on this planet knows your might? The man who had
 been the vilest man of the race of men, engaged in robbery,
Became by your grace immortal, immortal as the lord of
 Umā! O boon-giver,
By your boon the robber Ratnākar is the poet who is
 the mine of the gems of poetry! By your touch, the
 poison-tree takes on the goodness of the beautiful
 sandal-tree!
Alas, mother, is there such piety in this servant?
But towards him who is meritless, the fool among her
 offspring, a progenitrix has all the more affection.
So descend, descend, kindly enchantress of the universe!
I shall sing, mother, swimming in heroic sentiment,
A mighty song. Descend and give your servant your
 foot's shade. And you come,

§1

Bhārati name for Sarasvati, goddess of the arts and learning, here invoked by M as his muse as he starts his epic. See VI.158.

tongue of Vālmiki the allusion here is to the famous story of how Vālmiki, formerly the robber Ratnākar, was shocked when a heron fell into his lap after being shot by a hunter while it was making love to its mate, cursed the hunter, and found that the words of his curse emerged in a metre that became the metre of his epic poem the *Rāmāyaṇa*.

lord of Umā i.e. Siva, husband of Umā (Durgā, Pārvati).

mine of the gems of poetry M puns here on Vālmiki's former name and *ratna-ākar*, 'jewel-mine'.

Goddess, honey-making Imagination! Having taken
    honey from the flowery wood of the poet's heart,
Build a honeycomb from which the people of Gauṛ,
    in joy, will drink nectar for ever.

§33

The great Dasānan sits on his aureate seat, like the topmost
    spur on the golden heights of Hemkuṭ, packed with light.
Hundreds of ministers and councillors and the like sit in
    obeisance all around. The chamber is unparalleled on
    earth, shaped from crystal.
Gems adorn it, like fresh-blooming lotus on Lake
    Mānas. Rows of white,
Red, blue, yellow pillars support the high gold roof,
In the same way that the chief of snakes, spreading his
    ten thousand hoods, lovingly cradles the globe.
Pearls, rubies, emeralds and diamonds glitter on hanging
    tassels,
Just as leafy garlands (studded with buds and flowers)
    hang in festive houses.
Beams born of gems wink repeatedly like lightning,

§1

honeycomb *madhucakra*; M puns on his own name here.

Gauṛ old name for Bengal or part of Bengal; for more than three centuries after the Muslim conquest of Bengal in 1198, the city of Gauṛ in the Malda district of West Bengal was used as a capital.

§33

Dasānan 'ten-faced one', i.e. Rāvan, who has ten heads and twenty arms.

Hemkuṭ a range of mythical golden mountains to the north of the Himalayas, in the direction of Mount Meru, the Hindu Olympus.

Lake Mānas sacred lake, famous for its wild geese, on Mount Kailās, where Siva dwells.

chief of snakes i.e. Ananta, Vāsuki or Sesha, king of the serpents or Nāgas. Vishnu when he sleeps rests his head on his chest, shaded by his ten thousand hoods, and he was used as a rope when the Ocean was churned.

dazzling the eye! Soft-eyed maidservants wave softer fly-whisks:
Moon-visaged, they swing their lotus-stem arms in joy.
The umbrella-bearer bears his umbrella,
As if, ah! Kāma himself stood in the chamber in the form of an umbrella-bearer,
Unburnt by the fire of Hara's anger! The door-keeper patrols the door, awesome in appearance,
Like trident-bearing Rudra at the gate of the Pāṇḍav camp! An unending spring-breeze gently blows, blowing fragrance,
Bringing a ripple, oh ecstasy! of playful chirping.
It captivates, like the ripple of Krishna's flute in the Gokul woodlands! What chaff compared to this,
O Maya, lord of the Dānavas, was that bejewelled chamber that you fashioned with your own hand at Indraprastha to please the Pauravas!

§33

Kāma himself in the famous myth that was the basis of Kālidāsa's *Kumārasambhava*, the god of love Kāma (Madan) is blasted to ashes when he attempts to wake Siva out of his trance. Book II of *MBK* describes his successful waking of Siva.

Hara Siva.

trident-bearing Rudra in the *Mahābhārata* Siva in his stormy form (Rudra) stands guard outside the Pāṇḍav camp.

Gokul woodlands the district near Mathurā, also known as Vraj, where Krishna grew up and sported with Rādhā and the other Gopis (milkmaids).

Maya, lord of the Dānavas the Dānavas are a race of demonic anti-gods, often not distinguished from the Asuras, Daityas, Karburas or Rākshasas. In the *Mahābhārata* Maya is saved by Arjun from the blazing Khāndhav forest, and in gratitude constructs a magnificent hall at Indraprastha, the Pāṇḍav city on the bank of the Yamunā.

Pauravas used here to mean the Pāṇḍavas, but actually it means the descendants of King Puru who were the ancestors both of the Pāṇḍavas and the Kauravas.

§62

In such a chamber sits the lord of the Raksha race, speechless with grief for his son! An incessant stream of tears drips down in drops,
Soaking his robe, just as a tree, if a keen arrow strikes its juicy body,
Weeps silently. With hands clasped, a messenger of defeat stands before him,
Grey with dust, his whole frame wet with blood. Of the hundreds of soldiers who sank,
With Virbāhu, in the ocean of battle, only one hero survives.
The fatal wave that swallowed them all spared him, a Rākshas named Makarāksha, equal to the lord of the Yakshas in strength.
At hearing from this messenger's lips of his heir's destruction, alas, the jewel of the race of kings,
The child of Nikashā, is distraught with grief today! The court is sorrowful at the king's sorrow.
The world is dark, alas! when clouds cover the sun!
At length, collecting himself, Rāvan heaved a sigh of sadness and said:

§80

'This news of yours is as a nightmare, O messenger! Did the beggar Rāghav kill in open battle the archer

§62

Makarāksha the name means '*makar*-eyed'. The *makar* is a mythological aquatic animal, equivalent to Capricorn in astrology. The sea-god Varuna rides it, and it is a symbol of virility on Kāma's banner.

lord of the Yakshas i.e. Kuber, elder half-brother of Rāvan. He is the god of wealth and lord of the Yakshas, a supernatural clan famous for their horde of riches.

child of Nikashā Nikashā was the mother of Rāvan, Kumbhakarna and Vibhishan.

whose strength of arm was the torment of the immortals?
Can God cut down a great *śālmalī* tree with a mere petal? O son, O Virbāhu,
Crest-jewel of heroes! By what sin have I lost such a treasure as you? O harsh Fate,
What sin did you see in me to steal this treasure? Oh alas, how can I bear this pain?
Who is there left to preserve the honour of our race in this deadly conflict? Just as the woodcutter in the middle of the wood, before he finally fells a tree,
Cuts its branches one by one, so this fierce foe, O God,
See, is relentlessly making me as weak! I shall be uprooted root and branch by his arrows!
Otherwise would my brother Kumbhakarna, the equal of trident-bearing Sambhu, ever have died before his time through my error?
And all the other soldiers too, protectors of the Rākshas race? Alas,

§80

śālmalī tree the silk-cotton tree.

By what sin . . . O harsh Fate for the key concepts of sin (*pāp*) and Fate (*bidhi*) in *MBK* see Introduction, pp. lii–lvi.

Kumbhakarna 'pot-ear'. Rāvan's monstrous brother used to sleep for six months at a time and wake up for only one day. It took hours to rouse him for the battle against Rām, and 2000 jars of liquor; but he was defeated and Rām cut off his head.

trident-bearing Sambhu i.e. Siva. For his trident, see II.447.

through my error Rāvan woke Kumbhakarna before he had completed his six months of sleep, which was in breach of a boon granted by Brahmā. All three brothers—Rāvan, Vibhishan and Kumbhakarna—were granted boons by Brahmā to stop them performing austerities that were a threat to the power of the gods. Kumbhakarna asked for perpetual sleep. Rāvan, knowing that he might need his brother's aid, asked for this to be modified. Brahmā allowed him to wake up every six months, but ruled that if was woken up prematurely he would be slain.

Surpanakhā, unlucky that you are, evil was the time that
you saw in the black Panchavaṭi wood that venom-filled viper!
Evil was the time that (incensed by your distress) I
brought to this shining abode the fire-flame-formed Jānaki!
Oh that I could leave golden Lankā, and enter the dense
forest, to soothe my burning mind with solitude!
This beautiful city of mine, ah! was like a dancing-house,
Lit by the light of massed lanterns, bedecked with
strings of flowers! But now,
One by one, the blooms are fading, the lamps are going
out:
Silent are the violin, the *vīṇā*, the drum,
The flute: so why then do I still remain here? Does
anyone desire to dwell in darkness?'

§114

Thus the lord of the Rākshas race, Rāvan, lamented
convulsively:
Alas and alack like the blind king at Hastinā, when he

§80

Surpanakhā Rāvan's sister, whose lust for Rām in the Panchavaṭi wood set off the chain of events that led to the war between Rām and Rāvan. When she tried to devour her rival, Sitā, Rām asked Lakshman to attack her. His missile chopped off her nose and ears. Humiliated and furious, she returned to Lankā and persuaded Rāvan to punish Rām by abducting Sitā.

venom-filled viper i.e. Rām.

Jānaki Sitā, daughter of Janak, king of Mithilā.

Lankā Rāvan's island kingdom, the home of the Rākshasas and mythical precursor of modern Sri Lanka. In the *Rāmāyaṇa* as well as in *MBK* the name can refer either to the whole island or its capital.

§114

blind king at Hastinā Dhritarāshṭra, the blind ruler of Hastinā, patriarch of the Kauravas, brother of Pāṇḍu, father of a hundred sons by Queen Gāndhāri.

heard from the lips of Sanjay how many of his dear sons had been slain by the blows of tremendous-armed Bhimsen, in the battle of Kurukshetra.

§119

Then councillor Sāran (most learned of ministers) rose with folded palms and began humbly to speak:
'O king, famous in the world, diadem of the Rākshas race,
Forgive this servant! Who on earth has the power to comfort you? But think,
Master, and consider it in your mind, that if a sky-piercing peak is pulverized by a thunderbolt,
The mountain rebels not a whit at that affliction. Indeed, this world is full of illusion:
Vain are all its sorrows, and its happinesses. Ignorant are those deceived by the devices of illusion.'

§130

To this the ruler of Lankā replied: 'What you have said is true, O councillor-in-chief Sāran!
I know well that this world is full of illusion, that all its sorrows are vain, and its happinesses.
But though I have heard and know this, my unreflecting soul still weeps. Death has torn away the flower that bloomed on the stem of my heart,
And my heart thus ruptured drowns in an ocean of grief, like a lotus-stalk in water, when somebody steals its blue treasure.'

§114

Sanjay a charioteer and advisor to Dhritarāshṭra, who brought news of the catastrophic defeat of the Kauravas at the battle of Kurukshetra.

Bhimsen (Bhim), second eldest of the five Pāṇḍav brothers, son of Kunti by Vāyu, the Wind.

§119

Sāran chief minister and councillor in Rāvan's court.

§139

Saying this, the king turned towards the messenger, and commanded:

'Tell us, messenger, how did the god-scaring warrior Virbāhu fall in battle?'

§142

With obeisance to the feet of the king of kings, and with clasped palms, the messenger of defeat began:

'Alas, lord of Lankā, how shall I tell a tale that has no precedent?

How shall I describe the heroism of Virbāhu? Bearing his bow, the mammoth hero burst through the ranks of the enemy,

Like a must elephant through a clump of reeds. My heart still shudders, remembering that fearful uproar!

I have heard, Rākshas lord, the booming of the clouds,

The roaring of the lion, the crashing of the ocean's waters; I have seen,

Sire, swift lightning chasing the wind. But never have I heard,

In the three worlds, dreadful rattling twanging of bowstrings like to this! Never have I seen such terrifying arrows!

§156

'Supreme warriors entered the fray with Virbāhu, like a herd of elephants with their herd-leader. Dust rose aloft in thick cloud-shapes;

As if clouds had come to cover the sky in fury; hissing darts, glinting like lightning flashes,

Flew to celestial regions! Wonderfully skilled was the hero Virbāhu! Who can count how many enemies died?

§142

the three worlds i.e. heaven, earth and the underworld.

§164

'Thus did your son and his army, O King, fight amongst their opponents.

In time Rāghav, foremost of men, came and joined in the struggle,

A golden crown on his head, a vast bow in his hand, inlaid with manifold gems like Indra's rainbow—'

Here the messenger of defeat wept silently, as the bereaved weep when they recall past sorrow! The court wept silently.

§172

With eyes full of tears, Rāvan, the beloved of Mandodari,

Spoke once more: 'Tell me, O news-bearer,

Tell me, I am listening, how did the seed of Dasarath destroy the valiant seed of Dasānan?'

§176

'How, O Lord of the earth,' again began the messenger of defeat,

'How, O fount of the Raksha race, shall I tell you this,

And how will you listen? Just as a fiery-eyed lion, gnashing its terrible teeth in rage,

Pounces on a bull's shoulders, so Rāmchandra attacked

§164

Rāghav see above, §1. **Indra** the god of the sky or heaven; king of the gods; the Hindu Zeus or Jupiter.

§172

Mandodari Rāvan's chief queen, mother of Meghnād and daughter of Maya (see §33 above).

Dasarath '[owner of] ten chariots', father of Rām, Bharat, Lakshman and Satrughna, husband of Kausalyā (mother of Rām), Kaikeyi (mother of Bharat) and Sumitrā (mother of Lakshman and Satrughna).

Dasānan Rāvan (see §33 above).

§176

Rāmchandra Rām is sometimes known by this fuller name.

the prince in battle! Waves of fighting now swelled all around,
As when the sea quarrels tumultuously with the wind!
Innumerable swords scintillated, like tips of flame amidst a smoke-swirl of massed shields!
Conches boomed loud as billows—what more shall I say, sire?
Through my errors in births past, I alone survived.
O God,
Alas, for what sin have you dealt me this agony today?
Why did I not lie down on a bed of arrows,
With Virbāhu, the ornament of golden Lankā, in the battlefield?
But I am not a sinner through my own sin. Look, it is my chest that is wounded,
Jewel of monarchs, by the aggressor's weapons; there are no steel-marks on my back.'
§195
Saying this, the Rākshas fell mute with mental anguish.
The lord of Lankā,
Between gladness and sadness, said: 'Praise to you,
Messenger! Oh does any hero's heart, on hearing your words,
Not wish to enter the war? Does the deadly serpent, when he hears the sound of the tabor,
Ever remain lazily in his hole? Blessed is Lankā, bearer of brave sons.
Come, all of you, let us go,
O persons of the court, let us see how Virbāhu, crest-jewel of heroes,
Has fallen in battle. Come, let us assuage our eyes by seeing.'

§205

The Rākshas lord climbed to the top of the palace, radiant as the dawn sun rising from its aureate mountain home. Captiving Lankā,
Crowned with golden pinnacles, sparkled all around: rows of gleaming mansions,
Set amidst flower-groves; lotus-spread lakes; brilliant silver fountains;
Trees; blooms as gorgeous to the eye as a girl's youthfulness; diamond-towered temples;
Multi-coloured shops, laden with many gems: as if the world had gathered,
As a divine offering, its varied treasures, and placed them at your feet,
O lovely Lankā, world's desire, you abode of joy.

§218

The lord of the Rākshasas looked down at a high rampart, mountainous in its solidity. Guards,
Drunk with valour, patrolled it like lions on a mountainside. The stealer of Sitā surveyed the four lion-gateways
(Now closed), where chariots, charioteers,
Elephants, horses, innumerable footsoldiers were at the ready.
The king beheld his enemies outside the city, like grains of sand along the sea-shore, or the ring of stars round the circle of the sky.
At the east gate was encamped the warrior Nila, unbeatable in battle; at the south gate was Angad,
Fresh in strength as a young elephant, or like the poison-bearing serpent who, at the end of winter,

§218

Nila warrior from the southern kingdom of Kishkindhyā, which has formed an alliance with Rām against the Rākshasas.

Angad nephew of Sugriv and crown prince of Kishkindhyā.

Sporting his bright scales, roves with hood outstretched,
arrogantly brandishing his trident-shaped tongue!
At the north gate was King Sugriv himself, lion of
heroes. Rām was at the west gate,
Now grieving, alas, to be parted from Jānaki,
Like the lotus-delighting moon when robbed of its light!
With Lakshman were Hanumān, son of the wind,
And Vibhishan, most trusted friend. The gold city of
Lankā had been encircled a hundredfold by her foes,
As a lioness in the deep forest, gracious to behold,
formidable in strength as Bhimā,
Is encircled by the stealthy nets of the hunt! And now the
Raksha lord surveyed the nearby battlefield: jackals,
Vultures, curs, ghouls prowled clamorously.
Some flew; some settled; some squabbled;
Some, flapping their wings, drove off their rivals in greed;
Some hooted with pleasure as they stanched the fires of
hunger; some sucked from streams of blood.
Awesome-looking elephants had fallen in heaps;
Storm-swift horses, alas, were swift no longer!

§218

King Sugriv with Rām's assistance his elder brother Vāli (father of Angad) was overthrown and slain, so that Sugriv could accede to the throne of Kishkindhyā. He had earlier taken the throne when he thought Vāli had been killed by an Asura. Vāli then returned, turned him out of the kingdom and seized his wife Rumā. After Vāli was overthrown, Sugriv took Vāli's own wife Tārā as his queen and adopted their son Angad as heir-apparent. Sugriv is supporting Rām in the war against Rāvan in return for his earlier help.

Lakshman son of Dasarath by Sumitrā, and Rām's half-brother.

Hanumān monkey-god and warrior from Kishkindhyā, son of Vāyu (Pavan), god of the winds, and therefore able to travel as fast as the wind.

Vibhishan Rāvan's younger brother; he defects to Rām when his advice that Sitā be returned is roundly rejected by Rāvan.

Bhimā 'ferocious', a name for the goddess Durgā when she is angry.

Smashed chariots galore, mahouts, horsemen,
Spearmen, charioteers, footsoldiers lay tumbled together!
Armour, shields, swords,
Bows, javelins, quivers and arrows,
Clubs, axes coruscated here and there; and jewelled crowns and helmets,
And burnished warrior-dress. Musicians lay amidst their instruments. Fallen was the banner-bearer,
Gold-bannered-sceptre in hand, struck down by the sceptre of Yama. O alas!
Just as the gold-tipped corn falls to the scythe of farmers in the field, so, by the arrows of Rāghav,
Sun of suns, had countless Rākshasas been toppled!
Virbāhu had fallen, crest-jewel of heroes,
Crushing strong opponents with his fall, like he whom Hiḍimbā reared so lovingly, Garuḍa-like Ghaṭotkach,
When Karna, bearer of the Kālprishṭha, shot the Ekāghni missile to save the Kauravas.

§218

sceptre of Yama the god of death carries a staff or sceptre (*daṇḍa*) to mete out punishment.

Crushing strong opponents with his fall when mortally wounded in the battle of Kurukshetra, Ghaṭotkach expanded at his father Bhimsen's bidding to enormous size, crushing the Kauravas until he was slain by Karna: hence the simile here.

Hiḍimbā a Rākshasi (female Rākshas), whose union with Bhimsen (see above, §114) produced the massive warrior Ghaṭotkach.

Guruḍa-like Ghaṭotkach can fly through the air like Garuḍa, the gigantic bird who is Vishnu's vehicle.

Karna Ghaṭotkach fought with Bhimsen on the Pāṇḍav side in the battle of Kurukshetra, and was slain by Karna, the warrior who fought on the Kaurav side, even though he knew he was the son of Kunti by the sun-god Surya before her marriage to Pāṇḍu, and therefore a half-brother of the Pāṇḍavas.

Kālprishṭha 'black-back', Karna's bow.

Ekāghni 'single-slayer'; Indra, king of the gods, was so impressed by Karna's golden skin-colour (derived from his father, the sun) that he

§269

With huge anguish, grief-stricken Rāvan spoke: 'The bed on which you have lain today,
Most beloved prince, is where heroes always long to lie! Can anyone,
In the trampling of hostile forces in battle to defend the land of his birth, dread death? He who dreads it is a base coward;
A hundred curses on him! But the heart, dear one,
That is drunk with love, is soft as a flower. How cruelly it is hurt by this thunder-stroke is known to the One who reads minds;
I have no words for it. O Fate, this earth is your play-room;
But can it be that you are happy at another's pain? When a son grieves, a father always grieves too.
You are the father of the world—is not this your way? Ah son!
Ah Virbāhu! Supreme lion of heroes! How shall I live without you?'

§285

Thus did Rāvan, ruler of the Rākshasas, lament.
Turning, he cast his gaze towards the sea, home of the *makaras*.

---

persuaded him to give it to him in exchange for a missile that could only be shot once but would never miss. For the effect of this elaborate simile, see Source Notes, p. 315.

§269

One who reads minds *antaryāmī*, 'one who goes within'. *antar* ('interior') can also mean heart, so *antaryāmī* is often used for the God who knows one's inmost feelings.

Fate *bidhi*: see above, §80.

§285

makaras see §62 above. Originally the *makar* was a large crocodile, but in Hindu mythology it takes on the character of the Greek dolphin or biblical Leviathan.

Motionless as a row of clouds, the stones floated on the water, bound by firm bonds.
Foaming waves on both sides, swelling like the many-hooded king of snakes, surged unceasingly with a deep roaring.
A bridge made like no other; ample as a royal pathway; streaming with enemies noisy as the waters of a stream in the rainy season.

§295

Outraged, great Rāvan, proudest and best of heroes,
Looked at the sea and said: 'A fine garland you have put round your neck today, O clever Varuna!
Fie on you, ruler of waters! Does this befit you,
You who cannot be crossed or conquered? Alas, O mine of gems,
Is this your ornament? What quality, tell me,
Master, I am listening—what quality in Rām bought you?
You are the storm-wind's foe, fierce as a storm in your attack! Tell me through what sin then do you wear these fetters?
A magician can chain a worthless bear, and play with it; but who has power to bind in a bird-net the royal paws of a lion?

§285

the stones floated on the water in the *Rāmāyaṇa*, Rām solves the problem of how to transport his massive army across to Lankā by praying to the Ocean-god Varuna, who accepts the weight of a bridge of floating stones.

many-hooded king of snakes i.e. Ananta, Vāsuki or Sesha. See §33 above.

§295

Varuna Vedic god who became the god of the ocean in classical Hinduism, analogous to Poseidon in Greek mythology. He was originally identified with thunder and rain too, until Indra took those powers away from him.

This Lankā here, gold-built city, gleams on your breast,
O spouse of blue waters, like the Kaustubh jewel on the breast of Krishna; why are you now so harsh towards her?
Rise, I say, and smash this dam with your might;
Banish the scandal of it; by sinking this massive adversary in bottomless water, cool my torment.
Keep not this line of shame on your forehead, sea-god, I beg you at your feet.'

§317

Saying this, Rāvan, mightiest of rulers,
Came and sat once more on his golden throne in his council-chamber. He sat silently, sunk in grief.
Ministers and councillors and the rest of the court sat all around him, ah! in silent mourning.

§322

Then, suddenly, the sound of feminine weeping flooded in from all sides,
Mingled with the tinkling of anklets, and the sonorous jingling of girdle-bells. Chitrāngadā-devi came into the chamber,
With her gold-complexioned attendants. Her hair was unplaited, alas,

§295

Kaustubh jewel one of the 'fourteen jewels' that were produced by the churning of the ocean. In this famous myth, Indra and the other gods were cursed by the sage Durvāsas to lose their vigour. Vishnu restored it by directing the gods to churn up the ambrosial ocean that surrounded him, using Mount Mandar as a churning rod and the serpent Vāsuki as a rope. Vishnu thereafter wore the Kaustubh on his chest, so it was also worn by Krishna, his incarnation.

§322

Chitrāngadā-devi one of Rāvan's queens and mother of the recently killed Virbāhu. The honorific suffix 'devi' ('goddess') is often added to the names of high-born females, or is used on its own when addressing them.

Loose and dishevelled! Her body was without ornament, like a forest-adorning creeper in the snow,
Bereft of its jewel-like blossoms! Her eyes were full of tears, like petals of a lotus brimming with night's dew!
The queen was benumbed with grief for Virbāhu, like a mother-bird after a deadly snake enters her nest and devours her young! A storm of grief swept through the court!
The golden skin of her women flashed all around like lightning; their unbound hair was a bank of clouds; their heavy sighing was a hurricane wind;
Their tears streamed like a cloudburst; their weeping and wailing boomed like thunder! The lord of Lankā on his golden throne started!
Handmaidens dropped their fly-whisks as their eyes moistened; the weeping umbrella-bearer dropped his umbrella; shocked,
Angered, fearsome guards at the door unsheathed their swords; councillors,
Ministers and the rest of the court were all alarmed, all in tears, all sobbing noisily!

§345

At length, chaste Queen Chitrāngadā looked towards Rāvan and murmured: 'Fate favoured me with a single gem;
I was defenceless, I placed it with you, jewel of the Raksha race,
For safe-keeping, like a bird that keeps her young in the hollow of a tree. Tell me,

§345

for safe-keeping there is wordplay here on *rakṣaḥkulamaṇi* ('jewel of the Raksha race') and *rakṣā* ('protection, safe-keeping').

Lord of Lankā, where have you put him? Where is my
precious gem?
It is the duty of kings to protect what the poor possess;
you are king of all kings; tell me,
King, where have you put that wealth of mine, beggar
that I am?'

§356

The mighty Dasānan replied: 'Why, dear one,
Do you serve me this pointless rebuke? Beautiful
Chitrāngadā, can someone who errs because his stars
are ill-fated be blamed?
Alas, devi, I suffer this anguish through Fate's power!
See, this golden city, mother of heroes,
Is empty of heroes now; just as forests are empty of flowers
during drought, and rivers are empty of water!
Like a porcupine entering a betel-leaf farmer's
plantation and tearing it to shreds, the son of
Dasarath is laying my Lankā waste! Even the ocean,
At his request, wears shackles on his feet! You,
Lady, are distressed with grief for a single son; day and
night my own breast is rent with grief for a hundred
sons!
Alas, devi, like tufts of cotton blown away when silk-
cotton pods burst open and the wind is fierce in the
woods,
So fall the finest of our mighty race in this fatal battle. I
tell you, Fate is stretching out its arms to destroy
my Lankā.'

§356

Fate's power *bidhi* is used again. Rāvan consistently attributes his predicament to the workings of fate or the stars. He is *grahadoṣe doṣī* ('at fault because of planetary fault'), not through any conscious ill-doing. See above, §80, and Introduction, pp. lv–lvi.

§375
The Raksha lord fell silent; moon-faced Chitrāngadā, child of a Gandharva,
Face lowered in grief, wept—overwhelmed,
Ah! with the memory of her noble son! The enemy of Rām began to speak once more.
§379
'Is this lamentation, devi, worthy of you?
By killing his country's enemies in battle, your noble son has gone to the city of Svarga. You are mother of a hero—
Is it right to weep for a son slain in doing his heroic duty? This race of mine is glorified, yes,
By your son's valour; so why do you cry, why do you drench your moon-like visage with tears?'
§386
But lovely-eyed Chitrāngadā-devi replied: 'Happy is the birth of one who kills his country's enemies in battle. I accept that the mother of such a hero is indeed blessed.
But reflect, lord, on where your Lankā lies and where the city of Ayodhyā lies.
For what cause, and desiring what—tell me,
King—has Rāghav come to this land? This golden Lankā is the envy of the king of the gods,

§375

child of a Gandharva Chitrāngadā's father Chitrasen was a Gandharva. The Gandharvas are a race of heavenly singers and musicians, the husbands of the Apsarāses. They can appear on earth as handsome men whom women fall in love with at first sight, resulting often in a 'Gandharva marriage' (marriage without parental consent and without a priest officiating).

§379

city of Svarga Indra's heaven.

§386

Ayodhyā capital city of Dasarath and Rām; Rām's birthplace. Soon after Rām went into exile in the forest, accompanied by Sitā and Lakshman,

Without compare in the world. All around it, the sea
shines like a silver rampart.
I have heard that Rām resides on the banks of the
Sarayu river—a mere human. Is the son of Dasarath
fighting in hope of your golden throne?
Does a dwarf wish to grasp the moon? So why, I say,
Do you call him your country's enemy? A serpent's head
is always low; but if anyone assails it,
It rears its hood and bites the assailant. Tell me who has
ignited the city of Lankā today with deathly flame?
Alas,
Lord, through the fruits of your own actions you are
drowning the Rākshas race, drowning yourself.'

§406

With this the mother of Virbāhu, Chitrāngadā,
weeping,
Returned with her attendants to the inner quarters of
the palace. In grief and outrage, Rāghav's enemy,
Ruler of the earth, rose from his golden throne and
roared out: 'Warrior after warrior has gone,
Emptying my Lankā. Who is there left to send into this
dread battle? Who will now save the honour of the
Rākshas race?

Dasarath died, leaving his second son Bharat in charge of the kingdom. But when Bharat found Rām and urged him to return to Ayodhyā to become king, he refused, because his father—incited by the jealous Queen Kaikeyi (Bharat's mother)—had exiled him for fourteen years.

Sarayu river Ayodhyā is located on its banks.

a mere human although in classical Hinduism Rām is regarded as the seventh incarnation of Vishnu, in *MBK* he is depicted as thoroughly human, and regarded contemptuously by the Rākshasas as human.

through the fruits of your own actions *nij karmaphale.* This moral principle is accepted by all the characters in *MBK* (gods included) other than Rāvan and his son Meghnād. See Introduction, pp. lv–lvi.

I shall go myself. Arm, O champions,
Ornaments of Lankā! Let us see what metal there is in this jewel of the race of Raghu! The world will lose either Rām today or Rāvan.'

§417

At these words of the lion of heroes, the scion of Nikashā, battle-drums thundered in the chamber,
Booming like storm-clouds. At that awesome sound, the Rākshasas,
Scourge of gods and demons and men, took up their arms, wild with war-lust.
Elephants (unstoppable in strength as a torrent) emerged at speed from their stables,
And horses arching their necks, furiously champing at their bits. Gold-topped chariots hurtled,
Flooding the city with their gleam. Batallions of footsoldiers followed, golden turbans on their heads,
Swords in glinting scabbards, battle-proof shields on their backs, the spears in their hands like sky-piercing *śāl*-trees,
Their bodies covered in iron armour. The mahouts that came were like Indra the thunderer high on his cloud-seat; horsemen that were like the horse-riding Asvins brandished terrifying missiles,

§406

race of Raghu King Raghu, the son of Dilip who was descended from the sun-god Surya, was Rām's great-grandfather, and gave his name to his lineage.

The world will lose either Rām today or Rāvan *arābaṇ, arām bā habe*: 'will be Rāvan-less or Rām-less'.

§417

śāl-trees a large tree (*Shorea robusta*) that produces very strong timber.

horse-riding Asvins the twin-horsemen or Gemini, sons of the sun-god Surya. His wife Samjñā ran away to escape his heat and took the form

World-destroying axes. A gleam rose skywards, as from a fire when it grips a forest.
The mighty banner-bearer, bearer of the colours of the Raksha race, unfurled his jewel-studded master-banner,
Like Garuḍa spreading his wings as he soars into the welkin. Martial bands played all around with solemn din; massed horses neighed excitedly;
Elephants bellowed; conches boomed loudly; the clattering of swords and the twanging of bowstrings made an ear-splitting clangour!

§443

Golden Lankā shuddered with the tramp of warriors' feet; the ocean roared in anger; and the uproar penetrated to the place at the bottom of the sea where,
In a golden lotus-garden, on a coral throne, the lovely Vāruni sat,
Binding up her hair with pearls. The divine nymph started and looked about her; she turned to her moon-faced companion and said in sweet tones:
'Tell me, O friend, why is the lasso-swinging lord of waters suddenly disturbed?

---

of a horse (*aśvinī*). He chased her, impregnated her, and she gave birth to two charioteers who also became famous for their skill as medical practitioners to the gods.

Garuḍa Vishnu's vehicle. See §218 above.

§443

Vāruni this is M's own name for the wife of Varuna, the sea-god. In a letter to Raj Narayan Basu on 3 August 1860, he wrote: 'The name is *Vāruṇānī* but I have turned out one syllable. To my ears this is not half so musical as *Vāruṇī*, and I don't know why I should bother myself about Sanscrit rules.' But see Source Notes, p. 317.

her moon-faced companion i.e. her *sakhi* (companion, attendant, confidante) Muralā.

lasso-swinging lord of waters *jaleś pāśī*: Varuna has a *pāś* or noose in which he catches wrong-doers.

See, the tops of our pearl-crusted dwellings are trembling violently: the mischievous winds must have re-appeared,
To fight with the waves. Fie on the god of storms! How,
My friend, can the wind-lord forget his promise of only a few days ago? In the court of Indra I asked him that day to chain the winds,
To shut them all in prison. The god laughed and said, 'Allow me,
Lady of the waters, to dally forever with your handmaidens—with all the clear-watered streams in the world;
Then I shall meet your demand.' And I gave him permission, friend.
So why, today, have the winds come to cause me this distress?'

§468

Her companion replied in liquid tones: 'In vain do you rebuke the wind, O Queen of the waters.
This is no storm; but King Rāvan in his palace is whipping himself up like a storm, to reduce by force of arms Rāghav's prowess!'

§472

Vāruni spoke again: 'It is true, O friend,
That Rām and Rāvan are fighting over Sitā. The guardian goddess of the Rākshasas is my special friend. Go quickly to her home—

§443

god of storms named in the text as Prabhañjan, i.e. Pavan, god of the winds and father of Hanumān.

§472

guardian goddess of the Rākshasas *rājlakṣmī*: i.e. the goddess Lakshmi as guardian of the prosperity of a king and his kingdom or, in this case, of Rāvan and the Rākshasas.

I long to hear some news of the battle. Give this golden lotus to Kamalā: tell the moon-visaged one that here,
Where, when she sat on her lotus-throne, she placed her rosy feet,
This flower bloomed, after she left for her home, darkening this ocean-dwelling.'

§483

Her friend Muralā rose, at the request of Vāruni; left the ocean-floor,
Like a nimble flying-fish rising to display to the sun the seductive wealth of its shining silver scales. The messenger landed in the place where, in a lotus-patch,
On a lotus-seat, and lotus-like in beauty, the beloved of Vishnu sits in the city of Lankā.
Standing for a while at the door, Muralā drank in with her eyes the vision before her—of the sweet beauty that enraptures the one who infatuates Madan himself.
A spring zephyr—her eternal follower—murmured with longing for the fragrance of the goddess's lotus-feet.
There were blossoms all around, like jewels in Kuber's

§472

Kamalā name for Lakshmi, with wordplay on *kamalā* (lotus).

left for her home i.e. to join her husband Vishnu. See below, §513.

§483

beloved of Vishnu *keśab-bāsanā*: Keshav ('having long or handsome hair') is a name for Lakshmi's husband Vishnu or his incarnation Krishna.

the sweet beauty that enraptures the one who infatuates Madan himself Lakshmi's beauty enraptures Vishnu/Krishna who in turn enchants Madan, 'the maddener', i.e. Kāma, the god of love.

Kuber *dhanad* ('wealth-giver') in the text, i.e. Kuber, god of riches (*dhan*) and lord of the Yakshas (see §62 above).

mountain store. Sandalwood and other exquisite
essences burned in a hundred golden censers,
Filling the temple with perfume. There were rows of assorted
gifts on golden plates, and various *pūjā*- ingredients.
Golden lamps shone, full of fragrant oil—yet modest in
their lustre,
Like glow-worms in the blaze of full moon! With face
turned away, moon-like Lakshmi sat in sadness,
Sat as moon-visaged Umā sits when *Bijayā-daśamī*
dawns in the homes of Bengal with imminence of loss!
With cheeks slumped in her hands, lustrous Kamalā sat on
her lotus-throne: must grief enter a heart as tender as this?
§509
The lovely messenger Muralā gently entered the temple;
did obeisance at Indirā's feet, head bowed.
The guardian goddess of the Raksha race, blessing her,
began to speak:
§513
'Why have you come today, tell me, O Muralā?
Where is my beloved friend, the empress of the waters? I
constantly think of her.
When I was in her home, what kindness Vāruni showed
to me: how can I ever forget it?

§483

pūjā offering to a deity; worship. **Umā** Siva's consort (Durgā, Pārvati). ***Bijayā-daśamī*** ('Victorious tenth'), the last day of Durgā-pujā, Bengal's main Hindu festival, which starts with Durgā's coming from her husband's home to her parental home, and ends with her tearful return to her husband. Images of Durgā are immersed on that day, so that they can return to the clay from which they are made.

§509

Indirā another name for Lakshmi (Kamalā, Ramā).

§513

When I was in her home Lakshmi was herself one of the 'fourteen

My longings find their home in Vishnu's breast: lacking him then, only Vāruni's loving medicine healed me.
Tell me, is my dear friend well, the queen of the ocean?'
The beautiful Muralā answered: 'Vāruni is safe at the bottom of the sea. There is strife between Rām and Rāvan over Sitā;
She desires to hear news of the conflict. This lotus, chaste one,
Joyously bloomed on the spot where you placed your feet. The beloved of Varuna has sent it to you, thus.'

§530

Kamalā, that moonlight of Vishnu's heaven, heaved a sigh and said in sorrow: 'Alas,
O friend, day by day the wretched Rāvan grows weaker, like the seashore crumbling from the blows of the waves!
You will be shocked to hear that the mighty Kumbhakarna, awesome to behold, and Akampan,
As stalwart in battle as a mountain, have fallen with the charioteer Atikāya, and countless other Rākshasas,
More than I can describe. Virbāhu has died—crest-jewel of heroes.
Hear the wailing, Muralā, inside the palace:
It is Chitrāngadā weeping, prostrated with grief for her son. I'm desperate now to leave this city.

---

jewels' produced by the churning of the ambrosial ocean (see §295 above). Before that she lived in the abode of Varuna, the sea-god: hence her nostalgia here for Vāruni's hospitable care.

§530

Kumbhakarna see above, §80.

Akampan 'unwavering': name of one of Rāvan's generals.

Atikāya 'huge-bodied': son of Rāvan by Dhānyamālini (one of his queens).

My heart breaks at the sound day and night of women
wailing! In every home, messenger,
Mothers without sons, wives without husbands, weep!'
§545
Muralā asked: 'Please tell me, great goddess,
Which hero is preparing to fight today, proud in his
valour?' Vishnu's beloved answered:
'I do not know who is preparing today. Come, O
Muralā, let us see who is going into battle.'
§550
Saying this, Ramā and Muralā together, disguised as
Raksha women,
Went outside, in silk garments. Their anklets tinkled softly;
Bangles on their wrists glinted; on their slender waists,
ravishing girdles gleamed!
They stood by the door of the temple and saw soldiers
in battalions on the royal road, swiftly moving, like
sea-waves driven by the wind.
Chariots raced by, their whirling wheels clanking.
Horses galloped,
Frightening as storms. Elephants charged, shaking the
earth with their pounding,
Brandishing their trunks, like Yama wielding his club.
Bands played with martial clangour.
Hundreds of flags flew, studded with flashing jewels. On
both sides,
At the windows of golden houses, the world-enchanting
women of Lankā stood, raining down flowers,

§550

Ramā another name for Lakshmi (Kamalā) that conveys her beautiful and womanly (*ramaṇīya*) qualities.

Yama wielding his club see §218 above.

Cheering the army on. Turning to moon-visaged Indirā,
Muralā said:
§569
'The riches of heaven, goddess, are visible on earth today!
I feel as if Indra himself, ruler of the gods, has entered
Lankā today with his heavenly armies.
Say, kind goddess, say to me kindly,
Which warriors are ready for battle now, drunk with
heroic wine?'
§575
Chaste, *kamalā*-eyed Kamalā said: 'Alas,
Friend, golden Lankā is empty of heroes! Those who
were the finest of charioteers,
The terror of gods and demons and men, have perished
in this crushing battle!
See, in a gold-crested chariot, that awesome charioteer?
He is the Raksha lord Virupāksha, bearer of an iron
bow and invincible in battle! See,
On an elephant's back, Kālnemi, Rāvan's mother's
brother,
Whose strength is death to his enemies, hurler of the
bhindipāl-missile!
See that horse-rider, Tāljanghā, lofty as a palm-tree,
Club in his hand like club-wielding Vishnu. See
Pramatta, drunk with battle-frenzy,

§575

kamalā-eyed Kamalā see §472 above.

Virupāksha 'deformed-eyed': name of a Rākshas warrior.

Kālnemi M makes this Rākshas warrior the father of Meghnād's wife Pramilā (see below, III.413).

bhindipāl it is not known what sort of weapon this was exactly.

Tāljanghā another Rākshas, with wordplay on *tāl* ('palm-tree').

Pramatta another Rākshas; the name means 'drunken'.

Another formidable Rākshas, his chest tough as rock.
See all the others,
More than I can describe! Hundreds of such fighters have been slain in battle, as when fire enters the dense forest,
And unsurmountable trees, overwhelmed by flames, shrivel into ashes.'

§594

The messenger Muralā asked, 'Tell me, great goddess,
Why do I not behold Meghnād, lion of the Rākshasas in battle, defeater of Indra?
Has that warrior been killed, chaste one, in fatal combat?'

§598

Lovely-eyed Ramā answered: 'I believe the prince is blissfully dallying in a pleasure-garden, unaware that Virbāhu has been killed today in battle.
Go back to Vāruni, Muralā: tell her I shall abandon golden Lankā and speed back to heaven.
The king of Lankā is sinking through his own fault.
Alas, like a pure lake that,
In the rainy season, gets filthy with mud, golden Lankā is oozing with sin!
How can I live here longer? Go, my friend,
To the pearly palace where, on a coral throne, Vāruni sits.
Let me go to Indrajit: I shall bring him to gold-built

§598

The king of Lankā is sinking through his own fault *nijdoṣe maje rājā laṅkā-adhipati*: this echoes Chitrāngadā's opinion above, §386.

oozing with sin for the concept of sin in *MBK*, see Introduction, pp. lii–lvi.

Indrajit i.e. Rāvan and Mandodari's son Meghnād, the vanquisher of Indra. See above, §1.

Lankā. The fruits of past actions will quickly ripen in
this city.'

§612

With obeisance to the goddess's feet, the beautiful envoy
Muralā took leave; she rose into the air,
Like a peahen soaring through gorgeous green glades,
thrilling the eyes with her shine, as Indra does with
the mixed jewels of his rainbow!

§618

Alighting on the ocean shore, she entered the blue
waters. Meanwhile,
Speeding through the air, the goddess of the Raksha
race, the lotus-eyed beloved of Vishnu,
Travelled to the presence of Meghnād, crest-jewel of
heroes, the terror of Indra.

§623

She of the lovely hair, the beloved of sense-delighting
Vishnu, soon landed by the ever-victorious Indrajit.
Like Indra's abode was his palace: diamond-topped columns
of gold in its porticoes; fabulous forests all around,
Like Indra's Nandan-grove. *Koel*-birds were cooing on
the branches; bees were buzzing about;
Flowers were blooming; leaves were rustling; a spring-
breeze blew;

§598

The fruits of past actions will quickly ripen . . . cf. above, §386.

§623

Indra's Nandan-grove this name for Indra's paradise-garden means 'delightful, pleasing'.

***Koel*-birds** the *kokil* or *koel*-bird is often called 'cuckoo' by translators but is actually different from either the European or the Indian cuckoo (called *bau-kathā-kao* in Bengali), though it belongs to the same family. Its call—a common sound in Bengal—is quite strident and high-pitched, and more complex than the 'perfect fifths' with which it is associated.

Babbling springs burbled. Entering the golden mansion,
the goddess saw martial-looking women fearlessly
patrolling the golden doors,
Bows in their hands. Plaits hung down their backs
with their quivers, with jewels in the plaits flashing
like lightning;
The arrows in the quivers were like jewel-studded
serpents! On their buxom breasts, golden coats of
mail were like the sun's tracery of rays on a full-
bloomed lotus.
There were sharp arrows in their quivers, but even
sharper were the arrows of their elongated eyes.
Tipsy with the wine of their fresh youth,
They paced up and down, like female elephants on heat
in the spring. On their large buttocks,
Girdles tinkled sweetly—and anklets on their feet.
Mixed with that sound,
Viṇās, drums, flutes and water-pots played;
A wave of music, swelling all around, ravished the
heart!
The great hero frolicked here amidst fine-limbed women,
like the moon with Daksha's daughters; or,
O Yamunā, daughter of the sun, as Krishna the
herdboy,

§623

Vīṇās originally a generic term for a number of stringed instruments, but now applied to those of the lute-type. The *vīṇā* is supposed to have been invented by Nārad, chief of the Gandharvas, See §375 above.

Daksha's daughters Daksha is the father of the twenty-seven stars who are the wives of Chandra, the moon.

Yamunā famous river that joins the Ganges at Allahabad. Krishna sported with the Gopis on its banks (see §33 above). Personified, Yamunā is the daughter of the sun. For the effect of the comparison with Krishna, see Source Notes, pp. 318–19.

Dancing at the foot of the *kadamba*-tree, flute on his
lips, frolics with milkmaids on your charming
banks!

§654

Taking the form of Meghnād's Rākshasi nurse
Prabhāshā, Ramā, the beloved of Vishnu,
Appeared—leaning on a stick, dressed in white.
Leaving his golden couch, Indrajit, lion of heroes,
Took the dust of his nurse's feet and said: 'Why,
Mother, have you come to this place? What news of
Lankā do you have?'

§661

Kissing his brow, the disguised Lakshmi, daughter of the
waters,
Replied: 'Alas, son,
How can I speak to you of golden Lankā's state! In
horrible battle, your dear brother,
The mighty Virbāhu, has been slain! The lord of the
Rākshasas is distraught with grief:
He is arming, with his soldiers, to enter the battle
himself today.'

§667

Meghnād asked in horror: 'What are you saying, dear nurse?
Who could have killed my dear younger brother and
when? I beat back Rām in a night battle; I cut our
enemies to pieces,

§623

***kadamba*-tree** large tree with tiny florets set on a yellow-orange ball. It is sweet scented, grows in the rainy season and is associated with Krishna.

§654

Prabhāshā Meghnād's childhood nurse, so he greets her as a much-loved nanny-figure.

§661

daughter of the waters see §513 and §295 above.

Raining down massive arrows; so this news, this baffling news,
Mother, where did you get it? Tell me quickly.'

§673

The beautiful Indirā, finest jewel of the jewel-giving ocean, replied:
'Alas, son! Sitā's husband has magic powers;
Though slain by your arrows, he lives. Go now quickly;
Save the honour of your race, O crest-jewel of the Rākshasas, in this mortal conflict.'

§678

In fury, mighty Meghnād ripped off his flower-garland, threw off his golden bracelets;
His discarded earrings flashed at his feet, like the blooms of an *aśoka*-tree when fallen at its foot! 'Shame on me,'
He boomed, 'Oh! shame on me.
Golden Lankā is encircled by enemies; what am I doing here among women? Does this befit me,
I, Indrajit, son of Dasānan?
Bring my chariot at once; by slaying our enemies, I shall wipe out this disgrace.'

§689

Prize-bull-charioteer Meghnād put on his hero's armour, like Kārttikeya preparing to destroy Tārak, greatest of anti-gods;

§673

Indirā i.e. Lakshmi (Kamalā, Ramā). See §550 above.

§678

***aśoka*-tree** the name of this evergreen tree means 'free of grief'. Its clusters of lightly scented flowers are at first orange, then scarlet.

Dasānan see §33 above.

§689

Kārttikeya the god of war, also known as Skanda. Various myths tell of how he was born of Siva with no mother, in order to rid the world of the demon Tārak (see II.491).

Or else like diademed Arjun disguised as Brihannalā,
arming together with Uttar at the foot of the *śamī*-tree, to rescue the stolen cattle.
His chariot was like a storm-cloud in colour; its wheels
were like flashes of lightning; its banner was like Indra's bow;
Its horses were swift as the wind. As the crest-jewel of
heroes confidently climbed into his chariot, the lovely Pramilā clutched at his hands
(Alas, like a golden creeper clinging to a massive tree)
and wailed: 'Where,
Love of my life, tell me, will you leave me when
you go?
How will I live without you, unlucky that I am?
Alas,
Lord, when a creeper in the deep forest lovingly binds
itself round the feet of an elephant, if the elephant ignores its affection and moves off,
It still finds a refuge round its feet. So why are you,
fount of virtues,

§689

diademmed Arjun disguised as Brihannalā in the *Mahābhārata*, the five Pāṇḍavas, during their thirteenth year of exile, live in the palace of King Virāta, disguised as servants. Arjun took the form of a eunuch called Brihannalā, and taught Uttarā, the king's daughter, songs and dances. Arjun is given the epithet *kirīṭī* ('crowned, diademmed') here, because of the *kirīṭ* or crown that Indra gave him.

arming together with Uttar Arjun and Virāta's son Uttar joined forces to retrieve 60,000 cattle stolen by the Kauravas.

***śamī*-tree** previously the Pāṇḍavas had hidden their weapons amidst the branches of a *śamī* (acacia)-tree. When, at Arjun's request, Uttar fetched the weapons down, Arjun was so moved that he revealed his true identity, throwing off his eunuch's bangles and putting on his armour instead. Meghnād has been idling among women, dressed in a garland and bracelets; hence the simile here.

Pramilā Meghnād's wife. See Introduction, p. lxxiii and Source Notes, p. 331f.

Deserting your servant today?' Meghnād smiled and replied: 'You have conquered Indra's conqueror,
Darling, by binding me with these bonds: who can untie them?
I'll return speedily, O gracious love, having vanquished Rāghav through your grace.
Give me, O moon-like one, leave to go now.'

§714

The huge chariot rose into the air with a rushing noise, like the Maināk mountain spreading its golden wings and lighting up the sky!
Furiously, the mighty hero tugged at his bowstring; its terrifying,
Ear-splitting twang was like the flapping of Garuḍa's wings in the clouds. Lankā trembled; the ocean shook.

§720

King Rāvan was arming too, frenzied with war-lust. As bands blared,
Elephants trumpeted, horses neighed, infantry and cavalry bellowed,
Silk flags fluttered, and the dazzle of golden breastplates rose up into the sky, Meghnād arrived in his chariot at top speed.

§726

Swelling with pride, the Rākshasas cheered when they saw the great hero. Bowing to his father's feet and with hands folded in greeting,

§689

Rāghav i.e. Rām: see §1 above.

§714

Maināk mountain a mythological mountain winged as all mountains were until Indra clipped their wings to stop them landing on towns and villages. Mount Maināk escaped, and received sanctuary in the ocean.

Garuḍa see §218 above.

He said: 'O Lord of the Raksha race, is it true what I have heard,
That Rāghav has died, and then revived? This sorcery,
Father, I cannot understand! But give me your permission to uproot root and branch that miscreant today!
Let me pulverize him with devastating arrow-fire, drive him to the winds; or else drag him bound before your royal feet.'

§735

Embracing the prince, kissing his head, the lord of golden Lankā then replied:
'You are the crown of the Rākshas race, my boy; all the hopes of our race rest on you.
Yet my heart does not want to send you again into this dreadful war. Alas, Fate is against me!
Who has ever heard, son, of stones floating on water?
Who has ever heard of a man, slain, but living again?'

§743

Proudly the enemy of the Asuras' enemy answered: 'That man is trash! How,
O King of kings, can you fear him? If I stay away,
And you go into battle, the scandal of that will be proclaimed worldwide. Indra will laugh;

§726

Rāghav has died in a previous battle Meghnād has himself slain both Rām and Lakshman, but magic herbs brought from the Himalayas by Hanumān (see I.218) have revived them and many other fallen warriors.

§743

the enemy of the Asuras' enemy i.e. Meghnād, enemy of Indra, who is the enemy of the Asuras or anti-gods.

Agni will be outraged. Twice I have defeated Rāghav; command me,
Father, once more: let us see by what medicine he will survive this time!'

§751

'My brother Kumbhakarna—' said the Rākshas lord, 'in a panic I woke that great warrior,
At the wrong time. Alas, his body,
See, lies fallen on the seashore, like a tree or a mountain felled by a thunderbolt!
So if, my child, you are set on entering this dire conflict,
Do a *pūjā* first to your *iṣṭadeva*: perform a sacrifice in the Nikumbhilā grove, O jewel of heroes!
I appoint you to the post of general. See—the sun is about to set;
Fight at dawn, dear boy, with Rām.'

§743

Agni will be outraged Agni, god of fire, is Meghnād's *iṣṭadeva* or patron god to whom he offers special prayers. See below, §751, and also Book VI. 7, 418.

Twice I have defeated Rāghav once Meghnād defeated both Rām and Lakshman and bound them with Nāgas or snakes (see above, §33). They thought that this would definitely finish them off, but they were able to escape with the help of Garuḍa (see above, §218). The second time, he attacked them and their armies at night with a shower of invisible arrows. Only Hanumān and Vibhishan appeared to survive. But then Hanumān fetched four special herbs from the Risyamuk mountain and revived Rām and Lakshman and all the others who had been slain.

§751

Kumbhakarna see §80 above.

your *iṣṭadeva* i.e. Meghnād's patron deity Agni. Brahmā, or in some accounts Brihaspati (the planet Jupiter), gave Meghnād the boon that if he completed a *pūjā* to Agni before going into battle he would be invincible. See above, §1, and Source Notes, pp. 306–8.

Nikumbhilā a cave or grove at the western gate of Lankā where oblations or sacrifices (*yajña*) are offered.

§761
Saying this, King Rāvan took Gangā-water and
annointed Prince Meghnād, in the prescribed way.
§763
At once a court-singer broke into song, plucking his *vīṇā*
in joy: 'In your eyes,
O Lankā, Rākshas city, there are tears;
You have let down your hair in grief; your bejewelled
crown, alas,
Has fallen to the ground, and your royal ornaments too,
O lovely Queen!
Rise, rise, chaste lady,
And master your grief. The sun of the Raksha race is
about to dawn! Your night of sorrow is ending!
Rise, Queen, see,
In his massive left arm there is a bow, at whose twang
Indra in his heavenly palace goes pale! See his
quiver,
In which there is a weapon like Siva's that can terrify the
great god himself! See Meghnād, most skilled of all
skilled fighters,
Lion of heroes, whose handsomeness smites all women!
Blessed is Queen Mandodari!
Blessed is the ruler of Lankā, Nikashā's son! Blessed is
Lankā,
Nurturer of heroes! Listen, O Echo,

§761

Gangā-water the Rākshasas are very devout Hindus in *MBK*, offering oblations and using sacred Ganges-water in the correct way. See Introduction, p. lxxxiiif.

§763

O Lankā, Rākshas city Lankā is personified as a Queen here.

Queen Mandodari Meghnād's mother: see §172 above.

Daughter of the sky! Call out to all with open throat:
enemy-vanquishing Indrajit is arming for battle.
Let the Raghu lord tremble in his tent with dread, and
the traitor Vibhishan,
And all the paltry monkey-inhabitants of the Danḍak
forest.'

§784

The Rākshas band played; the Rākshasas bellowed;
golden Lankā filled with shouts of victory.

Here ends 'The Annointing', the first book
of *Meghnādbadh kābya.*

§763

Raghu lord i.e. Rām. See §406 above.

the traitor Vibhishan see §218 above.

Danḍak forest Hanumān and his army of monkeys come from this huge forest in South India, in which are located Sugriv's kingdom of Kishkindhyā as well as the smaller Panchavaṭi wood in which Rām, Lakshman and Sitā were exiled. See §218 and §80 above.

BOOK II

§1

The sun set; twilight fell; a jewel-like star hung on the brow of evening.
Night-lotuses burgeoned; day-lotuses closed their tired dry eyes on the lake; twittering birds returned to their nests;
Cattle hurried lowing to their byres. Gracefully-starred Night arrived, smiling,
Together with the moon; a perfumed breeze stirred all around, whispering amorously to all,
Stealing, oh! what riches by kissing flower upon flower.
The goddess of sleep came; like tired infants seeking rest in the nest of their mothers' laps, creatures of land and water took refuge at her feet.

§14

Moon-loving night descended over heaven, where Indra sat on his golden throne surrounded by the gods; lovely-eyed Sachi,
Daughter of Puloman, sat to his left. A royal umbrella,
Encrusted with jewels, gleamed above Indra's head. Maidservants delicately waved begemmed fly-whisks,
A sweet breeze blew, playfully wafting the honeyed scents of the Nandan-forest. Heavenly musicians played on all sides!
The six main *rāgas*, each with their thirty-six embodied *rāgiṇīs*, began their music.

§14

Sachi,/ Daughter of Puloman Puloman was a Dānav (see I.33) who cursed Indra when he seduced his daughter Sachi. Indra then killed Puloman and took Sachi as his wife. Unlike Siva's consort Pārvati/Durgā/Kāli, Sachi—also known as Indrāni—does not feature in Hindu mythology as a power or personality in her own right.

Nandan-forest famous paradise-garden or forest in Indra's heaven.

six main *rāgas* in the standard classification of the *rāgas* or modes of

Urvasi, the sweet-smiling Rambhā, Chitralekhā and fine-haired Misrakesi came and danced,
Enchanting the gods with their jingling ornaments! Gandharvas supplied nectar on golden plates! Other attendants brought divine food;
Or saffron, musk, *keśar* or sandalwood;
Or garlands stitched from fragrant *mandār*-flowers. As Indra, king of the gods,
Together with the other inhabitants of heaven, wallowed in pleasure, Lakshmi,
The patron-goddess of the Raksha race, alighted there, lighting heaven's city with the glow of her beauty.

§35

The husband of Sachi respectfully bowed before Ramā's feet. Blessing him,
Taking her seat on a golden chair, the lotus-eyed habituée of white-lotus-eyed Vishnu's embraces said, 'O Lord of the gods,
Hear, with full attention, why I have come to your presence today.'

§40

Indra answered: 'O offspring of the sea, enchanter of all,
Your crimson feet are the object of the longings of the

Indian music, each of the six main *rāgas* has six wives or *rāgiṇīs* or secondary modes. Here they are personified as heavenly musicians.

Urvasi, Rambhā, Chitralekhā, Misrakesi heavenly nymphs or Apsarāses, celebrated for their dancing, of which Urvasi is the most famous.

Gandharvas see I.375.

***mandār*-flowers** the *mandār* is a mythological flowering tree that grows in heaven. **Lakshmi** see I.472, 483, 513, 550.

§35

Ramā one of Lakshmi's names. See I.550.

§40

offspring of the sea see I.513, 295.

whole universe, truly! Anyone who is favoured by your look of favour,
O favour-filled one, will triumph in life! What virtue in me,
Tell me, mother, has won this pleasure?'
§45
Lakshmi spoke again: 'For a long time, O ruler of the gods,
I have been in golden Lankā. The king of the Rākshasas has worshipped me with great care,
With many precious gifts. Alas, Fate has been against him now for so long!
Through his own bad actions, the sinner is drowning along with his race; yet I cannot desert him,
Lord. Can a prisoner, sire,
Ever escape from gaol if he cannot open the door? For as long as Rāvan lives, I shall remain tied to his house.
O slayer of Vritra, Rāvan's son Meghnād is certainly known to you. He is the one warrior left now in Lankā;
So many other warriors have died in this war. That mighty lion of heroes will attack Rāmchandra tomorrow;
Rāvan has once again appointed him as general. Rāghav is beloved of the gods—please think about how you will save him!

§45

Through his own bad actions cf. I.598, 386 and see Introduction, p. lii.

slayer of Vritra Indra slew the Asura (see I.743) Vritra with his thunderbolt. As the demon of drought, he was constantly at war with Indra.

Rāmchandra i.e. Rām.

Rāghav see I.1.

If proud Meghnād starts the battle after completing a *pūjā* in the Nikumbhilā-grove, I assure you that Sitā's husband will be in dire straits. Mandodari's son is invincible in the world,
O divine Lord! Just as Garuḍa is the mightiest of birds, so is he the jewel of the Raksha race!'
§70
Saying this, Ramā, the desired of Vishnu,
Fell—silent—fell silent, ah!
Like a *vīṇā* does after charming the mind with its sweet music—its six *rāgas* and thirty-six *rāgiṇīs* and more! On listening to Lakshmi's message,
Everyone forgot their own work—like birds in the budding gardens of spring, when they hear a *koel*-bird's hoot!
§77
The Ruler of the gods spoke: 'Who, mother,
Other than Siva himself, can save Rāghav from this grave danger? Rāvan's son is formidable in battle!
I fear him more than a snake fears Garuḍa! This thunderbolt, that smashed the head of Vritra,
Was turned back by Meghnād's weapons; that is why he is known in this world as Indrajit. By all-purifying Agni's boon,

§45

pūjā see I.483. **Nikumbhilā-grove** see I.751.
Garuḍa see I.218.

§70

desired of Vishnu *keśab-bāsanā*: see. I.483. ***vīṇā*** see I.623.
***koel*-bird's hoot** see I.623.

§77

Vritra see above, §45.
that is why he is known in the world as Indrajit. See I.1, 598.
by all-purifying Agni's boon because Agni, god of fire, is Meghnād's *iṣṭadeva* or patron god. See I.743.

He is all-conquering. At your command, let me hasten to the palace on Mount Kailās!'

§87

The Vishnu-loving daughter of the Ocean said: 'Then go, lord of gods,
Go quickly. On the crest of Mount Kailās, at the feet of moon-crowned Siva,
Present, Lord, this whole message.
Tell him that chaste Mother Earth weeps all the time, unable to bear this weight; tell him that Ananta too is weary.
If the Raksha lord is not overturned and uprooted, the world will sink to the lowest hell! Great Siva loves Lakshmi dearly.
Tell him how she has lived alone in Lankā, exiled from Vishnu's heaven! How often,
In her loneliness, has she thought of him: what wrong has she done,
That he should not think of her at least once? What father keeps his daughter away from her husband's home for so long? Ask him,
Ask the wise matted-haired one! And if you cannot see him, make your appeal at the feet of Durgā.'

§77

palace on Mount Kailās where Siva dwells.

§87

Ananta the massive snake on whom Vishnu rests his head when he sleeps. The name means 'endless'. See I.33.

exiled from Vishnu's heaven . . . What father keeps his daughter away from her husband's home for so long? It was Durvāsas' curse that confined Lakshmi to the bottom of the ocean, until she was raised from it by the churning of the ocean (see I.295), but there seems to be no mythological reason for her presence in Lankā, exiled from her husband Vishnu, or why M implies here that her father (the creator-god Brahmā) has kept her there.

matted-haired one *jaṭādhar*: a common epithet for Siva because of his *jatā* or pile of matted hair.

Durgā i.e. Siva's wife.

Saying this, the moon-browed beloved of Hari took her leave. The lovely-haired Vishnu-enchanting goddess flew downwards through the sky,
Like an image of gold, when it sinks into a pure lake, ensparkling the waters with its shine!
§109
Mātali—Indra's groom—brought his chariot;
Indra turned to Sachi and said to her softly, privately: 'Come,
Devi, with me; when a breeze blows perfumed with nectar,
It is doubly effective! A lotus-stalk takes its elegance from its flower, believe me,
Dear wife!' Smiling at her husband's loving words, beautiful-buttocked Sachi took his hand and climbed into his chariot.
§117
The chariot swiftly descended to the golden gates out of heaven, with opened of their own accord, and with a sweet sound!
Emerging at speed, the vehicle shone in the sky; the world woke up in amazement,
Thinking the sun-god had dawned! *Phiṅgā*-birds chirruped, and all the other birds;
They filled the woodlands with their dawn chorus! Shy new wives rose from their flowery bridal beds, started their housework!

§87

beloved of Hari epithet for Lakshmi, because Hari is a name of her husband Vishnu.

§109

Devi see I.322.

§117

***Phiṅgā*-birds** the drongo: a black passerine songbird with a forked tail.

§126

The radiant peak of Mount Kailās loomed over Lake Mānas; on top of it, Siva's abode,
Like the peacock's-tail-crown on Krishna's brow! The mountain was green with verdure; golden flowers girdled it,
Like a gorgeous yellow loincloth! Mountain-springs burbled in places—flecking the body of the mountain like smears of white sandal-paste!

§133

Leaving the chariot, Indra and Sachi entered Siva's abode of joy on foot. His wife Durgā was seated there on a golden throne,
Like an empress; her companion Vijayā was waving a fly-whisk, and another companion,
Jayā, held a royal umbrella! Oh how can a poet describe the riches of Siva's palace?
With your mind's eye, O those who can imagine, see them!

§140

Great Indra and his queen bowed with deep respect before the feet of Durgā. She blessed them and asked: 'What brings you both here today?
Tell me, god, your good news.'

§144

With his palms pressed humbly together, thunderbolt-throwing Indra began: 'What do you not know,
Mother, in this wide world? God-defying Rāvan,
Alarmed at the progress of the war, has again appointed

§126

Mount Kailās the great silver mountain in the Himalayas where Siva dwells. In some myths it is also the site of Alakā, capital city of Kuber, god of wealth (see I.62).

Lake Mānas see I.33.

his son Meghnād today as general. At dawn tomorrow,
The enemy-tormenting prince will re-enter the battle, after doing a *pūjā* to his *iṣṭadeva* Agni to procure a boon from him. Mother,
You are not unaware of his prowess. Lakshmi, guardian goddess of the Raksha race,
Came to Vaijayanta to give me this news, O gracious one! The beloved of Vishnu said:
"Earth is weeping—she cannot support this unsupportable load; and earth-bearing Sesha is tired."
Lakshmi herself is restless all the time now to leave the golden city of Lankā. She requested me, O Annadā,
To lay this message at your feet! The heroic Rām—jewel of the race of Raghu—
Is favoured by the gods. But what warrior, from among the gods,
Can fight in a battle with Rāvan's son? He can render powerless even my world-smashing thunderbolt, and is therefore known in the world as Indrajit!
By what means will you save Rāghav? Please think about this, *Mā*.
If you do not take protective action, the world will be made Rām-less tomorrow by Meghnād, Rāvan's son.'
§168
Durgā replied: 'Rāvan is Siva's chief devotee; the Trident-bearer has great affection for him.

§144

after doing a *pūjā* to his *iṣṭadeva* See I.743, 751, 1. **Vaijayanta** Indra's palace in heaven, also known as Amarāvati. **Sesha** i.e. the great snake Ananta or Vāsuki. See I.33. **Annadā** epithet for Durgā, meaning 'giver of food'. **race of Raghu** see I.406. ***Mā*** 'mother': can be used when respectfully addressing a goddess, as well as one's mother or even a young girl.

How, O King of the gods, can I do harm to him?
The master of *tapas* is at present immersed in *tapas*; that is why Lankā has reached such a pass, O Lord.'
§173
With hands pressed together, Indra spoke again: 'The Lord of the night-faring Rākshasas is an inveterate defier of *dharma*—
A rebel against the gods! You can judge that for yourself, O daughter of the mountains.
That miscreant stole a poor man's sole possession; can your favour towards him ever be right, Mother?
The noble Rāghav, to honour his father's decree, abandoned all material pleasures and went in beggar's garb to the deep forest!
He had but one jewel with him, precious beyond value; I have no words to describe how he cherished it.
That jewel was stolen by that criminal, by spreading a net of deceit! Alas,
Mother, my heart burns with anger as I think of it! Armed with Siva's indulgence towards him, he holds the gods in contempt!

§168

master of *tapas* as the ash-smeared, bark-clad 'Great Ascetic', Siva is supreme at *tapas*: feats of austerity or asceticism.

§173

dharma a word so notoriously difficult to define that it is sometimes best to leave it untranslated. See Introduction, pp. liv–lvi. Rāvan is an *adharmācārī* or defier of *dharma* because he does what is morally wrong. On the other hand, the reason why he does not himself understand that to abduct Sitā was wrong is because it is actually the *dharma* (natural tendency or duty) of Rākshasas to do such things!

to honour his father's decree Rām's step-mother Kaikeyi, as the favourite wife of King Dasarath, persuaded him to grant her two boons: one was that Rām should be exiled from Ayodhyā for fourteen years; the other was that her own son, Bharat, should be made Crown Prince. See I.386.

one jewel with him i.e. his wife Sitā.

That devil is perpetually greedy for others' wealth, others' wives. So why,
Kind goddess (I cannot understand) are you kindly towards him?'

§190

The king of the gods fell silent; his wife now started to speak, in tones as sweet as a *vīṇā*'s.
'Whose heart, devi, does not break at the plight of Sitā?
Day and night that beautiful moon-visaged lady sits in the Asoka wood (like a woodland-loving bird in a cage)
Sobbing with grief! The anguish she suffers without her husband, Mother,
Is not unknown to your rosy feet. If you do not punish the vile Raksha ruler, who,
Devi, will punish him? Destroy Meghnād and return Sitā to the one she adores;
Expunge my shame, O you who has the moon on your brow! I die,
Mā, with humiliation, when I hear people talk about how Meghnād is the master in battle of the king of heaven!'

§204

Durgā smiled and said: 'You loathe Rāvan, great Indra!
And you—O sweet-spoken Sachi—are desperate for Indrajit to be slain!
The two of you are asking me to destroy golden Lankā.

§190

Asoka wood the grove on Lankā where Sitā is being held captive.

§204

sweet-spoken Sachi the original printed editions of *MBK* have *mañju-nāśinī* here, but I agree with editors who suggest it should be emended to *mañju-bhāṣinī*, though other emendations meaning 'sweetly smiling' or 'beautiful-haired' have also been suggested. (See Dinanath Sanyal's edition of *MBK*, p. 115.)

But I am not empowered for such a task. The
Raksha race is protected by Siva.
Without him, who—tell me,
Indra—can achieve this purpose in this world? My
husband—
O King of the gods—is immersed in yoga at present. The
peak where he sits,
Yogāsan by name, is terrifying, swathed in thick clouds;
The lord of yoga is in solitude there. How will you get to
him? Even the lord of birds Garuḍa is unable to fly there!'

§217

The son of Aditi humbly answered: 'Who apart from
you,
O *mukti*-granting Mother of the universe, can go there,
to the awesome slayer of Tripura?

§204

The Raksha race is protected by Siva why this should be so is a complex matter. If one of Siva's oldest identities is that of god of the forest and lord of the animals, then hunters would have had to placate him to protect themselves against the mysterious creatures of the forest: spirits, demons and dwarfs. As the 'Destroyer' of the triad of classical Hinduism (Brahmā the Creator, Vishnu the Preserver and Siva the Destroyer), he also acquired the character of a god of death whose death-dance destroys the world so that it can be created anew. As such, he is surrounded by corpses and attended by the demons who inhabit cremation grounds—i.e. the Rākshasas. See also Source Notes to II.425, pp. 328–9.

Yogāsan 'seat of yoga': i.e. both the sitting position for yogic meditation, and (here) the peak or plateau where Siva sits in meditation.

§217

son of Aditi Aditi, goddess of the firmament, is the mother of Indra and all the gods. She is the antithesis of Diti, who is the mother of the anti-gods (the Asuras, Dānavas, Rākshasas, etc.).

mukti 'freedom', implying spiritual liberation or moksha.

Tripura 'three cities', personified as the Asura Tripura, whom Siva destroyed along with all the other Asuras who lived there. Built by Maya (see I.33), one (of gold) was in the sky, one (of silver) was between earth and sky, and the third (of iron) was on earth.

Save the three worlds, devi, by crushing the Rākshasas;
Increase the power of *dharma*; relieve the Earth of her burden; calm down Vasuki,
Bearer of the Earth; rescue Rāghav—' Thus did demon-defying Indra plead with the chaste goddess.

§225

Then suddenly the heavenly city filled with a sweet fragrance; conches and bells sounded all around,
And sounds of praise as sweet as when birds gather and sing in a distant flower-forest. Durgā's gold throne quaked. Tenderly addressing her companion Vijayā,
Siva's consort asked, 'O moonlike one, who and where—
Tell me quickly—is worshipping me so exceptionally, and why?'

§233

Singing out mantras, doing calculations on the ground with chalk, Vijayā smilingly replied:
'It is Dasarath's son, O daughter of the mountains, who is doing *pūjā* to you in Lankā.
Having painted in vermilion, on two water-filled pots, an image of your beautiful feet,
The Raghu lord is worshipping you with blue lotus-

§217

dharma see above, §173. It can be understood here as 'righteousness'.
the three worlds see I.142.
Vāsuki,/ Bearer of the Earth i.e. the great snake Sesha or Ananta. See I.33. He bears the whole earth as well Vishnu, because the earth is wrapped round by his tail. In some versions of the churning of the ocean myth (see I.295), Vāsuki—used as a rope—is distinguished from Ananta/Sesha, but M treats all three as one.

§233

Dasarath's son i.e. Rām. See II.173 and also I.172, 386.

flowers—I can see that through my calculations. Give him a gift of fearlessness,
O fearless one! The son of Kausalyā, the greatest of the line of Raghu,
Is your supreme devotee. Rescue him from danger, O rescuer!'

§241

Rising from her golden throne, the queen of queens stood up and spoke again to her chaste companion:
'Give due hospitality, Vijayā, to Indra and his consort.
I shall go to where, on awesome Mount Yogāsan, my matted-haired husband sits in meditation.'

§247

With that, elephant-gaited Durgā entered her golden apartments. The lovely Vijayā, with charming words of welcome,
Seated King Indra and heaven's Queen Sachi on golden chairs. They received with great pleasure divine food from her. Jayā laughingly hung a garland of star-like flowers round Sachi's neck;
On her bound-up hair, she placed eternally charming, eternally blooming jewel-flowers;
Musicians played on all sides; nymphs sang and danced. Kailās city was enchanted;
The three worlds were enchanted! Children hearing that ravishing sound in their dreams smiled in their mothers' laps, eyes closed!
Sleepless pining women woke up startled, thinking they heard beloved footsteps at their door! *Koel*-birds fell silent in the woods!

§233

fearlessness *abhaya*. See below, VIII.83.

son of Kausalyā, the greatest of the line of Raghu i.e. Rām. See I.172, 406.

Yogis jumped up, thinking their *iṣṭadevas* had arrived, in response to prayers for a boon!

§265

Entering her golden apartments, Siva's beloved thought: 'How shall I gain an audience today with my lord?'
She pondered for a while, then thought of Rati. Her desire to reach her travelled in a trice—
In the form of a perfume-filled wave of air—to the place where the lovely-faced delighter of Kāma was dallying with him, in a flower-garden.
Rati's heart danced, like a *vīṇā*-string at the touch of a finger! She flew swiftly through the air to Mount Kailās.
Like a blooming lotus at dawn, bowing at the feet of the sun's envoy the dawn, Kāma's beloved bowed before the feet of the beloved of Siva!

§278

Blessing Rati, Durgā smiled and said: 'The lord of yoga is immersed in *tapas* on Mount Yogāsan;
How, with what ploy, do I break his trance,
Tell me, O moon-faced one?' Bowing,
Lovely-haired Rati replied: 'Take on, devi,
A captivating guise. If you so command, I shall bring various adornments and dress your beautiful body.
As soon as he sees you, Siva will be transfixed—just as Spring,
The lord of the seasons, is transfixed, when he sees a flower-braided forest!'

§247

iṣṭadevas patron-gods. See I.743.

§265

Rati wife of Kāma, the god of love. Her name means 'passion, coitus'.

§278

tapas see above, §168.

§287

Saying this, Rati rubbed Durgā's hair with sweet-scented oil, and plaited it exquisitely.
She supplied a variety of ornaments, studded with diamonds and pearls; she brought sandal-paste,
And musk, and saffron mixed with *keśar*; and silk garments gleaming with gems.
The lovely-eyed one then painted the goddess's feet with lac. Taking on world-ravishing form, the daughter of the lord of the mountains got ready,
Glorious as gold when polished to double radiance! She looked at her moon-like face in a mirror, like a full-bloomed lotus when it sees its own beauty in a clear lake.
Smiling, Siva's beloved looked at Kāma's beloved and said: 'Call the lord of your life.'
At once (like the queen of *koel*-birds when calling out to the Spring!) Rati called out to Madan.
The flower-bow-bearer came running, came like an exile abroad when he hears with oh! what delight the music of his native land!

§306

The daughter of the lord of the mountains said, 'Come with me, O Kāma;
I shall go to where the master of yoga is immersed in yoga now. Let us go quickly, my child.'

§287

keśar technically, the pollen-tube of a flower; or a synonym for *kuṅkum* (saffron); but M probably just means (sweet-scented) pollen.

The daughter of the lord of the mountains *Nagendrabālā*: 'daughter of Nagendṛa'. Nagendra ('lord of the mountains') is a name for Himavat or Himālaya, father of Pārvati/Durgā. **Madan** 'the maddener'; a name for Kāma, god of love. **flower-bow-bearer** like Cupid in Greek and Roman mythology, Kāma pierces his victims with arrows. His bow is made of sugar-cane strung with a row of bees, and his arrows are flowers.

§309

The son of Māyā, the ever-joyous Madan, replied at the feet of fearless Durgā:
'Why, devi, do you command me to do this?
When I recall what happened before, I die, mother,
With dread. When, chaste one,
Through foolish Daksha's fault, you abandoned your body to be born in Himālaya's house, and Siva in grief and yearning withdrew from the burden of the universe and began to meditate,

§309

The son of Māyā Madan (Kāma) is the son not of Māyā-devi, the goddess who guides Lakshman and Vibhishan through the Rākshas defences in Book VI of *MBK* (and Rām down to the Underworld in Book VIII), but of Māyāvati, who was 'mother of Madan' according to a myth recounted in the *Annadāmaṅgal* of Bharatchandra Ray (1712–1760). After Madan was destroyed by the fire of Siva's anger (see I.33), his wife Rati assumed the name 'Māyāvati' and went to work as a cook in the house of Sambar, a Dānav associated with drought and compared sometimes to Vritra (see II.45). Meanwhile, Madan was born again in Dvārakā as the child of Krishna and his wife Rukmini. When Sambar heard about this from the sage Nārad, he seized the child and hurled him into the sea. He was swallowed by a fish, which was caught in a fisherman's net. The fisherman presented the fish to Sambar, and Māyāvati took it to her kitchen-hut. When she cut the fish open and found the child, she adopted it as her son.

When I recall what happened before i.e. how he was burnt to ashes by a blast from Siva's third eye. See Source Notes, pp. 326–7.

When, chaste one, / Through foolish Daksha's fault you abandoned your body . . . Daksha is the father of the twenty-seven stars who are wives of Chandra, the moon. He is also the father of Sati, an early form of Siva's *śakti* or consort. Daksha organised a grand sacrifice, but forgot to invite his father-in-law, Siva. Sati died from the shame of this, and Siva went wild with grief, killing Daksha and staying by Sati's dead body in a state of deep mourning. Worried that this would distract Siva from his responsibilities to the universe, the other gods sent Vishnu to dismember Sati with his discus into fifty-one parts, which were then scattered to become places of pilgrimage to the goddess. Still in mourning, Siva withdrew to the mountains to meditate. The gods then persuaded the goddess to incarnate herself as Pārvati (Durgā), daughter of Himālaya, and Madan (Kāma) was enlisted by Indra to break Siva out of his trance so that he could be attracted to her.

Indra, King of the gods, ordered me to break his trance.
I went at a bad time, mother, to the place where Siva
was deep in *tapas*;
I released my flower-arrow from my flower-bow at an
inauspicious moment. Like a lion when he suddenly
attacks a king elephant, filling the jungle with his roaring,
The fire-god devoured me in fury—he whose dwelling,
great goddess,
Is on the great god's brow. Alas, *Mā*,
The agony I suffered: how can I narrate it at your rosy
feet? I howled,
Screamed out to Indra and the moon and the wind and
the sun; none of them came; I was soon burnt to ashes!
I feel nearly broken with fear when I think of Siva; I beg
you to have mercy, O merciful one!'

§330

Siva's wife smiled reassuringly at Kāma and said: 'Come
with me cheerfully, O bodiless one,
Be fearless in your heart. Through my boon you will be
ever-victorious! The Agni who,
At that bad time, so fiercely burnt you will do service to
you today, just as life-destroying poison can save life
if used with medical skill.'

§337

Kāma bowed down before Umā's feet and said: 'When
you give a gift of fearlessness, O fearless one,
What fear can he who receives it feel in these three
worlds? But I ask at your lotus-feet: how,

§309

tapas see II.168.

he whose dwelling, great goddess,/ Is on the great god's brow i.e. in Siva's fiery third eye.

§337

Umā a common name in Bengal for Durgā/Pārvati.

O daughter of the mountains, will you leave your home, tell me,
In so ravishing a form? The world will at once go mad, mother,
I tell you truly, when they see your sumptuous beauty! It will immediately achieve the opposite of what you intend.
When the gods and anti-gods stirred the ocean to extract its nectar, the anti-gods in their wickedness started to fight with them over it. Vishnu then came in equally seductive form!
When Vishnu as Mohini was seen by the three worlds, everyone succumbed to my arrows! Gods and anti-gods forgot the ocean's nectar through longing for the nectar of her lips;
Snakes hung their heads in shame, at seeing the snake-like plait down her back; even the flying Mount Mandar fell motionless,
At the sight of her lofty breasts! To remember this, chaste one,

§337

When the gods and anti-gods stirred the ocean to extract its nectar see I.295. The last of the 'fourteen jewels' raised by the churning of the ocean is the divine doctor Dhanvantari, who emerges with a bowel of the precious nectar, which makes anyone who drinks it immortal. The Asuras, who have taken one end of the churning rope, drop their end and rush at Dhanvantari to grab the bowl. To stop a full-scale brawl between gods and anti-gods, Vishnu intervenes in form of Mohini, a beautiful and seductive damsel. Her beauty enchants the Asuras, and they agree to share the nectar with the gods. Mohini, however, as befits her name, which means 'bewitching', tricks them by serving all the gods first and then running off with the bowl. The Asuras furiously attack the gods, but are easily defeated because the nectar has restored the gods' strength.

flying Mount Mandar the mountains of Hindu mythology originally all had wings (see I.714). In the myth of the churning of the ocean, Mount Mandar is used as a rod and the serpent Vāsuki as rope (see II.217). Mountains, like breasts, have peaks—hence Mandar's shame on seeing Mohini.

Makes me smile. If copper takes on such beauty by being gilded with gold, devi,
Think of the beauty of pure gold!' At once Durgā, worker of illusions,
Magically created a thick golden cloud to envelop her fabulous body—alas, like a lotus at day's end,
Covering its moon-visage! Or like a flame concealing its smile under a pile of ash! Or like the moon when eclipsed by Indra with a discus to safeguard its nectar!

§367

Sweet-smiling Durgā emerged through the ivory portals of her palace, like dawn hidden by clouds! Kāma was with her,
Flower-bow in his hand, and a quiver on his back that was full of sharp flower-arrows—a thorny stalk for her lotus-like beauty.

§372

On the crest of Mount Kailās is an awesome, cliff-like peak: world-renowned Yogāsan;
Earth-delighting Durgā arrived there elephant-gaited. At once tumultuous waters, confined to deep caves,

§337

Or like the moon when eclipsed by Indra . . . Vishnu had to protect the moon from Garuḍa (see I.218), who tried to steal its nectar to rescue his mother Vinatā from slavery. Vinatā's husband Kasyapa was also the husband of Kadru, mother of the race of snakes. Vinatā and Kadru were arch-rivals, and had a fierce dispute about whether sun's horses were black or white. They agreed that whoever was wrong should become the slave of the other. The horses were actually white, but Kadru won the wager by getting her snake-sons to spurt black poison over them. The snakes then became greedy for the nectar of the gods, and offered to release Vinatā if Garuḍa could give them some. Indra stopped him from stealing nectar from the moon, but Vishnu allowed him to take a cupful from the ambrosial ocean.

§372

Yogāsan see above, §204.

Fell silent, like the sea turning calm after a storm; clouds retreated,
Like darkness at the smile of dawn! Durgā gazed at her matted-haired meditating husband: body smeared with ash,
Eyes closed, he was sunk in an ocean of *tapas*, robbed of all external awareness!
§383
Lovely-haired Durgā smiled and said to Madan: 'Why delay any more, O enemy of Sambar?
Let fly your flower-arrow.' At the goddess's command, Kāma bent his knee,
Released with a twang his bowstring, pierced her husband with an arrow of rapture! The tangle on his head shuddered,
Like trees on a mountain cracking and crashing when shaken by an earthquake! Lord Siva was disturbed! The fire on his forehead crackled,
Flared up with a dazzling glare! Kāma took terrified refuge in Durgā's breast, like a lion-cub rushing to its mother's embrace when storm-clouds thunder,
And eye-blinding lightning flashes with world-smashing power! Siva now opened his eyes. The daughter of the mountains threw off her illusory covering of cloud.
§400
Overwhelmed by Durgā's ravishing beauty, Lord-of-the-animals Siva said: 'Why,

§383

O enemy of Sambar see above, §309. **tangle on his head** i.e. Siva's matted locks. See above, §87. **daughter of the mountains** because Durgā is the daughter of Himālaya. See II.309.

§400

Lord-of-the-animals Siva see above, §204.

O mother of Ganesa, do I see you alone here, in this deserted place?
Where, wife, is your servant the lion?
Where are Vijayā and Jayā?' Umā smiled her graceful smile and replied: 'You have been,
O Lord of yoga, in solitude here for a long time, oblivious of me;
That is why I have come, Lord, in hope of a glimpse of your feet.
Does a woman who loves her husband come to him with attendants? The mate of a heron goes alone at dawn to her life's love!' Smiling a little with affection,
Siva seated his wife on a deerskin mat. Immediately, flowers burst into bloom all around;
Sting-barbed bees came wildly rushing for honey; a spring breeze blew; *koel*-birds sang;
A shower of night-dew-moistened blossoms covered the mountain-peak! In Umā's breast (what dwelling-place suits Madan better?)
The flower-bow-bearer, sitting there eagerly, joyously pulled back his bowstring and released a bevy of arrows—
Which maddened the Trident-bearer with passion! In shame at this, Rāhu came and swallowed the moon on Siva's brow,

§400

mother of Ganesa the elephant-headed god Ganesa is the son of Siva and Pārvati (Durgā).

your servant the lion Durgā in her form as the ten-armed slayer of the buffalo-demon Mahish has a lion as her vehicle.

***koel*-birds** see I.623.

Trident-bearer i.e. Siva. See below, §447.

Rāhu an Asura who causes eclipses of the moon by swallowing it. It always re-emerges, because Vishnu cut off Rāhu's head with his discus when he drank some of the nectar grabbed by the Asuras at the churning of the

And the god Agni coyly withdrew into a swathe of ash.

§425

Raised by the beauty of Durgā to his fully aroused form,
Siva laughed and said: 'I know,
Goddess, what is in your mind; why Indra and Sachi have come to Mount Kailās;
Why the jewel of the race of Raghu is performing a *pūjā* to you at an abnormal time. Rāvan is my most fervent devotee; but the wretch is sinking through his own misdeeds;
It breaks my heart to think of this, great goddess! Alas,
Devi, where in god or man is there power to stop the results of past actions? Send Kāma,
Umā, to the king of the gods. Order him,
Queen, to hasten to the house of Māyā-devi. The warrior Lakshman will slay the warrior Meghnād through her grace!'

§439

Fish-bannered Kāma departed, like Garuḍa soaring from his nest, with constant backward glances at that pleasurable dwelling!

---

ocean (see II.337). Only his head remained immortal, which means the moon always passes out of his throat and can never be consumed. He can also cause solar eclipses in the same way.

the god Agni the fire-god Agni dwells in Siva's third eye. See above, §309.

§425

pūjā see I.483.

Māyā-devi when Durgā veils Kāma in a cloud in §337 of this book, she is described as *māyāmayā*, 'full of magic power or *māyā*'. So any goddess can be identified with *māyā*. But M makes Māyā-devi a separate goddess, and gives her a very important role in his epic. See Source Notes, p. 329.

§439

Fish-bannered Kāma Kāma has a fish or *makar* (see I.62) as his symbol, because its *rasa* or juice gives men virility.

Thick golden clouds, emitting thick gusts of fragrance as they rained down flowers—red lotus,
White lotus, jasmine, *sẽutī*,
Jāti, pārijāt and others—enveloped and surrounded great Siva and his wife.

§447

Moon-visaged Rati, the beloved wife of Kāma, had been waiting at the ivory-inlayed golden gates of Mount Kailās,
Pining for her lord! Kāma now arrived, and at once and with ecstasy swept her into his arms,
Delighting her with sweet love-talk. Her tears dried, like drops of dew on the petals of a lotus when the sun rises over the crest of dawn.
Receiving her life's treasure, pressing her face against his (like a parrot and her mate when spring's sap flows)
She said in loving tones: 'It has saved my life to have you back with me, O enjoyer of me!
I have thought of you so much: how can I describe it? I always tremble,
Lord, at great Siva's name, remembering what happened before!
The Trident-holder is horribly violent! Do not go to him again, swear to me,

§439

sẽutī a kind of white rose.

Jāti, pārijāt the *jāti* is another kind of white flower; the *pārijāt* is a never-fading heavenly flower that was one of the 'fourteen jewels' churned up from the ambrosial ocean (see I.295 and II.337).

§447

remembering what happened before see I.33 and II.309.

The Trident-holder the three prongs of Siva's *triśūl* or trident are associated with his three main functions: creation, preservation and destruction; and also his three virtues or *guṇas*: *sattva* (truth), *rajas* (activeness, will-power) and *tamas* (inertia, quietude, gloom).

My Lord!' Five arrowed-Madan smiled fondly and answered: 'Who,
O Beauty, need fear the sun when protected by shade? Let us go now to the king of the gods.'
§467
Kāma arrived at where Indra was sitting on a seat of gold, bowed and told him what Siva had commanded. Mounting his chariot,
The warfaring king of the gods sped to Māyā's abode. His horses hurtled through the sky, powerful as fire,
Manes unmoving; the wheels of the chariot clattered tumultuously, ripping through clouds.
§475
Thousand-eyed Indra soon landed where Māyā dwelt. Leaving his mighty chariot, that mightiest of divine charioteers entered her temple.
Who can describe what the god saw? On a golden throne whose shine was like the united scorching rays of the sun, powerful wonder-working Māyā sat.
With his hands pressed together, Indra stooped low and said: 'Give me your blessing, O enchantress of the universe!'
§483
The goddess blessed him and asked: 'Tell me what brings you here today, O son of Aditi?

§447

Five arrowed-Madan Madan (Kāma)'s flower arrows (see above, §287) are five in number and are made from the flowers of the mango, *aśok*, jasmine, *bakul* and myrtle, and produce respectively beguilement, burning, dessication, paralysis and stupefaction.

§475

Thousand-eyed Indra see V.478.

§483

son of Aditi see above, §217.

§485

Indra answered: 'At Siva's command, great Māyā,
I have come to your home. Tell me, by what trick will
 the son of Sumitrā defeat the son of Dasānan
 tomorrow morning?
By your grace (so Siva said) the heroic Lakshman will
 destroy the heroic Meghnād in fierce combat.'

§491

The goddess thought for a moment, then said to Indra:
 'When the monstrous demon Tārak,
O Master of the gods, grabbed hold of heaven after
 beating you in battle, Kārttikeya,
Nursling of the six Pleiades, was born from the womb of
 Pārvati. Bull-emblemed Siva himself armed that hero
 for the slaying of the Dānav king,
By creating weapons with his furious energy. See, deva,
This shield, embellished with gold; see this sword,

§485

son of Sumitrā i.e. Lakshman. See I.172.

son of Dasānan i.e. Meghnād. Dasānan is Rāvan. See I.33.

§491

monstrous demon Tārak . . . born from the womb of Pārvati Tārak was a mighty Asura who captured heaven. Brahmā, the Creator, declared that only the six-headed war-god Kārttikeya, born of Siva's seed, would be able to defeat Tārak. M describes Kārttikeya as 'born from the womb of Pārvati', but in the best known versions of the myth Siva does not beget Kārttikeya in the normal way. Instead, he places his seed inside Agni, god of fire. It grows into a six-headed embryo too hot even for Agni to bear, so he drops it into the Ganges. It is rescued by the Ganas, Siva's attendants, and taken to a cave on Mount Meru (see I.33), where Gauri arranges for the infant to be wet-nursed by the six Krittikās or Pleiades.

Bull-emblemed Siva Siva's emblem is the bull and he is accompanied always by his faithful bull Nandi, guardian of all four-footed animals.

the Dānav king i.e. Tārak. 'Dānav' is often used by M as a synonym for the Asuras generally. See I.33.

See, deva,/ This shield . . . through her magic power, Māyā-devi is

Which Death himself inhabits; see, O champion,
This formidable quiver, inexhaustibly full of arrows, as full as the realm of the Nāgas is with poisonous snakes!
See the bow, Lord.' The powerful husband of Sachi,
Smiling at the beauty of the bow, said: 'What chaff my own bejewelled bow is,
Compared to this! The shield is refulgent as the sun, eye-dazzling!
The sword gleams bright as a flame! Where in the world, mother,
Is there a quiver like this?' 'Listen, Lord,'
(Māyā-devi spoke again) 'six-faced Kārttikeya destroyed Tārak with the power of these weapons. By that same power,
O mighty one, Meghnād will die, I promise you!
But there is no hero in the three worlds—whether divine or human—who can kill Rāvan's son in fair combat.
Send the weapons to Rām's younger brother. I myself will go to Lankā tomorrow; I shall guard Lakshman,
Lord, against Rākshas attack. You go to the realm of the gods, O protector of the gods.
When Dawn, friend of all flowers, opens the golden gates of the East tomorrow with her lotus hands,
Lion-hero Lakshman will free you of the fear of Indrajit, your eternal enemy, and Lankā's lotus-sun will set!'

---

able to summon up the weapons that Siva gave to the war-god Kārttikeya to use against Tārak.

realm of the Nāgas the Nāgas are snake-like demigods and their realm is underground. See I.33.

Rām's younger brother i.e. Lakshman.

Lankā's lotus-sun will set i.e. Meghnād will die. Cf. the song of praise

§525
Praising the goddess with joyous gratitude, Indra
returned to heaven, weapons in hand.
§527
He took his seat on a golden throne in the court of the
gods, and spoke to his charioteer Chitrarath:
'Carefully carry the weapons,
Great hero, to Lankā's golden realm. The leonine son of
Sumitrā will slaughter Meghnād tomorrow through
Māyā's grace.
Māyā-devi will explain to him how. And say to Rām, O
Lord of the Gandharvas,
That the gods all greatly desire his welfare; even Pārvati,
Siva's beloved,
Is well disposed to him now. Tell him, wise one,
Not to be afraid! If Rāvan's son dies in battle, Rāvan
will surely die too;
The jewel of the race of Raghu—chaste Sitā's delight—
will delight in her again.
O noblest of charioteers, climb into my chariot and go.
In case the Rākshasas create an uproar when they see
you in Lankā,
I shall arrange for clouds to cover the sky; I shall call up
Pavan, the lord of the winds,

---

to Meghnād at the end of Book I: 'The sun of the Raksha race is about to dawn' (§763). M was fond of the compound *paṅkaj-rabi* ('lotus-sun') as an image of power and glory.

§527

Chitrarath the king of the Gandharvas (see I.375). His name means '(having a) colourful chariot' and he also serves as Indra's charioteer.

jewel of the race of Raghu i.e. Rām. See I.406.

Pavan god of the winds and the father of Hanumān (see I.218). He is also known as Vāyu.

And bid him to let loose the winds; lightning will break out into dance; I shall fill the world with stupendous thunderclaps.'

§548

Touching King Indra's feet, carefully picking up the weapons, the charioteer Chitrarath set off down to earth.

§550

Then the ruler of the gods called to Pavan and said: 'Whip up at once a cataclysmic storm over Lankā, O Lord of the winds;

Let loose quickly the imprisoned winds; bring clouds; fight for a while with your enemy the sea!'

The wind-god rushed off merrily, like a leaping lion breaking his chains, to where the winds were imprisoned in a dark dungeon,

Deep inside a mountain. He heard their booming howl from a long way off; he saw the mountain inwardly wrestling with their assault,

Powerless to restrain their force. Pavan opened the stone doors at a touch. Bellowing,

The winds charged out, like waters suddenly bursting through a dam. Earth shook;

The ocean roared! Wave after wave surged, rising to mountain-high peaks,

Crazed by their battle with the winds! Rumbling clouds raced in all directions; lightning-streaks flared;

Thunderclaps boomed. The moon—lord of the stars—

Fled with the stars. Clouds swathed Lankā; banks of flames belched forth;

Trees in the forest fell crashing to the ground; a tempest raced through the sky;

Rain cascaded, as if to inundate Creation. Battering hail rattled down.

§576

The panic-stricken Rākshasas took refuge in their houses. In the place where the noble lord of the Rāghavas held court in his tent, Chitrarath suddenly alighted,
Royally apparelled, like the sun garlanded with rays! His girdle glittered round his middle,
Its jewels as brilliant as the zodiac; his great sword dangled from it—corruscatingly bright!
How can a poet describe that divine quiver, bow and shield, that armour and spear,
That golden crown solar in its glare? His divine radiance was blinding to the eye; the whole area was suddenly filled with the scents of heaven.

§587

Humbly abasing himself at the feet of the divine messenger, Rām asked: 'O dweller in heaven,
What region apart from heaven, ah! befits such grandeur and beauty?
Why—tell me—have you deserted the gardens of Nandan to be here today?
I have no gold throne, Lord, so where shall I seat you?
But if you feel kind towards me, sit on this *kuś*-grass mat and receive water for your feet and these *pūjā*-offerings. Alas,
Rām is but a beggar.' Chitrarath blessed him, sat down on the mat and courteously said:

§576

lord of the Rāghavas i.e. Rām, lord of the descendants of Raghu. See I.1.

§587

gardens of Nandan see above, §14.

***kuś*-grass** a kind of sacred grass used in religious ceremonies, so a mat made of it is auspicious.

§597
'My name is Chitrarath—hear me, son of Dasarath;
I serve King Indra with unstinting loyalty; I rule the race of Gandharvas. I have come to this city at Indra's behest.
He and all the other gods wish you well. These weapons that you see, jewel of men,
Have been sent by Indra for your younger brother. At dawn, the great goddess Māyā will appear and tell you by what stratagem brave Lakshman will annihilate mighty Meghnād tomorrow.
You are loved by the gods, jewel of the race of Raghu! Durgā herself is very well disposed to you!'
§609
The Raghu prince replied: 'I float in a sea of joy, O best Gandharva,
At this wonderful news! I am, alas,
An ignorant human being; how can I express my gratitude? I ask you that.'
§613
The messenger smiled and said: 'Listen, jewel of the Raghus,
To what defines gratitude to the gods: care for the poor, control of the senses,
Keeping always to the path of *dharma*; constant service to the goddess of Truth. Sandalwood,
Flowers, silken garments and other *pūjā*-offerings are ignored by a god if the giver is unrighteous. This essential thing I say to you.'
§626
Rāmchandra bowed; the charioteer Chitrarath blessed him, and went in his divine chariot back to heaven!

§613
dharma see above, §173, 217

The huge storm died down; the ocean grew calm; on
seeing once again the moon with his attendant
stars,
Golden Lankā smiled. Moonlight once again washed her
silvery body in the rippling waters; lotuses smiled at
the fun of this.
Corpse-eating jackals returned apace to the battlefield,
and flocks of vultures, and other vile flesh-eaters.
The Rākshasas emerged once again, seething with
blood-lust, frightening weapons in their hands!

Here ends 'The Receiving of Weapons',
the second book of *Meghnādbadh kābya*.

BOOK III

§1
The youthful Pramilā, daughter of the Dānavas, weeps
in her pleasure-garden,
Distraught at her husband's absence. Sometimes she
tearfully roams through its groves of flowers, like the
women of Vraj,
Deprived, alas, of the sight of Krishna in his yellow loincloth,
At the foot of the *kadamba*-tree, flute on his lips!
Sometimes she goes indoors,
Only to emerge again, mournful as a dove on finding an
empty nest! Sometimes she climbs the turret of her home,
To stare fixedly at distant Lankā, dabbing at her
ceaseless tears with the end of her sari! Silent are the
flute and *vīṇā*,
The drum and cymbals, the sounds of song! Glum-faced
are her companions around her,
Grieving for her, wilting, ah!
Like flowers burnt up, at spring's departure, by drought.
§17
The goddess of Night descended on the pleasure-grove.
The lovely Pramilā, trembling,

§1

Pramilā Meghnād's wife Pramilā is largely M's own creation, because no wife is named in Vālmiki's *Rāmāyaṇa* and in the medieval Bengali *Rāmāyaṇ* of Krittibās none of the 9,000 wives he is said to have are named. Her Dānav father Kālnemi (see below, §413) is identified as a maternal uncle of Rāvan. See also below, §85. **Dānavas** see I.33. **Vraj** the area round Mathurā and on the bank of the Yamunā river where Krishna grew up and sported with the *gopīs* (milkmaids). ***kadamba*-tree** large tree with tiny, sweet-scented florets set in a yellow-orange ball. It is associated with Krishna and the rainy season. For the effect of the simile here, see Source Notes, p. 331. ***vīṇā*** see I.623.

§17

The goddess of Night *niśā-debī*: Night personified in the European manner rather than a goddess from Hindu tradition.

Said with a tremulous moan to her spring-scented friend
Vāsanti, arms round her neck and weeping: 'See here,
My dear, dark night has come to bite me like a snake!
Where is the royal and invincible Meghnād at this dangerous time?
He went away saying he would come back at once; why this delay? I cannot understand;
If you can, friend, please tell me.'

§27

Vāsanti answered, like Spring's friend the *koel*-bird cooing in spring: 'How can I say why the lord of your life is delaying today?
But do not worry, O vermilion-wearer! He will soon crush Rām and return.
What do you fear, my darling? Who can be a match in battle for one whose body cannot be pierced by the arrows of gods or anti-gods?
Come, let us go into the forest. Let us pick fresh flowers,
Let us stitch a lustrous garland. Let us hang it cheerfully round the neck of your beloved, in the way that victory-flags are merrily tied to the crests of victorious chariots!'

§40

With this, the two friends entered the forest, walked to where moonlight playing on the surface of a lake made the lotuses smile;
Bees buzzed; *koel*-birds cooed; flowers bloomed;

§17

Vāsanti the name means 'of the Spring', and there is wordplay with *basanta-saurabhā* ('spring-scented').

§27

***koel*-bird** see I.623. **vermilion-wearer** *sīmantinī*: because Pramilā is married, she wears vermilion in her *sīmanta* or parting, in the Bengali fashion.

Lines of fireflies glittered, like vermilion sparkling on the joyful brow of the goddess of the forest; leaves rustled in the spring breeze.

§47

They filled the ends of their saris with blossoms. Who can describe how many petals were bepearled by Pramilā's tears? A little way off,
She saw a sorrowing sunflower, pale-faced, alas,
Without the light of the sun. She approached it gently and said: 'The anguish that you,
O beloved of the sun, suffer in night's thick darkness, is mine too!
How dark the world is now to my gloomy vision! I am burnt to the core with the fire of separation! The sun by whose image I daily live has set behind the mountains of the west!
When shall I get back—as you will get back through the grace of dawn—the lord of my life?'

§61

Having gathered flowers in that wood, heaving deep sighs, chaste Pramilā said to her companion:
'See what heaps of flowers we have picked; see what lustrous garlands we have stitched, my friend;
But where shall I find those feet at which I long to offer them? Who, I wonder,
Has ensnared the lion? Come, let us all go back to Lankā.'

§40

goddess of the forest another literary personification, not a Hindu deity.

§47

Without the light of the sun cf. the identification of Meghnād with the sun in I.763 and II.491.

§61

the lion i.e. Meghnād.

§68
'How,' said Vāsanti, 'will you enter the city today?
The Rāghav armies have encircled it like an uncrossable sea! Thousands of enemies patrol all around with weapons in their hands, like club-wielding Yama himself.'
§74
Stupendous Pramilā grew angry! 'What have you said, Vāsanti?
When a river leaves its mountain-home to flow to the sea, who has the power to hold it back? I am the daughter of a Dānav,
The wife of a Rākshas; Rāvan is my father-in-law; Meghnād is my husband;
Why should I be afraid of the beggar Rāghav? I shall enter Lankā today through my own strength of arms; let's see how that jewel of men can stop me!'
§83
With that, and moving like a champion elephant, chaste Pramilā furiously went back into her golden palace.
§85
As when great Arjun, scourge of his enemies, arrived—with a horse for sacrifice—

§68

club-wielding Yama himself see I.1, 218.

§74

the beggar Rāghav i.e. Rām. See I.1.

§85

As when great Arjun . . . Arjun is the third of the Pāṇḍav brothers in the *Mahābhārata.* His elder brother Yudhishṭhir organises an *Aśvamedha* or 'horse-sacrifice' ritual, and the horse is brought by Arjun. Preparations for the sacrifice took over a year, during which the sacrificial horse was allowed to wander at will. All the territory it crossed became the possession of the king performing the sacrifice, unless his sovereignty was successfully challenged in battle.

In the land where women alone lived, and roused them
with his god-given conch, so Pramilā's warrior-
women joyously armed themselves for battle;
War-trumpets blared on all sides; maddened with war-
lust, the women streamed out,
Brandishing swords, twanging their bow-strings,
flashing their shields!
The dazzling glare of burnished armour lit up the city!
Horses in their stables neighed, pricking up their ears
at the jingle of the women's anklets,
Or the rattle of their waistbands, as when serpents
dance to the rat-a-tat-tat of a drum. Elephants in
their stalls let out ear-splitting roars,
Like massive thunderclouds booming from afar! Echoes
on the mountain-tops, in the forests,
In caves, waking with rapture, suddenly filled the land
with a fearsome din.

§102

A demoness, haughty embodiment of wrath,
Nrimunḍamālini by name,

§85

In the land where women alone lived there is no mention of this in Vyāsa's *Mahābhārata*, but in the *Aśvamedha-parba* of the medieval Bengali *Mahābhārat* of Kasirām Dās, Arjun's travels with the sacrificial horse take in a *mahāban* ('great forest') called Pramilāpuri, whose inhabitants are all *bīrāṅganā* (Amazon-like, warrior-women). Their chief, who is called Pramilā, initially refuses to let the horse free again without a fight. M must have got his name for Meghnād's wife from there. See Source Notes, p. 332.

the women although Pramilā and her companions are Rākshasis (demonesses), M refers to them with ordinary words for women, such as *nārī* and *bālā*. The comparison between Pramilā's army and the *bīrāṅganā* of Pramilāpuri recalls his dramatic monologues by heroic women, *Bīrāṅganā kābya* (see Introduction, p. lxxiii).

§102

Nrimunḍamālini 'she who is garlanded with human heads'. An epithet for the goddess Kāli, but the name here of Pramilā's most warlike attendant.

Girded a hundred horses in varied liveries, brought them joyously out of their stables to the porch of the palace. A hundred guardswomen mounted them:

Swords in scabbards clattered at the horses' sides. Tassels on the helmets of the women danced; their bejewelled plaits swung along merrily with the quivers on their backs.

Spears were in their hands, like the thorny stalks of a lotus. Excited horses whinnied,

Like Siva's shouts of ecstasy when demon-pounding Kāli's lotus-feet press upon his breast! A martial band played; gods in heaven,

Nāgas in the underworld, people on earth, all were taken aback!

§115

Too angry to be frightened or modest, resplendent Pramilā dressed. Beams from the crown on her hair shone,

Ah! like a rainbow on a cloud! There was a streak of collyrium on her brow,

Like the eye-enchanting crescent moon on the brow of Durgā! She had a breastplate on her high bosom, a many-jewelled golden girdle carefully strapped round her waist.

A quiver swung on her back with a shield round as the sun and as bright to the eye! Gleaming against her thighs (ah!

Plump as forest-adorning banana-tree trunks), a razor-

§102

Like Siva's shouts of ecstasy . . . Kāli dominates her husband Siva, making love to him in the superior position, and killing him, even, so that she can dance on his dead body. M's editor Dinanath Sanyal disapproves of M's simile here. See Introduction, p. lx. **Nāgās in the underworld** see I.33, II.491.

§115

collyrium *añjan*: normally eye-salve or *kajjal*, but M very clearly implies a line or streak (*rekhā*) on the brow (*bhāle*). **Durgā** M calls her Bhairavi here, wife of Siva in his terrifying (*bhairav*) aspect.

sharp sword in a golden scabbard shone; a long spear was in her hand;
Various sparkling ornaments bedecked her limbs!
Thus Pramilā dressed—like Durgā,
Maddened with war-lust, preparing to destroy in horrible battles the buffalo-demon or the brothers Sumbha and Nisumbha; and like Durgā's attendant goblins,
Armed horsewomen circled her. Then she mounted her own steed Vaḍabā, who was fiery as the fire that burns underseas!

§135

Like a cloud booming in the sky, elephant-buttocked Pramilā hailed her assembled companions: 'Invincible Indrajit—
Listen, O Dānav women—seems trapped like a prisoner in Lankā today!
I cannot understand why the lord of my life so neglects me with delay! I shall go to him; I shall smash through formidable armies to enter the city,
Crushing by my own force of arms the chief of the Rāghavas. This I promise, O warriors!
Or else I shall die in battle—if that is my fate! We are born of the Dānav race;
It is the Dānav destiny to slay in battle—or drown in the

§115

the buffalo-demon i.e. Mahish. See II.400. **or the brothers Sumbha and Nisumbha** Asura-brothers who were both slain by Durgā. **her own steed Vaḍabā** there is wordplay here with Vāḍaba, the 'mare's fire' that burns beneath the southern seas. It is supposed to emerge from a cavity called the 'mare's mouth' under the South Pole, and Vaḍabā is also a name for this submarine horse-head.

§135

Invincible Indrajit i.e. Meghnād, the 'vanquisher of Indra'. See I.1. **Dānav women** *dānabi*: female Dānavas. See I.33. **chief of the Rāghavas** i.e. Rām. See II.576.

blood of our enemies! We have honey on our lips and poison in our eyes;
Is there not strength in our lotus-stalk arms? Come, everyone—
Let's see what stuff Rām is made of! We shall see the man that my aunt-in-law Surpanakhā fell for so madly in the Panchavaṭi wood;
We shall see the warrior Lakshman; we shall bind and bring back Vibhishan—that blot on the Rākshasas—
In ropes made of snakes! Like she-elephants in a reed-bed, we shall pound her enemies.
You are stunning as lightning, my dears: move like lightning and strike your enemies!'

§158
The Dānav women roared tumultuously, like a herd of she-elephants, on heat in spring!

§160
Violent as a forest-fire whipped up by its friend the wind, Pramilā set off to find her husband. Golden Lankā shuddered;
The sea roared; dust flew around in thick clouds; but how can the thickest fogs of the night envelop a fire?
Pramilā-devi, with her Amazon army, travelled with the speed of a fire!

§167
Moon-like in radiance, she soon arrived at the western gate of the city. The sound of hundreds of conches boomed from her army, and hundreds of bowstrings were twanged in anger!

§135
Surpanakhā see I.80.
Vibhishan—that blot on the Rākshasas because of his defection. See I.218.

Lankā trembled in panic; mahouts on elephants,
 charioteers in their chariots,
Horsemen on their horses; kings on their thrones;
 women in their purdah-quarters;
Birds in their nests; lions in their mountain-layers;
 elephants in forests;
All trembled, all quaked—and sea-creatures dived to
 the bottom of the sea!

§176

Hanumān, son of the wind, mighty to behold,
Advanced in fury and roared, 'Who are you, coming to
 die this night?
Hanu is awake at this gate, he at whose name the Lord of
 the Rākshasas shudders on his throne! The jewel of the
 Rāghavas himself is awake with his councillor Vibhishan,
And lion-like Lakshman, and countless other heroes—
 unmatchable in battle.
What are you playing at, got up as women yet looking so
 fierce? I know that night-prowlers work fearsome magic,
Yet I cut through all magic with my prowess; whatever
 enemies I confront, I smash them!'

§188

The haughty Nrimunḍamālini, twanging her bowstring
 and howling with anger, answered:
'Bring Sitā's husband here quickly, you villain! Who is
 interested in you,
Small fry that you are? We do not choose to use our weapons
 on creatures like you. Does a lioness fight with a jackal?
You're free to go; run for your life, tree-dweller!

§176

Hanumān see I.218.

§188

tree-dweller as a monkey-god, Hanumān is contemptuously described here as *banabāsi*, 'living in forests'.

What point is there in killing you, fool! Push off,
Call Sitā's husband here, and Lord Lakshman, and that traitor to the Rākshasas Vibhishan.
You have heard of the invincible Indrajit: the beautiful Pramilā is his wife—she will enter Lankā today through her own might,
To do homage at the feet of her lord! Idiot, what power has anyone to stop us?'

§202

Son of the wind Hanumān, who is mighty through the might of the wind, advanced and saw in terror Pramilā resplendent amidst her army of women.
The brightness of her crown flashed like lightning; her armour was set off by her beauty, like jewellery brought to life by the radiance of the sun!
Amazed, Hanumān said to himself, 'When I vaulted the impassable sea to alight in Lankā, I saw the formidable Bhimā,
Ghastly to behold, sword and skull in her hand, a garland of heads round her neck!
I saw Mandodari and Rāvan's other lady-loves, Dānav daughters all. I saw numerous Rākshas women,
Rākshas wives (moon-sliver-like in their beauty) as I wandered alone from house to house in the darkness of the night.

§202

the formidable Bhimā i.e. Durgā in her wrathful aspect. Also known as Ugrachaṇḍā or Chāmuṇḍā, this is the form in which Durgā, at the command of her husband Siva, stood as a guard outside the gates of Lankā. When Hanumān secretly crossed over to the island at night, he was stopped by her from entering the city.

Mandodari Meghnād's mother. See I.172.

Rākshas women,/ Rākshas wives the Rākshasis are humanized here as elsewhere with ordinary words for woman and wife (*bālā, badhū*). See above, §85.

I saw in the Asoka wood that lotus of the Rāghav race,
Sitā, alas so desolate!
But never have I seen in this world such ravishing beauty! Lucky is the warrior Meghnād, that to his cloud such lightning is forever bound by love!'

§222

Thinking this to himself, the son of Anjanā, in a voice as profound as the wind,
Said, 'Having shackled the sea with stones, fine lady,
My master—that sun of suns—came to this city with thousands of warriors.
The Rākshas king is his enemy; you are women; why,
Tell me, have you come at this unsafe time? Speak without fear;
I am Hanumān, Rām's servant; that fount of the Rāghavas is a sea of compassion.
What quarrel has he with you, lovely-eyed as you are? Tell me quickly,
What favour do you desire? Why have you come here? Speak,
And I will lay your petition, goddess, at Rām's feet.'

§235

Pramilā answered—the sweetness of her message sounding in Hanumān's ears like the message of a *vīṇā*—'The Rāghav lord is my husband's enemy;
But that does not mean that I would fight with him. My husband is a lion of heroes, he triumphs in the world through his own strength;

§202

Asoka wood see II.190.

§222

Anjanā she only seems to be known as Hanumān's mother.

What point would there be in *my* making war on his enemy? We are all of us women, feeble women;
But remember, lord, how a man dies at the touch of the lightning that delights his eyes.
Take with you my messenger Nrimunḍamālini. She will explain what I seek from Rām; go quickly with her.'

§248

The messenger Nrimunḍamālini, like Kāli in appearance, moved fearlessly through the enemy army,
Like a ship with sails forging blithely through the waves, alone on a limitless sea! Hanumān strode before her,
Showing the way. The soldiers were alarmed at the sight of her, like householders seeing their houses on fire at night!
She laughed to herself at their fear. They stared at her aghast as they hurriedly huddled into groups. Her anklets jingled,
And the belt round her waist. Terrifying spear in hand, she moved with the gait of an elephant,
Reducing everyone to panic with the sharp arrows of her stare. On the crown on her head, a crest of peacock-feathers danced gaily;
A necklace glittered between her plump breasts! Her gem-studded plait swung behind her back, like Kāma's banner flying in springtime!
She moved as seductively as an elephant-calf, spreading lustre all around, like moonlight

§235

We are all of us women, feeble women cf. III.85, 202.

§248

like Kāli in appearance cf. III.102. Nrimunḍamālini is described as *nṛmuṇḍamālinī-ākṛti* ('like Nrimunḍamālini in appearance'), and Nrimunḍamālini is a name for Kāli, Siva's consort in her must terrifying guise.

Kāma's banner Kāma has a fish or *makar* on his banner. See II.439.

(Close friend of the lotus) shining in the pure waters of a lake, or radiant dawn between mountain-peaks!

§271

Lord Rām, crest-jewel of the Raghus, was sitting in his tent; the lion-hero Lakshman faced him with cupped hands; Vibhishan was next to him;

And all the other heroes, fiery as the Rudras, awesome to behold!

The weapons that Indra gave him gleamed on a votive stool, ruddy with sandal-paste, covered with an offering of flowers;

Censers burnt with offerings of incense; rows of lanterns flickered all around. Everyone gazed at the weapons in amazement!

Some praised the sword; some the supreme shield—plated with gold,

Like clouds at the end of the day graced by the gold of the sun; some the quiver; some the pile of lustrous armour!

Noble Rām himself, taking the bow in hand, spoke:

'At Sitā's *svayambar* I broke Siva's bow with my bare hands; yet this bow I cannot even string!

How about you, brother Lakshman, can you bend it?'

§288

Suddenly the troops cheered; shouts of '*Jay* Rām' rose deafeningly into the sky,

§271

Rudras Rudra was originally a Vedic storm-god. He became identified with Siva in his angry aspect, and the Rudras are the furious winds that are his progeny. **The weapons that Indra gave him** conveyed by Chitrarath in Book II. See II.597f. *svayambar* the ritual by which a prospective bride can choose her own groom, often from suitors required to perform a test.

§288

***Jay* Rām** 'Victory to Rām'.

Like an ocean wave! Startled, Vibhishan looked towards Rām and said,
'Look outside the camp, O finest of Rāghavas. What dawn has descended here at midnight?'

§294

Everyone gazed in astonishment. 'Look carefully, my friend,'
Said Rām, 'at whether that formidably beautiful lady is a goddess or a demoness. Lankā is full of sorcery—
A mesh of illusions; your elder brother Rāvan can change his shape at will. Look closely;
Such trickery is not unknown to you. Finest of Rākshasas, I acquired you in the nick of time!
Without you, friend, who,
At its hour of peril, will save this inadequate army of mine? You are the eternal protector of Rām in this Raksha city!'

§304

At that moment the messenger arrived at the tent with Hanumān. She bowed before Rām with her hands pressed together, and then,
In a voice as lovely as the thirty-six *rāgiṇīs* strung into one song, said: 'All homage to Rām and to all his peers.
My name is Nrimunḍamālini; I wait on the lovely demoness Pramilā, the beloved of the lion of heroes Meghnād.'
Blessing her, the heroic son of Dasarath asked, 'Why,
O messenger, have you come here? Tell me precisely,
What service should I do your mistress, to make your visit good? Tell me quickly.'

§304

thirty-six *rāgiṇīs* see II.14.
Dasarath see I.172.
Bhimā-like messenger see above, §202.

§315
The Bhimā-like messenger answered, 'You are the finest of warriors, my lord.
Either come and fight with her, or let her pass; she wishes to enter golden Lankā today to do homage to her husband!
You have killed many Rākshasas through your own prowess; a Raksha wife wants to fight you; do battle with her,
Great hero! We are a hundred women; whoever you choose is willing to fight with you alone.
Take bow and arrow if you wish, sir, or shield or sword or club;
And we constantly practise wrestling! Whatever means you like, lord—
But hurry: my lady is making her army wait merely on your permission, like a huntress holding back a leopardess, champing to attack a herd of deer she has seen.'
§329
Saying this, the lovely messenger tilted her head, like a full-bloomed flower
(Studded with dew) tilting its head to salute a soft breeze! The Rāghav lord answered,
'Listen, lovely-haired one, I never quarrel with anyone without cause.
The Rākshas king is my enemy; you are all women, all wives;
What have you done that I should behave like an enemy to you? You can joyfully enter Lankā with no fear in your hearts! Rām,
Madam, was born of the heroic race of Raghu; your mistress and all her warlike companions,
O lovely-eyed messenger, are the wives of heroes. Tell her,
Extolling a thousandfold her wifely devotion, her

power and valour, that I concede victory without a fight.
All praise to Indrajit! All praise to the beautiful Pramilā!
Through a quirk of Fate,
Messenger, Rām is known in the world as a beggar, a penniless forest-dweller;
What favour worthy of you can I do you today, peerless as you are? I bless you and wish you well.'

§349

With this Lord Rām said to Hanumān, 'Let them through, I say!
With highest respect, with humble courtesy, permit what they ask.'

§352

Bowing to Sitā's lord, the messenger withdrew from the tent. Councillor Vibhishan said with a smile:
'Look at Pramilā's strength, look outside, my lord!
I do not know who, in battle, could match these women,
Awesome as Durgā when she fought against Raktabij!'
Rām replied, 'When I saw how the messenger looked I quailed in my heart,
Great Rākshas! I gave up the fight forthwith! To stir up such a tigress would be madness;
Come, my friend, let us see the wife of your nephew.'

§364

Like when a distant forest-fire spreads through the forest and blazes all around, the radiance that Rām saw filled the clear sky, turned cloud-wisps to gold!

§352

Raktabij Raktabij commanded the army of Sumbha and Nisumbha (see above, §115). Whenever a drop of his blood fell to the ground a full copy of himself immediately sprang up. Fighting him, therefore, meant fighting innumerable Raktabij clones.

He listened in alarm to shouting, deafening bow-twanging, clip-clopping horses,
Clanking swords in scabbards. Mixed with the din was the tooting of a martial band, like birdsong blown by a storm!
Banners flew—gleaming with inlaid gems; fleet-footed horses trotted,
Their strings of ankle-bells jingling. Files of soldiers stood on each side, stock-still as cliffs;
The female army passed between them, like elephants through a valley, filling the land with trumpeting and rocking the ground!

§378

Proud Nrimunḍamālini was at the front, on a black stallion, golden ensign in her hand;
Behind her were musicians, ah! like Vidyādharis in beauty,
Incomparable in the world! *Vīṇās*, flutes
Drums and other instruments joined in sweet consort! Behind them, surrounded by spear-carrying guardswomen,
Was Pramilā, like the moon amidst stars! Massive in strength was she!
Beams from her jewels sported all around. Rati's husband followed invisibly at her side with his flower-bow, repeatedly landing his flower-arrows on target!
Like buffalo-trampling Durgā on her lion-mount, or Indra's consort Sachi riding on flying Airāvat, or Lakshmi,

§378

Vidyādharis a race of heavenly female beings, famed for their *bidyā*, i.e. their mastery of the arts and sciences, as well as for their beauty.

Rati's husband i.e. Kāma or Madan. See II.265, 287.

buffalo-trampling Durgā on her lion-mount see II.400.

flying Airāvat Indra's flying elephant, seemingly borrowed here by his wife Sachi (Indrāni).

Beloved of Vishnu, on the back of Garuḍa, valiant
Pramilā rode on her horse Vaḍabā—
Vaḍabā, empress of horses, adorned with jewels!
As if ignoring their enemies, the Amazon army slowly advanced. Some twanged bowstrings,
Some whooped as they unsheathed their swords; some brandished their spears; some let out howls of laughter;
Some roared—like a lioness roaring in deep forest with lust for the fray, or like Durgā maddened with desire!

§402

Turning to that finest of Rākshasas Vibhishan, Rām said, 'How amazing,
Son of Nikashā. I've never seen this, never heard of this in any of the three worlds!
Have I woken from a dream? Tell me truly, O jewel of friends!
I'm perplexed; this illusion has unsettled me—do not add to my confusion.
I heard from the charioteer Chitrarath that Māyā-devi would arrive to help me; is it she who has come to Lankā, to work this deception?
Tell me, friend, whose trickery is it?'

§413

Vibhishan answered, 'It is not a dream, O husband of Sitā,
I assure you. There is a demon, famous in the world and hostile to the gods,

§378

Garuda see I.218. Like Sachi, Lakshmi here has borrowed her husband's vehicle. **Vaḍabā** see above, §115.

§402

Son of Nikashā as brother of Rāvan, Vibhishan is also the son of Nikashā. See I.62, 218. **the three worlds** see I.142. **I heard from the charioteer Chitrarath** see the last part of Book II, from §576.

Called Kālnemi; the beautiful Pramilā is his daughter. By her birth,
My lord, she partook of the power of Durgā; she is equal to Durgā in strength!
Who can match this demoness in battle? That lion-warrior, the Rākshas lord who vanquished thunderbolt-wielding Indra in battle,
O lord of the Rāghavas, is kept underfoot by that enchantress, like Siva under Kāli's feet!
To impede the mighty Meghnād and save the world, the Creator created this impediment, like chains on a rampaging elephant!
Pramilā keeps on controlling his volcanic power with her amorous talk, like streams of rain controlling a fierce forest-fire (the forest's enemy).
A deadly serpent, savage in its bite, is enveloped in the fragrant waters of the Yamunā!
Thus all in the universe are safe—gods in heaven, Nāgas underground and people on earth.'

§413

Kālnemi Kālnemi in the *Rāmāyaṇa* is Rāvan's maternal uncle. Rāvan promises him half of his kingdom if he can slay Hanumān before Hanumān can fetch the herb that will restore the fallen Lakshman to life. He fantasizes about gaining his half, including half of his many wives, but is defeated by Hanumān. M makes this well-known Rākshas the father of Pramilā.

like Siva under Kāli's feet! the mother-goddess Kāli, as the most aggressive manifestation of Siva's *śakti* or consort, is often depicted as dominating him: standing naked on his chest. Cf. above, §102

A deadly serpent . . . is enveloped in the fragrant waters of the Yamunā Kāliya, often described like Ananta, Vāsuki or Sesha as the king of the Nāgas or serpents, lives in the river Yamunā. He is also an incarnation of Kālnemi (see above). When Krishna goes to bathe in the Yamunā, he is almost strangled by Kāliya. But M's comparison here is merely with the beautiful Pramilā, who holds her husband in her power just as the waters of the Yamunā holds Kāliya.

Nāgas underground see II.491.

§432

The Rāghav lord responded, 'It's true, what you said,
Dear friend. Meghnād is the greatest of charioteers. I've
never seen greater skill anywhere in the three worlds.
I have seen Bhrigurām, immovable in war as a plateau-
topped mountain! But your brother's son,
Friend, is even luckier with bow and arrow. What shall I
do now,
Tell me, jewel of the Rākshasas? A lioness has come to
the forest today with her mate:
Who will save this herd of deer? Look, look around,
At the poisonous sea that roars and surges on all sides!
Like Siva (beloved of world-saving Durgā)
Drinking up poison to rescue the universe, rescue this
army through your good advice, my friend.
Keep in mind, hero, that your elder brother is as lethal as
a snake; the warrior Meghnād is his venomous fang.
If I can somehow gouge out this fang, my wishes will be
accomplished; otherwise my journey to golden Lankā,
Bridging the sea, I tell you, has been a pointless quest.'

§451

Then Lakshman said, bowing to the feet of his brother:
'Why should we fear the Rākshasas any more,
O Lord of the Raghus? What fear need anyone have in
the world, who has God on his side?

§432

Bhrigurām, immovable in war as a plateau-topped mountain a name for Parasurām, axe-wielding sixth incarnation of Vishnu who managed once to slay the entire Kshatriya (warrior) caste. There is world-play here with *bhrigu*, a plateau.

Like Siva . . . Drinking up poison before the churning of the ambrosial ocean (see I.295), Siva drank up the poison it contained, acquiring the name Nilkanṭha ('blue-throated') because the poison turned his throat blue.

Rāvan's son will certainly be destroyed tomorrow, by my hand. Where and when can unrighteousness triumph?
The lord of the Rākshasas is an evil-doer; because of his sin, Meghnād will be overcome on the battlefield;
The son dies through the sin of the father. The lotus-sun of Lankā will set tomorrow—that was what the divine charioteer Chitrarath said.
So why, lord, are you so worried?'

§463

Vibhishan answered, 'It's true what you have said, O elephant of heroes!
There is victory where there is righteousness. The Lord of the Raksha race is drowning, alas,
Through his own sin! Meghnād, the enemy of Indra,
Will be killed by your arrow; but be cautious nonetheless. The demoness Pramilā is immensely powerful—
And Nrimuṇḍamālini, strung round with heads, loves battle too!
Anyone who lives near a forest that a fierce lion enters should always be watchful. Who knows when and where and whom that fell beast will attack! Let's get through the night safely and attack at dawn.'

§475

Rām said to wise Vibhishan: 'Be so good, O finest of Rākshasas,

§451

unrighteousness *adharma*: see II.173.
the lotus-sun of Lankā see II.491.
that was what the divine charioteer Chitrarath said in Book II, §597.

§463

The Lord of the Raksha race is drowning, alas,/ Through his own sin *nij pāpe maje, hāy, rakṣaḥ-kul-pati*. See Introduction, p. liif.
strung round with heads see above, §102.

As to inspect with Lakshman the armies at each gate—check who is on guard where. Everyone is weary after fighting with Virbāhu.
Look all around—see what Angad is doing; where the hero Nila is;
Where the loyal Sugriv. I myself shall keep watch at the west gate, bow and arrow in hand!'

§483

'As you command,' said Vibhishan, and went with Urmilā's husband Lakshman.
They shone like Indra accompanied by Kārttikeya, slayer of Tārak, or like the ambrosial moon accompanying the sun!

§487

Devoted Pramilā arrived at Lankā's golden gate. Horns sounded; kettle-drums rolled;
Formidable Rākshasas roared, like clouds of destruction or a herd of elephants! The Rākshas Virupāksha glowered,
Lance in hand; and Tāljangha—carrying a club the size of a palm-tree;
And dangerous-looking Pramatta! Horses neighed; elephants trumpeted;
Chariot-wheels rattled and whirred; spearmen brandished their spears; javelins flew so thickly they covered the moon.

§475

after fighting with Virbāhu see I.1.
Angad . . . Nila . . . Sugriv see I.218.

§483

Urmilā's husband Lakshman see I.1.
Kārttikeya, slayer of Tārak see II.491.

§487

Virupāksha . . . Tāljangha . . . Pramatta see I.575.

The sky filled with fire and hubbub, just as during a night-time earthquake a volcano belches out thunderous streams of fire. Lankā trembled at the onslaught!

§501

Enraged, Nrimunḍamālini shrieked, 'Who are you hurling weapons at in the dark,

You cowards? We are not your enemies; we are Rākshas wives,

Open your eyes and look.' At once the gatekeeper drew the squeaking, slithering bolt.

The gate opened thunderously! Greeted with shouts of triumph, beautiful Pramilā entered golden Lankā.

§508

Like insects eagerly rushing at a flame, the citizens came crowding all around; women cheered her,

Raining down flowers; musicians joyfully serenaded her. She proceeded through them,

Bright as a wave of fire through a dense jungle. Vidyādharis played *vīṇā*s, flutes,

Tom-toms, cymbals; neighing horses galloped;

Swords clattered in their scabbards. Babies woke up in terror in their mothers' laps! Many young Rākshasis opened their windows,

Gazed at Pramilā, joyously praised her prowess. Soon she arrived where her husband was staying,

Bursting with love for him—like a serpent whose jewel was lost, when the jewel is recovered!

§523

All-conquering Indrajit said jokingly, 'Are you, O moon-faced one,

§508

Vidyādharis see above, §378.

Chāmuṇḍā—arriving at Mount Kailās, after slaying
Raktabij? If you command me,
I shall fall at your feet at once, ever your servant!' Smiling,
Pramilā replied: 'By your feet's grace, lord,
Do I triumph in the world; but I cannot defeat Kāma. I
ignore war's fiery arrows,
But I live in dread of the fierce fire of separation; that is
why I have come to the one my heart longs for all the
time. The river delights in reaching the sea.'

§534

With this, she entered the house, took off her warrior's garb;
She decked her limbs in a jewel-edged sari, tied a bodice
round her bulging breasts; a girdle adorned her hips.
Diamonds hung round her neck, pearls across her
bosom; a jewel in her parting sparkled like a star;
Gemstones gleamed in her hair, earrings in her ears.
Beautiful Pramilā dressed herself gorgeously.
Meghnād, crest-jewel of the Rākshasas, floated in a sea
of rapture;
The two sat down on a golden throne. Singers sang;
dancers danced,
Like singing Vidyādharas and dancing Vidyādharis in
heaven; birds, forgetting their imprisonment,
Sang in their cages; fountains swelled, like the tidal
waters of the sea at the touch of the moon's rays.
A spring breeze blew softly, as when the Lord of the

§523

Chāmuṇḍā name of Durgā in her frightening aspect—derived from the gigantic demons Chaṇḍa and Muṇḍa, whom she slayed.

Raktabij see above, §352.

§534

Vidyādharas husbands of the Vidyādharis: they sing while their wives dance.

Seasons secretly sports with wood-nymphs, in the sweet season of spring.

§552

Outside Lankā, lion-hero Lakshman made his way to the north gate, together with Vibhishan;

Wise Sugriv was keeping watch there with his army, massed like the Vindhyā mountains, staunch in battle!

Fierce-looking Nila was at the east gate; the Goddess of Sleep assailed him in vain. At the south gate Prince Angad patrolled,

Like a ravenous lion in search of pray; or like trident-wielding Nandi on the top of Mount Kailās. Hundreds of fires burned all around,

Their smoke invisible in the dark; Lankā was in their midst, like the moon in a clear sky surrounded by stars.

Batallions of warriors kept watch at each gate; like farmers on careful look-out from platforms by fields which are flush with crops brought on by the rain, ready to drive away deer,

Fierce buffaloes, all kinds of herbivores, so did these Rākshas-frightening fighters keep watch round Lankā.

§571

Reassured by this, the two returned to where Rām was in his tent, patiently waiting.

§534

Lord of the Seasons *ṛturāj*, i.e. the Spring.

§552

Sugriv see I.218.

Vindhyā mountains mountain range that divides north from south India.

Fierce-looking Nila . . . Prince Angad see I.218.

trident-wielding Nandi Nandi is Siva's bull (see II.491), though *śūl-pāṇi* ('trident-wielding') is also often an epithet for Siva himself (see II.447).

§573
On Mount Kailās Durgā turned to Vijayā and said,
'Look towards Lankā, my moon-like friend!
Pramilā is entering the city in warrior-garb, an army of women following her. The gleam of their golden army is lighting up the sky!
See how the jewel of men Rām gazes in astonishment, and Lakshman, their friend Vibhishan and all the other heroes!
Who in the world of men is more beautiful than she? I dressed like that myself to destroy demons in the Satya-yuga. Hear the din she is making!
How she angrily pulls at her bowstring and twangs it noisily! A whole vast army quakes at the sight of her! Look how the crown on her bound-up hair dances!
How her lovely frame bobs up and down with the trotting of her horse, ah! like golden lotus on Lake Mānas,
Bobbing in the waves!' Vijayā answered, 'It's true what you have said,
O Daughter of the Mountain. Who has seen such beauty in the human world? I know that Pramilā,
Valiant daughter of a Dānav that she is, is your servant; but think,

§573

Vijayā in Book II, §133 Durgā was described as seated on her golden throne, with her companion Vijayā waving a fly-whisk and her other companion Jayā holding a royal umbrella.

Satya-yuga Hindus have tradionally recognised four *yugas* in the history of the world, each one shorter than the last. The Satya-yuga was the first, the Golden Age of Truth. We are currently living in the Kali-yuga, the age of discord and immorality.

Lake Mānas see I.33.

Daughter of the Mountain *Haimabati*: name for Durgā because she is the daughter of Haimavat (Himālaya).

Valiant daughter of a Dānav see above, §1.

Goddess, how you will keep your promise? By himself,
Meghnād is impossible to defeat; when Pramilā is with
him, he is even more powerful,
Just as fire—friend of the wind—is augmented by the wind!
Victor over Mahish though you were, how will you save
Rām? How will brave Lakshman destroy such a
Rākshas?'

§598

Thinking for a while, Siva's wife answered: 'The
beautiful Pramilā took a part of me at her birth;
I can take that power away from her tomorrow. The
jewel that is radiant at the touch of the sun's rays
becomes, alas,
At the setting of the sun, lustreless: likewise I shall
weaken Pramilā tomorrow.
The hero Lakshman will definitely overcome Meghnād!
Pramilā and her husband will come to us here;
Meghnād,
Rāvan's son, will wait on you, and Pramilā too will be
welcome here as my bosom-companion.'

§573

Victor over Mahish though you were Durgā is here given the epithet *Kātyāyani*. Kātyāyan, one of the authors of the *Dharmaśāstras* (treatises on Dharma) was a sage who worshipped Durgā, and according to one myth it was in his ashram that Brahmā, Vishnu and Siva created Durgā from their own bodies so that the buffalo-demon Mahish (see II.400) could be destroyed. It is this feat that is recalled by the choice of epithet here, with the implication that defeating Meghnād and the Rākshasas will require even greater strength and courage.

§598

The beautiful Pramilā took a part of me at her birth . . . there are multiple implications here. Durgā will weaken Pramilā by taking away the *tej* (fire, power) that came from Durgā in the first place, and this will weaken Meghnād himself; but the death of Meghnād, who is often compared to the sun (see II.491), will also diminish Pramilā like a sunset taking away lustre from a jewel.

§609

With that, Durgā went back to her palace. The goddess of sleep came to Mount Kailās with gentle steps;
Its inhabitants rested on beds of flowers; illuminating Siva's brow, the moon filled the great god's pleasure-dome with silvery radiance.

Here ends 'The Reunion',
the third book of *Meghnādbadh kābya*.

§609

illuminating Siva's brow Siva carries the moon in his hair.

BOOK IV

§1

I bow to your lotus-feet, master poet Vālmiki! O crest-jewel of India,
I follow after you, like a humble subject journeying to a distant pilgrimage-place for a sight of his king! Many pilgrims,
By meditating day and night on your footprints, have entered the temple of fame, have conquered world-conquering,
Pitiless Death there and are now immortal! Bhartrihari, author of the *Bhaṭṭikāvya*;
Sweet-voiced, learned Bhavabhuti; honey-tongued Kālidās,
Famed in India as Bhārati's favoured son; Murāri, whose music is as enchanting as Krishna's flute;
Fame-dwelling Krittibās, ornament of Bengal! O father,
How can I ever play with all these swans in poetry's

§1

Vālmiki legendary author of the *Rāmāyaṇa*, M's main source for *MBK* See I.1.

Bhartrihari, author of the *Bhaṭṭikāvya* the poet and grammarian Bhartrihari, who died in 751 AD, is deemed to be the author of the *Bhaṭṭikāvya*, a poem in 22 cantos that illustrates the forms of Sanskrit grammar but which also tells the story of Rām.

Bhavabhuti Sanskrit dramatist whose play *Uttararāmacarita* is about the 'later fortunes' of Rām.

Kālidās Kālidāsa is regarded as the greatest poet and dramatist of Sanskrit literature. His dates are uncertain, but he is traditionally supposed to have been the most brilliant of the 'nine gems' of literature at the court of Vikramāditya in Ujjain.

Bhārati's favoured son i.e. favoured by Sarasvati, goddess of arts and learning, invoked by M as his muse at the beginning of *MBK*. See I.1.

Murāri i.e. Murāri Misra, Sanskrit poet, author of *Anargharāgava* ('The priceless Rāghava'), a play about Rām.

Krittibās author of the best-known medieval Bengali *Rāmāyaṇ*—the version that M was brought up on. In this paragraph, M firmly allies himself with a succession of great poets who have written about Rām.

lake, if you don't teach me! I shall stitch a new garland,
Having carefully picked flowers in your poetry-garden; I want to adorn with a manifold array my language; but where shall I find
(Unworthy as I am) those ornaments, unless you give them, O fount of ornaments?
Be generous, O master, to one who has nothing.

§21

Golden Lankā was floating in a sea of joy, garlanded with golden lamps—like an empress in a jewelled necklace!
Instruments played in her houses; dancers danced; singers sang mellifluously;
Lovers dallied with their mistresses, bringing out peals of laughter from their sweet lips!
Some were having sex; some were drinking mead. Garlands of fruits and flowers hung round their doorways;
Flags flew from turrets; there were lamps at windows; streams of people flowed noisily along the streets,
As if at a great festival, when the townsfolk revel. Clumps of flowers rained all around—
Filling the city with fragrance. Lankā was awake today at midnight; Sleep wandered from door to door—
No one would allow her in, for all her soothing pleas!
'The mighty hero Indrajit will kill Rām tomorrow;
He will kill Lakshman; with his lion's roar he will drive the jackal-like hordes of the enemy into the sea; he will bring back Vibhishan as captive;
He will release the moon from the jaws of Rāhu; all eyes

§21

Indrajit i.e. Meghnād. See I.594, 1.

Vibhishan Rāvan's younger brother and traitor to the Rākshasas. See I.218.

in the world will bask again in the glory of her nectar-like rays.' Illusory Hope was singing this song that day in the city of Lankā—
In her streets, at her *ghāṭs*, in houses,
Temples, gardens; so why should the Rākshasas not be floating in a lake of joy?

§46

Alone in the Asoka wood, distraught with grief, Rām's beloved wept silently in her hut!
Her formidable guards had gone to join the drunken festivity, like a tigress when it leaves a half-dead doe, and roams far away in the forest,
Without fear of its escape! Sitā was wan-faced, alas,
Like a sun-loving gemstone deep in the darkness of a mine, where the sun's rays cannot penetrate; or like *bimba*-lipped Lakshmi pining at the bottom of the sea!
A breeze wafted from afar, like a sighing expression of lament! Rustling leaves wrestled with their sorrow!
Birds perched silently on branches! Flowers fell in clusters to the base of trees, as if the trees were throwing off their garments in the heat of their distress!
Distant streams rushed towards the sea, sobbing loudly

§21

He will release the moon from the jaws of Rāhu during a lunar eclipse, the demon Rāhu is said to swallow the moon, releasing it again when the eclipse is over. Rām's armies, encircling Lankā, are likened here to Rāhu. See II.400.

ghāṭs steps down the water: mooring or bathing places.

§46

Asoka wood see II.190.

***bimba*-lipped Lakshmi** the *bimba* is red-coloured fruit that M. Monier-Williams in his Sanskrit dictionary identifies with 'Momordica Monadelpha (a plant bearing a bright-red gourd)'. For Lakshmi see I.472, 483, 513. As to why she is 'pining at the bottom of the sea', see II.87.

as they flowed, as if to tell Sitā's sad story to the lord of waters!

No moonshine entered that dark forest. Can a lotus bloom in a turbid lake? Yet the wood was lit up by Sitā's extraordinary beauty!

§67

She sat alone, shining as if the wife of the sun were in Death's dark realm! Then lovely Saramā,

Vibhishan's wife, beautiful as Lakshmi herself in the dress of a Rākshasi, arrived and sat down tearfully at Sitā's feet.

§72

In a while, wiping her tears, the lovely-eyed one said in gentle tones,

'The cruel guards have left you on your own and are back in the city: everyone is in festive mood tonight; that is how I have been able to slip away to worship your feet.

I have filled a small box with vermilion for you; if you allow me, I shall mark your beautiful brow with it.

What's this? Do these garments befit you? The wicked king of Lankā is brutal,

Alas! Who tears off the leaves of a lotus? Why were your ornaments ripped off you? I do not understand.'

§83

Tenderly opening the box, Saramā placed a drop of vermilion in Sitā's parting; it gleamed there,

§46

to the lord of waters *bārīśe*: i.e. to Varuna. See I.443.

§67

shining as if the wife of the Sun were in Death's dark realm Sitā is compared here to *Prabhā*, name of the wife of Surya, the sun-god, but also a word meaning 'radiance', and the gloomy Asoka wood is compared to *tamomaya dhām*, i.e. the 'abode of darkness', Yamapuri, Death's realm.

§83

Saramā Vibhishan's wife. See Source Notes, p. 339. **Saramā placed a**

Like a jewel-like star, ah! on the brow of twilight.
§86
Then Saramā took the dust of her feet. 'Forgive me, goddess,
For touching a body so desired by the gods; but I am
forever a slave to your feet.' Saying this,
She sat down again at Sitā's feet—ah! like a glowing
lantern at the foot of a tamarind tree,
Casting light all around! Sitā replied gently, 'You are
wrong to blame Rāvan,
O moon-like Saramā! I myself threw off my ornaments,
when the villain abducted me from the forest ashram.
I shed them all along the way, to leave a trail. That
bridge of adornments has brought him
—My loyal husband Rām—to golden Lankā! Jewels,
Pearls, gems—what is there in the world,
Pray, that I would not forsake, to get back that ultimate
treasure?'
§101
Saramā said, 'Devi, I have heard about your *svayambar*
from your ambrosial lips,
And why Lord Rām, the jewel of race of Raghu, took
you off into the forest.
Tell me now kindly, how did the Raksha king abduct
you, Lady? I beg you—
Satisfy my thirst with your shower of nectar! The vile
guards are far away; seize this moment to tell me—

---

drop of vermilion in Sitā's parting the mark of a (Bengali) wife, and an act of extreme devotion and respect for Saramā to place it there.

§86

like a glowing lantern at the foot of a tamarind tree the *tulsi* or tamarind tree is sacred to Hindus, so the simile emphasises Sitā's purity.

§101

svayambar see III.271.

And why Lord Rām . . . took you off into the forest see I.386, II.173.

I am listening. By what deceit did the thief deceive Rām and Lord Lakshman? By what sorcery did he enter Rām's house to steal such a jewel?'

§112

Like sacred waters burbling from the mouth of the Gomukhi cave, sweet-voiced Sitā addressed Saramā: 'You are Sitā's supreme well-wisher,

Dear friend! I'll gladly tell you what happened to me earlier, if you listen attentively.

§118

'We were living, O lovely-eyed one, on the banks of the Godāvari river,

Like a dove and its mate nesting contentedly high up in a tree. We were in a dense wood, Panchavaṭi by name,

Like a divine woodland brought down to earth! Wise Lakshman attended on us constantly. Do you imagine that anyone can lack anything who has the Danḍak forest at his disposal?

Daily, the brave Saumitri brought us fruits and roots; my husband sometimes brought deer;

But the mighty Rāghav lord is always averse to killing creatures, my dear, famed as he is in the world as an ocean of kindness!

§112

Like sacred waters burbling from the mouth of the Gomukhi cave the source of the sacred Ganges is said to be in the Gomukhi ('cow-faced') cave in the Himalayas, so the simile (like the tamarind tree in §86 above) emphasises Sitā's purity.

§118

Godāvari river . . . Panchavaṭi . . . Danḍak the Godāvari ('cow-granting') river is in the Deccan in southern India and runs through the Danḍak forest, which contained the Panchavaṭi wood where Rām, Sitā and Lakshman were exiled. **Saumitri** i.e. Lakshman, son of Sumitrā. See I.172. **Rāghav lord** i.e. Rām. See I.1.

§128

'I forgot my former luxuries! I am a princess, married
into the Raghu tribe;
But in that forest, dear Saramā, I found the highest happiness!
How can I describe the flowers that perpetually
bloomed all around our hut? In the Panchavaṭi forest
there was constant spring! The king of the cuckoos
woke us each morning with his sweet cooing!
What queen—tell me, O moon-like one—
Opens her eyes to such a charming dawn hymn? The
peahen danced joyously with her mate outside my
door! Where in the world,
Dear lady, dances a pair like them? Baby elephants and
deer used to come constantly as our guests—
And birds, some gold in colour, some white,
Some black, some as colourful as Indra's rainbow on the
crest of a fine cloud.
They were all unaggressive; I waited on them lovingly:
like a river in a desert quenching the thirsty,
I gave them water, by the grace of the rain clouds.
A lake was my mirror! I picked blue lotus (like peerless gems)
To wear in my hair; I dressed myself in flowers; my
husband smiled,
Merrily called me the goddess of the forest! Alas, friend,
Shall I ever see my life's lord again? Will these worn-out
eyes of mine ever see, in this miserable existence,
His feet once more, those lotus in the lake of my hope,
those jewels in my eyes?
Through what sin, O harsh Fate, am I a sinner in your sight?'

§128

Raghu tribe see I.406.

Indra's rainbow *Vāsaber dhanuḥ*: 'Vāsava [Indra]'s bow'. Indra is the original Vedic god of skies, rain, thunder and lightning, and rainbows in India are seen as his bow.

§158
With this Sitā wept quietly, and Saramā wept, drenching her with her tears.
§160
A little while later the Rākshas bride Saramā dried her eyes and said at the feet of Sitā: 'If it pains you to remember the past, devi,
Then leave it; what point in remembering? I want to die when I see your tears.'
§165
Lovely-voiced Sitā answered (as sweet in tone as a *kādambā*-bird): 'O beloved of your husband,
If I do not weep, then who else in the world will weep? No one is more wretched than I.
I will tell—hear me—the story of my past.
In the rainy season, friend, under pressure of floods,
Turbulent rivers batter both their banks with pouring waters; in the same way, a mind that is sorrowful must speak of its grief to another.
That is why I speak and you listen, O Saramā! Who else does Sitā have in this horrible city?
§175
'We were living happily in the Panchavaṭi wood on the banks of the Godāvari. Alas, friend,
How can I describe its sylvan beauty? In my dreams, I would hear the woodland *vīṇā* in the hands of the goddess of the woods;

§165
***Kādambā*-bird** *kādambarī* would be a more usual name for a female *kokil* or *koel*-bird, but M probably liked the long *ā* vowel at the end. Cf. his choice of the 'incorrect' name Vāruni for the wife of Varuna (I.443).
§175
vīṇā see I.623.

Sitting on the edge of a lake, I would sometimes see
heavenly maidens dressed in sunbeams cavorting in
the lotus-beds! Sometimes the virtuous wives of sages,
Perfect in their smiles, would come to my hut, like rays
of the moon in a dark house!
We would sometimes spread a deerskin (painted with so
many ravishing colours!) at the foot of a tall tree,
Welcoming the shade as our friend. Sometimes we would
merrily dance in the woods with a hind; we would
sing songs in imitation of the *koel*-bird's tune!
We would marry young creepers, good Saramā, to trees;
When the pair produced buds, we would kiss them,
joyfully addressing them all as our granddaughters!
When bees hummed, we would honour them as husbands
for our granddaughters! Sometimes I would blissfully
roam with my husband along the river-bank;
I seemed to see in its flowing water a new sky, a new
array of stars, the grace of a new moon!
Sometimes we would climb a hill, my friend, and I'd sit
at my husband's feet,
Like a humble creeper entwined round a mighty mango-
tree; who can I tell of the nectar that his loving conversation
rained down on me—how can I describe it?
I've heard that sky-haired Siva sits with Gauri on a
golden throne in their dwelling on Mount Kailās, and
tells her stories from the Āgamas, Purānas,
Vedas through his five mouths; I used to hear such
things too, lovely Saramā!

§175

koel-bird see I.623. **Gauri** name for Siva's wife Pārvati (Durgā). **Āgamas, Purānas, Vedas** the Āgamas are Sanskrit texts couched in the form of instructions by Siva to his wife; the Purānas (the word means 'ancient') are the texts in which most (non-Vedic) Hindu myths are

Even now, in this lonely wood, I think of them,
As if told by his sweet voice! Is that music ended for me,
O harsh Fate?'
Wide-eyed Sitā fell silent in her sorrow. Then the beautiful
Saramā spoke: 'To hear you speak of all this,
O Beloved of Rām, makes me hate my royal luxuries! If
I could,
I would leave my palace, go and live in simplicity in the
forest! But when I think about it further,
I feel afraid! When the sun, devi,
Enters a dark wood, its rays light it up; when night
comes to any land,
Everyone looks gloomy at its arrival! Wherever you set
foot, sweet lady,
How can everyone not be happy? You are the joy of the
world, enchanter of the universe!
Tell me, goddess, by what device did Rāvan abduct you?
I have heard the sound of a *vīṇā*, and the cuckoo's cry
amidst new-furled leaves in the verdant months of
spring; but I have not heard,
Anywhere in the world, a voice as sweet as yours! See in
the sky how the moon,
Whose radiance pales beside yours, drinks up smilingly
the nectar of your voice, fount of nectar though he is!
The *koel* and all other birds—I assure you—are silent
now in anticipation of your story.
Satisfy the longings of all, O virtuous one, by telling it to us!'
§235
Rām's wife spoke: 'Thus we passed many months in joy,
in the Panchavaṭi wood,

---

incorporated; the Vedas are the primary scriptures of Hinduism, revered as 'not of human origin', and generally regarded as including the Mantras, the Brāhmanas, the Āranyakas and the Upanishads.

Till your sister-in-law, the mischievous Surpanakhā, came and caused a mighty upset!
I cringe with shame, my friend, when I think of her.
Fie on her! Blot on the female sex! Tigress!
She wanted to kill me and make Rām her husband!
Lion-like Lakshman drove her off furiously.
Rākshasas came running,
A horrendous battle broke out in the forest. I huddled in my hut in terror. How can I describe my wails,
Dear friend, at the twanging of bows? I shut my eyes,
Clenched my hands in prayer to the gods to protect my husband! Roars and screams rose up into the sky. I fell to the ground in a swoon!

§251

'I do not know how long I was in this state, my dear; the finest of the Raghus awoke me with his touch.
In his gentle voice (as soft, alas,
As a breeze through a garden in spring), he said: "Arise,
Empress of my life, treasure of the scion of Raghu! Joy of the royal Raghu house!
Does this bed befit you, gold-limbed as you are?" O dear Saramā,
Shall I hear those sweet tones again?' Sitā suddenly fainted—Saramā caught her.

§261

As when a hunter in thick woodland, when he hears melodious birdsong in the branch of a tree, shoots his arrow in the direction of the song,
And the bird flutters down to the ground, writhing in agony at the blow; so Sitā suddenly fell into Saramā's lap!

§235
Surpanakhā see I.80.

§266
In a while she came to again. Saramā said tearfully,
'Forgive me,
Maithili lady! I needlessly caused you this torment, alas,
Stupid as I am!' The lovely-haired darling of Rāghav
replied gently, 'What have you done wrong,
My friend? Listen carefully as I speak again of my past.
You have heard from Surpanakhā of the trick that Mārich
(Deceitful as a mirage in a desert) played on me. Alas,
Evil was the time, my dear, that I begged for a stag,
Crazy with greed for it! Lord Rām set out with his bow
in hand, leaving his brother Lakshman to guard me.
The illusory deer ran like lightning, flashed through the
forest; my lord sped after it,
Swift as a lion; wretch that I was, I lost my eyes' star!
§282
'Suddenly I heard, friend, cries in the distance—
"Where is my brother Lakshman—rescue me! I'm dying."
Lion-like Lakshman was alarmed! I panicked, gripped
his hands,
Pleaded, "Go, great hero;
Run through the forest like the wind; don't you know who
is calling you? My heart bursts at the sound of his cries!
Go quickly—it is Rām who is calling you, O charioteer!"

§251

finest of the Raghus i.e. Rām. See I.406.

§266

Maithili lady Sitā came from the kingdom of Videha, whose capital was Mithilā.

Rāghav i.e. Rām. See I.1.

Mārich a Rākshas whom Rāvan engaged to take the form of a golden stag. When she sees the deer, Sitā is captivated by its beauty and asks Rām to capture it for her. Rām follows it deeper and deeper into the forest, leaving Sitā in Lakshman's care. Rām realizes that Mārich is a Rākshas in disguise, and shoots an arrow at it. Wounded, it cries out in Rām's voice.

§290
'Lakshman answered, "Devi, how can I carry out your command?
How can I leave you alone in this lonely forest? Who can say how many spell-working Rākshasas are wandering here? But what are you worried about?
Who in the three worlds can harm the ornament of the Raghu clan, so mighty that even Bhrigurām hailed him as his guru?" Again I heard cries—
"I'm dying! Where is my brother Lakshman, to help me at this moment of peril?
Where is Sitā?" I could not bear it any longer, dear Saramā!
I let go of Lakshman's hand, I yelled at him in my madness, "Who can claim that my gracious mother-in-law Sumitrā gave birth to you,
You villain? God made your heart from stone! A cruel tigress must have borne you and raised you in the jungle,
You wicked man! You coward, you insult to the warrior race,
Shall I go myself, to see who is so pitifully calling for me in the distant forest?" Enraged,
With reddened eyes, the jewel of heroes seized his bow, bound in a trice his quiver to his back,
And said to me, "I revere you, daughter of Janak,
Like a mother! Yet I suffer this abuse! I shall go.
Take care of yourself indoors. Who knows what might happen today? It won't be my fault.

§290

Bhrigurām see III.432 and Source Notes, p. 341.

I yelled at him in my madness. In the *Rāmāyaṇa* Sitā also accuses Lakshman (revealing an aspect of her character that M does not choose to include here!) of wanting to stay with her out of lust for her.

Janak king of Videha and Sitā's father.

I'm leaving you by your command." Saying this, the hero went off into the forest.

§317

'How shall I tell you, dear friend, of all that went through my mind as I waited there alone?
The day wore on; with cries of delight, young elephant,
Birds, baby-deer, used to being fed by me,
All came as usual. Among them I was startled to see a yogi, radiant as the god of fire,
His body smeared with ash, water-pot in his hand, matted hair on his head!
Alas, my dear, if I had known the wicked deadly snake that lurked beneath the flowers,
The poison in the spotless lake, would I ever have bowed my head, ever have grovelled on the ground before him?

§335

'The false one said, "Give alms, Raghu wife,
Rice-giving Durgā of the woods, to your guest, famished as he is!"

§337

'Covering my face with my veil, friend, I said with clasped hands,
"Sit on this deerskin mat, sir, and rest under the tree;
My husband will return very soon, with his brother Saumitri." The fiend snarled
(I didn't understand that his anger was just a device), "I am a hungry guest, I tell you.

§290

Saying this, the hero went off into the forest leaving Sitā alone and defenceless, as Rāvan has planned.

§335

The false one said the yogi (holy man) is Rāvan in disguise. **Rice-giving Durgā of the woods** *Annadā*: an epithet of Durgā as a provider of food.

Give me alms; or say if you will not, so that I may go elsewhere.
Are you unwilling to serve a guest today, O daughter of Janak? Do you want to blacken the house of Raghu with the scandal of this,
Married into it though you are? Tell me, what arrogance is this in you that you should want to discount a Brahmin's curse?
Give me alms, lest I leave you with a curse, namely,
That the fell king of the Rākshasas will from now on be the enemy of Sitā's beloved!" Suppressing my shyness, alas,
Dear friend, I timidly came outside with offerings to him, not knowing I was stepping into a trap.
Immediately, laughing horribly, your brother-in-law grabbed hold of me.

§350

'Once, O moon-like Saramā, I was wandering with my husband in the forest.
A doe was grazing near a distant bush. Suddenly I heard a frightful roar; I looked and saw a tiger,
Awesome and swift as lightning, attacking the doe! "Save her!"
I cried to my lord, falling at his feet. With the fire of his arrow he pulverized the tiger instantly.
I lovingly helped that belle of the forest back on to her feet, my friend! The king of the Rākshasas,
In the manner of that tiger, snatched me! But no one,
My darling, came to save the stricken deer at this perilous time! I filled the forest with my desperate screams!
I heard weeping—the goddess of the forest must herself have been weeping in motherly distress at my plight! But her tears were in vain!
Iron melts only with the heat of fire; can a stream of water soften it? Does a heart that is cruel pay attention to tears?

§367

'The false matted hair of the yogi vanished; the water-pot too! In the garb of a royal charioteer,
The villain lifted me into his golden chariot. He spoke to me so foully—sometimes with violent aggression,
Sometimes more seductively. I want to die when I recall it, Saramā!

§372

'He drove me along. Like a frog squeaking in the jaws of a snake, I cried,
Happy lady, in vain! The noisy clatter of the golden chariot's wheels filled the woods,
Drowning, alas, my wretched wails!
When trees shudder in terror at the impact of a storm, who can hear if a dove coos? Desperately,
Friend, I tore off my bangles, bracelets,
Necklace, tiara, earrings,
Anklets and girdle; I scattered them on the path; that is why,
O Raksha wife, I'm devoid of ornament now. You were wrong to blame Rāvan for that.'

§384

Moon-like Sitā fell silent. Saramā said, 'I'm still thirsty for more,
O lady of Mithilā! Give me more nectar. My ears have been so enriched today!'
Sitā began again, radiant as the moon, sweet-voiced as ever.

§389

'Hear if you really want to hear, dear lady. Who else will listen to my tale of woe?

§372

You were wrong to blame Rāvan for that see above, §86.

§391
'As cheerful as a hunter when he traps and brings home a bird, the king of Lankā drove me in his chariot; and like a bird squawking and struggling to break its bonds,
I too, sweet Saramā, wept.
§395
'"O sky, I have heard that you carry sound" (I prayed).
"Carry the sound of my plight to the crest-jewel of the Raghus, and to my brother-in-law Lakshman, triumphant in the world!
O wind, bearer of fragrance, I beg you at your feet,
Speed to where my lord wanders! O cloud, you are thunderous;
Call to my lord with your sonorous boom! O bee, lover of honey;
Leave the flowers, and hum, in the groves where Rām is,
News of Sitā! O *koel*-bird, Spring's companion,
Sing a song of Sitā's sorrow in your perfect fifths! My lord will listen, ah!
If you sing." Thus I lamented, but no one heard!
§408
'The golden chariot hurtled on, whisking past sky-piercing mountain-tops, amid forests,
Streams, rivers of various lands. You have seen with you own eyes,
Saramā, the speed of the Pushpak chariot; what need to describe it?

§395

perfect fifths see I.623.

§408

Pushpak chariot the Pushpak chariot, capable of flying through the air at great speed, formerly belonged to the god Kuber, Rāvan's elder half-brother (see I.62). When Rāvan defeated Kuber in battle, he took his chariot as a victory trophy. The chariot was made by the divine architect and

§413
'Soon I heard the terrifying roar of a lion ahead of me!
The horses bucked in alarm—the chariot jolted!
I saw, when I opened my eyes, a warrior high up on a mountain,
Awesome as Siva, massive as a storm-cloud at the world's destruction! "I know you,"
Said the warrior in a booming voice. "You are Lankā's thieving Rāvan! What wife have you abducted this time,
You rogue? Whose house have you darkened by stamping on the lamp of love? This is what you always do—
I know that. I shall now expunge this insult to all warriors, by killing you with my sharp arrows!
Come, you idiot! I despise you,
King of the Rākshasas. Is there anyone as shameless as you, anywhere in the world?"

§427
'The warrior than roared again, my dear. I slumped senseless in the chariot!

§429
'When I came to again, I found myself lying on the ground. Rāvan in his chariot was fighting with the warrior along the sky's paths,
With blood-curdling yells. How can my feeble tongue, my darling,
Describe that battle? I clenched my eyes shut in terror. I appealed to the gods,

---

craftsman, Visvakarmā, who also (among many other feats) built the city of Lankā itself.

§413
a warrior i.e. Jaṭāyu. See below, §600.

Weeping and wailing, to side with the warrior to destroy
  the Rākshas, my enemy;
To rescue me from desperate danger! I stood up,
  thinking I would flee into the forest,
To somewhere far off; alas, I stumbled and was thrown
  down again,
As if by an earthquake! I prayed to Earth—"Let your
  breast split open,
Chaste mother, in this lonely place, and swallow me up,
Wretched as I am. How can you endure your miserable
  daughter's torments? Come quickly.
Alas, mother, the villain will soon return,
Like a robber returning at dead of night to the place
  where he has secretly buried his stolen hoard! Come
  and rescue me quickly, mother."

§448

'The clangour of battle rang out through the sky, lovely
  Saramā; the earth shuddered;
The region was filled with the noise! I passed out again. Listen,
Dear lady, with close attention, to an amazing tale.
I saw in a dream chaste Earth, my mother! She came
  close to me in her kindness,
Took me in her lap and said in her gentle voice: "It is the
  will of Fate, my child,
That the Raksha king has carried you off; because of
  you, the wretch will drown,
Along with all his race! Because I cannot bear the weight
  of his evil, I gave birth to you so that Lankā can be
  destroyed!
At the evil moment when Rāvan laid hands on you, I

§448

It is the will of Fate *bidhir icchāy*: no one in *MBK* has a more comprehensive conception of Fate than Earth.

knew that Fate was smiling at me at last; I blessed you!
You have banished your mother's agony, O daughter of Mithilā! Look now as I open the door of the future."
§464
'I saw before me, friend, a soaring mountain; five warriors were there,
All of them sunk in sorrow. Then Rām arrived, with Lakshman.
I cannot tell you, my friend, how it distressed me to see how pale he was with pining for me,
How it made me weep! The five warriors paid homage to Rām and to his brother. Together they invaded a beautiful city.
§473
'Rām killed the king of that city in a fierce battle, and placed on its throne Sugriv, noblest of the five.
Messengers were sent in all directions, and thousands of warriors assembled, bellowing like lions!
Earth trembled, my friend, at the pounding of their feet!
I fearfully clenched my eyes! Mother Earth smiled and said to me, "Who are you afraid of,
Jānaki? King Sugriv, Rām's best helper, is arming himself for your rescue.

§464

five warriors were there i.e. Nala, Nila, Hanumān, Jāmbuvān and Sugriv. See I.218. Nala and Jāmbuvān (leader of the bears—see Source Notes, p. 353) are warriors from Sugriv's kingdom of Kishkindhyā. Nala was also said to be the son of Visvakarmā (see below, §491).

§473

Rām killed the king of that city Rām assisted Sugriv in the overthrow of his elder brother Vāli, so that Sugriv could accede to the throne of Kishkindhyā and marry his brother's wife Tārā. See I.218.

Jānaki i.e. Sitā, daughter of King Janak.

The king your husband defeated was King Vāli, renowned
throughout the world. That city is Kishkindhyā.
See all those Indra-like soldiers arming now!" I looked,
and saw a mighty army on its way,
Like a tumultuous river in the rainy season! Close-
packed trees crashed down; rivers ran dry;
Terrified animals ran into the undergrowth; the whole
world was filled with the din, dear Saramā!

§491

'The army arrived at the shore of a sea. I saw, my friend,
Stones floating on the water! The soldiers were grabbing and
uprooting whole mountains, throwing them into the water.
Craftsmen constructed an astounding bridge out of
them. At my husband's command, Varuna himself
put on shackles!
Wild with war-frenzy, the army passed over the
impassable sea! The golden city of Lankā shuddered
at the tramp of enemy feet—
"Victory, victory to Rām," cried all! I wept with delight,
My dear! I saw the king of the Rākshasas sitting on a golden
throne in a golden temple; there was but one righteous,
Wise hero amidst Rāvan's courtiers; he was saying, "Pay
homage to Rām,
Give Sitā back; otherwise you and your race will die!"
Drunk with worldly ambition,
Rāvan kicked and hurled abuse at him. Hurt by this
insult, that elephant of heroes went to where the lord
of my life was encamped.'

§491

Stones floating on the water the famous stone bridge that, when Rām commanded the sea-god Varuna to let him pass, was built on Varuna's instruction by Nala, Visvakarmā's son, to enable Rām and his forces to cross over to Lankā.

there was but one righteous,/ Wise hero i.e. Vibhishan. See I.218.

§509
Saramā said, 'What more shall I tell you about the sorrow
Rāvan's brother felt at your sorrow? Who can describe,
Dear lady, how he and I wept to think of you?' 'I know,'
replied beautiful Sitā;
'I know that Vibhishan has been my saviour! And you
too, dear Saramā!
That I am still alive here, wretched though I am, is only
through your kindness,
Kind friend! But let me speak, listen to my amazing dream!
§520
'The Rākshasas armed in readiness for battle; the
Rākshas band played; battle-cries lifted the sky.
I trembled, friend, at the sight of those warriors,
Like Agni in their energy, like lions in their assault! How
can I describe the battle?
Rivers of blood flowed! I saw corpses piled high in
horrifying heaps! Headless goblins came,
And ghosts, demons and Dānavas; there were vultures
and other kinds of carrion-eating birds;
There were packs of jackals, and innumerable dogs.
Lankā was filled with tumult!
§531
'I saw the Karbur king in his council-chamber again,
ashen-faced now, tears in his eyes,
Grief-stricken! His pride had been dashed, my friend,
By Rām's atack! "Ah Fate," he groaned,

§520

Agni god of fire. See I.743. **Dānavas** see I.43.

§531

the Karbur king i.e. Rāvan. 'Karbur' is another name for Rākshas, and can also be used for other kinds of anti-gods—Asuras, Daityas, Dānavas.

Āh Fāṭe *hāy bidhi*: see Introduction, pp. lv–lvi.

"Is this what was in your mind? Go, all of you,
Wake up if you can my Siva-like brother Kumbhakarna.
Who can save the Rākshas race, if he cannot?"
Some Rākshasas ran to fetch him; the band played
noisily; womenfolk triumphantly ululated.
The gigantic charioteer Kumbhakarna (who in the world
is as skilled as he?) entered the battle—
And my husband sliced off his head with a single sharp
arrow! Unlucky was that fearsome warrior's
awakening—he died before his time.
I heard glorious shouts of "*Jay* Rām", my friend! Rāvan
and all of golden Lankā howled despairingly!

§548

'It unnerved me, Saramā, to hear such wailing all around!
I said to Mother Earth, clutching her feet, "My heart
breaks at the sufferings of the Raksha race,
Mā! It always distresses me to see someone else's
distress. Forgive me!"
Smiling, Earth said, "It's true what you have seen,
O wife of Rām! Your husband will rout and destroy Rāvan
and Lankā utterly. Open your eyes and look again."

§556

'I saw, friend Saramā, a group of celestial maidens,
With ornaments in their hands, and a garland of
mandār-flowers, and silken garments!

§531

Wake up if you can my Siva-like brother Kumbhakarna see I.80.

§548

Mā! see II.144.

§556

***mandār*-flowers** a celestial tree that grows in the gardens of the gods, but also sometimes associated with the brilliant scarlet blossoms of the *mādār* or coral-tree.

They surrounded me smilingly. One of them said, "Rise,
Virtuous lady, Rāvan has at last been slain in battle!"
Another said,
"Rise, treasure of the scion of Raghu, rise quickly.
Bathe your body in scented water, devi, put on these ornaments.
Sachi, queen of the gods, will return Sitā to her lord today!"
§565
'With my hands folded, dear Saramā, I replied,
"Why, O maidens, should I need this finery?
I'll go, if you allow, to my husband in this state.
Sitā is a beggar; let the jewel of men see her as she is, in beggar's garb."
§570
'The maidens replied, "Listen, O daughter of Mithilā!
A jewel is grubby when it's in the mine; but before giving it to a king, it should be cleansed!"
§573
'Weeping, laughing, my dear,
I dressed myself hurriedly. I saw my husband nearby, like the sun,
Ah! when it rises above its golden eastern mountain. Nearly mad,
O sweet-faced Saramā, I ran to embrace his feet! But then,
Suddenly, I woke up, like a lamp going out in a pitch-dark house;
My own state was like that—the entire universe seemed dark to me! Ah Fate,
Why didn't I die there? Why did my tormented soul remain in my body? To what end?'

§556
Sachi wife of Indra, the king of the gods. See II.14.

§583
Moon-like Sitā ceased, like a *vīṇā* when a string has snapped! Saramā
(Beautiful as Lakshmi in the form of a Raksha wife) said tearfully, 'Janak's daughter will get her lord!
This dream of yours is true, I tell you! Stones are indeed floating in the sea;
Gigantic Kumbhakarna, the terror of gods and demons and men, has indeed fallen in battle;
Vibhishan is advising triumphant Rām and his thousands of soldiers. Rāvan will receive his rightful punishment; the villain will go under—
Along with his race! Now tell me what happened next. I am longing to hear the rest of your story.'
§595
Chaste Sitā began again in her gentle voice: 'O moon-like Saramā, when I opened my eyes I saw Rāvan before me;
The leonine warrior who had fought him was lying on the ground, alas, like a mountain-top smashed by a thunderbolt!
§600
'Rāghav's enemy roared, "O moon-like Sitā, open your lotus eyes and see Rāvan's might!
World-renowned Jaṭāyu lies senseless today through my assault! The stupid son of Garuḍa is dying through his own folly! Who told that idiot to fight with me?"
§605
'"I died in a fight for justice and righteousness," murmured the hero. "I have fallen in open combat,

§600

World-renowned Jaṭāyu . . . son of Garuḍa Jaṭāyu is the king of the vultures and son of Garuḍa (see I.218). His name means 'shaggy-hair-aged' and therefore implies longevity. He is famous for defeating Indra and

And so I will go to heaven. Think what will happen to you! You became a jackal,
And greedily fell upon a lioness! Who can save you, Rākshas?
By stealing this jewel of a woman, Lord of Lankā, you have caused your downfall."

§612
'With that the hero stopped speaking. Lankā's ruler again hauled me into his chariot. With hands clasped together,
I called between tears to that noble hero, "My name is Sitā, daughter of Janak,
Married into the clan of Raghu, sir! This sinner found me alone in my hut,
And stole me; if you see my husband, tell him what has happened."

§619
'The chariot took off again with a deafening clatter. I heard a roaring; I saw an ocean before me with its blue waves!
Bottomless, shoreless waters swelled unceasingly! I wanted to throw myself into the water and drown,
Dear friend, but the villain stopped me! I called in my mind to the ocean and the creatures in it;
No one listened. They ignored my misery! The golden chariot flew through the sky as swiftly as thought.

§628
'Soon the city of Lankā gleamed before me. This golden city, my dear,
Is a line of gems on the brow of the sea! But does a cage made of gleaming gold please a pining prisoner's eyes?
Is a caged bird happy because its cage is made of gold?

---

attacking Surya, the sun-god. He was slain by Rāvan when he tried to prevent him from taking Sitā to Lankā in his chariot.

A bird of the forest is always wretched when it is encaged! Unlucky was my birth, O beautiful Saramā!

Whoever heard of such a thing, my friend? I am the daughter of a king; and married into a royal house—

Yet I am trapped in a prison.' The weeping Sitā threw her arms round Saramā's neck; Saramā wept too.

§641

In a while, lovely-eyed Saramā wiped away her tears and said, 'Devi,

Who can cut through the bonds of Fate? But it is true what Earth said. It was Fate's will that the king of Lankā stole and brought you here!

That criminal will die along with his race! How many fighters are there left in this city, mother of fighters though she is?

Where are there fighters who can defeat the three worlds? See—on the shore of the sea—

How corpse-eating creatures prowl in delight amidst heaps of corpses! Listen to the wailing of widows in their homes! Your night of sorrow will end soon!

Your dream will come true, I tell you! Bands of Vidyādharis will come with garlands of *mandār*-flowers and joyously place them round your neck!

You will appear before Rām, like Earth appearing before her lover, the spring,

At the lush arrival of spring! Don't forget me, chaste Sitā!

For as long as I live, I shall joyfully worship your image in the temple of my mind, like a lake delighting in the worship of moonlight's treasure when night comes.

§641

Vidyādharis see III.378.

***mandār*-flowers** see above, §556.

You have suffered greatly, lovely-haired one, since coming to this land.
But I am not to blame.' Sitā said tenderly, 'Darling Saramā!
Who in the world has been kinder to me than you? You have been like a stream in the desert to me, Raksha wife.
When I am burnt up by the sun, you soothe me with your cool shade. You are the embodiment of kindness in this cruel land!
A lotus in Lankā's muddy water! A jewel on the head of this deadly snake that is golden Lankā! What more shall I say,
My dear! To the beggar Sitā you are a priceless jewel! When a poor person finds a jewel,
How, my treasure, can she not safeguard it?'
§676
Falling at Sitā's feet, Saramā said, 'Let me take leave of you now,
Kind Sitā! My heart doesn't want to leave you, O lotus of the race of Raghu!
But my husband serves Rāghav; I have put myself in danger by coming to speak at your feet; the king of Lankā will be furious when he hears of this.'
§681
Sitā replied, 'Dear Saramā! Go quickly to your house;
I hear footsteps approaching; the guards are returning to this wood, I think.'
§684
Saramā sped away like a frightened deer; Sitā remained alone, like a single flower in the forest.

Here ends 'The Asoka wood',
the fourth book of *Meghnādbadh kabya.*

BOOK V

§1

Star-studded night smiled in the realm of the gods—but the great Indra, king of the gods,
Was anxious now in his palace; forsaking his bed of flowers he sat down glumly on his jewelled lion-throne; all the other gods were asleep in their golden mansions.

§6

Sachi, empress of the gods, murmured plaintively,
'Of what error, my lord, am I guilty of before you?
Why have you not set foot in our bedroom? Look at how Menakā opened her eyes again immediately after shutting them, alarmed at your gloom!
And Urvasi, see, is frozen with alarm!
Lovely Chitralekhā is like a painted doll! In dread at your dread, the rest-giving goddess of sleep stays away from you,
And who else does she fear but you? Tell me who would stay awake anywhere so late at night; is an army of demons encamped at heaven's gate?'

§18

The enemy of the Asuras replied, 'I am wondering, goddess,
How the hero Lakshman will destroy Meghnād. Rāvan's son is invincible in the world, chaste wife.'

§6

Sachi see I.14. **Menakā . . . Urvasi . . . Chitralekhā** *Apsarāses* or nymphs who live in Indra's heaven and act as handmaidens to Sachi. Menakā is famous as the mother of Sakuntalā in Kālidāsa's celebrated play. Urvasi is famous for her dancing. See II.14. **Lovely Chitralekhā is like a painted doll** there is wordplay here on *citra-puttalikā* ('painted doll').

§18

The enemy of the Asuras i.e. Indra, enemy of all anti-gods and demons. *Suras* means devatās or gods, and 'a' is a negative prefix.

§20

'You acquired the weapons, great husband,' said the eternally youthful daughter of Puloman,
With which Tārak was killed by Kārttikeya; in having Siva on your side, you are fortunate;
When I appealed to noble Durgā, she herself promised your desire would be realized tomorrow; that goddess-queen Māyā herself would arrange for Meghnād to be slain.
So why, lord, are you so worried?'

§29

The foe of the Daityas replied, 'It's true, queen of the gods,
What you have said; I have sent weapons to Lankā; but I cannot imagine,
Great-eyed one, by what trick Māyā will save Lakshman in his fight with the Rākshasas. I know Sumitrā's son is a great warrior;
But how can an elephant withstand a lion's assault? I do not turn a hair, my beauty,
At blasts of thunder, at rampaging clouds; I can stare at volcanic sea-fire;
Lightning flashes perpetually suround my vehicle; but my heart quakes, goddess,
When the great bow-bearer Meghnād bellows with rage,

§20

daughter of Puloman see II.14. **with which Tārak was hilled by Kārttikeya** see II.491. **you are fortunate in having Siva on your side** see Book II, §425 and the passages preceding it for the process by which Siva is brought round to abandoning his earlier support for Rāvan and the Rākshasas.

§29

The foe of the Daityas M uses Asuras, Daityas, Dānavas, Karburas or Rākshasas fairly interchangeably for demons or anti-gods. **by what trick** *ki kauśale*: see I.1 and the events in Book VI. **Sumitrā's son** i.e. Lakshman. See I.172.

and aims with a battle-cry volleys of fire-arrows from his bow; even my flying elephant Airavat is cowed by that ghastly onslaught.'

With a mournful sigh Indra fell silent; sighing too (distressed as a good wife always is at her husband's distress)

The goddess Sachi sat beside her lord. Urvasi, Menakā,

Rambhā, lovely Chitralekhā stood all around, like moonbeams silently encircling a closed-up lotus on a night-dark lake!

Or like lamps round Durgā's throne at her autumn festival, when Bengal rejoices at her longed-for arrival! The couple sat silently.

Then Māyā-devi arrived. The jewels in the palace doubled in their lustre, as do the golden *mandār*-trees in Indra's garden in the rays of the sun!

§57

The god and goddess did respectful obeisance to Māyā's lotus-feet. Blessing them, she sat down on a golden seat.

With his hands pressed together, the king of the gods asked, 'What,

O mother, is your desire? Please tell me.'

§61

Loving Māyā replied, 'I'm going, O son of the sun,

To Lankā; I shall carry out your wish; by a trick

I shall pulverize the crest-jewel of the Rākshasas today. See, night is ending.

§29

Airavat Indra's flying elephant Airavat was one of the 'fourteen jewels' produced by the churning of the ambrosial ocean. See I.295 and II.337.

Rambhā another Apsarās or heavenly nymph.

Or like lamps from Durgā's throne . . . a reference to Durgā-pujā, Bengal's main Hindu festival. See I.483.

Māyā-devi see II.425.

***mandār*-trees** see IV.556.

Soon, O Destroyer of Cities, world-delighting Dawn will smilingly rise above her mountain-top,
And Lankā's lotus-sun will set behind its peak! I shall guide Lakshman, O Foe of the Asuras,
To the temple in the Nikumbhilā grove. I shall enmesh the Rākshasas in a web of illusion. Weak and weaponless,
The warrior will helplessly die (like a lion in a trap) by force of divine arms;
Who can evade the prescriptions of Fate? Meghnād will die violently; but when the Raksha king gets news of this,
How will you protect Rām's brother, Rām himself, and steadfast Vibhishan,
Friend of the Raghus? Insane with grief for his son, mighty-armed Rāvan,
O lord of the gods, will enter the fray like Death! Who has the power to oppose him?
Think, divine lord, about what I have told you.'

§80

Sachi's husband, vanquisher of the demon Namuchi, replied:
'If Lakshman slays Meghnād with his arrows, Māyā, I shall enter the battle against the Rākshasas myself,
With my army of gods, to protect him. I shall not fear Rāvan,
Goddess, by your grace! First kill Meghnād,
The pride of the Rākshasas, violent in battle, by spreading your web of illusion,

§61

Lankā's lotus-sun see II.491.
temple in the Nikumbhilā grove see I.751.
the prescriptions of Fate *bidhir bidhi*: see Introduction, pp. lv–lvi.
Vibhishan,/ Friend of the Raghus see I.218.

§80

vanquisher of the demon Namuchi this demon's only claim to fame, it seems, is that he was slain by Indra!

Mother! Rām is loved by the gods; the immortals will fight with all their might on his behalf.
I will go down to earth tomorrow; I shall burn up the Rākshasas, with swift lightning fire.'

§91

'Just is this work of yours, O thunderous son of Aditi,' said Māyā;
'I am cheered by what you say, O greatest of gods! Permit me now to go to Lankā.'
With that, all-powerful Māyā blessed the pair and departed. Sleep now came to bow down at Indra's feet.

§97

Merrily taking Sachi's lotus-hand, great Indra entered their bedroom, that room of pleasure!
Chitralekhā, Urvasi, Menakā and Rambhā all quickly withdrew to their rooms.
They took off their anklets, girdles, bangles and other ornaments;
They took off their bodices; beautiful as sun-beams, the nymphs of heaven lay down on their flower-beds.
A fragrant breeze wafted, lingering sometimes over their tresses, sometimes over their pert breasts,
Sometimes over their moon-like faces, like a honey-drunk bee, when it gathers honey from full-bloomed flowers in a forest!

§109

The great goddess Māyā proceeded to the golden gate of heaven; it opened of its own accord, with a musical sound.

§91

O thunderous son of Aditi goddess of the firmament and mother of the gods including Indra and even Vishnu. Her antithesis is Diti, mother of the Daityas or anti-gods.

The enchantress of the universe emerged through the gate; calling in her mind to the Goddess of Dreams, she said to her softly:

§113

'Go to Lankā, where the hero Lakshman is resting in his tent. In the guise of his mother Sumitrā,

Sit at his pillow and tell him, playful one, this:

"Rise, my son, the night is ending.

In a grove by the north gate of Lankā there is a lake; in its bank there is a temple to Chanḍi, encased in gold;

Bathe in that lake, pick a variety of flowers, and worship reverently that demon-defying mother-goddess.

By her grace, you will easily crush vainglorious Meghnād, O famous one.

Go alone to that wood, my dear." Go quickly with these instructions to Lankā,

O Svapna-devi. See how night is fading—it will brook no delay.'

§126

Svapna-devi went on her way, lighting up the dark blue sky, falling to earth like a star!

Rapidly arriving in the tent where Rām's brother lay, she sat down by his pillow dressed as Sumitrā, and murmured in her magical,

§113

temple to Chanḍi Chanḍi or Chanḍikā is Durgā in her ferocious aspect, the slayer of the buffalo-demon Mahish. See II.400. Her victory over him is celebrated during Durgā-pujā in Bengal, and depicted in the large images of Durgā that are constructed for it. It is central to the *Devīmāhātmya,* the famous Sanskrit poem that forms a major part of the Mārkanḍeya Purāna. Chandi also slew the Asura brothers Sumbha and Nisumbha (see III.115) and their self-replicating general Raktabij (see III.352).

Svapna-devi *svapna* means 'dream'. The 'Goddess of Dreams' is a personification influenced by Western literature, not a figure from Hindu mythology. See Source Notes, p. 343.

Gentle voice: 'Rise, my son,
The night is ending. In a grove by the north gate of Lankā there is a lake; in its bank there is a temple to Chandi,
Encased in gold; bathe in that lake, pick a variety of flowers,
And worship reverently that demon-defying mother-goddess. By her grace, you will easily crush vainglorious Meghnād,
O famous one. Go alone to that wood, my dear.'

§139

Waking with a start, the warrior looked all around him, and at once,
Alas, his chest was dampened with tears! 'O Mother,' he sobbed,
Why have you so cruelly disappeared? Show yourself again, that I may worship your feet;
Let me fulfil my heart's desire by taking their dust, dear mother! When I had to take leave of you,
How you wept—my heart breaks to recall it! Will I ever,
Devi, see your feet again in this vain life?' Wiping away his tears,
That elephant of heroes, moving like an elephant, went to where the king of the Raghus held court.

§151

Lakshman bowed to his elder brother's feet and said, 'I have had a strange dream, O Lord of the Raghus!
Sitting at my pillow, my mother Sumitrā said, "Rise,
My son, the night is ending. In a grove by the north gate of Lankā there is a lake;

§139

king of the Raghus i.e. Rām. See I.406.

In its bank there is a temple to Chanḍi, encased in gold; bathe in that lake,
Pick a variety of flowers, and worship reverently that demon-defying mother-goddess. By her grace,
You will easily crush vainglorious Meghnād, O famous one. Go alone to that wood,
My dear." Saying this, my mother vanished.
I cried out after her, but received no answer. What,
O Raghu jewel, should I do now? Please tell me.'
§165
The enjoyer of Sitā asked Vibhishan, 'What do you say, O best of counsellors?
In Raksha territory, you are Rāghav's protector, renowned throughout the world!'
§168
That finest of Rākshasas answered: 'There is indeed in that forest a Chanḍi temple, lord,
Beside a lake. The Rākshas king himself worships the goddess in that grove; no on else dares go there—
It is a hideous place! I've heard that Siva, no less,
Guards the temple-door—his terrifying trident in hand! Anyone who worships the mother there is victorious in the world!
What else shall I tell you? If the son of Sumitrā has the courage to enter that forest, your desire will ride,
O great charioteer, like a chariot, to success!'
§178
'I am at my brother's command, O noblest of Rākshasas,' said heroic Lakshman;

§165
Rāghav i.e. Rām. See I.1.
§168
his terrifying trident in hand see II.447.

'If he gives his order, I shall easily penetrate the forest. Who will prevent me?'
Gently, Rām said, 'When I think,
Dear brother, of all you have suffered for my sake, my heart does not want to cause you further torment!
But what can I do? How can I set aside the decrees of the gods? Go carefully,
Empowered by the power of *dharma*! May the favour of the gods protect you, like armour!'

§189

Touching Rām's feet and saluting Vibhishan, mighty Lakshman set off fearlessly and swiftly to the north gate, sword in hand.
Loyal Sugriv, fiery as Agni, was on guard there with his army.
Hearing the sound of footsteps, he called out sternly, 'Who are you?
Why are you here at dead of night? Tell me quickly if you want to live! Otherwise I shall smash your head with a stone!'
Lakshman replied with a laugh, 'Smash the Rākshasas, O jewel of heroes;
I am a follower of Rām.' Advancing quickly, Sugriv greeted his friend Lakshman.
Pleasing the king of Kishkindhyā with his sweet speech, the enjoyer of Urmilā proceeded onwards, through the north gate.

§203

Strong-armed Lakshman soon arrived at the entrance to

§178

dharma see II.173, 217 and Introduction, p. livf.

§189

Sugriv see I.218. **Agni** see I.743. **the enjoyer of Urmilā** i.e. Lakshman. See I.1.

the grove, and saw with amazement a terrifying figure nearby! The moon shone on his forehead,
Like a jewel on the brow of a huge snake! His hair was matted, and marked by the flow of the foaming Ganges through it,
Like a cloud on an autumn night shot through with silvery lightning! His body was smeared with ash; a trident as big as a *śāl*-tree was in his right hand!
Lakshman recognised him as Siva! Unsheathing his gleaming sword, the lion-hero said:
'Chariot-driving Dasarath, son of Aja son of Raghu, is famous in the world.
I, his son, humbly bow to your feet,
Moon-crested one! Let me through; I want to enter the forest and worship Chaṇḍi;
Do not attack me. The king of Lankā is perpetually engaged in unrighteous acts;
But if you want to fight in his support, O supreme-eyed Siva, attack me without delay.
In the name of *dharma* I invite you; if *dharma* is true, I shall surely be the victor.'

§223

Like a mountain-peak loudly echoing the thunder, bull-bannered Siva sonorously replied: 'I praise your courage,

§203

His hair was matted, and marked by the flow of the foaming Ganges through it Siva's *jaṭā* or matted hair is a symbol of his asceticism; he also prevented India from being flooded by the waters of the Gangā by catching them in his hair as they flowed down from heaven. ***śāl*-tree** a tree that grows in the dry climate of West Bengal or Bihar, and noted for its height as well as its hardwood and resin. **Chariot-driving Dasarath . . . Raghu** see I.172, 386, 406. Aja, Rām's grandfather, completes the lineage.

§223

bull-bannered Siva see II.491.

Crest-jewel of heroes Lakshman! Why should I fight with you? Chaṇḍi is well-disposed towards you today—
You are in luck.' Matted-haired Siva opened the door he was guarding; the son of Sumitrā entered the forest.

§230

The hero started at the sudden roar of a lion! The dense jungle rumbled all around! A red-eyed lion came charging towards him,
Swishing its tail, grinding its teeth! Shouting '*Jay* Rām,' Lakshman whipped out his sword.
The phantom lion vanished, like darkness before a flame. Circumspect Lakshman edged forward calmly.
Suddenly thunderous clouds covered the moon! A wind howled! Lightning fleetingly lit up the sky,
Making the land seem doubly dark with its momentary flare! One after another thunderbolts crashed down to earth! A storm uprooted trees with its strength!
Fire swept through the forest! Golden Lankā quaked; the sea moaned in the distance,
Like thousands of conches, blown on the battlefield, their booming mixed with the twanging of bowstrings!

§247

Immovable as a mountain, the hero stood firm amidst this uproar! All at once,
The forest-fire died down; the violent storm ceased; stars twinkled in the sky;
Their husband the moon was visible again! Flower-tressed earth smiled with delight! A gently murmuring breeze brought a rush of fragrance.

§230

a red-eyed lion the lion, the storm and the forest-fire are all illusions worked by Māyā-devi as tests for Lakshman.

§253

Amazed, wise Lakshman proceeded cautiously. Suddenly the wood was filled with a sweet jingling!

A flute sounded, with *vīṇā*, drum,

Cymbals and the seven-vesselled *sapta-svarā*; and a woman's voice rising above it, beguiling the mind!

§258

The hero saw in front of him, in a flowering grove, a group of women,

Like stars fallen to earth! Some were bathing in a translucent lake, like moonshine at night!

Silk saris and bodices glittered on the bank; their bodies in the clean water were like golden lotuses, ah!

On Lake Mānas! Some picked flowers; some preened their hair to entangle the God of Love!

Some took ivory-carved, gem-studded *vīṇās* into their hands! Golden strings—

A dwelling for music's feelings—glistened on the *vīṇās*! Some were dancing happily;

Jewel-necklaces swung between their plump breasts, anklets jingled with their steps, girdles jangled on their round buttocks!

Men can die from the deadly bite of a poisonous cobra; but the heart would be stricken by love's potion, even at the sight of the jewelled snake-plaits swinging down their backs!

Anyone who sees Death's messenger the snake crossing his path flees in dread; alas, on seeing those plaits,

§253

vīṇā see I.623. ***sapta-svarā*** a musical instrument made of seven water-pots filled with varying amounts of water and struck on the rims.

§258

a group of women a further illusion worked by Māyā, to tempt Lakshman this time. **Lake Mānas** see I.33.

Who would not want to wrap them round his neck, like
the snake that Siva, trident-holder,
Umā's beloved, wears round his head? *Koel*-birds were
awake with a song in the branches of trees;
Fountains gurgled nearby; a breeze blew ecstatically,
stealing from flowers the treasure of their scent!

§283

Soon the women were surrounding invincible
Lakshman, and singing: 'Welcome,
O crest-jewel of the Rāghavas! We are not night-
wanderers; we live in the sky!
Our home is a golden palace in the heavenly forest of
Nandan, O hero; we joyously drink nectar;
Eternal spring lives in that garden of youth; our lotus-
breasts are forever full-bloomed; the flavour of nectar
never dies from the lake of our lips;
We are immortal, lord! We all choose you as our husband;
Come with us, dear master! For ages on end,
Men perform harsh austerities to win this delightful
pleasure: we give it to you, jewel of virtue!
The worms of disease and grief that devour life's flowers
in this world do not enter the realm where we dwell
forever in joy!' With his palms pressed together,
Lakshman replied:

§258

like the snake that Siva . . . wears round his head the snake-king Vāsuki (see I.33) is draped round Siva's head and neck. It symbolizes the anger that Siva unleashes during his destructive phases, and its poison accounts for his blue neck. He drank up the poison to stop the destruction of humanity, but had to keep it in his throat otherwise it would have destroyed him too.

Umā's beloved Umā is a name Durgā or Pārvati that is commonly used in Bengal; it is also used in Kālidāsa's *Kumārasambhava* (see I.33).

***Koel*-birds** see I.623.

§283

heavenly forest of Nandan see I.623.

'O heavenly beauties, forgive me! My brother is the world-renowned charioteer Rāmchandra;
Sitā is his wife; the Rākshas king found her alone in the woods and abducted her. By destroying Meghnād in fierce combat,
I shall rescue chaste Sitā; grant, O lovely ladies,
That this vow of mine may be fulfilled! I was born not as a god but as a man; only as mothers to me can I honour you all!'
Saying that, great-armed Lakshman raised his eyes and saw that the forest was deserted! The nymphs had gone, as in a dream;
Or like a water-bubble that only lives for a moment! Who in this illusory world can understand the illusions that Māyā works? The astonished warrior again proceeded slowly on his way.

§313

In a while noble Lakshman saw a lake nearby; there was a temple to Chaṇḍi on its bank; its many golden steps were studded with gems.
He saw lamps burning in the temple; there were heaps of flowers round the seat of the deity; cymbals,
Conches and bells were sounding; there was water in pots! Incense burning in censers perfumed the area,
Mixing its fragrance with the scent of the flowers. Stepping down into the lake, the hero bathed;
Reverently, he picked some blue lotus; they scented the air all around.

§323

Leonine Lakshman then went into the temple,

§283

Rāmchandra see I.176.

worshipped lion-riding Chanḍi in the proper way. 'O boon-giver,
He said, spreading his whole body before her, 'Give me your boon!
I pray, mother, that I may destroy the Rākshas warrior Meghnād.
Can a human tongue, alas, speak of all that you know about the human mind,
You who can see into all hearts? Fulfil all my longings, kind Chanḍi!'
Clouds rumbled far off! Lankā was shaken by a clap of thunder! The forest,
Temple, lake all quavered and quivered, as if struck by an earthquake!

§335

Looking in front of him, Lakshman saw the great goddess on her throne. Bursts of divine fire dazzled his eyes amidst flashes of lightning!
Stunned, he turned his eyes to the darkened temple around him! The chaste goddess smiled;
The darkness sped away; clear sight returned to wise Lakshman! A wave of sweet music filled the air!

§342

Then he heard great Māyā speaking: 'O sun of virtuous

§323

lion-riding Chanḍi Chanḍi's *vahana* or vehicle when she rides into battle against demons is a lion.

§342

great Māyā *Mahāmāyā*: this can be a name for Chanḍi, so it might at first seem unclear whether Chanḍi or Māyā is speaking. But it is clear from what she says about the weapons, the Nikumbhilā rite, etc. that she is the Māyā whose assistance leads to the killing of Meghnād in Book VI, and that M is deliberately conflating her with Chanḍi here. See also Source Notes, pp. 344–5.

Sumitrā, all gods and goddesses are favourable to you today!
Indra has sent you divine weapons; I myself have come here, at Siva's request,
To help you achieve your task. Taking the divine weapons, hero,
And with Vibhishan accompanying you, go into the city, to the place of the Nikumbhilā rite,
The temple where Meghnād is worshipping Agni. Attack him without warning, like a tiger,
And kill him! Through my boon, you will both enter the place unseen;
Like a sword in its scabbard, I shall shroud you both in a net of illusion. Go with no fear in your heart,
O famous one!' The jewel of heroes bowed to Māyā's feet, and set off rapidly back to where Rām was.
Birds were awake and twittering in the flowering woods, like musicians filling the land with cheerful music during a great festival! Trees rained down clusters of flowers on his head;
A breeze blew softly. A message rang out from the sky: 'Happy was the time,
Lakshman, when your mother Sumitrā gave birth to you! Today the three worlds will fill with a song of your renown—
I assure you! You are about to achieve what is beyond the gods to achieve, dear son of Sumitrā!
You will gain godlike immortality!' Sarasvati's words ceased; birds sang even more sweetly in the forest-glades.

§342

Indra has sent you divine weapons see Book II, §527f. **the place of the Nikumbhilā rite** see I.751. **Agni** see I.743. **Sarasvati** see I.1.

§369
The music of those birds entered the bower of bliss where the mighty Indrajit was lying on a bed of flowers in a house of gold. The elephant-hero awoke to that woodland song. He took the lotus-hand of his wife Pramilā,
And ever so like a bee whispering love's secrets in the ear of a lotus, he said (kissing her closed eyes),
'The birds are calling you, my darling, with their cooing,
You who are the golden dawn! Open, my love,
Your lotus-eyes! Rise, my eternal joy!
My heart, dear wife, is like the jewel that is the sun's spouse;
You are the rays of the sun; I am without lustre when you close your eyes. In my world,
You are the supreme fruit on the tree of fortune! O light of my eyes! Jewel beyond price!
Arise, see, moon-like one,
How the flowers are blooming by stealing from the ravishing garden of your beauty!' Prāmila sprang up—like a milkmaid roused of a sudden by the sound of Krishna's flute!

§389
With a delicate smile, she covered her body modestly. Her husband lovingly spoke again:
'Dark night is ending at last; otherwise would you, my lotus-flower,
Be blooming now to enchant my eyes? Come, beloved,
I must now bid farewell, after touching my mother's feet! Then,

§369

Indrajit i.e. Meghnād. See I.594, 1.

Pramilā see I.689 and III.1, 85, 413.

like a milkmaid roused of a sudden by the sound of Krishna's flute see I.33. For the effect of the link here and also at the end of this book (§599) between Pramilā and the *gopis*, see Source Notes, p. 331.

After worshipping Agni fitly, I shall meet Rām's wish for a battle, by raining down arrows as heavily as thunderbolts!'

§397

Rāvan's daughter-in-law dressed, and Rāvan's son: both incomparable in the world;
Pramilā, supreme among females; Meghnād,
Supreme among males! They left their bedroom—like the morning star accompanying the sun!
Pale with shame, fireflies flew away (abandoning the nectar of dew they were enjoying in the petals of flowers);
Bees came rushing in hope of honey; in the branches, *koel*-birds sang in delectable fifths;
Rākshas musicians played; guards did obeisance; '*Jay* Meghnād' resounded in the sky.

§409

The couple joyously took their seats in a bejewelled palanquin! A gang of bearers carried them to Queen Mandodari's golden palace—a radiant abode,
Fashioned from emeralds and diamonds and ivory, unparalleled in the world! Everything adorned it that God has created to delight the eyes!
Female guards protected its doors, holding weapons like Death's club; some were mounted;

§389

After worshipping Agni fitly because Agni is Meghnād's *iṣṭadeva* or patron god. See I.743, 751.

§397

delectable fifths see I.623, and cf. Book IV, §395.

***Jay* Meghnād** 'Victory to Meghnād'.

§409

Queen Mandodari Meghnād's mother and Rāvan's chief queen. See I.172.

weapons like Death's club Yama, god of death, carries a *daṇḍa* or sceptre: see I.218.

Some were on foot. Lamps festooned the palace like strings of stars. A spring breeze blew,
Bringing the fragrance of thousands of forest-flowers. Gentle *vīṇā*-music welled up, ravishing as in a dream!

§422

Invincible Meghnād strode into the golden palace, with beautiful Pramilā at his side. A Rākshasi named Trijaṭā came running.
The lion-hero said, 'Hear me, O Trijaṭā—
Today, after completing the Nikumbhilā rite, I shall fight with Rām at my father's behest,
And annihilate that enemy of the Rākshasas. I want, therefore,
To worship the feet of my mother first. Go with this message; say,
"Your son, O empress of Lankā, is waiting with his wife at your door!"'
Prostrating herself before him, Trijaṭā—that formidable Rākshasi—
Replied, 'Queen Mandodari is at present in the Siva-temple, O prince!
Sleepless and forgoing all food, she prays to Siva for your welfare. Who in this world has a son like you,
O hero? Who has such a mother?' She then sped away with the speed of lightning.

§422

A Rākshasi named Trijaṭā her name implies that she has three *jaṭā* or piles of matted hair. She acts as a maidservant to Rāvan and Mandodari.

the Nikumbhilā rite i.e. Meghnād's *pūjā* to Agni before going into battle. See I.751.

Queen Mandodari is at present in the Siva-temple because 'Rāvan is Siva's chief devotee'. See Book II, §168.

§439
A chorus of singers now sang to harmonious instruments: 'O Krittikā, O Durgā-like mother!
Come and see your Kārttikeya at your door with Senā, his lovely-eyed wife! Come and delight in her,
She who puts Rohini to shame; and your son whose looks make the moon look drab. Blessed is your fortune—
That mighty Indrajit should be so world-conquering; and chaste, beautiful Pramilā so world-ravishing!'
§446
The queen of Lankā emerged from the Siva-temple. The couple bowed down at her feet. The empress tearfully and joyously hugged them,
Kissed their heads! Oh the heart of a mother, fount of love in the world,
Just as flowers are founts of nectar, oysters are the homes of pearls, and mines are full of gems!
§452
A son like the autumn moon; his wife like autumn moonlight; the queen of the Rākshasas herself like the night with a crown of stars!
The stream of her tears was like dew, falling, glistening on her leaf-like cheeks!
§457
Heroic Meghnād said, 'Devi, give me your blessing.

§439

O Krittikā . . . Kārttikeya . . . Senā see II.491 for the complicated way in which Kārttikeya, the war-god, is the son of Pārvati (Durgā) but was wet-nursed by the six Krittikās or Pleiades. Here the singers are comparing Meghnād to Kārttikeya and Mandodari to both Durgā and the Krittikās. Pramilā is compared to Kārttikeya's wife Senā—the name has a military ring, as it also means 'army'.

Rohini the most beautiful of the twenty-seven stars who are the wives of Chandra, the moon.

After carrying out the Nikumbhilā rite with all due ceremony,
I shall go into battle today, and destroy Rāghav!
My brother Virbāhu was but a child: the scoundrel slew
him. I'll see what he can do against me!
Give me the dust of your feet, mother! By your grace I
shall rid Lankā of danger with a shower of sharp arrows!
I shall bind and bring back my uncle Vibhishan—that
traitor! I shall drive Sugriv into the bottomless sea,
And Angad too!' Wiping her tears with her jewel-
studded sari, the queen replied:

§468

'How shall I say goodbye to you, my darling? The sky of
my heart will turn dark,
Full moon to me that you are. Sitā's husband is fearsome
in battle—and Lakshman likewise;
Pitiless Vibhishan is like a poisonous snake! Maddened
with ambition, the villain kills his own kin without
compunction,
Like a ravenous tiger swallowing its young! Evil was the
time, I tell you,
My child, that my mother-in-law Nikashā conceived
such a miscreant! It is he who has vilely brought
golden Lankā to ruin!'

§478

Smiling before his mother, the warrior replied: 'Why,
Mother, do you fear our enemies Rām and Lakshman?
Twice at my father's command I have repulsed them
in savage battle,

§457

Virbāhu see I.1.
Angad see I.218.

§468

Nikashā see I.62.

With a network of fiery arrows! Through your noble grace, I shall always prevail in fights with gods,
Demons or men! My uncle Vibhishan knows, devi,
The violence of my attack; and thunderbolt-throwing, thousand-eyed Indra too,
With his divine army; and Ananta in the underworld, and the great kings of the earth!
So tell me why are you afraid today, mother? Why should trash like Rām alarm you?'

§490

Lovingly kissing Meghnād's head, the queen said: 'This husband of Sitā, my child,
Has magic powers; or else all the gods are aiding him! When you bound him and Lakshman with snakes as lassoes,
Who undid those bonds? Who brought Rām back to life, when you slaughtered him with his army in a night battle?
I cannot understand any of this! I have heard that at Sitā's lord's command stones float on water, fires are put out by downpours!

§478

thunderbolt-throwing, thousand-eyed Indra *dambholi-nikṣepī* ('thunderbolt-throwing') and *sahasrākṣa* ('thousand-eyed') are both epithets for Indra, king of the gods (see I.164). Indra has a thousand eyes to enable him to see the whole universe at once, and there are myths to explain how he acquired them, notably the story of Ahalyā. Indra seduced her by taking on the guise of her husband, who then cursed Indra by covering him with a thousand *yonis* (vaginas). The curse was later modified, and the *yonis* became eyes.

Ananta king of the serpents or Nāgas. See I.33, II.491.

§490

When you bound him and Lakshman with snakes as lassoes . . . for the two occasions when Meghnād thought he had killed Rām and Lakshman, only to find them restored to life, see I.743.

stones float on water see IV.491.

fires are put out by downpours i.e. the weapons of Agni, god of fire, have proved powerless against Rām.

Rām is a sorcerer! How, my darling,
Can I let you go to fight with him again? Alas, Fate,
Why did foul-faced Surpanakhā not die in her mother's womb?' With this, Queen Mandodari gave way to speechless tears.

§504

The elephant-hero spoke: 'You needlessly distress yourself, mother,
By dwelling on the past! The enemy is at the gate of the city; till I have defeated him in battle,
I shall enjoy nothing! If fire attacks, who can go on sleeping indoors?
The Rākshas race is celebrated, the terror of gods and demons and men throughout the three worlds, devi!
Can I, Indrajit the son of Rāvan, allow such a race to be besmirched by Rām?
What will your father Maya, Danu's great son, say when he hears this?
Or your valiant brothers? The universe will laugh! Command me,
Mother, to go into battle to eradicate Rāghav! Hear how the birds are cooing in the woods.
Night is ending. I shall worship my *iṣṭadeva*, then enter the fray with my army of indomitable Rākshasas.
Return now, devi, to your own house.
I shall soon return in triumph to worship lovingly your lotus feet! I have received my father's order—please give me yours.

§490

Surpanakhā see I.80.

§504

your father Maya see I.33. **Danu** mother of Maya and thus of all the Dānavas. ***iṣṭadeva*** see I.743, 751.

Who can obstruct me, devi, if I have your blessing?'
§524
Wiping her tears with the jewelled end of her sari, the queen of Lankā replied: 'If you go,
May Siva, the guardian of the Rākshas race, protect you in this ghastly conflict;
This is what I pray at his feet! What more shall I say? You are leaving me in this house,
Alas, without the apple of my eye.' The grief-stricken queen turned to Pramilā and said: 'Stay here with me,
Mā; I shall ease my bitter heart by gazing at your shining face! Earth can be lit by a star when there is no moon.'
§535
Touching his mother's feet, strong-armed Meghnād bade farewell. The desolate queen withdrew to her own house,
Along with her daughter-in-law. Leaving the palanquin, the prince proceeded on foot through the forest—
Slowly and alone, along a flower-delineated path, towards the entrance of the place of sacrifice.
§541
Suddenly anklets jingled behind him—ah! instantly recognizable,
To a lover's ears, are the steps of his beloved! The hero smiled,
Joyously flung his arms round lotus-faced Pramilā. 'Alas, lord,'
She said, 'I thought I would go with you to the place of sacrifice—that I would then dress you for battle.

§524

May Siva, the guardian of the Rākshas race see Book II, §168.

Mā see II.144.

§535

flower-delineated path because worshippers carrying flowers for use in *pūjā* at the temple often drop petals along the way.

What can I do? My mother-in-law insists on confining me to her palace. But I could not stay without one more sight of your feet!
I have heard that the moon shines only because of the fire of the sun; that is true of me too, O sun of the Rākshas race.
Deprived of you, my world is dark, lord,
I tell you.' Her eyes rained down on to her pearl-adorned breast tears that were brighter than pearls! They made dewdrops on lotus petals seem pallid in comparison.

§557

The great warrior replied: 'I shall return, O diadem of Lankā,
After smashing Rāghav in battle! Go back, my love,
To Lankā's queen; Rohini appears, dear wife,
In advance of the moon. Did Fate, my treasure,
Make those lotus eyes for weeping? Why are dark clouds massing in those vessels of brightness? Let me go,
My beauty. See how rapidly Night is fading: duped by your radiance,
It thinks you are the dawn. Chaste wife, let me go to the place of sacrifice.'

§567

Like valiant, flower-arrowed Kāma leaving Rati behind—at Indra's command—

§557

Rohini see above, §439.

§567

Like valiant, flower-arrowed Kāma leaving Rati behind for the famous story of how Kāma—leaving his wife Rati behind—first made an unsuccessful attempt to break Siva out of his trance, see I.33, and for his second, successful attempt, see Book II of *MBK*, §265f.

In his ill-fated attempt to break Siva's trance, so, alas,
Did mighty Indrajit, handsome as Kāma, leave chaste
Pramilā,
Who was as beautiful as Rati! Kāma went at an
inauspicious time; so also did great Meghnād—
The hope of the Rākshas race, invincible in the world!
Who has the power,
Alas, to resist the workings of Fate? The youthful
Pramilā wept like Rati.

§577
Wiping her tears at last, she gazed at her husband
disappearing into the distance, and said gently:
'I know, O king of elephants, why you withdraw into
distant forests! You're ashamed to show your face,
On seeing my husband's gait! And who would call your
waste slim, O lion,
Who has set eyes on the lion of the Rākshasas? You too
slink away. You can kill an elephant;
That lion-hero with his massive weapons has vanquished
Indra, enemy of all demons, king of the gods.'

§588
Saying this, and pressing her palms together, faithful
Pramilā tearfully appealed to the sky:
'Pramilā your servant, O daughter of the king of the
mountains, implores you;
Turn your merciful gaze towards Lankā, O merciful one!
Protect the greatest of Rākshasas in this conflict!
Cover him with impenetrable armour! The creeper that
is always, chaste one,

§588
O daughter of the king of the mountains *nagendra-nandinī*: i.e. Durgā, whose father is Himavat (Himālaya). See II.287.

Under your protection, depends for its life on that great tree! Make sure,
Mother, that the tree suffers no axe-blow! What more shall I say? You are a reader of minds!
Who but you, O ruler of the world, can save him?'
§599
Like a breeze blowing a wealth of fragrance into a royal palace, the air carried Pramilā's plea to Mount Kailās.
Indra quaked in terror! At the sight of his fear, the lord of winds blew her words away with the speed of the wind!
Drying her eyes, chaste Pramilā made her way, like a pining milkmaid on the shore of the Yamunā returning with emptiness in her heart,
After saying goodbye to Krishna, to her empty abode. Tearfully she re-entered her mother-in-law's home.

Here ends 'The Undertaking',
the fifth book of *Meghnādbadh kābya.*

§599

Mount Kailās where Siva and Pārvati (Durgā) dwell. See I.33 and II.126.

lord of the winds *Vāyupati*: see I.114, 218.

like a pining milkmaid . . . Yamunā . . . Krishna see I.33, 623.

BOOK VI

§1

Leaving Chanḍi's grove, Lakshman, lion of warriors,
Returned to where Rām was waiting in his tent. Swiftly he went, like a hunter who has seen a lion in the forest,
And runs to his armoury to choose, for dangerous combat, his sharpest weapons.

§7

Arriving soon, falling at the feet of the great Raghu warrior, and greeting his chief adviser Vibhishan,
Wise Lakshman said: 'Through your blessing, Lord,
Your royal servant has been successful! Keeping you humbly in mind, I entered the grove,
And worshipped Chanḍi in her golden temple. How can I describe to you, limited as I am,
All the snares that she laid for me? Moon-crested Siva was on guard at the gate: through the force of your virtue,
Lord, he made way for me without giving fight, like a great snake fleeing when robbed of its strength by a powerful antidote!
Inside the grove, a roaring lion charged at me: I warded him off.
Then a mighty storm arose, with fearsome thunderclaps; a forest-fire like the end of the world filled the land;
Trees burned all around, till suddenly the fire died down of its own accord, and the wind-god vanished.

§1

Chanḍi's grove see V.113 and the events described in Book V, §189–§342.

great Raghu warrior i.e. Rām. See I.1, 406.

Vibhishan see I.218.

Moon-crested Siva see III.609.

Then I saw a crowd of divine forest-maidens before me: folding my hands, asking for their favour,
I bade them all farewell. The temple close by gleamed in the forest, lighting up the whole land.
I washed my body in a lake, then humbly worshipped the mother-goddess with an offering of blue lotuses. Māyā appeared,
And granted me a boon. Kindly she said: "The gods and goddesses are all pleased with you today,
O son of the chaste Sumitrā. Indra has sent you divine weapons. I myself have come here,
At Siva's command, to ensure that this task of yours is achieved. I tell you,
Take the divine weapons, and go with Vibhishan into the city, to Nikumbhilā,
The place of sacrifice, where Meghnād is worshipping Agni. Attack him suddenly like a tiger and kill him!
Through my favour, you will both be invisible as you enter. I shall cover you both,
Like a sword in its scabbard, with a web of illusion. Go with fearless heart,
O famous one!" Tell me, jewel of men,
What do you desire? Night is ending; there is no time to lose.
Will you order me, lord, to kill Meghnād?'

§47

The Raghu lord replied: 'Alas, how can I send you,
O more than life, into the hole of a snake from which all creatures flee like the wind, panting in terror of their lives,

§7

Māyā see II.425, 309.

son of chaste Sumitrā see I.172.

Nikumbhilā,/ The place of sacrifice where Meghnād is worshipping Agni see I.751 and V.61, 409.

As soon as they see that messenger of death? His poison annihilates gods and men! What point is there in trying to rescue Sitā?
Vainly, O ocean, did I bind you with stone!
I have killed innumerable Rākshasas in battle; I have brought Sugriv with his army to this golden city; a stream of blood,
Alas, like monsoon water, has drenched the earth to no purpose!
I lost, through ill luck, kingdom,
Wealth, father, mother and friends;
Only Sitā was left like a lamp in a dark house, and now (O Fate,
What fault am I guilty of before you?) misfortune has extinguished her! Who else in my family do I have left,
Brother? Whose face, when I see it,
Keeps me alive, makes my existence bearable? Let us go back,
Let us live in the forest again, Lakshman! Evil was the time,
Brother, that we came to this Rākshas city, lured by false hope.'

§68

To this the lion-like son of Sumitrā responded with hero's pride: 'Why, O Lord of the Rāghavas,
Are you so frightened? Who in the three worlds can alarm one who is empowered by the gods?
Thousand-eyed Indra,

§47

Vainly, O ocean, did I bind you with stone! see I.285 and IV.491, and Source Notes, p. 355. **Sugriv** see I.218. **lured by false hope** see Source Notes, p. 356.

§68

O Lord of the Rāghavas see II.576. **Thousand-eyed Indra** see V.478.

King of the gods, is on your side; and Kailās-dwelling Siva;
And mountain-born Durgā, promoter of *dharma*! Look towards Lankā:
Divine anger envelops its golden splendour with black clouds! But see how the gods light up your tent with their smiles, Lord!
Order me to take your divine weapons into the Rākshas abode. By your grace, I shall certainly kill Meghnād.
You are the wisest of men. Why do you spurn a divine behest? You move always along the path of *dharma*.
Why do you act today in a way that is against *dharma*, master? Should anyone anywhere stamp a holy water-vessel to pieces?'

§84

The noble Vibhishan said soothingly: 'What he has told you is true, O Rāghav chief.
Rāvan's son Meghnād is like a terrible messenger of death when he attacks, invincible in the world, the terror of Indra.
But there is no need to fear him today. I saw in a dream, O jewel of the Raghus,
The guardian goddess of the Rākshas race. She sat at my pillow,
Lighting the tent, Lord, with her pure radiance,
And said: "Alas, your brother is wild with war-lust,

§68

Kailās-dwelling Siva see I.33 and II.126. **Mountain-born Durgā** see II.287. **promoter of *dharma*** see II.173, 217 and Introduction, pp. liv–lvi. **Should anyone anywhere stamp a holy water-vessel to pieces?** i.e. not to rescue Sitā by destroying Meghnād would be like smashing a holy water-vessel, because she is herself the vessel of all virtues.

§84

invincible in the world, the terror of Indra see I.1. **the guardian goddess of the Rākshas race** i.e. Lakshmi. See I.472.

Vibhishan! What wish do I have to stay in this place of sin, hater of sin that I am!
Can a lotus bloom in filthy water? Whoever sees stars in a cloud-covered sky? But because of your actions in past lives,
The gods are gracious towards you. You will gain the empty throne of Lankā, with its sceptre and royal unbrella!
As decreed by Fate, I anoint you today as lord of the Rākshas race, O famous one!
Tomorrow the leonine son of Sumitrā will kill your nephew Meghnād; you will assist him! Follow carefully the commands of the gods,
O future king of the Rākshasas!" I woke; I saw that the tent was full of heavenly fragrance;
I heard sweet heavenly music, far off in the sky. At the door of the tent I beheld,
With wonder, Lakshmi, the goddess whose beauty would infatuate even Madan.
A beautiful plait covered her neck like a bank of clouds; in her hair glittered jewels, compared to which—
Ah!—lightning flashing through clouds would be pallid. Suddenly that mother of the world vanished.
I stood for a long time with thirsting eyes, but my longings came to naught—the goddess did not reappear!
Mark all of this well, son of Dasarath. Order me to go with Lakshman,
To the sacrificial place where Meghnād is worshipping

§84

As decreed by Fate *bidhir bidhāne*: cf. I.80, 269, 356, IV.448, 531, V.57 and Introduction, pp. lv–lvi. **Madan** i.e. Kāma, god of love. See I.483. **son of Dasarath** i.e. Rām. See I.172.

Agni. O guide of men, follow well the guidance of the gods!
I assure you, supreme Rāghav, that you will achieve your goal.'

§123

Sitā's lord answered with tears in his eyes: 'When I think about former times, O finest of Rākshasas,
My soul weeps with anguish! How can I throw this jewel of a brother into bottomless water? Alas,
My friend, when Queen Kaikeyi, fated to be cruel by my own ill fortune,
Acted on Mantharā's evil advice; and when I, upholding the honour of my father,
Abandoned the pleasures of the kingdom; my beloved brother, impelled by fraternal love,
Willingly left them too! His mother Sumitrā wept! The piercing wails of his wife Urmilā could be heard from the purdah-quarters.
And all the citizens—how can I describe how they begged him not to go? He paid no heed;
He followed me joyfully to the forest, like a shadow, blithely sacrificing his tender youth.

§84

supreme Rāghav see I.1.

§123

when Queen Kaikeyi . . . Mantharā's evil advice Kaikeyi, one of Dasarath's three wives (see I.172), was urged by her malicious maidservant Mantharā to persuade Dasarath to install Bharat (Kaikeyi's son) as crown prince instead of Rām (son of Kaikeyi's co-wife and rival Queen Kausalyā), and to send Rām into exile for fourteen years. **upholding the honour of my father** i.e. by carrying out his command. Even when Dasarath died, and Bharat sought out the exiled Rām to urge him to take over as king, Rām insisted on remaining in exile for the full fourteen years. **my beloved brother** i.e. Lakshman. **Urmilā** see I.1.

His mother Sumitrā said, "You have stolen the jewel of my eye, Rāghav!
Who knows with what sorcery you have enchanted my darling? I have sacrificed this treasure to you. I beg you to look after him well."

§143

'It is useless, O finest of counsellors, to try to rescue Sitā:
Let us return to the forest! Meghnād, chief of charioteers,
Terror of gods and men and demons, is invincible in battle! Mighty-armed Sugriv;
The good Prince Angad, so skilled in fighting; son-of-the-wind Hanumān,
Fierce in attack as his father; Dhumrāksha, fiery as a comet on the battlefield;
Nala and Nila; Kesari, who attacks his enemies like a lion;
And all the other warriors, godlike in looks, godlike in courage;
And you too, great warrior; if with all this support I cannot stop Meghnād,
Then how can Lakshman alone fight him? Thus I say, alas,
It is with illusory hope, O friend, that we have crossed the uncrossable sea.'

§158

Suddenly, in the sky, sky-born Sarasvati boomed out sweetly:

§143

Sugriv . . . Prince Angad . . . son-of-the-wind Hanumān see I.218.

Dhumrāksha a general in Hanumān's monkey-army whose name means 'smoke-eyed'.

Nala and Nila see I.218 and IV.464, 491.

Kesari another general in Hanumān's army. His name means 'lion-maned'.

§158

Sky-born Sarasvati see I.1. All the gods are, in a sense, 'sky-born', but Sarasvati as the goddess of poetry, music, speech and all the fine arts, as inventor of Sanskrit and its divine script *Devanāgarī*, and as the spouse of

'What right have you, tell me, O Lord of Sitā,
To doubt the message of the gods, loved by the gods as you are? Why,
I say, do you go against heavenly advice? Look at the sky.'
The Raghu king looked at the sky in wonder, saw a peacock fighting with a snake. As its squawks mingled with the snake's hisses,
The land all around was filled with a terrifying noise! The shadow of its wings covered the sky like massed clouds—while deadly poison,
Fierce as annihilating fire, flashed in its midst! Both fought ferociously!
The earth quaked continuously with terror; the ocean swelled tumultuously! Soon the peacock fell lifeless to the ground,
And the snake, victorious in battle, deafeningly hissed.
§174
Rāvan's brother said: 'You have seen with your own eyes a wondrous event today; it is not without meaning,
I tell you, O husband of Sitā, mark this well.
It is not just a phantom: by this portent, the gods have shown you that lion-like Lakshman will strip Lankā of her hero today!'
§180
Then the jewel of the Raghu race entered his tent and armed his beloved brother with the divine weapons. Ah! he shone,

---

the creator-god Brahmā, has for M especially high status. Cf. his invocation to her at the beginning of Book I.

a peacock fighting with a snake see Source Notes, p. 357.

§174

Rāvan's brother i.e. Vibhishan. See I.218.

§180

the divine weapons see Book III, §576f.

That handsome warrior, like Skanda, slayer of Tārak!
He put on a breastplate, studded with stars; a dazzling bejewelled sword glittered in its scabbard,
A shield wide as the sun shone on his back—carved out of ivory, plated with gold;
A quiver hung with it, full of arrows. In his left hand,
The great bowman clasped a heavenly bow; on his head, a helmet gleamed
(As if made of sunbeams); a tuft on the helmet quivered, like a mane quivering on a lion!
Rām's brother armed himself joyfully, fire-bright, like the sun in the afternoon.
§196
The hero strode speedily from the camp—eager, like a horse when it hears war-trumpets,
And thunderous waves of battle roll. The hero emerged, and with him came Vibhishan,
In warrior's dress, fearsome in battle! The gods rained down flowers;
Festive welcoming music rang out through the sky; air-borne nymphs danced; heaven and earth and hell filled with the noise of victory!
§204
Gazing at the sky and with cupped hands, the Raghu chief said in prayer: 'Humble Rāghav asks Durgā's lotus-feet for protection today!
Do not forget, goddess, this servant of yours!
The trials I have suffered, mother, in upholding *dharma,*
Are not unknown to your rosy feet. Feed the fruits of *dharma,* O beloved of Siva,

§180

Skanda, slayer of Tārak Skanda is another name of the god of war, Kārttikeya. See II.491.

To this wretched petitioner! Guard, chaste one,
In battle with Meghnād, the brother who is more than life to me, young Lakshman!
O Deliveress, by stamping on the fearsome demon Mahish, you saved the gods!
Save your servant, O trampler of Mahish, by trampling on a wild Rākshas!'

§216

The enemy of the Rākshasas prayed to the goddess thus. Like a breeze flowing fragrance into a palace, the air carried Rām's prayer,
Up to Mount Kailās. King Indra smiled in heaven; at once the wind blew the words even faster.
Hearing that pious prayer, mountain-daughter Durgā accepted it joyfully, and gave her blessing.

§224

Dawn arose smilingly, like hope, ah!
When it banishes sorrow from a darkened heart. Birds twittered in the glades; honey-feeding bees buzzed all around;
Night withdrew gently with her company of stars; on dawn's brow a single star shone with the brightness of a hundred stars! A string of new stars bloomed in her hair like flowers!
Turning to Vibhishan, finest of Rākshasas, Rāghav said:
'Go carefully, friend. Wretched Rām commits to your care his most precious jewel,
O master-charioteer! No more words need be wasted; today my life and death are in your hands.'

§237

The mighty Vibhishan encouraged the master-archer:

§204

by stamping on the fearsome demon Mahish see II.400 and V.113.

'You are loved by the gods, O jewel of the race of Raghu.
Whom do you fear, master? The hero Lakshman will certainly kill in battle the mighty Meghnād.'

§241

Touching Rām's feet, Lakshman departed, together with friendly Vibhishan.
Thick clouds surrounded them both. As if in a dismal freezing mist enveloping a mountain-peak when night ends, the two of them made their way invisibly towards Lankā.

§246

Dressed as a Rākshas wife, Māyā-devi now entered the golden temple where Kamalā—guardian goddess of the Rākshas race—
Sat on a lotus-throne. The lovely beloved of Vishnu smiled and said: 'Why,
Great goddess, have you come to this city? What,
O sportive one, tell me, is your desire?'

§251

All-commanding Māyā smiled sweetly and answered: 'Restrain your power today, daughter of the ocean;
The godlike charioteer Lakshman will enter this golden city; he will kill, at Siva's behest,
In the Nikumbhilā place of sacrifice, the proud Meghnād. Your power is like annihilating fire,

§241

Thick clouds surrounded them both because of the protection that Māyā-devi is giving them.

§246

Kamalā—guardian goddess of the Rākshas race i.e. Lakshmi. See I.472.

The lovely beloved of Vishnu *Keśab-bāsanā*: see I.483.

§251

daughter of the ocean Lakshmi was one of the 'fourteen jewels' produced by the churning of the ambrosial ocean. See I.513, 295.

O powerful one; what enemy can enter this city? I implore you,
Goddess, be gracious towards Rāghav! Save,
By your boon, righteous Rām from danger, O beloved of Mādhav!'

§262

Kamalā sighed sadly and said, 'Who, O worship of the world,
Has power to refuse your command? But how my soul weeps when it thinks of all that has happened! Alas,
The devotion with which that most excellent of Rākshasas—and his queen Mandodari—worship me,
What words would describe it? But the fount of the Rākshas race is drowning through his own fault! Goddess,
I shall restrain my power; who can prevent the consequences of past actions? Tell Lakshman that he can enter the city without fear.
I gladly grant this boon: the valiant son of Sumitrā will destroy Meghnād, the invincible son of Mandodari!'

§269

The beautiful beloved of Vishnu moved off to Lankā's west gate, like a flower when it blooms at dawn, wet with dew-drops!
On she went, followed by Māyā. Banana trees wilted;
Pots of holy water broke; earth drank up the water!
Lankā's glories were quickly reabsorbed into Kamalā's rosy feet,

§251

Mādhav another name for Vishnu/Krishna.

§262

Mandodari see I.172.

through his own fault . . . the consequences of past actions *nij-doṣe . . . prāktaner gati*: for this crucial moral principle in *MBK*, see Introduction, pp. lii–liii.

Like the moon's rays re-entering the rays of the sun, at
the end of night. The beauty of Lankā vanished,
As the beauty of a cobra vanishes when it loses its
adorning jewel! Distant clouds suddenly rumbled
with sonorous thunder; the sky wept torrents of
rain;
The ocean heaved; the earth quaked—in anguish at your
plight,
O Lankā, world's ornament, city of gold!

§288

The two ascended the city wall and saw, not far off, the
godlike Lakshman,
Like the sun-god covered by a storm, or like fire enveloped
in smoke! The noble Vibhishan accompanied him—
Like wind accompanying fire—fearsome in battle. Alas,
Who will protect Meghnād today, the hope of the
Rākshasas? Like a tiger in a dense forest,
When he spots a fine stag, and slinks into the
undergrowth, seeking his chance;
Or a deadly crocodile, when he sees a distant bather in
the river, and speeds towards him invisibly;
So the valiant Lakshman, with his friend Vibhishan,
advanced swiftly to slay the Rākshas.

§302

Sighing with grief, bidding farewell to Māyā, chaste
Kamalā returned to her temple.
How Vishnu's beloved wept! Earth happily lapped up
her tears, like an oyster from whose essence priceless
pearls flower,
Carefully drinking your tears, O clouds, when the chaste
star Svāti shines in the sky!

§302

Svāti one of twenty-seven stars who are the wives of Chandra, the

§309

The two heroes entered the city, empowered by powerful Māyā. The gates opened thunderously at a touch from Lakshman.

But whose ears did the noise enter? Alas, the Rākshas guards were all blinded by Māyā's trickery;

None of them saw those two enemies, fearsome as Death's messengers; the snake invaded the flowers by stealth!

§316

Amazed, Lakshman beheld from the gate the fourfold army all around: mahouts on elephants,

Cavalry on horseback, charioteers in chariots, infernal infantry on the ground—

Frighteningly warlike in appearance, unbeatable in battle! Their brilliant lustre rose into the sky like annihilating fire.

§322

The hero beheld in terror the great Rākshas Virupāksha, bright as hell's fire, brandishing a mighty iron javelin,

---

moon. It is said that if, at the times when she is with her husband, rain falls on the ocean, oysters drink it up and make pearls out of it.

§309

by stealth *kauśale*. See I.1 and V.29.

§316

fourfold army *caturaṅga*: i.e. the 'four-limbed' army that in Hindu tradition is considered to be complete. It consists of elephants, cavalry, chariots and infantry.

Frighteningly warlike in appearance *bhīmākṛti bhīmbirya*: i.e. like Bhimā in appearance (a name for Durgā in her warlike aspect). See Source Notes, p. 358.

§322

Virupāksha . . . Tāljangha . . . Ranpriya . . . Pramatta . . . these particular Rākshasas are given descriptive epithets appropriate to their names, which mean, respectively, 'having deformed eyes', 'having legs as long as palm (*tāl*) tree', 'battle-loving', 'drunken'. Cf. I.575, III.487.

Riding in a colourful chariot; and the hero Tāljangha, tall as a *tāl*-tree,
Mighty as club-wielding Vishnu; and elephant-riding Kālnemi, massive destroyer of enemies;
And Ranpriya, expert in warfare; and Pramatta,
Constantly drunk with valour; and Chikshur, mighty as the Lord of the Yakshas;
And all the other warriors, the perpetual terror of gods and demons and men! Slowly,
Slowly, the two advanced; Lakshman observed hundreds of golden buildings on either side,
And temples and shops; and gardens, lakes and fountains;
Horses and elephants in stables; countless fire-coloured chariots; armouries;
Elegant theatre-halls, studded with gems—ah!
A city like heaven! Who can describe all the glories of Lankā, the desire of the gods,
The envy of the demons? Who can count the jewels in the ocean, or the stars in the sky?

§341

In the middle of the city the hero saw with wonder the king's royal palace. Rows of gold and diamond pillars shone; towers reached up to the sky;
Gleaming like the peaks of Hemkuṭ! Doors and windows sparkled with the beauty of gold and ivory, charming to the eye—
Like sunbeams sparkling on frost at dawn! Renowned

§322

Kālnemi in *MBK* he is the father of Meghnād's wife Pramilā. See I.575 and III.413.

Chikshur, mighty as the Lord of the Yakshas another Rākshas, compared here to Kuber, Rāvan's elder half-brother. See I.62.

§341

the peaks of Hemkuṭ see I.33.

Lakshman turned to the noble Vibhishan and said, 'O best of the Rākshasas,
Your elder brother is favoured among kings, an ocean of greatness in the world. Oh who on this earth is as glorious as he?'

§353

The mighty Vibhishan heaved a sorrowful sigh and said: 'What you say is true, jewel of heroes!
Who on this earth is as glorious as he? But nothing lasts for ever in this world; that one should go and another should come is the law of the world,
Like the waves of the sea! Come quickly and complete your purpose by killing Meghnād; O charioteer,
By drinking the nectar of fame, lord, achieve immortality!'

§361

The two proceeded swiftly, invisible through Māyā's grace. The Rākshas wives whom Lakshman saw by the edge of lakes,
Colourful pitchers at their hips, smiles on their sweet lips, would shame the loveliest of deer-eyed women!
Lotus flowers were blooming in the dawn streams! Here and there charioteers were emerging rapidly, awesome in appearance;
Breastplated footsoldiers left their flowery beds; horns were being blown, breaking sleep with their blast;
Grooms prepared horses; elephants roared, brandishing clubs with their trunks,
Pearl-tasselled silk liveries gleaming on their backs. Charioteers carefully loaded various weapons into gold-bannered chariots. In the temples,
Dawn music played—enchanting, ah!

As the music of *holi* in Bengali homes, when the gods appear on earth to worship Lakshmi's husband! Plucking flowers,
Flower-maidens wandered here and there, enriching the streets with flower-fragrance, spreading light all round with their beauty,
Like Dawn, the friend of flowers! In other places porters bustled,
Loaded with curds and milk. Gradually the hubbub increased; all the citizens of the city woke up.
Some said, 'Come, oh come,
Let us climb to the city-walls. We shall not get a place if we do not go early, to watch such amazing fighting.
Let us feast our eyes on seeing the Prince in his battle-dress, and all the other great heroes.' Some of them answered haughtily,
'What point is there, pray, in going to the walls?
The Prince will destroy Rām in a trice, and the young Lakshman: who in the world can withstand his arrows?
He will burn up his enemies, like fire burning dry grass, trampler of enemies that he is!
He will punish his uncle Vibhishan with his mighty blows and bind up that the scoundrel. He is certain to come victoriously to receive the king's salutation: let us go to the audience-hall!'

§397

What more can the poet say of all that the hero heard, all that he saw? Smiling in his mind,

§361

holi *deb-dol-utsab*: the swing festival when the child Krishna is swung in a *dol* or swing, and people throw coloured power at each other, in imitation of Krishna sporting with the Gopis (see I.33). **Lakshmi's husband** i.e. Vishnu's incarnation Krishna. See I.483. **the Prince** *yubarāj*: i.e. Meghnād.

Renowned Lakshman proceeded, godlike in valour and
appearance, bearing his divine weapons,
Accompanied by Vibhishan, the valiant charioteer. The
temple in the Nikumbhilā grove gleamed not far off.

§401

On a seat of *kuś*-grass, Meghnād worshipped in
seclusion his *iṣṭadeva;* dressed in silk,
With a silk *cādar,* a sandalpaste mark on his brow, a
garland round his neck.
Incense glowed in the censer; lamps of holy ghee shone
all around; there were piles of flowers,
And, with its spoon, a boat-shaped *koṣā* made of
rhinocerous-horn,
And full of your water, O Gangā, purger of sin!
To one side, there was a golden bell, and various
presents on gold dishes;
The door was closed—the hero sat alone, like Siva,
Lord of Yoga, immersed in meditation, on the high peak
of Mount Kailās!

§413

Through the power of Māyā, and like a ravenous tiger

§401

kuś-grass a type of grass with long pointed leaves that is regarded as sacred.

iṣṭadeva see I.743, 751, 1.

cādar a a sheet of cloth carried over the shoulder or worn round the shoulders like a shawl.

ghee clarified butter. Because of its purity, it is crucial in Hindu rituals, and is offered as oblation into the sacred fire.

koṣā a vessel shaped like a canoe that is used in Hindu rituals.

Gangā the river Ganges, sacred to all Hindus. All these accoutrements emphasise what a devout Hindu Meghnād is. See Introduction, pp. lxxxiii-lxxxiv.

Siva, Lord of Yoga *Yogīndra*: name for Siva as the Great Ascetic, renowned for his feats of *tapas*. See II.168.

entering a cow-byre like a messenger of death,
mighty-armed Lakshman entered the temple.
His sword gleamed in its scabbard; his quiver banged against his shield; the temple shook as it filled with the sound of his warlike tread!

§418

Meghnād opened his prayer-closed eyes in alarm. He saw the godlike charioteer in front of him—brilliant as the sun-god at mid-day!
Prostrating his body in obeisance, the champion cupped his hands and said: 'O God of Fire,
Your servant has worshipped you at the right time today: this is why, Lord,
You have honoured the city of Lankā today with your feet! But tell me, why,
O fiery one, have you come to honour your servant in the form of Lakshman, the enemy of the Raksha race?
What game of yours is this, O shining one?' The warrior bowed right down to the ground again.

§429

Furious, Dasarath's son answered with warlike pride: 'Son of Rāvan,
I am not the god of fire—look at me closely! Lakshman is my name,
Born to the lineage of Raghu! I have come here, O lion-hero,

§418

Prostrating his body in obeisance thinking that Lakshman is the god Agni himself, Meghād does a *praṇām* or obeisance *sāṣṭāṅge*, i.e. with 'eight limbs', hands, breast, forehead, knees and feet.

cupped his hands *kṛtāñjali-puṭe*: i.e. with palms held forward and cupped, the gesture that in Hindu tradition indicates a sacred and humble offering, though this expression is also often used by M for the placing of the palms together in a gesture of greeting or *namaskār*.

To subdue you in battle. Fight with me at once.' Like a wayfarer when he suddenly sees a king cobra on the path with raised hood,
And is paralysed with fear, so the warrior stared at Lakshman! His fearless heart was frightened today—
Molten like a ball of iron in a furnace, alas! Rāhu had swallowed the sun,
Had suddenly darkened his glory! Drought had sucked up the ocean! Kali had entered Nala's body by deceit!

§442

In amazement the champion answered, 'If you are truly the brother of Rām, then tell me,
O charioteer, by what deceit have you entered today the city of the Raksha king? Hundreds of Rākshasas,
Whose strength would frighten the lord of the Yakshas, are guarding the city-gates, mighty weapons in their hands.
The wall of this city is high as a mountain; ten thousand soldiers patrol that wall, circle within circle;

§429

Rāhu has swallowed the sun see II.400.

Kali had entered Nala's body by deceit! An allusion to the famous story of Nala and Damayanti. The beautiful princess wanted to marry King Nala, but several of the gods wanted to marry her too. They asked Nala to convey this to her, and he obligingly did so. Damayanti then arranged a *svayambar* (see III.271), to which the gods came disguised as Nala, but she was able to pick out the real Nala nonetheless. The gods accepted this, but Kali—a personification of evil who is also the losing single spot on a dice and the name for the fourth and most degenerate of *yugas* or ages in the history of the world—thought that Nala had betrayed the gods. He entered his body, which made him addicted to dice-playing, so that he lost his kingdom and everything he owned, except for the faithful Damayanti. (Nala here is not the warrior Nala from Kishkindhyā who fought for Rām: see IV.464.)

§442

Whose strength would frighten even the lord of the Yakshas cf. Book I, §62, in which the Rākshas Makarāksha is described as 'equal to the lord of the Yakshas' (Kuber).

Through what magic power, pray, have you bamboozled them?
What fighter is there in this world, born of men or of gods, who can defeat single-handed such a mass of Rākshasas?
So why, I ask you, are you fooling your servant with this deception,
O Agni, consumer of all? What are you playing at,
O playful one? Lakshman is not invisible, O Lord;
How can he enter this temple? See, the door is still closed!
Grant a boon, lord, to this servant:
May I free Lankā of fear by killing Rāghav today; may I drive far away the king of Kishkindhyā; may I bring that traitor Vibhishan to the feet of King Rāvan in chains.
Listen to the battle-trumpets sounding all around! The zeal of Raksha army will fade if I delay; permit me to go.'
§464
The godlike lion-hero Lakshman replied: 'I am your destroyer, O fierce son of Rāvan!
A snake crawls through the grass to bite a doomed man! You are mad with battle-lust, strong through the strength of the gods—
Yet you often show contempt for the gods! Your wickedness has brought you down at last. Come,
I invite you, by divine command, to fight.'
§471
With these words, the hero unsheathed his lethal sword. Dazzling to the eyes as annihilating fire,
That sword of swords shone like the lightning-filled thunderbolt in Indra's hand! Meghnād said, 'If you are truly Rām's brother,

§442
King of Kishkindhyā i.e. Sugriv. See I.218.

Mighty-armed Lakshman, I shall certainly fully meet your desire for battle; has Indrajit ever been unwilling to fight?
But first, O finest of warriors, stay and take a guest's refreshment in this house—
You are the enemy of the Rākshasas, yet you are now a guest. Let me put on my armour.
It is not the custom of warriors to fight an unarmed enemy; this rule, O excellent hero,
Is not unknown to you. You are a Kshatriya: what more need I say?'

§485

Lakshman roared like thunder in reply: 'If a hunter finds a tiger in a trap, does he ever release him?
I shall kill you now, you fool! You are born of the Raksha race;
Why should I observe the Kshatriya code with you, O Sinner? Let me kill my enemy by whatever trick I can!'

§491

The vanquisher of Indra spoke, as red-hot in his anger as Abhimanyu when he faced the seven

§471

Indrajit see I.1.

Kshatriya the second of the four *varṇas*—the main 'colours' or caste-divisions of Hindu society. They are the kingly or warrior caste, and to attack Meghnād while he is engaged in a sacred ritual and before he has a chance to arm is an outrage to the Kshatriya code of behaviour. See Introduction, pp. lv–lvi.

§485

trick *kauśal*: see I.1, V.29 and above, §309.

§491

Abhimanyu famous warrior and hero in the *Mahābhārata*, Arjun's son by Subhadrā, tragically killed by the Kauravas in the battle of Kurukshetra. See Source Notes, p. 359.

Kaurava charioteers: 'O blot on the Kshatriya clan,
A hundred curses on you, Lakshman! You are shameless!
At the sound of your name, all Kshatriya warriors will block their ears in horror! You have entered this house like a thief,
I shall finish you off now with a thief's punishment. If a snake enters Garuḍa's nest, does it ever,
O sinner, return to its own hole? Who brought you in your villainy here today?'

§502

In the blink of an eye, the mighty armed one picked up the *koṣā* vessel and hurled it at Lakshman, roaring terribly.
The hero fell to the ground with the force of the impact, like a mighty tree crashing down in a storm! His divine weapons clattered,
And the temple rocked, as if from a huge earthquake! A stream of blood flowed.
Meghnād instantly seized the divine sword—but he could not lift it. He pulled at the bow—
It remained in Lakshman's hand. He angrily grasped the shield, but his efforts were useless.
As vainly as an elephant wrapping his trunk round an outcrop of rock and trying to pull it, that greatest of heroes dragged at the quiver. Who in the world can fathom the magic power of Māyā?

§491

the seven Kaurava charioteers i.e. Drona, Kripa, Karna, Asvatthāman, Duhsāsan, Sakuni and Jayadrath, who surrounded Abhimanyu in battle and killed him.

Garuḍa's nest see I.218, 743.

With wounded pride, proud Meghnād looked towards the door. In horror he saw before him—
With a terrifying axe in his hand—his uncle Vibhishan, ominous as a comet and fearsome in battle!
§520
'At last I know,' grieved the vanquisher of enemies, 'how Lakshman has entered the Raksha city!
Alas, uncle, are your actions right?
The virtuous Nikashā is your mother! The Rākshas chief is your brother! And Siva-like Kumbhakarna too!
Your nephew is the vanquisher of Indra! Would you show a thief how to enter your own home, uncle?
Would you seat a *caṇḍāl* in a king's palace? But I shall not insult you, senior as you are to me,
Equal to my father. Open the door; I shall go to my armoury;
I shall send Rām's brother to Death's abode. I shall rid Lankā of shame today, through combat.'
§532
Vibhishan answered, 'Clever though you are, this aim of yours is futile!
I am Rāghav's follower: how can I be persuaded to act against him?' Meghnād answered in anguish,
'O uncle, your words make me want to die! Can you be Rāghav's follower?

§502

with wounded pride *abhimāne*: it is notoriously difficult to translate the Bengali concept of *abhimān*, which is a combination of pride and hurt feelings—often a feeling of being hurt by someone you love. It is the betrayal by his uncle Vibhishan that is particularly hurtful to Meghnād's feelings.

§520

Nikashā see I.62.

Kumbhakarna see I.80.

caṇḍāl i.e. someone from the lowest castes, entrusted with burning the dead or executing criminals; an untouchable.

How can you bring such a thing to your lips? O tell me, uncle!
Fate has ordained that the moon be placed on Siva's brow; does the moon then fall and roll in the dust? O Raksha warrior,
How can you forget who you are, or the noble line into which you were born, or how low-born Rām is?
A swan is at ease on a pure lake, in a lotus garden; does it ever,
Lord, swim in muddy waters, to dwell with scum?
Does a lion—king of beasts—O lion of heroes,
Ever converse on friendly terms with a jackal? I am ignorant; you are wise;
Everything is known to you. Lakshman is a mean-minded man, O hero:
Would he attack an unarmed warrior otherwise? Tell me, O great charioteer,
Is this the custom of warriors? There is not a child in Lankā who would not laugh at such an idea! Let me pass;
I shall return immediately! We shall see today by what divine force wicked Lakshman will face me in battle. You have seen with your own eyes,
O finest of Rākshasas, my fighting strength against gods or demons or men! What is there in this feeble man to frighten me?
He has arrogantly entered the Nikumbhilā temple; command me to punish him for his insolence! Uncle,

§532

Fate has ordained that the moon be placed on Siva's brow cf. III.609.

how low-born Rām is? because—especially in M's interpretation of the *Rāmāyaṇa* story—Rām is a *nar* or human being, not a god, even though Hindu tradition has also regarded him as as the seventh incarnation of Vishnu. See Introduction, pp. lxix–lxx.

A forest-dweller has set foot in the city of your birth! O
God, an evil devil is at large in your paradise garden!
A worm has penetrated a full-bloomed lotus! Tell me, uncle,
How (son of your brother that I am) shall I bear such shame?
And how can you, O jewel of the Rākshasas, bear it?'

§568

Like a snake brought low by the power of a mighty
mantra, pale-faced with shame, Rāvan's brother
answered Rāvan's son:
'It is not my fault, my dear; you are wrong to berate me!
Through his own sinful actions is the King sinking
golden Lankā, alas, and sinking himself!
The gods are always opposed to sin; and now the city of
Lankā is full of sin; like the earth at the time of its
destruction,
Lankā is drowning in a sea of death! I have thus sought
Rāghav's protection in order to save my soul! Who
wants to die through another's wrong-doing?'

§579

The terror of Indra grew furious! Like a thunder-cloud roaring
angrily in the sky at night, the hero of heroes said:
'You are renowned throughout the world, O brother of
the Rākshas king, for following the path of *dharma*.
By what sense of *dharma*—tell me, I am listening—

§568

mantra technically, the Mantras are part of the Vedas (see IV.175), but the term is also used for any sacred verse used in Hindu ceremonies or rituals. Here it conveys the immense moral power of Meghnād's passionate complaint to his uncle in the previous paragraph.

Through his own sinful actions *nij karma-doṣe*: see Introduction, pp. lii–liii.

§579

The terror of Indra i.e. Meghnād as Indrajit, the vanquisher of Indra. See I.1.

Do you sacrifice utterly kinship, fraternity, lineage?
The Sāstras say: "If an enemy is virtuous, and a kinsman is without virtue,
Nevertheless a virtueless kinsman is best—an enemy is always an enemy!" O best of Rākshasas,
Where have you learnt the evil you are doing? But it is futile to rebuke you! In such company,
O uncle, who would not learn such barbarism? He who keeps low company becomes low himself!'

§592

Through Māyā's aid, Lakshman now recovered consciousness, and noisily twanged his bowstring.
He aimed and shot a viciously sharp arrow at the invincible Indrajit, like the great archer Kārttikeya shooting a shower of arrows at Tārak! Alas,
A stream of blood flowed (like a stream pouring down a hill during the monsoon) drenching his clothes,
Drenching the ground! Writhing in pain, the hero grabbed at the conch,
Bell, votive dishes, everything that was there in the place of sacrifice,
And hurled them furiously one after another—like the warrior Abhimanyu, weaponless in battle through the might of the seven charioteers,
When he hurled his chariot-crest, his chariot-wheels, his broken sword,
Torn shield, ripped armour, whatever he could grasp!

§579

Sāstras the Hindu scriptures, both *śruti*—'heard' or revealed, i.e. the Vedas—or *smṛti*—'remembered' texts considered to be of purely human origin.

§592

Kārttikeya . . . Tārak see I.689, II.491.

Abhimanyu . . . seven charioteers see above, VI.491.

But wonder-working Māyā, by the might of her arm, deflected them all,
Like a mother driving away mosquitoes from her sleeping son, with a sweep of her lotus-hand!
Meghnād rushed at Lakshman,
Bellowing with rage—like a lion when he sees beaters encircling him! Through Māyā's sorcery,
He saw, all around him, awesome Death on his terrifying buffalo,
Siva holding his trident, four-armed Vishnu with his conch and discus and club. In terror,
He saw the whole race of gods riding in their beautiful vehicles. Sighing in grief, he stood dispirited,
Like the moon at the jaws of Rāhu, alas, or a lion caught in a trap!
§621
Casting his bow aside, Rām's brother unsheathed his lethal sword: its flashing blade dazzled the eyes!
Alas, it blinded the invincible warrior Meghnād, and with one blow of the sword he fell to the ground,
Wet with blood. The earth trembled; the sea surged and roared;
The universe was suddenly filled with terrifying noise! In heaven, on earth and in the nether world,
Creatures both mortal and immortal were thrown into a panic! Rāvan's golden crown suddenly slipped from his head, as he sat on his gilded throne,
Like a chariot-crest when an enemy cuts it to the

§592

awesome Death on his terrifying buffalo Yama, god of death, rides a buffalo, called Mahish here, and therefore identifiable with the buffalo-demon that Durgā slew. See II.400.

Like the moon in the jaws of Rāhu see II.400.

ground. The Lord of Lankā prayed in alarm to Siva!
 Pramilā's right eye fluttered!
Forgetting herself, alas, she suddenly rubbed out the
 vermilion mark on her beautiful forehead!
Mandodari, queen of the Rākshasas, fainted in horror!
Babies, sleeping in their mother's laps, cried out loudly:
Like the children of Vraj, when radiant Krishna,
 darkening the land, departed for Madhupur!

§642

Falling in unfair combat, the scourge of the foes of the
 Asuras, the hope of the Rākshasas,
Said in harsh tones to Lakshman: 'You are a blot on the
 race of warriors, O son of Sumitrā!
A hundred curses on you! I am Rāvan's son—I do not
 fear death!
But oh what perpetual pain it will be in my mind, O
 miscreant, that I died today from your sword's blow!

§621

Rāvan's golden crown suddenly slipped from his head . . . Pramilā's right eye fluttered!/ Forgetting herself, alas, she suddenly rubbed out the vermilion mark on her beautiful forehead!/ Mandodari . . . fainted in horror all these are very inauspicious signs of the loss of power and sovereignty that will arise from the dastardly slaying of Meghnād, Rāvan's noblest son. In Indian tradition, if a woman's right eye flutters it is inauspicious; if her left eye flutters it is auspicious. For men, it is the other way round.

Vraj the area where Krishna grew up and sported with the Gopis. See I.33.

departed for Madhupur another name for Mathurā, whose wicked king Kams is Krishna's uncle (M may have liked the name because of the pun on his name: see I.1 and Introduction, pp. xvii–xviii). Kams tries to have Krishna slain when he is born, but he is smuggled out, and is brought up by foster parents. When Krishna is grown up, another uncle, Akrur, calls him to Mathurā to kill Kams. He does not return to Vraj after achieving that feat. See also Source Notes, p. 362.

§642

The scourge of the foes of the Asuras i.e. Meghnād, because the foes of the Asuras are the Suras or gods. See V.18.

Did I defeat Indra—conqueror of demons—to die at your hand?
How shall I understand why God has dealt this torment to me? What sin I have committed? What else shall I say to you?
When the Rākshas lord gets news of this, who will save you, miserable man that you are?
Even if you dive to the bottom of the sea, his royal anger, volcanic in its power,
Will reach you there; it will burn you up like a forest-fire if you hide in forest, O evil one!
Night will not conceal you, you fool. Who among demons or men or gods has power to rescue you,
Son of Sumitrā, from Rāvan's fury? Who can expunge your shame from the world,
O sinner?' Dying as he spoke, noble Meghnād recalled the lotus-feet of his father and mother.
In anguish he thought of Pramilā, his eternal joy! A stream of tears mixed with blood,
Flowing unrestrainedly, drenched the earth! The lotus-sun of Lankā set!
Like a flame snuffed out, or the fading sun itself, his mighty strength lay on the ground.

§671

Rāvan's brother, Vibhishan, said with tears in his eyes:
'You are used to soft silk beds, O mighty-armed one: oh what induces you now to lie on the bare ground?
What will the Raksha king say when he sees you on this bed? Or Mandodari, queen of the Rākshasas?

§642

Did I defeat Indra? see I.1.
What sin have I committed? see Introduction, p. lvi.
The lotus-sun of Lankā set cf. II.491 and III.598.

Or Pramilā, lovely as the autumn moon? Or their maidservants—
Who put goddesses to shame by their beauty though demon-born? Or Nikashā, your old grandmother?
What will the Rākshasas say? You are their crest-jewel! Rise,
My darling! Vibhishan, your uncle,
Calls you! Why do you not hear, O more than life?
Rise, my darling, and I shall immediately open the door at your request!
Go to your armoury—wipe out this stain on Lankā today in battle. O pride of the Rākshasas,
Does the radiant sun, who delights the eyes of all, ever set in the afternoon?
Oh why then do you fall to the earth today, O famous one, in this unarmed state?
Listen, battle-horns sound, inviting you;
Elephants roar and horses neigh tumultuously; the Raksha army arms itself eagerly for battle. The enemy is at the gate:
Rise, O conqueror of enemies, and save the great honour of our race in this war!'

§694

Thus did the mighty Vibhishan lament in grief. The lion-hero Lakshman grieved with his friend, and said:
'Restrain your sorrow, crest-jewel of the Rākshasas! What purpose is there in vain grief?
I killed this warrior at the dictate of Fate; the fault is not yours! Come,

§671

Nikashā see I.62.

§694

I killed this warrior at the dictate of Fate *bidhir bidhāne badhinu e yodhe āmi*: cf. §84 above and earlier references to *bidhi*.

We shall go to the tent where Rām, jewel of thought, is anxious without you.
The music of celebration is playing in heaven: listen, O hero.'
Vibhishan heard the sound of a heavenly orchestra—enchanting as in a dream. The two emerged swiftly,
Like a hunter who has killed a tiger-cub in its mother's absence, and runs like the wind, panting for his life,
In case the tigress suddenly attacks, frantic with grief, on seeing her dead offspring.
Or like Asvatthāman, son of Drona, after slaying the five sleeping boys in the Pāṇḍav tent at night,
Rushing with the speed of desire, excited and fearful, to where Duryodhan,
Leader of the Kauravas, lay with his thigh broken from the battle of Kurukshetra! Invisible through the grace of Māyā,
They both returned to the tent where Rām, Sitā's delight, was waiting.

§716

Touching his lotus-feet, the lion-son of Sumitrā spoke with clasped hands: 'Through the grace of these feet,

§694

Asvatthāman, son of Drona, after slaying the five sleeping boys . . . in the *Mahābhārata,* the Kaurav warrior Asvatthāman, during the battle of Kurukshetra, stole at night into the Pāṇḍav tent where Draupadi, joint-wife of the five Pāṇḍav brothers, and her five infant sons were sleeping. He slew all five, and other people in the camp too.

excited and fearful excited because of his daring exploit, but fearful of the revenge the Pāṇḍavas will wreak on him.

Duryodhan,/ Leader of the Kauravas, lay with his thigh broken Duryodhan is the eldest of the hundred sons of the blind and ailing King Dhritarāshṭra, and the leader of the Kauravas in the battle of Kurukshetra. His thigh is broken by Bhim, the second of the Pāṇḍav brothers. For the effect of this simile, see Source Notes, p. 364.

O ornament of the Raghus, your servant has been victorious in battle! The great Meghnād,
Vanquisher of Indra, has lost his life!' Kissing his head,
Clasping his brother in love, Rām said tearfully: 'I have regained Sitā today through your strength of arms,
O master of arms! Glorious are you among heroes! Glorious is your mother Sumitrā!
Glorious is Dasarath, our father, fount of the Raghu race!
Favoured am I to be your elder brother! Glorious is Ayodhyā, the land of your birth!
Your fame will be proclaimed forever throughout the world! But offer a *pūjā* to the gods who gave you your power, O dearest;
Through his own powers, man is always weak: good results are achieved only through the grace of the gods.'
§731
Addressing respectfully his great supporter Vibhishan, Sitā's husband said: 'In good time did I find you,
Friend, in this Rākshas city. You are the blessing of the Raghu race in Rākshas guise!
O jewel of virtue, you have, through your own virtue,
Won over the Raghus today. I call you king of all friends, as the sun is king of the planets!
Come, let us all worship Durgā, who brings forth goodness!'
In great joy, the gods rained down flowers from the sky; the army cheered with delight:
'Victory, victory to Sitā's lord!' Golden Lankā woke in terror at the noise.

Here ends 'The Killing of Meghnād',
the sixth book of *Meghnādbadh kābya*.

§716

Ayodhyā the kingdom and capital of King Dasarath, and Rām's rightful inheritance.

BOOK VII

§1

The sun arose now at dawn, like lotus-born Brahmā emerging from sleep in the petals of Vishnu's lotus-navel, contentedly opening his lotus-eyes to gaze at the earth!
With flowers in her hair, and a garland of dewy pearls round her neck, Earth smiled ecstatically!
Like festive music filling a temple with praise, melodious birdsong swelled in forest-arbours; lotuses beautified pure pond-waters;
On land, with equal longing, golden sunflowers turned towards the sun.

§10

Like a flower bathing in the dew of night, chaste Pramilā bathed in perfumed water, and plaited her hair beside her plump breasts.
She attached a string of pearls to her glossy hair, like a thin crescent moon amidst dark clouds in autumn! She took a jewelled bracelet to adorn her lotus-stalk arms:
It pained her arm, alas, as if too tight!
And her delicate gold necklace pinched her delicate throat! Turning in surprise to her spring-fragrant companion Vāsanti, Pramilā said:

§1

like lotus-born Brahmā . . . in Hindu chronology—which is on a truly cosmic scale—one *kalpa* or 'day of Brahmā' lasts 1000 *yugas* (see III.573, VI.418). Twelve months of such days constitute his year, and 100 of these years his lifetime. We are currently in the *sveta-vārāha-kalpa* of the fifty-first year. At the end of each *kalpa* the world is annihilated. The *pādma* or 'lotus' *kalpa* is one of these *kalpas*. M calls the creator-god Brahmā 'Padmayoni' here, which means 'born of a lotus' At the start of the *pādma-kalpa* Brahmā is asleep in Vishnu's 'lotus-navel': hence M's striking simile here for the rising sun.

§10

Pramilā Meghnād's wife. See III.1. **Vāsanti** her name means 'of the spring', so there is wordplay on *basanta* ('spring') here.

'Why, O friend, can I not wear my ornaments?
Why do I hear distant wailing in Lankā, the sound of
grief? My right eye flutters all the time;
My heart palpitates! I do not know, dear friend,
I do not know, alas, what plight will befall me today!
My husband is at the place of sacrifice; go to him, Vāsanti!
Stop that jewel of heroes from going into battle on this
evil day. Tell the lord of my life that his wife implores
him not to go, that she clings to his feet!'

§31

The *vīṇā* of her words ceased; her friend Vāsanti replied:
'The keening is steadily growing—
Listen keenly, O beautiful one! How can I say why the
citizens are wailing?
Let us go quickly, to where Queen Mandodari is
worshipping Siva in his temple. Mad with battle-fever,
Chariots, charioteers, elephants and horses are pouring
along the royal road;
O vermilion-wearer, how can I go alone to the place of
sacrifice, to where your ever-victorious husband is
putting on his armour?'
The two set off together to moon-crested Siva's temple,
to where—in vain!
The queen of the Rākshasas was begging the god to

§10

My right eye flutters all the time cf. Book VI, §621. Pramilā's right eyelid inauspiciously started to flutter when her husband was killed, and is still fluttering.

the place of sacrifice i.e. the Nikumbhilā grove (see I.751) where Meghnād was doing a *pūjā* to Agni before Lakshman and Vibhishan broke in and he was slain (as described in Book VI, §413f.).

§31

vīṇā see I.623.

Queen Mandodari Meghnād's mother. See I.172.

protect her son. With anxious hearts, the pair
hastened there.

§44

In his palace on Mount Kailās, the Lord of the Mountains
was wan-faced now. Heaving a deep sigh of grief,
Matted-haired Siva turned to his mountain-born wife and
said: 'O goddess, your desire has been satisfied; the great
warrior Indrajit has been slain in grim combat!
Strong Lakshman slew him in a place of sacrifice through
Māyā's trickery! Rāvan—the fount of the Raksha race—
Is my chief devotee, O moon-faced one! I always feel
distressed when he is distressed.
You see this trident in my hand, wife; grief for a dead
son strikes far more heavily than its blow!
That pain is permanent, alas; even all-taking Death
cannot take it away!
What will Rāvan say, my dear, when he hears that his
treasured son has been slaughtered?
He will instantly die himself, if I cannot save him through
the gift of my own furious power! I satisfied Indra,
Lady, at your request; give me permission now to give
solace to ten-faced Rāvan.'

§31

to where . . . The queen of the Rākshasas was begging the god to protect her son. See Book V, §422f.

§44

Mount Kailās see I.33 and II.126.

Lord of the Mountains *Giriś*: an epithet of Siva.

Matted-haired Siva see II.87 and V.223.

Indrajit see I.1, 594.

fount of the Raksha race see I.1.

You see this trident in my hand see II.447.

I satisfied Indra,/ Lady, at your request see Book II, §247f.

ten-faced Rāvan see I.33.

§61

Durgā replied: 'Do as you wish, O enemy of Tripura!
My humble plea was for Vishnu's desire to be fulfilled;
that has been accomplished. But the hero Rām,
Lord, is devoted to me; keep this in mind,
O master of the universe! What more can I say, at your
lotus-feet?'

§67

Smiling, Siva called for the warrior Virbhadra. With the
fierce-looking follower humbly spreadeagled at his feet,
Siva said, 'Indrajit has lost his life in combat today, my friend!
Lakshman entered the place of sacrifice and slew him
there, by Umā's grace. Messengers are terrified of
giving this news to the Rākshas king—
And especially because they do not know the trick by
which strong Lakshman destroyed awesome
Meghnād in combat. Apart from gods, warrior,
Who in the world can understand the power of Māyā?
Go quickly to golden Lankā, mighty-armed one,
In the guise of a Rākshas messenger. I command you: fill
now Nikashā's son Rāvan with the fire of my rage.'

§80

Mighty Virbhadra sped through the sky, furious to look
at; birds dropped down to earth in terror;
At the radiance of his beauty, the sun looked pallid, just as
the moon looks pale compared to the fire of the sun!

§61

O enemy of Tripura see II.217.

§67

the warrior Virbhadra a servant of Siva.
by Umā's grace i.e. by Durgā's grace. See I.483, II.337.
the trick *kauśal*: cf. VI.485, V.29 and I.1.
Nikashā's son see I.62.

The shadow of his massive spear lay across the earth! The
lord of the oceans sonorously roared salutations to the
mighty messenger. He alighted from his chariot at Lankā;
The golden city quaked at the pounding of his footsteps,
like a branch of a tree, when the king of birds
Garuḍa lands on it!
Entering the temple, the hero saw the lord of warriors lying
on the ground—like a full-bloomed *kiṃśuk*-tree,
Flattened, alas, on the floor of the forest by a massive storm!
Virbhadra wept when he saw the prince! At the sight of
such mortal tragedy, his immortal heart ached!

§95

Where the crest-jewel of the Rākshasas, ten-faced Rāvan
sat on his golden throne, Virbhadra arrived in the guise
of a messenger, his radiance subdued now,
Like fire hiding under ashes. Blessing the Rākshas with a
show of humility, he stood before him with his palms
pressed together, and tears in his eyes.
Surprised, the king asked: 'Why,
O messenger, does your tongue hold back from
performing its task? Rām is but a man—
You cannot be his servant; so why, O news-bringer,
Is your face so pale? Lankā's lotus-sun, victor over
demons and gods,

§80

Lord of the oceans *amburāśi-pati*: i.e. Varuna. See I.295, 443, 62.

Garuḍa see I.218.

***kimśuk*-tree** Flame of the Forest; tree with bright orange-red flowers like a parrot's beak, growing in clusters. It flowers in spring, and is associated with spring festivals, so there is a poignant irony here. Meghnād has been killed in his prime.

§95

Rām is but a man cf. Meghnād's scornful reference to 'low-born Rām' in Book VI, §532.

Is arming for battle today; what bad news can you bring to me? If Rāghav has died in battle from a blow like a dreadful thunderbolt,
Tell me that news—I shall honour you for that.'
Disguised Virbhadra slowly replied:
'Alas, lord, how can a humble creature like me lay terrible news at your feet?
O Karbur king, first gift me with a promise of no ill-treatment!' Nervously,
Great Rāvan answered, 'What need you fear, messenger?
Speak quickly—in this world, both good and bad are fated to occur.
No harm will befall you, I promise; give me your news at once.'

§118

Siva's strong attendant, disguised as a Raksha messenger, then said:
'O finest of Rākshasas, today, in combat,
The warrior Meghnād, the pride of the Karburas, was slain.'

§121

As when a hunter, in the deep forest, strikes with a deadly arrow the king of the beasts,
And it falls to the earth with a desperate roar, so the Rākshas king keeled over in his council-chamber! Howling with alarm,
His courtiers rushed to his side all around; some brought cooling water in vessels; some fanned him.

§95

Lankā's lotus-sun i.e. Meghnād. Cf. II.491 and III.598.
O Karbur king see IV.531.

§127

By infusing him with Siva's fury, Virbhadra brought him round quickly. Like gunpowder at the touch of a spark,
Rāvan leapt to his feet, and commanded Virbhadra: 'Tell me,
Messenger, who slew the ever-triumphant Indrajit in battle today? Tell me at once.'

§132

Virbhadra replied: 'The leonine son of Sumitrā, your Majesty,
Entered the Nikumbhilā place of sacrifice in disguise, and wickedly killed brave Meghnād in unfair combat! Like a blooming *kiṃśuk*-tree felled in the woods by a storm,
I saw the hero in the temple! You are the greatest of warriors, my lord—
Bury your grief today in heroic action. There are Rākshas women, sir,
To soak the earth with tears! Avenge the citizens, great archer,
By slaying today, with a mighty assault, the foul enemy who has murdered your son!'

§143

In a trice the divine messenger vanished; the chamber was filled all over with heavenly fragrance. The Rākshas lord saw the matted locks of Siva himself,
And the shadow of his huge trident. Bowing

§127

By infusing him with Siva's fury i.e. with *rudra-tej*, the fiery power of Siva as Rudra. See I.33.

§132

The leonine son of Sumitrā i.e. Lakshman. See I.172.

like a blooming *kimśuk*-tree see above, §80.

§143

And the shadow of his huge trident particularly in his angry form as Rudra, Siva carries a *triśūl* or trident. See I.33 and II.447.

with pressed palms, Siva's devotee Rāvan now
 said:
'Have you remembered at last your wretched servant, O
 master? How can a fool like me,
Alas, understand this mystery, O mysterious one?
First, O knower of all, I shall carry out your command;
Then I shall lay—at your lotus-feet—all that is in my heart.'
Enraged—incandescent now with Siva's anger—the
 Rākshas chief bellowed:
'Let all the bowmen there are in this golden city form an
 army, with all speed. In the drama of battle I shall
 forget this torment—
If I can, alas, forget torment so bitter.'

§158

The booming of war-trumpets blasted the council-
 chamber, like Siva's blowing of his horn at the
 world's destruction, with deafening din!
And like his attendant goblins rushing to arm the top of
 Mount Kailās, the Rākshasas got ready all around;
 Lankā shuddered with the tramp of their violent feet!
Fire-coloured chariots poured out, with banners of gold;
 and smoke-coloured elephants,
Brandishing massive hammers with their trunks; horses
 charged out neighing; Chāmar came out in force,
The terror of the gods; with the charioteers there was
 Udagra, foremost in battle;

§143

Siva's devotee Rāvan cf. Durgā's comment in Book II, §168. For the reasons for the link between Siva and the Rākshasas, see II.204.

§158

like Siva's blowing of his horn at the world's destruction Siva announces the destruction of the world by blowing his *śṛṅga* or horn, often depicted as a *śaṅkha* or conch. **his attendant goblins** in his form as the Destroyer and frequenter of cremation-grounds, Siva has a retinue of *bhūtas* or goblins.

With the elephants there was Vāskal, like cloud-riding
Indra amidst the clouds with an awesome thunderbolt in his hand! Master-horseman Asilomā came roaring;
And Biḍālāksha with his footsoldiers, that formidable Rākshas, frenzied in combat!
Heralds came too; their banners flashed through the sky like sudden comets; Rākshas bandsmen played on all sides!

§178

As when divine fire-born, demon-destroying Chanḍi takes up her divine weapons with whoops of delight, the terrifying army of the Rākshasas assembled in Lankā's city,
Like the goddess herself on the war-path. Its elephants were vigorous as her arms; its horses were speedy as her feet;
Its golden chariots were like her crown; its jewel-studded banners were like her sari; its drums,
Bugles and trumpets were like the roar of her lion!
Clubs, cudgels,
Pikes, spears, axes,
Swords, arrows and battering-rams gleamed like her teeth!
The armour of the army shone like her fiery eyes!
Earth quaked and rocked with its tramping; the ocean was turbulent with terror; mountains trembled at its roar—
Like Chanḍi reborn, again and again, it emitted a furious din!

§158

Chāmar . . . Udagra . . . Vāskal . . . Asilomā . . . Biḍālāksha names of various Rākshas fighters, meaning respectively 'fly-whisk', 'haughty', 'warrior', 'sword-haired, 'cat's eyes'.

§178

demon-destroying Chanḍi see V.113 and Source Notes, p. 366.

§192

In his tent, the sun of the race of suns—Rām,
Spoke in amazement to his ally Vibhishan: 'See, O friend,
Now, how Lankā is juddering, as if with a massive earthquake!
Clouds of smoke are covering the sun like thick clouds; the sky is lit up by a ghastly gleam, as if at the world's conflagration!
Listen to that noise of waves, as if the sea is advancing from afar to engulf the universe!' Pale-cheeked with alarm,
Vibhishan, crest-jewel of councillors, spoke:
'What more can I say, sir? The city quakes with the marching of Rākshas fighters;
It is no earthquake! It is not the blaze of the world's end that you see in the sky, O husband of Sitā;
It's the gleam of their golden armour, mixed with the sheen of their weapons, that shines on all sides!
The din that stops up our ears, I say, is not the roar of the sea,
But the Rākshas army yelling, crazed with battle-lust. Demented with grief for his son,
The king of Lankā is girding himself for war. Tell me, O hero,
How will you save Lakshman, and all your other heroes, from this terrible peril?'

§214

Rām said soothingly, 'Go quickly, good friend,
And call all my generals here. The gods always protect me. They will save me this time.'

§192

sun of the race of suns *rabikul-rabi:* because the ultimate descent of Rām and the Raghus was from the sun-god Surya. See I.406.

§218

Vibhishan took up his horn and blew on it loudly.
Sugriv came charging like a king elephant; and battle-skilled Angad;
Nala and Nila came, godlike to look at; and Hanumān,
Stormy in attack; the mighty Jāmbuvān, bull of heroes Sarabh,
Gavāksha and Raktāksha (scourge of the Rākshasas) and many other leaders came.

§225

Greeting them all appropriately, brave Rāghav said:
'Insane with grief for his son,
The Rākshas king is rapidly mustering his army; Lankā cannot stop shaking from the tramp of his soldiers' feet! You are all renowned in the three worlds for your prowess;
Arm immediately; protect Rām today, from this grave threat.
Ill-fortune drove me from my friends to exile in the forest; you are all I now have—my strength and my shield in battle!
Only one true fighter remains in Lankā—Rāvan himself; slaughter him today,
O heroes! With your assistance I shackled the sea; I killed in fierce battle Kumbhakarna,

§218

Sugriv . . . Angad . . . Nila see I.218.

Nala . . . Jāmbuvān see IV.464.

Hanumān see I.218.

Sarabh,/ Gavāksha and Raktāksha warriors in Hanumān's monkey-army. Sarabh is also a name for an eight-footed animal stronger than a lion or an elephant; Gavāksha means 'bull-eyed' and Raktāksha means 'blood-red-eyed'.

§225

Rāghav i.e. Rām. See I.1.

Kumbhakarna see I.80.

The equal of trident-wielding Siva; Lakshman slew mighty Meghnād, the terror of gods and demons and men!
By rescuing my wife—incarcerated through Rāvan's guile—save my race,
My honour, my life, O friends of the Raghus!
You have bought me by being so loving towards me; O south-country dwellers, bind the whole Raghu clan in bonds of gratitude now by giving me your aid.'
§245
The Raghu lord fell silent with tears in his eyes. In a voice like thunder Sugriv replied: 'I will either die or I will kill Rāvan—
This is the promise, O greatest of heroes, that I lay at your feet!
It is thanks to you, lord, that I enjoy the privileges of a king;
You bestow wealth and honour; it is I who am humbly bound to your lotus feet in gratitude! What more shall I say,
Sir? Anyone among my companions who fears death in carrying out your work is no soldier! Let the Rākshasas arm—
We will fight them fearlessly!' The generals all bellowed aggressively; the whole huge army shouted out '*Jay* Rām'.
§256
Incensed by that angry sound, the Rākshas army shouted fiercely, just as demon-trampling Durgā,

§225

O south-country dwellers i.e. allies from the southern kingdom of Kishkindhyā. See I.218.

§245

***Jay* Rām** 'Victory to Rām'. Cf. III.288.

§256

demon-trampling Durgā see II.400 and III.523.

When shouted at by demons, shouts back! Golden
Lankā filled with thunderous uproar!

§260

The noise reached the place where Kamalā, the guardian deity of the Raksha race, sat on her lotus-throne;
Startled, she sprang up quickly! She saw,
With her lotus eyes, the Rākshasas arming all around, blind with anger;
Rākshas banners were flying in the sky, boding ill to all living creatures! The Rākshas band was booming out music.
The goddess flew off through the sky; like the autumn moon in her beauty, she made for Indra's abode.

§269

Assorted instruments were playing in that celestial residence; nymphs were dancing; singers were singing melodiously;
The king of the gods was sitting on his golden throne, surrounded by gods and goddesses; to his left was Sachi,
Sweetly smiling. An unending spring breeze was wafting gently; Gandharvas were raining down clusters of *mandār*-flowers.

§275

The beloved of Vishnu entered the divine council-chamber. Indra bowed and said: 'Give me the dust of your feet,

§260

the place where Kamalā, the guardian deity of the Raksha race, sat on her lotus-throne as first described in Book I, §483, and last encountered in Book VI, §246.

§269

Sachi see II.14. **Gandharvas** see I.375. ***mandār*-flowers** see II.14.

§275

The beloved of Vishnu *Keśab-priyā*: i.e. Kamalā/Lakshmi, husband of Vishnu/Keshav. See I.483.

Mother; thanks to you my fear has gone; the terrifying son of Rāvan has lost his life today in combat!
I can enjoy the pleasures of heaven unthreatened now. Full of kindness as you are, what should anyone lack,
If looked on kindly by you?' The beautiful goddess, supreme jewel in the ocean's mine of jewels,
Answered with a smile: 'Your enemy, O enemy of demons,
Has fallen now; but the king of Lankā is mustering his forces, determined to avenge the death of his son!
Tens of thousands of Rākshasas are arming with him. I have come here, sir,
To give you this news. Wise Lakshman has done what you asked him to do; save him,
O son of Aditi! Great is he who goes to all lengths to save one who has done him a favour! O mighty upholder,
What more shall I say? You are not unaware of the strength of the Rākshasas! Think hard,
And see by what means, O husband of Sachi, you can save Rāghav.'

§294

The king of the gods replied: 'Look, O mother of the universe,
At the sky to the north of heaven: the gods are ready for war. If the bow-bearing king of the Rākshasas comes out intent on battle,
I shall fight with him myself, kind Lakshmi! I do not fear Rāvan,
Now that his son, Mother, is no more!'

§300

Kamalā saw with amazement Indra's army in the northern

§275

supreme jewel in the ocean's mine of jewels see I.513, 295.
O son of Aditi i.e. Indra. See II.217.

part of heaven. For as far as her divine sight roved, she saw with its keenness chariots and charioteers,
Elephants and their drivers, horses and their riders, and death-defying infantry,
Trimphant in battle. There were Gandharvas, Kinnaras and gods as fiery as the world's destruction;
Kārttikeya—enemy of Tārak—was in command,
A peacock banner flying from his chariot; the charioteer Chitrarath was in his colourful chariot. The sky blazed,
As if from a forest-fire; elephants were like clouds of smoke in it; spears flashed like flames,
Dazzling to the eye; banners gleamed like frozen streaks of lightning; shields—
Vying with the sun in size and brilliance—glittered; armour shone.

§313

The beloved of Mādhav asked: 'Tell me, O supreme son of Aditi,
Where is the Wind and the other masters of directions? Why do I see the divine army deprived of them?'
Sachi's great husband replied:

§300

Kinnaras a race of horse-headed, bird-bodied beings who are part of the entourage of Kuber, god of wealth (see I.62).

Kārttikeya—enemy of Tārak see I.689 and II.491.

Chitrarath king of the Gandharvas and Indra's charioteer. See II.527.

§313

The beloved of Mādhav i.e. Kamalā/Lakshmi. Mādhav is a name for Vishnu, and also for his incarnation Krishna.

the Wind and the other masters of directions in Hindu tradition the eight points of the compass (North, North-East, East, etc.) + 'up' (heaven) and 'down' (the underworld) each have a *dikpati* or 'master of direction'. Vāyu (Pavan, Prabhanjan: see I.114, 218) is master of the North-West; Yama is master of the south; Indra is master of the East, etc.

'I have ordered them today to guard their own regions, great Mother. In a battle between gods and Rākshasas,
(Both invincible) who knows what may happen? The earth will be overwhelmed,
Perhaps, as by a cataclysm; this whole vast creation may sink to bottommost hell!'

§323

The lovely-haired lover of Vishnu blessed the king of the gods; riding on a golden cloud, she sped back to Lankā.
She returned to her abode, sorrowfully sat again on her lotus-throne, lighting up her surroundings with the rays of her beauty;
Her face was pale, alas, with grief for the Rākshasas!

§329

Wild with battle-fever, the Rākshas king prepared for battle; the chariots around him gleamed like the golden crests of Hemkuṭ!
A band played nearby; Raksha banners fluttered in the sky; innumerable Rākshasas bellowed and howled.
Queen Mandodari now arrived in his presence, like a dove, alas,
Desperately finding its nest bereft of its young! A crowd of attendants ran behind her. She fell at the feet of the king.

§338

Gently raising her to her feet, Rāvan said mournfully: 'Fate has turned against us both,
O Queen of the Rākshasas! But for as long as I live, revenge will be my only desire!

§329

the golden crests of Hemkuṭ see I.33.

§338

Fate *bidhi*: see VI.84, 694 etc.

Return to your empty room; I am going into battle; why stand in my way?
We shall have endless time later, devi, to lament!
Let's abandon our royal pleasures, dear wife, and live in solitude,
Recalling Meghnād day upon day. Go back; why do you wish to extinguish the fire of my anger with your tears,
Queen Mandodari? The *śāl*-tree that was the glory of the forest has fallen today! The highest crest on the highest mountain has been smashed!
Our moon, our sky's gem, has been swallowed forever by Rāhu!'

§352

Supporting her on her arm, a companion helped the queen back to her quarters. Bursting with fury,
The Rākshas lord roared out to the Rākshasas: 'He by whose strength the Rākshas army was victorious against gods, demons and men;
He whose network of arrows petrified Indra himself, and the army of heaven, and the Nāgas in the underworld,
And people on earth: that noble hero has been slain today in unfair combat, O warriors!
Entering a holy place like a thief, Lakshman killed my son, when he was alone and unharmed!
Like when an exile dies in sorrow in a strange land, without any future sight of his loved ones—father,
Mother, brothers, wife—

§338

devi see I.322.
***śāl*-tree** see I.417.
Rāhu see II.400.

§352

Nāgas in the underworld see I.33 and II.491.

So the ornament of golden Lankā has died today! For many years I have cared for you all like sons; ask yourselves,
Is any race on earth more famous than the Rākshasas? But despite having vanquished gods and men, I have planted the tree of our fame in vain!
Cruel Fate has been against me for so long now; that is why the water-filled trough round the tree has dried up so prematurely! But I shall not lament;
What point is there in that? Will it bring him back? Can streams of tears,
Alas, ever soften the hard heart of death? Let me go into battle now and destroy that impious knave Lakshman,
That false fighter; if my effort is in vain, I shall not return—
I shall never set foot again in this city, in this present life. This is my vow,
O warriors! You are all the terror of gods, demons and men in battle,
And ever-victorious; with Meghnād in our hearts, come now to the battlefield;
At the news of his murder, who among our race now wants to live? He was the pride of the Karburas!'

§387

The great bow-bearer lapsed into silent grief. In sorrow and outrage, the Rākshas army howled,
Soaking the ground, alas, with the torrent of their tears.
Hearing that awesome sound, the Raghu army roared too, and Indra thundered in heaven!
Sitā's husband grew angry, and leonine Lakshman, and Sugriv,
Angad, Hanumān, and all the other leaders,

§387

Sugriv, Angad etc. see above, §218.

Deadly to the Rākshasas; and Nala, Nila and brave Sarabh—
The whole huge army shouted, '*Jay* Rām!' Thunderous clouds covered the sky;
Thunderclaps clattered; lightning dazzled the world; it beamed like Durgā when she laughingly killed gigantic Chaṇḍa and Muṇḍa and their crew,
Frenzied with battle-lust! The sun—that destroyer of darkness—
Was itself overwhelmed by dark clouds; winds blew on all sides in hot gusts; forest-fires lit up the forests;
Tumultuous floods suddenly swallowed up cities and villages; earthquakes brought down buildings and trees; animals perished with piercing cries as if at the end of the world!

§408

Panic-stricken, Mother Earth ran to Vishnu's heaven. She bowed humbly to the god where he sat on his golden throne,
And implored: 'Many times, O husband of Lakshmi,
Have you rescued me, by assuming various shapes, sea of kindness that you are;

§387

Durgā . . . Chaṇḍa . . . Muṇḍa see III.523.

§408

Mother Earth *Mahī*: a name for Prithivi, the Vedic goddess of the earth, comparable to the Greek goddess Gaia.

Many times . . ./ Have you rescued me, by assuming various shapes . . . these lines allude to three of Vishnu's ten *avatārs* (incarnations). As the tortoise *avatār* Kurma, Vishnu during the Satya-yuga (see III.573) formed a base at the bottom of the ocean for the Mandar mountain, which was then turned by the gods and Asuras using Vāsuki as a rope, so that the ocean could be churned and the 'fourteen jewels' that had been lost in the deluge that preceded the Satya-yuga could be recovered. See I.295. As Varāha, a wild boar, Vishnu made the land mass of the Indian subcontinent by digging mud out of the sea with his tusks: this was after the demon Hiranyāksha

You saved me from destruction by placing me on your tortoise-back! I rode on your white tusks (like a blot on the body of the moon)
When you took the shape of a boar, O friend of the humble! By becoming a man-lion,
You saved me by killing the demon Hiranya-kasipu! You reduced the arrogance of Bali by reducing yourself to a dwarf! I have survived,
Lord, through your grace. What more can I say,
Master? I look to you for protection! That is why I am here at your lotus-feet in this time of peril.'
§423
The smiling enemy of Mura asked kindly: 'What is upsetting you now, O world's earth-mother?
Please tell me. Who is tormenting you, my dear?'
§426
Tearfully Earth replied: 'What is there that you do not know, O knower of all?
Look towards Lankā, sir; the Rākshas king is avid for battle;
As is the great chief of the Raghus; and heaven's chief charioteer, Indra as well!
So three mad elephants are assailing me! That lion-like,

---

had dragged the earth down under the water. As Narasimha, a man-lion, Vishnu emerged suddenly from a stone pillar that the demon Hiranya-Kasipu had struck, scornfully wondering if the omnipresent Vishnu was inside it. Narasimha then tore the demon to pieces. As Vāman, a dwarf, Vishnu overthrew Bali, a demon-king of the underworld who had become ruler of all three worlds. He pretended to be a peasant in need of land, and asked Bali for as much as he could cover in three steps. When Bali agreed, Vāman grew to cosmic size, so that each of the three worlds was covered by a single step. Earth and heaven were thereby recovered from Bali, who was allowed to keep the underworld.

§423

The smiling enemy of Mura i.e. Vishnu, because Mura was a demon slain by Vishnu's incarnation Krishna.

godlike warrior Lakshman slew mighty Meghnād
today.
Demented with intense grief, the fount of the Rākshas
race has vowed that he will kill Lakshman in battle
today; Indra has vowed,
With heroic pride, that he will save him. Alas,
O yellow loincloth-wearer, in golden Lankā a furious battle
will soon begin between gods, Rākshasas and men.
Please tell me, lord, how shall I endure such horrible agony?'

§440

Lakshmi's lord smiled and looked towards golden Lankā.
He saw the Rākshas forces emerging, uncountable,
Blind with rage, in fourfold formation! News of their
power preceded them,
Terrifying the world; the din they made followed them,
shattering to the ear;
Thick clouds of dust accompanied them, blinding to the
eye! Golden Lankā quaked unceasingly!
Outside the city great Vishnu saw the Raghu army—like
waves on a beach, when the sea's eternal enemy the
wind shows itself from afar!
Heaven-dwelling Vishnu saw the gods rushing towards
Lankā too, like king-of-the-birds Garuḍa, swooping
with a skwark when he spies his snake-food below!
The universe filled with tumultuous noise! Yogis fled
from their meditation; terrified mothers hugged and
wailed over their children;

§426

O yellow loincloth-wearer *Pitāmbar*: an epithet of Krishna and therefore also of Vishnu.

§440

in fourfold formation i.e. elephants, cavalry, chariots and infantry. See VI.316.

Panic-stricken animals fled in all directions! Vishnu, jewel of thought,
Floating like a swan on the lake of Siva's meditations, reflected for a while and said to Earth: 'I see grave danger for you,
Chaste goddess! Siva himself, by the gift of his anger,
Has filled the Rākshas king with fiery aggression today! I see no other way—you must go to him,
Medini.' Earth replied in tears at his lotus-feet: 'Alas,
Lord, the trident-holder is impossibly destructive; he is constantly engaged in killing!
Tripura's enemy is full of limitless *tamas*! Stoked up by the fires of its poison, a death-dealing snake always longs to burn up the living.
Sire, you are a sea of kindness; you sustain the universe;
Tell me, who but you can carry its weight? Save me,
Humble as I am, O husband of Sri, I beg you at your rosy feet!'

§472

The great god responded tenderly: 'Go back to your home, Vasudhā;
I shall carry out your desire by restraining the power

§440

Floating like a swan on the lake of Siva's meditations Siva dwells near Lake Mānas (see I.33). But *mānas* also means 'mind', so for Siva as *Yogīndra* or 'Lord of meditation', Lake Mānas is also the 'lake of the mind'. The metaphor here says that Vishnu as *cintāmaṇi* or 'jewel of thought' is like a swan on that lake, and therefore always aware of what is going on in Siva's mind. **Medini** another name for Earth or Prithivi, because she is said to have been formed from the *med* or 'fat' of the demons Madhu and Kaitabh. **Tripura's enemy** i.e. Siva. See II.217. ***tamas*** the third of Siva's three *guṇas* or virtues, associated with his destructive power. See II.447. **O husband of Sri** i.e. Vishnu, as Sri is a name for Lakshmi.

§472

Vasudhā short for *Vasundharā*, another name for Earth or Prithivi.

of the gods; but Indra will not be able to save
Lakshman; Siva is mightily pained by the grief of the
Rākshasas.'

§476

Joyously, Earth returned to her home. Vishnu said to
Garuḍa:
'Fly into the sky, great bird, steal the fire of the gods,
As the dark-defying sun steals water—or as you, son of
Vinatā,
Stole nectar. Make the gods powerless, at my command.'

§482

Spreading his massive wings, the king of the birds
soared into the sky; a great shadow fell on the
earth,
Casting countless forests, mountains, rivers and streams
into gloom!

§485

Like when a fire sweeps through a house, and flames
pour out of windows and doors into the road, so
Rākshasas poured out from all gates,
Bellowing furiously; the Raghu army roared all around
them; the gods entered the fray too.
Airāvat, greatest of elephants, came,
Exuberant with battle-lust; on his back was thousand-
eyed Indra, with his thunderbolt missile,
Radiant as Mount Meru in the rays of the sun, or the
sun itself, in the afternoon;

§476

as you, son of Vinatā,/ Stole nectar see II.337.

§485

Airāvat, greatest of elephants Indra's flying mount. See III.378 and V.29.
thousand-eyed Indra see V.478.
Mount Meru see I.33.

Tārak's enemy Skanda came, as general of the army,
peacock-banner flying from his chariot;
Chitrarath came in his colourful car; and Kinnaras,
Gandharvas and Yakshas riding in their various vehicles.
Lankā listened in dread to heaven's war-band playing; at its
deathless booming, the land of Lankā trembled in alarm!

§499

Spreading his whole body in obeisance to Indra, Rām,
jewel of men,
Said: 'I am a servant of the gods, O lord of the gods!
What can I say about merit earned in my previous lives?
It must be because of that that I have gained your
feet's protection at this time of crisis, O Thunderer!
Only because of that do heaven's inhabitants, by the
touch of their feet, sanctify the earth today.'

§506

King Indra spoke to Rāghav in reply: 'You are beloved
of the gods, O jewel of the Raghus!
Take my divine chariot, O charioteer, and destroy with
the strength of your arms that evil-doing Rākshas.
Through his own misdeeds, the fount of the Raksha race
is sinking; who can save him?
As when we gods acquired nectar by churning the
ocean, so, O hero,
We will restore chaste Sitā to you by pummelling Lankā
and punishing the night-dwellers. How much longer

§485

Tārak's enemy Skanda see II.491. Skanda is a name for Kārttikeya, god of war.

peacock-banner Skanda/Kārttikeya also rides a peacock.

Kinnaras, Gandarvas see above, §269 and §300.

Yakshas see I.62.

§506

As when we gods acquired nectar by churning the ocean see I.295.

can she remain like Lakshmi at the bottom of the
ocean, darkening the world?'

§516

A tremendous battle now rang out, between the
Rākshasas and the gods and men! Thousands of
conches boomed all around like the waters of the sea.
Mighty bow-bearers deafened the ear with the twang of
their bows! Arrows covered the sky, split armour,
Shields and bodies with their lightning-fire; blood
poured in torrents! Raksha and human warriors fell;
Elephants keeled over like leaves blown off by a storm
in a forest; neighing horses collapsed; the battlefield
filled with uproar!

§526

Chāmar—terror of the immortals—attacked the gods
with the full strength of his army.
Great Chitrarath entered the battle in his sun-like chariot,
like a lion when he beholds his enemy the elephant!
Massive Udagra aggressively challenged Sugriv;
Chariot-wheels whirred noisily, like the churning of
hundreds of streams! Fierce as a king-elephant,
Vāskal drove his elephants, when he saw Prince Angad
from afar; and the prince grew furious,
Like a lion-cub when he sees a herd of deer! Asilomā, a
sharp sword in his hand,
Angrily surrounded with his horses Sarabh, that ox of a
warrior. Biḍālāksha

§506

like Lakshmi at the bottom of the ocean see I.513 and II.87.

§526

Chāmar . . . Chitrarath . . . Udagra . . . Vāskal . . . Asilomā . . . Biḍālāksha see above, §158.

Sugriv . . . Angad see I.218.

Sarabh see above, §218.

(Destructive as Siva) began to do battle with Hanumān.
Rām entered the fray in his heavenly chariot,
Ah! like a second thunder-wielding Indra! Peacock-bannered Skanda,
Enemy of Tārak, saw in amazement the handsome hero Lakshman, like an image of himself on earth.
Dust-clouds billowed all around; golden Lankā shuddered and shook; the ocean roared!
Indra, the beloved of Sachi, assembled a formidable army!

§548

The Rākshas king emerged, in his flying chariot; its wheels whirred deafeningly,
Spitting out sparks; its horses whinnied with delight. A jewel-induced radiance,
Dazzling to the eyes, shone out ahead of it, like the dawn,
When Āditya rises above his mountain-peak in his one-wheeled chariot! The Rākshasas cheered tumultuously, when they saw the Raksha lord.

§554

Addressing his chariot-driver, Rāvan said: 'That man Rām is not fighting unaided today,
My friend. Have a look! Like flames amidst clouds of smoke,
Gods are gleaming amidst the Raghu ranks! Indra has come to Lankā, having heard that Indrajit has been slain!'

§526

Peacock-bannered Skanda, enemy of Tārak see above, §485.

§548

Āditya name for Surya, the sun-god, who rises above a mountain-peak in the morning, travels across the sky in his one-wheeled chariot, and descends behind another peak in the evening.

§554

Raghu ranks see I.406.

Recalling his son, the royal fount of the Raksha race
howled with rage and bellowed out: 'Drive on,
O charioteer, like thunder-bearing Vāsav himself.' The
chariot sped forward with the speed of thought.
The Raghu army fled, like woodland-creatures panting
and fleeing at the sight of a mad king-elephant! Or
like an awesome cloud,
Full of thunder and lightning, when it flies with the
wind with tumultuous roaring, and birds and animals
flee on all sides in panic!
Drawing his bow, the lion of warriors sliced through
Indra's army with an instantaneous arrow, like a
massive flood when it easily smashes a dam of sand,
Or like a tiger at night breaking through to fenced-in cattle!
But Tārak's great enemy Skanda charged forward in
his chariot, furiously drew back his bowstring,
To obstruct Rāvan's advance. With hands pressed
together in respect, the king of Lankā bowed to that
hero and growled,
'I worship your parents day and night, sir! So why do I
see you today amidst Lankā's enemies?
Why do you do such a favour to that base man Rām,
prince? You are a master-charioteer;
Lakshman killed my son in unjust combat; I shall kill
that false-playing fool; let me past!'

§583

Pārvati's son replied: 'I am protecting Lakshman today,
O Raksha king,

§554

Vāsav name for Indra, king of the gods, who can in turn be called 'Vasus' or 'the good or bright ones'.

your parents i.e. Siva and Pārvati, though Skanda/Kārttikeya was not conceived in the normal way. See II.491.

By Indra's order. Meet strength with strength; you will not achieve your desire unless you fight me.'

§587

In a frenzy, resplendent now with the fire of Siva, the fount of the Rākshasas hurled his flaming weapons with a howl,
Impeded Skanda's attack with his mesh of arrows! Durgā—watching from heaven—
Said to Vijayā: 'Look, friend,
Towards Lankā, at how the Raksha king is cruelly peppering Prince Skanda with his lethal arrows! Look at the sky,
At how Garuḍa is stealing his power; go swiftly as lightning, my dear,
To protect the prince. It breaks my heart, my friend,
To see the stream of blood from my child's soft body. Siva is always indulgent towards his devotees; he loves them more than his son;
That is why Rāvan is now so ferocious in battle, my friend.' Moonlike Vijayā sped away through the sky,
Lovely as a sunbeam. Reaching the prince, she said in his ear:
'Hold back your weapons, O power-holder: the source of all power commands you.
The king of Lankā is full of Siva's fire today!' Cheerfully, Tārak's great enemy Skanda turned back his chariot.

§587

resplendent now with the fire of Siva for the power of Siva's *tej* or fire, see I.33 and II.309. **Durgā** because Durgā = Pārvati, she has maternal concern for Skanda/Kārttikeya. **Vijayā** see III.573. **Look . . . / At how Garuḍa is stealing his power** see above, §476, 482. **Siva is always indulgent towards his devotees** see Book II, §168, where Rāvan is described as 'Siva's chief devotee'. In his destructive aspect, Siva has a train of attendant demons, Rākshasas included. See II.204.

Roaring like a lion, cutting through innumerable forces, the lord of the Rākshasas hurtled to where thunder-wielding Indra rode on the back of Airāvat.

§610

Hundreds of Gandharvas encircled Rāvan; his roar was enough to ward them all off in a trice, like a forest-fire reducing trees to ashes!

Warriors fled, shamefully giving up the fight. The enemy of the Daityas came back

Furious as Karna, when he saw Arjun, in the battle of Kurukshetra.

§616

The Raksha king bellowed as he hurled a massive lance at the head of Airāvat. Indra instantly intercepted his attack, with a shower of arrows.

The lord of the Karburas yelled proudly to the king of the gods: 'He who was a constant terror to you in heaven, O husband of Sachi,

Has been killed today through your deceit, in unfair combat! I suppose that is why you have come to Lankā so shamelessly!

You are unkillable, immortal; otherwise I would crush you at once,

§587

Airāvat Indra's flying elephant. See III.378.

§610

Hundreds of Gandharvas see I.375. **the enemy of the Daityas** i.e. Indra, enemy of all demons and anti-gods. See V.29. **Furious as Karna, when he saw Arjun, in the battle of Kurukshetra** in the battle that forms the protracted climax of the *Mahābhārata*, Arjun, third of the five Pāṇḍav brothers, kills Vrishasen, son of the Kaurav hero Karna (see I.218), who attacks Arjun in fury, and is slain by him.

§616

The lord of the Karburas see IV.531.

As Death would himself. But you won't be able to save
Lakshman—that is my vow,
Sir!' Grasping an enormous club, Rāvan jumped from
his chariot to the ground;
The earth shook violently at the impact of his feet; in its
scabbard by his thigh, his sword rattled noisily!

§631

The bellowing Thunderer aimed his thunderbolt!
Immediately Garuḍa purloined its power; the
Thunder-thrower could not even move his thunder!
The Raksha king then struck at the head of the king of all
elephants with his fearsome cudgel, like the wind when
it hurls a storm at a mountain-top, uprooting trees!
Airāvat was crushed by the blow, sank to his knees.
With a laugh,
Rāvan returned to his chariot. Instantly the charioteer
Mātali supplied a new vehicle for Indra; shamefacedly,
The enemy of Diti's sons withdrew. Bow in hand and roaring
like a lion, Rām now entered the fray in his divine chariot.

§643

The Rākshas king said: 'I do not want to fight you
today, O husband of Sitā!
Live safely for one more day in this world! Where is
your brother, that false-fighting scoundrel?
I shall kill him; go back to your camp, O chief of the
Rāghavas!'

§631

Immediately Garuḍa purloined its power cf. §587 above, where Garuḍa steals power from Skanda, the god of war himself. Garuḍa is subject to Vishnu's command here: when Meghnād defeated Rām and Lakshman and bound them with snakes, Garuḍa rescued them. See I.743. **Mātali** Indra's charioteer Mātali instantly supplies a new chariot because Airāvat has been put out of action. **The enemy of Diti's sons** i.e. Indra, enemy of all demons or Daityas, whose mother is Diti (see II.217).

Bellowing loudly, great-archer-Rāvan saw Rām's brother from afar. Like a lion amidst a herd of oxen,
Lakshman was slaughtering Rākshasas; sometimes in his chariot, sometimes on the ground.

§652

The flying chariot whirled along with a spinning sound; its wheels rained sparks as if they were made of fire; a royal banner adorned its crest like a comet!
Like a royal hawk when it spreads its wings and swoops through the sky on seeing a distant dove, the Rākshas swooped on seeing the son of Sumitrā,
Slayer of men. Gods and men rushed up noisily to protect the hero. Rākshasas too came running, following their lord.

§661

Hanumān, son of Anjanā, having fought off the Rākshas Biḍālāksha,
Now came, fierce as a storm in his attack, his roars frightening to hear.

§664

Like bunches of cotton blown in all directions by the wind, the Rākshasas fled at top speed, at the sight of the Death-like hero.
The king of Lankā, enraged, assailed the hero with razor-sharp arrows!

§652

The son of Sumitrā i.e. Lakshman. See I.172.

§661

Hanumān, son of Anjanā see I.218 and III.222.

Biḍālāksha see above, §158.

§664

Death-like hero Hanumān is here described as a *yamākṛti bīr*: a hero shaped like Yama, god of death (see I.1, 218).

Hanu became agitated, like a mountain shaken by an earthquake! At this moment of danger,
He humbly remembered his father; joyfully the wind gave his own strength to his son, like the sun when it decorates with its rays the moon,
Fount of ambrosia, the lotus's desire! But the fiery son of Nikashā,
Filled with Siva's anger, stopped the son of the wind; Hanumān fled brokenly from the battlefield!

§676

King Sugriv of Kishkindhyā came next, after slaying in battle Udagra, lover of warfare.
The lord of Lankā laughed and said: 'At what unlucky time, you ruffian,
Did you leave the comforts of your kingdom to come to golden Lankā? Your brother's wife Tārā is as lovely as a star; why did you leave her,
To be here amongst fighters, O ruler of Kishkindhyā? I let you pass—
Go back to your kingdom! Why make her a widow again, you fool?
What other brothers-in-law does she have?' Brave Sugriv replied fiercely, 'Who is more sinful in the world than you,
O king of the Rākshasas? Through your lust for another's wife, you have dragged down your whole race,

§664

He humbly remembered his father i.e. Vāyu/Pavan, god of the winds (see I.218). **fiery son of Nikashā** i.e. Rāvan. See I.62.

§676

Udagra see above, §158. **Your brother's wife Tārā is as lovely as a star** Sugriv overthrew and killed his brother Vāli and married his wife Tārā. See I.218. Her name means 'star'.

§676

Through your lust for another's wife since Sugriv is guilty of the same offence, there is an irony here that shows M's sympathy for the Rākshasas.

You scoundrel! You are the ruin of the Raksha race, Rāvan!
Your death is now in my hands. I shall rescue my
friend's wife, by killing you today!'

§691

Saying this, the hero roared and threw a whole
mountain-peak. Darkening the sky,
The peak flew; with a piercing arrow, the battled-skilled
king of the Rākshasas intercepted it,
Smashed it to pieces. Drawing his bow again with a yell,
the crest-jewel of the Rākshasas now pierced Sugriv again,
With his sharpest arrow! In agony from the blow, the
good king retreated;
The Raghu armies too fled in all directions (like water
when a dam breaks), noisy in their terror;
The gods, spiritless now, fled with the humans,
Like sparks flying with smoke, when the wind blows
strongly! Rāvan saw Lakshman ahead of him,
Godlike in appearance! Frenzied with battle-lust, he
roared at him ferociously—
Lakshman shouted back at him fearlessly, like an
elephant in rut trumpeting at the noise of another
mad elephant! Angrily,
The bow-bearer twanged his god-given bow. 'Have I,
O Lakshman,
You wretch,' raged Rāvan, 'at last found you on the
battlefield?'
Where is Indra the Thunderer now? Where is peacock-
bannered Skanda? And the lord of the Raghus,
Your brother? Where is King Sugriv? Who will save you today,
You scoundrel? Think of your mother Sumitrā, and your
wife Urmilā,

§691
god-given bow see Book II, §475f. **Urmilā** see I.1.

At this hour of doom—think of them both! I shall feed your flesh to flesh-eating animals now;
Earth will suck up your stream of blood! You crossed the sea at a fatal time, you villain;
You entered Rākshas territory in thief's garb; you stole the jewel of the Rākshasas—whose value in the world was unparalleled.'

§721
King Rāvan bellowed aggressively, and fixed to his bow an arrow like a spike of fire; the loud-voiced lion-hero Lakshman answered with a leonine roar;
'I was born a Kshatriya, O king of the Rākshasas; I do not fear death;
Why should I be afraid of you? Grief for your son has unbalanced you today. Whatever you may try to do,
Warrior, I shall soon extinguish your grief, by sending you to join your beloved son!'

§729
A tremendous fight ensued; gods and men stared at the two of them in wonder; again and again roaring Lakshman deflected Rāvan's arrows!
Surprised, the Raksha ruler said: 'Your prowess does you credit, lion-like son of Sumitrā!
You are mightier than Skanda, and more skilful. But you won't escape from me now!'

§736
With Meghnād in his thoughts, Rāvan furiously hurled his great *śakti*-weapon! Upwards it whooshed,

§721
I was born a Kshatriya see VI.471.

§736
***śakti*-weapon** when Rāvan married Mandodari, her father Maya (see I.33, 172) gave him an infallible *mahāśakti* ('great power') weapon, which he had acquired through feats of *tapas* or austerity.

That awesome foe-destroyer: roaring like thunder, lighting the sky like lightning!
Gods and men trembled with fear! Like a star falling, Lakshman crashed to the ground as the wonder-weapon struck him;
His god-given weapons clattered, lustreless now from their smearing of blood; the hero fell like a mountain throttled by snakes!

§744

Like a hunter in the deep forest when he kills a lion with an infallible arrow, and rushes towards it, so the mighty Raksha king jumped down from his chariot and ran to claim the corpse!
Howls broke out all around! Divine and human forces surrounded Lakshman's body with cries of horror. On Mount Kailās,
At the feet of Siva, Durgā said: 'The Raksha king has killed Lakshman,
My lord, in battle. The son of Sumitrā is rolling now in the dust!
You have satisfied that Rākshas, loyal to your devotees as you are; you have swept aside Indra's boasting;
But I beg you, extra-eyed husband, to save Lakshman's corpse!'

§757

Smiling, trident-wielding Siva said to brave Virbhadra: 'Restrain,

§744

loyal to your devotees as you are see above, §143.

extra-eyed husband *Virupākṣa*: 'odd-eyed', an epithet for Siva because of the 'third eye' in his forehead.

§757

Virbhadra see above, §67f.

Hero, the king of Lankā.' Reaching him with the speed of thought,
Virbhadra said sternly in Rāvan's ear: 'Return, O Raksha king,
To golden Lankā. What point is there in fighting, now that your enemy is dead?'
§762
The divine messenger vanished like a dream! Lion-hero Rāvan got back into his chariot with a lion-like roar; the Rākshas band played,
The Rākshasas cheered tumultuously; the Raksha army re-entered the city—like fearsome,
Battle-triumphant Chanḍa-and-Munḍa-killing Durgā, returning after killing Raktabij, dancing victoriously,
Roaring and cackling through her blood-smeared lips, her body soaked in blood! In the same way that the gods assembled to praise her then,
So singers welcomed the Rākshas army, in joy, with songs of victory!
§772
Defeated in battle, Indra returned with his forces to heaven, greatly humiliated.

Here ends 'The Assault of the *Śakti*-weapon',
the seventh book of *Meghnādbadh kābya*.

§762

Chanḍa-and-Munḍa-killing Durgā, returning after killing Raktabij see III.352, 523 and Source Notes, p. 369.

BOOK VIII

§1

Like an emperor finishing his day of royal work, and carefully laying down his crown before entering his bedroom, the sun,
Dispeller of darkness, removed the jewels from its head at the end of the day, and laid them on the western mountain-peak.
Night came with her company of stars, and her calm husband the moon, fount of nectar.

§7

Hundreds of fires burned all around on the battlefield. Where the valiant son of Sumitrā lay on the ground, Sitā's lord lay silently also!
His tears, ceaselessly flowing to blend with his brother's blood, dampened the earth,
Like a spring mixing with ochre-coloured earth as it flows down a mountainside! Empty of heart, the Rāghav army mourned;
Vibhishan (fearsome in battle), Kumud,
Angad, Hanumān, Nala,
Nila, the mighty Sarabh, Sumāli
(Strong-armed as a lion) and Sugriv: all were sorrowful at their lord's sorrow!

§7

the valiant son of Sumitrā i.e. Lakshman. See I.172.
Rāghav army i.e. the army of Rām and the Raghus. See I.1.
Vibhishan see I.218.
Kumud warrior from the kingdom of Kishkindhyā, allied with Rām.
Angad, Hanumān . . . Nila see I.218.
Nala see IV.464.
Sarabh see VII.218.
Sumāli another warrior from Kishkindhyā.
Sugriv see I.218.

§18

Emerging from his swoon, Lord Rām said mournfully:
'When we left our kingdom,
And settled in the forest, Lakshman; when night came,
You always kept watch, bow in hand, to protect me,
O great bowsman! Today—today,
Here in this Raksha city—I am drowning in a perilous sea of enemies; yet do you,
Mighty as you are, forget me, to take your rest on the earth?
Who, tell me, will protect me today?
Rise up, I say! When have you neglected your brother's command?
But if through my misfortune—perpetually unlucky as I am—you have deserted me,
O more-than-my-life, then say—I am listening—
What wrong has my unhappy wife Sitā done to you? She thinks of you, her brother-in-law,
Constantly in her Raksha prison: she weeps for you day and night. How can you forget—
Dear brother, how can you forget today the one who continually cared for you with a mother's love? O crest of the Rāghav clan,
The grandson of Paulastya has enchained a wife of your clan! Is it right that you should lie here like this, without punishing in battle that vile thief—
You who in battle are as all-devouring as fire? Rise with your arms strong, O victory-banner of the Raghus!
I am helpless without you, like a charioteer in a chariot without wheels! Hanu is stricken where you lie,

§18

The grandson of Paulastya Paulastya was one of ten sages or *prajāpatis* created by Brahmā. He imparted the Vishnu Purāna to Parāshar, one of the poets of the Rig Veda and father of Vyāsa, author of the *Mahābhārata*. He

I tell you, like a bow without its string; Angad is moaning in sorrow;
Our wise friend Sugriv is bereft; that noblest of Karburas Vibhishan is horrified; the whole army is distraught!
Rise quickly; soothe my eyes by opening your eyes, my brother!

§49

'But if you are exhausted from this ghastly battle, great bow-bearer, let us return to the forest.
What hope is there, my dearest, of rescuing unfortunate Sitā?
What hope is there of defeating Rāvan? On the bank of the Sarayu river, where your mother Sumitrā weeps for her darling son,
How can I show my face, Lakshman, if you do not return with me?
What shall I say, when your mother asks: "Where,
Gentle Rām, is the jewel of my eyes, your younger brother?"
What shall I say to your wife Urmilā, and all the citizens? Rise,
My darling! Why oh why do you turn away today from your brother's request, though your love for him made you leave the comforts of the realm and withdraw to the forest?
You always used to weep with sympathy when you saw my tearful eyes; you tenderly stanched my flow of tears; I am drenched with tears now,

---

was the father of Visravās, who was father of Kuber (see I.62), Rāvan, Kumbhakarna (see I.80) and Vibhishan.

§18

Karburas i.e. the Rākshasas. See IV.531.

§49

Sarayu river river on whose banks Rām's city of Ayodhyā lies; a tributary of the Gogra (Gharghara). **your wife Urmilā** see I.1.

Yet will you not look at me, O more-than-my life? O Lakshman
(Famous in the world for loving your brother!), can this behaviour ever befit you, O brother,
My eternal joy? All my life I have followed *dharma*, I have worshipped the gods;
Is this the fruit they give me? O night, you are full of kindness;
With your drenching of dew, you perpetually refresh the flowers, withered from the day's heat;
Give the gift of life to this flower! You, O moon,
Are a fount of nectar; spread your life-giving nectar, revive Lakshman—
And restore too, by your compassion, this pleading Rām!'

§78

Lamenting in this way, the enemy of the Rākshasas cradled his beloved brother in his lap, on the field of battle;
His warriors sighed all around with grief, like trees sighing at midnight, when the wind blows through them in the deep forest!

§83

In her palace on Mount Kailās, Durgā, daughter of the mountain,
Was dejected at Rām's sorrow; with her head in husband's lap, she drenched his lotus-feet with her streams of tears,
Like dew soaking a lotus at dawn! Lord Siva asked: 'Why,
My beauty, are you upset today? Please tell me.'

§49

dharma see II.173.

§83

Mount Kailās see I.33, II.126.
Durgā, daughter of the mountain see II.287.

'What do you not know, my lord?' replied the fair-
skinned goddess;
'In grief for Lakshman, in golden Lankā, Rāmchandra—
Listen—is weeping pathetically! My heart is disturbed
by his lament!
Who, O lord of the universe, will worship me again in
this world?
You have caused me deep shame today, husband; you
have sunk my name in a lake of scandal!
I erred at your feet by breaking your trance, O master of
trance; is this why you have punished me in this way?
Unlucky was the time that Indra came to me! Unlucky
was the time I was worshipped by Rām, the husband
of Sitā!'

§100

The great goddess fell silent, tearfully wounded in her
feelings! Siva answered with a smile:
'Why, O daughter of the mountain, are you so glum
over such a small matter?
Send, with the aid of Māyā, the heroic Raghu chief to
Kritānta's city;

§83

Rāmchandra see I.176.

Who . . . will worship me again in this world? In II.225–233 Durgā receives the fragrance of Rām's *pūjā* to her, and grants him a boon of 'fearlessness' (*abhaya*). It is very important to protect him and make sure that her boon is effective. This is why, as advised by Siva, she sends Māyā to Rām as her representative.

I erred at your feet by breaking your trance see Book II, §265f.

Unlucky was the time that Indra came to me see Book II, §133f.

Unlucky was the time I was worshipped by Rām see Book II, §225f.

§100

with the aid of Māyā see II.425, 309.

Kritānta's city i.e. Yama's city, the realm of death (see I.1). This name for Yama means 'bringing to an end'.

Favoured by me, he will enter the land of ghosts in his mortal shape. His father,
King Dasarath, will tell him how his brother will come back to life again. Don't be downcast,
Moon-like one! O beautiful wife, give this trident of mine to Māyā:
It will light up the gloomy underworld like a pillar of fire; the ghosts will honour it, as subjects do a king's sceptre!'

§113

Durgā mentally called Māyā to the Kailās palace. In a trice, the sorceress was there,
Doing obeisance to Durgā; the goddess said to her in sweet terms: 'Go to Lankā,
O enchantress of the universe. Sitā's husband is crying, desolate at Lakshman's death;
Address him consolingly, and take him with you to the underworld; his father Dasarath will advise him—
Will tell him how wise Lakshman will come back to life; and all the warriors who have been slain in this dreadful conflict. Take this trident in your lotus hand,
Chaste one—it is from the Trident-holder himself. Finest of weapons that it is,
It will light up Death's gloomy realm like a pillar of fire!' Pranāming to Umā, Māyā set off.
Chāyā-devi, goddess of the Milky Way, fled far away,

§100

King Dasarath see I.172. **this trident of mine** the *Devīmāhātmya* (see V.113) describes how when Siva and the other gods created Durgā in order to destroy the demon Mahish, they each gave her a weapon. Siva gave her his trident, Krishna (Vishnu) gave her his disc, Agni gave her a flaming spear, etc.

§113

the Trident-holder himself from *triśūli*, a name for Siva (see II.447). **Umā** i.e. Durgā. See II.337 and I.483. **Chāyā-devi** *chāyā* means 'shade'.

Pallid beside Māyā's blazing beauty! Stars took on her shine—like jewels lit up by sunshine!
Leaving a trail of light behind her in the sky, like foam behind a boat, beautiful Māyā sped towards Lankā!
Soon she alighted there, where the jewel of the Raghus sat mournfully with his troops! Golden Lankā was filled with heavenly fragrance!

§134

Māyā said in Rāghav's ear: 'Wipe away your flow of tears, son of Dasarath—
Your brother will live; bathe in the sea-waters, then come with me quickly to Death's abode;
In your mortal frame, wise Rām, you will enter the city of ghosts today through Siva's grace.
Your father Dasarath will tell you how well-favoured Lakshman will come back to life. O great-armed one, come quickly with me.
I shall make a tunnel; go down it fearlessly, hero!
I shall go ahead of you, showing you the way. Tell Sugriv and the other generals to guard Lakshman.'

§147

Amazed, Rām told the generals to keep watch, then went to the seashore,
To the great bathing-place there. Washing his body in the sacred waters, that man of good fortune,
After honouring the gods and his ancestors with an offering of water, returned quickly and alone to the door of his tent. How bright it was now with Māyā's enveloping radiance!

She was created by Samjñā, wife of Surya the sun-god, as a sister-goddess who would stand between her and her husband and protect her from his heat. Samjñā then escaped into a forest disguised as a mare. Surya pursued her there, disguised as a stallion, and sired the Asvin twins (see I.417).

Cupping his hands, he made an offering of flowers to the goddess. Dressing his majestic body in formidable armour,
The hero of heroes cheerfully stepped into the tunnel: with the gods on his side, what had he to fear?

§158

The Rāghav chieftan proceeded, like a wayfarer along a dark forest path, when,
At night-time, moonshine dapples the trees. Māyā-devi walked silently ahead of him.

§162

After a while, Rām was startled to hear a surging sound, as of thousands of sea-waves angrily breaking!
Nervously he saw nearby a terrifying city, sunk in eternal night! The thunderous Vaitarani river encircled it like a moat;
Waves foamed tumultuously, like fire-shaken clouds of steam from milk boiled up in a pan! The sun doesn't shine in the sky of that land;
Nor the moon; nor the stars; dense clouds,
Belching out flames, scud in the wind overhead, thunderously roaring like Siva when he ends the world by furiously shooting from his bow!

§175

Rām saw with astonishment a weird bridge over the river, sometimes ablaze, sometimes covered in cloud,
And sometimes beautiful—as if made of gold! Souls rushed ceaselessly towards that bridge—

§162

Vaitarani river the river that separates Naraka or hell (where sinners are punished) from the 'three worlds' of heaven, earth and Pātāla, the underworld realm of the Nāgas (see II.491). It is roughly equivalent to the Acheron or the Styx in Greco-Roman mythology. See Source Notes, pp. 373–4.

Hundreds of thousands of them, some of them wailing, some of them laughing!

§181

Sitā's lord asked, 'Tell me, kind Māyā,

Why does the bridge keep changing in appearance? Why do innumerable souls rush towards it, like insects towards a flame?'

§185

Māyā-devi asnwered: 'It's the bridge of desires, Rām;

For sinners it is fiery and covered in smoke; for the virtuous, it is broad,

Beautiful, like the golden path to heaven! Those countless spirits that you see,

Jewel of men, have left their mortal bodies and are all on the way to the underworld, to receive the fruits of their actions there;

The followers of *dharma* take the bridge to the north, west and east gates; sinners,

With horrendous effort, have to keep swimming across; Death's henchman torments them on the banks;

Their sinful hearts burn in the water, as if in boiling oil! Come along with me;

You will soon see what has never, by human eyes, been seen before!'

§199

Slowly Rām followed, while magical Māyā led like a golden lantern, lighting that hideous land!

Next to the bridge he saw with horror Yama's towering envoy, a staff in his hand! Bellowing like thunder,

The brute demanded, 'Who are you? By what power,

§185

the bridge of desires for this and other aspects of hell as described by M, see Source Notes, p. 374f.

O braggart, have you entered this ghostly land in the flesh? Speak quickly,
Or else I shall smash you in a trice with a sweep of my rod!' Laughing, Māyā-devi held up Siva's trident before the envoy.
§209
Bowing, the envoy said meekly to the goddess, 'What power do I have,
Lady, to obstruct your path? The bridge itself is golden—
See—with delight, like the sky at dawn's arrival!'
§213
Rām and Māyā crossed the Vaitarani river. The Raghu lord saw ahead of him iron gates of a city; wheels of fire ceaselessly revolved on all sides,
Corruscating! The jewel of men saw on that awesome gate, written in flaming letters,
The message: 'By this road go sinners to a land of torment to suffer eternal torment; you who enter here must abandon all hope!'
§221
The hero saw Disease at the gate, reduced to skin and bone. Sometimes its emaciated body shuddered with cold;
Sometimes it was flushed with scorching heat, like the Lord of the Oceans scalded by Vāḍaba's fire! Biliousness,
Congestion, Flatulence violently assaulted it, robbing it of consciousness!
Next to it sat Gluttony, with a hugely distended belly; repeatedly vomiting undigested food,

§221
Vāḍaba's fire see III.115.

It scooped it again and again in its bare hands and
swallowed it greedily! Next Drunkenness raved,
cackling and rolling its eyes!
In turn it danced, sang, yelled abuse or lapsed into a
senseless stupor!
Next was foul Lust, decomposing like a corpse, yet
perpetually copulating—
Continually burning at its core with the flames of
passions! Next sat Consumption, retching up blood,
Coughing all the time; and Asthma, wheezing unbearably!
And Cholera, with lacklustre eyes; from mouth and anus
flowed a stream of blood,
Colourless as water! Virulent Thirst attacked it
constantly; its thin body was clutched by Cramp—
Death's horrible attendant—like a tiger attacking an
animal in the forest, falling on it,
Gleefully biting it to pieces. Nearby, next to that disease,
Sat Insanity—sometimes manic, like fire when ghee is
thrown into it,
Sometimes inert! And dressed in various styles—or
sometimes naked,
Like Siva's paramour Kāli in battle-frenzy! Sometimes
she crazily sang songs, clapping her hands;
Sometimes she howled; sometimes she laughed through
her hideous lips; sometimes she cut her own throat
with a razor-sharp dagger;

§221

ghee see VI.401.**or sometimes naked,/ Like Siva's paramour Kāli in battle frenzy** Kāli, the most ferocious manifestation of Siva's *śakti* or consort, is traditionally depicted as black and naked, with blazing bloodthirsty eyes, a lolling tongue, a string of skulls round her body, snakes writhing round her neck, and weapons in each of her ten hands. See also III.102, 248, 413.

Or swallowed poison; or drowned in a well or hanged herself! Sometimes—
Horrors!—whipped up with lust, her grotesque gyrations lured lovers to fornicate!
Mixing faeces and urine, alas, into her food,
She golloped it cheerfully! Sometimes restrained by chains; sometimes sluggish as a currentless stream,
When no wind blows; unending were her madnesses, beyond description!

§262

Valiant Rāghav saw War (his face smeared with blood, a sharp sword in his hand),
In a fire-coloured chariot! Anger sat at the front of the chariot, dressed as a charioteer—
A garland of skulls round his neck, a pile of human bodies at his feet! Then Rām saw Murder,
With a terrifying sword in his hand; his arms were perpetually raised, alas,
To commit a murder! Suicide was swinging dumbly from a noose round its neck attached to a tree; its tongue was lolling;
Its eyes were protruding horribly! Māyā-devi said soothingly: 'You have seen all those ghastly envoys of Death,
O Raghu warrior; they wander unremittingly over the earth in various guises, like a hunter in deep forest in pursuit of a deer!
Proceed into Kritānta's city, O husband of Sitā; I will show you today,
Alas, how ghosts in the land of ghosts live. This is the south gate;
There are eighty-four lakes in this region. Come, come quickly.'

§280

The great husband of Sitā entered Death's city, like, ah!
Spring, king of the seasons, when he enters a burnt-out forest;
Or like nectar reviving a lifeless body! The city was shrouded in darkness, with the sound of groaning all around;
Earthquakes shook land and water; clouds were furiously belching fire; a scorching breeze was blowing,
As if, in a cremation-ground, thousands of corpses were burning!

§288

In a while the finest of the Raghus saw a great lake ahead of him; fires were rolling across it like waves! Millions of souls were afloat in it,
Writhing and screaming: 'Alas, almighty God,
So cruel, have you created us all just for this? O tyrant,
Why did we not die of fiery hunger in our mother's womb? Where are you, O sun?
And you, Lord of the Night O moon? Shall we never soothe our eyes by seeing you two again?
Where are our sons, wives, relations?
Where oh where is the wealth that we went down path after crooked path to amass, abandoning *dharma* to do things that were wrong?'

§300

Thus did the ghosts of sinners lament without pause in that lake! Suddenly an answer boomed out of the void above, filled it with its terrible sound:
'Why this futile railing against Fate, you fools? You receive here the fruit of your actions on earth!
Why were you deceived by sin into forgetting righteousness?

You know that, in the fateful workings of *karma* in the world, there is no flaw.'

§308

The celestial message ceased; immense minions of Death swung cudgels down on to their heads; tapeworms gnawed at them;

Flesh-eating birds, with claws hard as adamant, swooped down on their shadowy bodies and raucously tore out their entrails!

The sinners filled, with their screams, the entire region!

§313

Māyā said sadly to Rāghav: 'This lake is called Uproar: listen to the noise,

Jewel of the Raghus, of its fiery waters! Those who wickedly steal from others dwell here for ever;

Judges who behave unjustly also end up here—and many other sinners, engaged in villainy.

Its flames never go out; worms gnaw perpetually! Rām,

I told you it was no ordinary fire that burnt the ghosts in this appalling hell; the anger of Fate burns here eternally! Come,

Warrior, come and see the circle of hell called *Kumbhipāk*: Yama's henchmen fry sinners there in boiling oil!

Listen, I tell you, to their howls nearby!

§300

Fate . . . fruit of your actions . . . fateful workings of *karma* see Introduction, p. liif. The last line of the paragraph is *subidhi bidhir bidhi bidita jagate*: literally, 'The law of Fate in the world (is) known to be a good law'.

§313

the anger of Fate *bidhi-roṣ*: cf. VI.84 etc.

Kumbhipāk in this region of hell, the damned are baked like a clay *kumbha* (jar, pot), or cooked like the contents of one.

I have blocked your nostrils with my magic; otherwise you would not be able to stand it here, O finest of Raghus!
Or let us go to where the ghosts of suicides groan in impenetrably dark wells, imprisoned there for ever!'
With clasped hands Lord Rām pleaded:
'Spare me, kind goddess! I shall die straightaway from horror if I see any more horrible sufferings like this!
Alas, mother, who would willingly be born on earth,
If this state ensues? Man is frail; who can withstand the blandishments of sin?'
Māyā replied: 'There is no poison, great archer,
In this vast world, for which there is no medicine! But if anyone rejects that medicine,
Who can save him? The good—those who battle against sin on the field of *karma*—
Are never let down by the gods; righteousness shields them with impenetrable armour! If you do not wish to see all these places of punishment,
Then come, warrior, along this road!'
§346
A little further on Sitā's husband entered a great forest—silent, vast and limitless;
No birds called there, no breeze blew in that frightful place, none of the flowers bloomed that normally bring beauty to woodlands!
Rays of light pierced the foliage in places—but wanly, like the smiles of the sick.
§352
Thousands of ghosts suddenly surrounded the Raghu

§313

on the field of *karma* *karma-kṣetre*: for this and also for M's conception of sin (*pāp*), see Introduction, p. liif. and lviiif.

righteousness *dharma*: see II.173.

prince, inquisitive as bees round a honey-pot.
Piteously,
Some of them asked: 'Who are you? Tell us,
By what miracle have you come to this place, with your body still intact? Whether you are god or man,
Speak quickly! Speak—give solace to us all,
O miraculous one, with the showering nectar of your voice!
Ever since Death's envoy abducted our sinful souls,
We have been deprived of the sound of the tongue's speech!
O hero, our eyes are comforted by the sight of your limbs;
Soothe our ears, sir, with your voice!'

§363

The enemy of the Rākshasas replied: 'I am of Raghu stock, O shades;
Valiant Dasarath is my father; his chief queen Kausalyā is my mother; my name is Rām;
I was unluckily exiled, alas, to the forest!
At Siva's command, I have come to visit my father: that is why I am in Kritānta's city today.'

§369

One of the ghosts replied: 'I know you, great leader;
I lost my life in the Panchavaṭi wood because of your arrow.' The jewel of men saw with amazement the Rākshas Mārich—bodiless now!

§373

Rāmchandra asked: 'What sin has brought you to this ghastly forest, Rākshas?

§363

I was unluckily exiled, alas, to the forest see I.386, II.173, VI.123.
Kritānta's city see above, §100.

§369

Panchavaṭi wood see I.80, 763.
the Rākshas Mārich see IV.266.

Tell me.' 'Rāvan, that wicked descendant of Paulastya,
Is the cause of my punishment, sir!' replied disembodied Mārich;
I led you astray at his behest—that was my crime!' The Rākshasas Khar and Dushan now appeared
(Khar, who was like the sharpest sword in battle when he was alive); seeing the Raghu lord,
The two shrank back again, in fury and shame, like a snake without fangs when it sees a mongoose,
And slinks back into its lair! Suddenly a clattering racket filled the wood: the ghosts sped away,
Like dry leaves when blown by a violent storm! Māyā said to great Rām: 'These ghosts,
Listen, jewel of the Raghus, live in various circles of hell;
Sometimes they come and wander in this wood of lamentation, to lament silently. Look over there,
Death's envoys are angrily driving them all back to their cells!'
Sitā's lotus-heart's sun gazed at the bands of ghosts:
Death's grim servants hounded them; they screamed as they ran, like a herd of deer being chased by a ravenous lion,
Breathlessly panting! That sea of compassion Rāmchandra sorrowfully proceeded with Māyā, tears in his eyes.

§398

Soon the hero was trembling at the sound of more

§373

that wicked descendant of Paulastya see above, §18.

The Rākshasas Khar and Dushan sons of Rāvan's mother's sister. They were appointed guards to Rāvan's sister Surpanakhā, who sent them to attack Rām and Lakshman in revenge for her humilation (see I.80). They were killed by Rām and Lakshman in the Panchavaṭi wood, along with their 14,000 strong army. *Khar* means 'sharp, keen'.

wailing! He saw in the distance thousands of women, unadorned,
Like the moon in the sky in daylight! Some of them were tearing their long hair and shouting, 'We were perpetually preening and binding you,
To bind our lovers, forgetting all decency, crazed with youthful lust!'
Some were lacerating their breasts with their nails, saying, 'Alas,
Vainly we spent our days adorning you with diamonds and pearls; what was the result of that?' Some women violently gouged their own eyes
(Like a pitiless vulture attacking a dead animal), crying: 'Smearing you with collyrium,
O eyes of sin, we aimed seductive glances in all directions; when we examined your gleam in the mirror,
We hated the eyes of deer! In the end, what was our reward for such vanity?'

§414

The women dispersed, weeping and wailing. Behind them a female envoy of Death was on guard;
Instead of tresses, vicious, hissing snakes hung down her back;
Her nails were like swords; her lips were bloody; her hideous,
Pendulous breasts hung down to her navel; dazzling fire belched out of her nostrils; the flames of her eyes mingled with its glare!

§421

Addressing Rāghav, Māyā said: 'You see before you,
O jewel of the Raghus, those women; they were all addicted to clothes and ornaments on earth.

Like trees in spring, they always lustfully decked themselves out, to infatuate the hearts of deluded lovers!
Alas, where is their gorgeous beauty now, the treasure of their youth?'
Immediately an echo sounded: *Alas, where is their gorgeous beauty now,*
The treasure of their youth? Wailing pitifully, the women went off to their respective hells.

§431

Māyā spoke again: 'Look in front of you again, O enemy of the Rākshasas.'
The jewel of men saw another troupe of women, of ravishing beauty! Their hair was entwined with fragrant flowers;
Flames of desire were in their deerlike eyes; nectar of infinite sweetness on their honeyed lips!
Their necks were adorned with jewels like Indra's conch! Bodices of thin gold thread covered their breasts only to reveal them, to arouse in the hearts of lovers still greater desire!
Their waists were wafer-thin; their heavy thighs, despising,
So it seemed, the flimsy blue silk that (very thinly)
Covered them, merrily displayed their banana-tree-like grace; like the naked limbs of nymphs in Lake Mānas when they gambol in the filmy waters.
Anklets jingled round their feet, and a girdle round their buttocks; *vīṇā*,

§431

Indra's conch *kambu* meaning a conch or shell has traditionally been used as a simile for a neck: hence its appropriateness here.

Lake Mānas see I.33.

vīṇā see I.623.

Violin, cymbals and *sāraṅgī* gently blended with the merry beats of a drum; the women were blissfully floating on waves of music.

§450

From the other direction, a handsome band of youths appeared, smiling fetchingly;

They were comely as the mighty Kārttikeya, the darling of the Krittikās; or,

O Rati, like Madan, your heart's desire!

§454

Maddened with desire at beholding that male company, the women shot coy glances from their eyes, and tinkled the bangles on their wrists.

Blown by their hot breath, the pollen in their flower-garlands quickly covered the sun of self-control in the men. They gave up the fight;

In such a battle where are there men, ah! with the power to win?

§461

Like a bird and its mate when they flit here and there in the sport of love, the amorous women whisked those lusty youths off into the forest—their intentions writ large in their eyes.

§465

Suddenly the forest filled with a howling noise! In horror Rām saw the men and women rolling horribly on the ground, scrabbling and scratching,

§431

sāraṅgī a stringed instrument played with a bow like a violin.

§450

The mighty Kārttikeya, the darling of the Krittikās Kārttikeya, god of war, was wet-nursed by the six Krittikās. See II.491. **O Rati, like Madan, your heart's desire** see II.265, 287 and the events in Book II, §265f.

Thumping and kicking each other. They tore at hair and
gouged at eyes, slashed at noses and faces with their
hard finger-nails.
A stream of blood soaked the earth. Both groups fought
viciously, like Bhim in the kingdom of Virāta,
Disguised as a woman and fighting ferociously with Kichak.
All the henchmen of Death who were there then pounced,
quickly drove both groups away with iron clubs.
In gentle tones, the beautiful Māyā spoke to Rām, the
joy of the Raghu clan:

§477

'In life—listen, my child—
The men were the servants of Kāma; and the women
too. Kāma satisfied their greed unceasingly,
Sinking *dharma*, alas, in the waters of *adharma*,
Discarding shame; now they are being punished in this
city of Yama! Like a mirage deceiving a thirsty man
in the desert;
Like a gold-skinned *mākāl*-fruit duping the hungry; that

§465

like Bhim in the kingdom of Virāta,/ Disguised as a woman and fighting ferociously with Kichak the *Mahābhārata* tells of how, during their thirteenth, last year in exile, the five Pāṇḍavas lived incognito in the kingdom of Virāta. A general there, Kichak, kept pestering their joint wife Draupadi for her affections. She appealed to Bhimsen, the second eldest of the brothers, and he dealt with the problem by dressing up as a woman. Draupadi agreed to an assignation with Kichak, but Bhim waited for him in her place. When Kichak bowed down in the dark and penitently invited the fake Draupadi to kick him in the head, Bhim was happy to oblige, and the ferocious fight that followed left Kichak dead.

§477

servants of Kāma i.e. servants of the god of love. See II.287, 439.

adharma the opposite of *dharma*: unrighteousness.

gold-skinned *mākāl*-fruit duping the hungry the bitter-apple or colocynth: a gourd-like fruit that looks beautiful but whose pulp is nasty-smelling and inedible.

is what happens when they fornicate; desire in both groups is vain.
What more shall I say, my child? Mark what you see.
This torment, O fortunate one, is suffered by many sinners on earth before they go to hell:
This is what Fate prescribes to them. Wanton waste in their youth; beggary in old age.
An inextinguishable fire of lust burns in their hearts; in the form of lust, Fate's unquenchable fury burns their bodies;
I tell you, great-armed one, this is the reward of these sinners in the end!'

§494
Bowing at the feet of Māyā, the jewel of men said: 'Many are the strange sights I have seen in this city,
Mother, by your grace: who can describe them all?
But where is my royal father? I want to beg at his feet for my young brother Lakshman; will you take me now to his blessed abode?'

§500
Māyā smiled: 'This city is endless, Rāghav,
I have shown you only a bit of it. If we roamed together unceasingly for twelve years in Kritānta's city, O hero,
We would not see the whole of it. At the east gate live chaste, devoted wives with their husbands;
That part of the city is unparalleled on earth or in heaven; there are beautiful mansions with fine gardens, and lovely lakes always full of lotuses;
A spring breeze wafts all the time with a charming murmur; *koels* sing perfect fifths without pause! The *vīṇā* plays without a player;

§500
***koels* sing perfect fifths without pause** see I.623.

As do the drum, cymbals, flute and sweet-sounding
sapta-svarā !
Milk, curds, ghee well up continuously from fountains
all around;
Undying fruits ripen in orchards; Durgā herself provides
delicious food! Everything one wants is supplied
there:
Things to chew, suck, lick and drink,
O great bow-bearer, as if by the ever-fruitful wishing-
tree in heaven. We need not go there;
Go to the north gate, I say: wander for a while in the
fair land beyond,
Where soon, jewel of men, you will see your father's
feet.'

§522

The two moved swiftly northwards. Sitā's lord saw
hundreds of mountains: barren,
Parched, ah! as if blasted by divine anger!
Some had layers of ice on their peaks; some belched
streaming lava, melting rocks with its fiery flow,
Hiding the sky with ash, filling all space with uproar!
Lord Rām saw hundreds of borderless deserts:
An unceasing, scorching wind blew, driving the sand like
sea-waves!
He saw an immense lake, boundless as a sea; in parts of it,
Storm-waves heaved mountainously, booming loudly;
elsewhere,
Motionless waters festered; gigantic frogs sported in it,
croaking harshly!

§500

sapta-svarā see V.253.

wishing-tree *kāmalatā*: a name for the *kalpataru*, a tree in heaven that grants every wish.

Vast snakes floated on it, like the infinitely long serpent
Ananta; venom gleamed in places,
As in the primaeval ocean at the time of its first
churning! Sinners wandered through all these regions,
moaning piteously!
Snakes bit, scorpions stung, poison-fanged bugs
gnawed!
There was fire on land, and excruciating cold in the air!
Alas,
Who is ever spared for a moment at the north gate? The
warrior hurried on, led by Māyā.

§546

As when a boatman, having skilfully navigated a jungle
of waters, is met,
As he nears the shore, by a breeze that is the friend of flower-
born fragrance; and birdsong and the noise of people—
After many days—soothe his ears, so that he steers into
a sea of joy;
Thus felt Rāghav too, when he heard the sound of music
nearby! He saw with amazement golden palaces all
around,
And verdant gardens full of golden flowers; and wide
lakes, abode of new-bloomed lotus!
Māyā said gently: 'At this gate, hero,
Many great warriors, fallen in open combat, enjoy
eternal bliss.
Their pleasures here, noble Rām, are unending!
O strong-armed one, come along this woodland path—
you will see famous men,

§522

Ananta see I.33.

As in the primaeval ocean at the time of its first churning see I.295.

And the City of Immortality that is filled with all their fame,
as a forest is filled with scents! On this virtuous land,
God's smile shines perpetually, like moon, sun and stars
together!'
Joyfully the hero pressed onward, Māyā ahead of him,
her spear in her hand!
In a while Rām saw a field in front of him—like a field
of battle. In places there were spears,
Long as *śāl*-trees; elsewhere horses neighed, arrayed in
armour;
King-elephants trumpeted too! Shield-holders were
practising there, swords and shields in their hands;
And wrestlers fought, rolling on the ground; chariot-drivers
in splendid chariots were twanging their bow-strings;
Flags fluttered as if with the joy of battle. Seated on
flowery seats, and holding golden *vīṇās*,
Poets were singing, delighting their listeners with songs
of heroes! Transfixed by the music,
Warriors hurrahed; someone—who could say who—
Rained heaps of paradise-flowers all around, filling the
area with perfume. Apsarāses danced;
Kinnaras, as in heaven, sang!

§582

Māyā said to Rāghav: 'All these heroes died in battle in
the Satya-yuga, in open combat;
See them on the field today, O crest-jewel of the
Kshatriyas! See Nisumbha,

§546

śāl-trees see I.417.
Apsarāses see II.14, I.375.
Kinnaras see VII.300.

§582

Satya-yuga the Age of Truth: see III.573. **Kshatriyas** see VI.471.

Golden in body as the peaks of Hemkuṭ;
The gleam of that noble warrior's crown rises into the sky. Divine-fire-born Chanḍi defeated that hero in formidable battle.
Behold Sumbha, like trident-wielding Sambhu when he attacks; and the fierce anti-god Mahish,
Fleeter than a horse; and brave Tripura, enemy of the enemy of himself;
And Vritra and other great Daityas, celebrated in the world. See Sunda and Upasunda,
Joyously floating again in a sea of brotherly love.' Wise Rāghav asked, 'Why,
Tell me, kind Māyā, do I not see Kumbhakarna and Atikāya,
And Narāntak (slayer of men), and Indrajit and the other Raksha fighters?'

§582

the peaks of Hemkuṭ see I.33.

Chanḍi see V.113.

Nisumbha . . . Sumbha see III.115.

Sambu a name for Siva, is used for the chime here with Sumbha.

Mahish see V.113, III.573, II.400.

Tripura, enemy of the enemy of himself i.e. the enemy of *Tripurāri*, an epithet for Siva, enemy of Tripura. See II.217.

Vitra see II.45.

Daityas see I.33, V.29, 91.

Sunda and Upasunda famous Asura-brothers who after performing extraordinary austerities asked Brahmā for the boon of immortality. He told them this was impossible, so they asked if they could be killed only by their own hands. He agreed to this, and they went on the rampage. Brahmā then called on Visvakarmā, the divine architect (see IV.408) to create Tilottamā, a woman formed from pieces of the most beautiful beings in all three worlds. The brothers quarrelled over her so violently that they killed each other. The creation of Tilottamā was the subject of M's poem *Tilottamāsambhab kābya*. See Introduction, p. xxxi.

Kumbhakarna see I.80.

Atikāya see I.530.

Narāntak a Rakshas whose name means 'man-killer'. Kumbhakarna, Atikāya and Narāntak are all sons of Rāvan.

§598

Magical Māyā replied: 'Until funeral rites are performed, none can come to this city,

O husband of Sitā. There are lands outside the city, and souls wander there,

For as long as the *śrāddha* has not been carefully completed by their kinsmen; this is as Fate decrees, I tell you.

O finest of heroes, look at that handsome hero approaching; I shall stay at your side invisibly,

O jewel of men; converse with him courteously.' With that Māyā vanished.

§607

Astonished, the Raghu chieftan saw an imposing warrior, fiery with might;

Round the crest of his crown lightning played; ornaments, dazzling to the eye,

Were strung round his massive body! In his hand there was a spear; he moved like a king-elephant!

§611

The champion advanced, bore down on Rām and asked: 'Why have you come here in the flesh,

O crest-jewel of the Raghus? In unfair combat you killed me to please Sugriv;

But do not be afraid; in Kritānta's city we do not know anger, everyone is master of the senses.

The river of man's life through the world is muddied; in this land it flows purely! I am Vāli.'

§598

śrāddha the funeral rites that have to be performed by the eldest son of a deceased Hindu, whose soul remains in limbo until they are performed.

Fate *bidhi*: cf. VI.84 etc..

§611

Vāli King of Kishkindhyā who was overthrown by his younger brother Sugriv and slain by Rām. See VII.676, I.218.

The jewel of men recognized with shame the battle-skilled king of Kishkindhyā! Vāli smiled and said:
'Come with me, O son of Dasarath! Do you see that garden over there,
Lord, full of golden flowers? The noble Jaṭāyu roams there all day,
Your father's friend! He will be so pleased to see you! He sacrificed his life in the cause of *dharma*—
To save a chaste lady from violation; so his glory is unlimited! Come to him quickly!'

§629

The enemy of the Rākshasas asked: 'Tell me, of your kindness,
O great charioteer, are all of you equally happy?' Vāli answered,
'In the depths of a mine thousands of jewels are born, Rāghav; under light,
I say to you, not all shine the same; but who is without some lustre,
Tell me, jewel of the Raghus?' Thus their courteous conversation continued.

§636

In a charming wood, where a nectar-pure river continually burbled along, the jewel of men saw Jaṭāyu,
Son of Garuḍa, godlike in appearance; he was seated on a jewel-studded throne,
Carved from ivory! *Vīṇā*-music welled all around! Clusters of luminous lotus gleamed in that wood,
Like rays of sunshine breaking through a festive awning!

§611

Jaṭāyu slain by Rāvan when he tried to stop him abducting Sitā. See IV.600, and Source Notes pp. 341–2 and 384.

§636

Son of Garuḍa see IV.600, I.218.

A spring breeze was wafting unending fragrance!
Jaṭāyu said lovingly to Rām:
'You have gladdened my eyes today, O jewel-like son of my friend! Praise be to you!
Your mother conceived you, O auspicious one, at an auspicious time.
Praise to my friend Dasarath for begetting you! You are favoured by the gods, that thus you have been able to come in the flesh to this city.
Tell me, dear boy, the latest news of the war!
Has the wicked Rāvan perished in battle?' Bowing, Lord Rām said humbly:
'By the grace of your feet, uncle, I destroyed many Rākshasas in fierce battle;
The Rākshas king Rāvan is the only hero left now in the Raksha city; by his arrow, my brave brother Lakshman has lost his life;
I have come to this impenetrable land today at the command of Siva. Please tell me, O warrior,
Tell me, where is your friend, my father?'
§661
Brave Jaṭāyu answered: 'At the western gate that sage-king can be found, among other royal sages.
It is not forbidden for me to go to that region; O vanquisher of enemies, come there with me.'
§665
Wise Rām passed with him through many lovely landscapes, with many gold palaces; there were countless godlike warriors;
On the shores of lakes, in flowering gardens, souls cavorted joyously,
Like bees buzzing through arbours during spring; or like glow-worms at night, brightening the dark all around!

The two proceeded swiftly! Encircling Rāghav, there were thousands and thousands of souls.

§673

Mighty Jaṭāyu said to them: 'This noble charioteer is of the race of Raghu! By Siva's command,

He has come in the flesh to this land of ghosts, in order to see the feet of his father; bless him,

And then go back to your own abodes, O spectres.' They all blessed him and departed.

The two proceeded rapturously. In places golden mountains soared into the sky, their peaks all forested—

Like Siva with his shaggy locks! Streams flowed musically! Diamonds,

Gems and pearls bloomed in their clear waters. In other, low-lying places,

Green meadows sported flowers; lakes were dotted with lotuses! Cuckoos cooed ceaselessly in the woods!

§686

The son of the son of Vinatā said graciously to Rāghav: 'See the western gate, O jewel of men,

Dripping with gold! The houses in that fair land are made of diamonds! See Dilip,

That jewel of men, on a golden throne at the foot of a golden tree, its emerald leaves forming an umbrella over his lofty head,

And with him his chaste wife Sudakshinā! Pay humble

§673

Like Siva with his shaggy locks see II.87 and V.203.

§686

The son of the son of Vinatā Vinatā was mother of Garuḍa, Jaṭāyu's father. See II.337.

Dilip descended from the sun-god Surya, Dilip was the father of Raghu, Rām's great-grandfather. See I.406.

Sudakshinā Dilip's chief queen. Her name means 'very dexterous'.

homage to this ancestor of yours. Countless royal sages sit in this region—
Ikshvāku, Māndhātā, Nahusha and others,
Renowned in the world. Advance and pay homage to your ancestor, O great-armed one!'

§697

The great charioteer advanced and spread his whole body in homage to Dilip and his spouse; Dilip blessed him and asked, 'Who are you?
Tell me, how did you come in the flesh to this land of ghosts, O godlike charioteer?'
My heart floats in a sea of joy on seeing your moon-like face again!' And then Sudakshinā said graciously: 'O fortunate one,
Tell me quickly, who are you? Like the eyes of strangers warming at the sight of their own countrymen,
So, at the sight of you, my eyes are gladdened!
What virtuous woman conceived you in her womb at a lucky time, wise sir? If you are born of gods and look like a god,
Why do you do homage to us? If you are not a god, whose race do you glorify by your man-god-beauty?'

§711

Rām replied with his hands pressed together: 'Your son Raghu, O royal sage,

§686

Ikshvāku the first king of Ayodhyā (see I.386), and son of the 'first man' and primary Hindu Law-giver Manu.

Māndhātā another king of Ayodhyā from the same lineage as Ikshvāku, and later the first king of Saptadvip too.

Nahusha father of Yayāti, kings of the 'lunar race' as opposed to Rām's 'solar' lineage, though M seems to lump him together with Rām's direct ancestors.

Is renowned in the world—for conquering the world by his own bodily strength; his son Aja—
Protector of the earth—was chosen by Indumati as her husband; great Dasarath was born of her womb;
His chief queen was Kausalyā; I was born of her. The lion-hero Lakshman was the son of her co-wife Sumitrā,
As was Satrughna—vanquisher of enemies! The third wife Kaikeyi gave birth to our brother Bharat, sir!'

§722

The royal sage replied: 'So you are Rāmchandra, the crown of the race of Ikshvāku!
I bless you! Your perpetual renown will be proclaimed throughout the world, for as long as the moon and sun ascend in the sky,
O renowned one! My race has been glorified on earth through your virtue, O noblest of the virtuous!
You see that golden mountain? Near to it, on the bank of the Vaitarani,
Is a banyan tree named Akshaya: everyone in this realm knows it. Your father performs constant *pūjās* to Dharmarāj at the foot of that tree,

§711

Aja Rām's grandfather. See V.203.

was chosen by Indumati as her husband Indumati, sister of Bhojarāj, founder-king of Vidarbha, where Damayanti came from (see VI.418), chose Aja at a *svayambar* ceremony (see III.271).

Kausalyā . . . Sumitrā . . . Satrughna . . . Kaikeyi see I.172.

§722

the crown of the race of Ikshvāku see above, §686.

Vaitarani see above, §162.

Akshaya the name means 'imperishable'.

pūjās see I.483.

Dharmarāj another name for Yama or Kritānta. See above, §100.

For your well-being. Go, great-armed one,
Ornament of the race of Raghu, to his presence. Great Dasarath is desolate at the troubles you have suffered.'

§734

Bowing in joy to Dilip's lotus-feet, the jewel of men said goodbye to brave Jaṭāyu and went on alone (with Māyā floating above him)
To the vicinity of the spectacular golden mountain. He beheld the Akshaya banyan-tree on the bank of the Vaitarani river, whose waters in this region are pure as nectar.
It had golden branches and emeralds for leaves; and its fruit—ah!
Who can describe them? A god-worshipped king of trees, a bringer of spiritual release!

§742

Seeing his son approaching, the royal sage Dasarath opened wide his arms, and dampening the earth with his tears cried:
'Is it you who, after so long, by divine grace,
Have come to this inaccessible country, O more than my life, to gladden my eyes?
Have I got you back today, my lost jewel? Alas,
How can I tell you how I have suffered without you, sweet Rām? Like iron melting in the fire,
I departed my life prematurely, out of grief for you! I closed my eyes,
Alas, because of the burning in my heart! Cruel Fate,
Dear child, through my misdeeds, inscribed suffering on your brow,
Always righteous as you are! That was why these events happened; why,

Alas, Kaikeyi trampled on the creeper of my hopes—the glory of my life's garden—
Like a rampaging she-elephant!' Great Dasarath wept; his son too wept silently.

§759

The Rāghav chieftan said: 'I am swimming now in a shoreless sea, father;
Who can save me in this peril? You are aware in this realm of what happens in the world, so it is not unknown to you why I have come here!
Alas, in a ghastly battle, my dear brother met today an untimely death!
If I cannot recover him, I shall not return to where sun, moon and stars shine!
If you so command, I shall die at once, O father,
At your feet! I cannot stand life without him!' The jewel of men wept at his father's feet.
Distressed at his son's grief, Dasarath said: 'I know why you have come to this city,
Dear son. I continuously worship Dharmarāj, sacrificing all pleasures for your well-being.
You will get fortune-blessed Lakshman back! Life is at present stopped in his body, like a prisoner trapped in a tumble-down gaol.
On the peak of beautiful Mount Gandhamādan, a golden creeper grows, my child,
Called Visalyakarani. It is a powerful medicine; fetch it,

§742

I departed my life prematurely, out of grief for you . . . Alas, Kaikeyi trampled on . . . my hopes see I.386, II.173.

§759

Mount Gandhamādan . . . Visalyakarani the mountain where the

And it will restore Lakshman to life. King Yama himself
has been kind today, and prescribed this means.
Your ally Hanumān, the son of the wind, is as swift as
the wind;
Send him; he will bring the medicine in a trice; when he acts,
He is as mighty as a storm. You will, all in good time,
Destroy Rāvan in a fierce battle; the villain will be
smashed along with his tribe, by your arrows;
Sitā, your wife, the Lakshmi of the Raghus,
Will return to light up Ayodhyā; but it is not in your
fortune to enjoy happiness for long, my child!
Just as incense has to burn to perfume a land, you will
fill the land of Bhārat with your fame, alas,
O famous one, only through intense suffering! Through
my sin,
Fate has condemned you; I myself died through my sin,
deprived of you.

§795

'Night is only half gone on the earth above. Divine
strength makes you strong; go quickly to Lankā;

---

medicinal herb called Visalyakarani grows is on the Indian mainland, away from Lankā. The name of the herb means 'making free of a wound caused by an arrowhead (*śalya*)'.

§759

Your ally Hanumān, the son of the wind see I.218.

but it is not in your fortune to enjoy happiness for long an allusion to the final part of the story of Rām and Sitā. After they are reunited, Rām dismayingly betrays his supposed divinity and nobility of character by rejecting the pregnant Sitā through suspicion that the child she is carrying has been begotten by Rāvan. Grief-stricken and humiliated, Sitā withdraws to the forest again. Although Rām eventually takes her back, she remains insecure and unhappy, and prays to Earth (Prithivi, see VII.408) for protection. Earth opens up at her feet, and she is swallowed up, leaving Rām to spend the rest of his life in loneliness and remorse.

Bhārat *Bhārat-bhūmi*: the ancient name for India.

Send the hero Hanumān at once, to bring the potent medicine, my child,
That will save your brother; let him bring it now, while night still lasts.'
Dasarath blessed his heroic son. Hoping to take the dust of his father's lotus-feet, Rām stretched his lotus-hand towards them:
In vain! He could not touch them! The son of the son of Raghu said gently:
'This is not my living body that you see, O more than life! It is just a shade!
How can you, flesh-formed as you are, touch a shade?
Like an image in a mirror, or in water, is this body of mine.
Go without delay, dearest, to Lankā.'
Abasing himself in wonder at his father's feet, brave Rām sped away, Māyā at his side.
In a while the hero arrived at the place where great Lakshman lay on the battlefield; warriors surrounded him, sleepless with sorrow!

Here ends 'The Realm of the Shades',
the eighth book of *Meghnādbadh kābya*.

BOOK IX

§1
The day dawned; all around Lankā the assembled armies burst into shouts of '*Jay* Rām'.
§3
Leaving his golden throne, the king of the Rākshasas, Rāvan,
Sat down in mourning on the ground, in a place where, alas,
That terrifying sound resounded like the waves of the sea! In amazement he turned to Sāran and asked: 'Tell me quickly,
O wisest and best of councillors, why our enemies are cheering, when during the night they were listless with grief?
Tell me at once! Has the villainous, false-fighting son of Sumitrā come back to life?
Who knows what favour the gods have granted! The Rām who so cunningly arrested the restless current of the sea; he whose sorcery floated stones on the water;
Who was slain yet revived twice in battle; is there anything in the world that he cannot do?
Best adviser—I am listening—tell me what has happened?'
§18
With folded hands, Sāran answered sorrowfully: 'Who understands the tricks of the gods in this world of illusion,
Great king? Mount Gandhamādan, king of peaks,

§1
Jay **Rām** see III.288.
§3
Sāran see Book I, §119f.
the villanous, false-fighting son of Sumitrā i.e. Lakshman. See I.218. For his 'false-fighting', see Book VI, §413f.
The Rām . . . whose sorcery floated stones on the water see IV.491.

Kin to the gods, came itself last night with a gift of
supreme medicine that revived Lakshman, O Lord;
That is why Rām's soldiers are cheering with happiness.
Like a snake doubly vigorous at the end of winter, the
heroic son of Sumitrā is whooping wildly with war lust;
And Sugriv's south-country forces are bellowing too, my
lord, like a herd of elephants when they hear their
elephant king!'

§28

Sighing with despair, the great king of Lankā said: 'Who
can break the laws of Fate?
The enemy that I slew in open combat, when I fought
against gods and mortals, has he come back to life
with divine assistance?
O Sāran, through my misfortune Death himself has
forgotten his own *dharma*! When it devours a deer,
Does a lion then ever let it free? But what point is there
in this futile lament? I understand fully:
The sun-like glory of the Rākshasas is sinking into
darkness! My brother Kumbhakarna, mighty as
trident-wielding Siva,
Has been slain—and Prince Meghnād, the vanquisher of
Indra,

§18

Mount Gandhamādan . . . came itself in the *Rāmāyaṇa*, Hanumān is sent to fetch the medicinal herb, and does so by bringing back the entire mountain. Dasarath's instructions to Rām at the end of Book VIII of *MBK* conform with this, as he tells him to send Hanumān (see VIII.759). But here, Sāran as presented by M is unaware of Hanumān's role, and seems to think that the mountain (winged, like all mountains in Hindu mythology: see I.714) has flown by itself.

Sugriv's south-country forces see I.218, 763.

§28

dharma see II.173 and Introduction, pp. liv–vi.

my brother Kumbhakarna see I.80.

A second Kārttikeya! How can I bear to live longer?
Can I ever get the two of them back in this world?
Go, O Sāran, to mighty Rāghav; tell him:
"Rāvan—the fount of the Raksha race—O great-armed one,
Begs this of you: 'Suspend—you and your armies—
All enmity in this land for seven days, O charioteer! The king wishes to complete proper funeral rites for his son.
Observe the true warrior-code, O lord of the Raghus! A warrior always honours true warriors on the opposing side.
Through the power of your arms, hero-conceiving golden Lankā is hero-less now, I tell you!
You are favoured amongst heroes! You took up the bow at an auspicious time, O jewel of men!
Fortune-granting Fate looks favourably on you; by divine edict, the lord of the Rākshasas has fallen into danger;
Fulfil your enemy's desire, today, great charioteer.'"
Go quickly with this message, O chief minister, to Rām's tent.'

§57

Bowing to the king of the Rākshasas, that wisest of councillors departed with his retinue. The gate-keepers immediately opened the gates with a terrifying creaking noise.
Slowly, sorrowfully, the Raksha minister proceeded to the seashore, with its perpetually rolling waves.

§62

The jewel of the race of Raghu sat in his tent, immersed in an ocean of joy; valiant Lakshman was before him,

§28

Kārttikeya see I.689, II.491.

Like a tree newly revived at frost's fading; or like a full moon smiling in the sky; or like,
At night's end, a lotus blooming! To his right was the mighty Rākshas Vibhishan,
And all around were his other generals—formidable in battle, surrounding him as divine warriors do the chief of the gods.

§70

A messenger said hastily to Rām: 'Sir, Sāran,
Prime Minister of the Rākshasas, famous in the world, is here with his companions at the entrance to your camp:
Tell me your command, O jewel of men.' The Raghu lord ordered:
'Bring him at once, O messenger; welcome him to this place.
Who does not know that, in a war, ambassadors must never be attacked?'

§77

Entering the tent, Sāran then said (saluting Rām's royal feet):
'Rāvan, the fount of the Raksha race, O great-armed-one,
Begs this of you: "Suspend—you and your armies—
All enmity in this land for seven days, O charioteer! The king wishes to complete proper funeral rites for his son.
Observe the true warrior-code, O lord of the Raghus! A warrior always honours true warriors on the opposing side.
Through the power of your arms, hero-conceiving golden Lankā is hero-less now, I tell you!
You are favoured amongst heroes! You took up the bow at an auspicious time, O jewel of men!

Fortune-granting Fate looks favourably on you; by divine
edict, the lord of the Rākshasas has fallen into danger;
Fulfil your enemy's desire, today, great charioteer."'

§91

The Raghu lord answered: 'Your master, O Sāran,
Is my supreme enemy; yet, I assure you,
I am greatly saddened by his sorrow.
Whose heart is not distressed when he sees the sun
eclipsed? A majestic tree that battled in the forest
with the sun's heat is pale and gloomy at that time!
In a crisis, friends and enemies are equal to me, great minister!
Return to golden Lankā; for seven days I and my armies
will not bear arms. Assure,
Wise minister, the Raksha king that a pious man never
strikes anyone engaged in a pious act!' With this the
champion fell silent.

§103

Humbly, the Raksha ambassador replied: 'You are the
finest of the race of men,
O jewel of the Raghus; in learning, intelligence and
strength you are without compare in the world!
High-minded sir, I tell you your decision is right. Do
good people ever act unrighteously?
Just as the mighty son of Nikashā is the Lord of the
Rākshasas, so you are the Lord of Men, O Rāghav!
Evil was the time—I beg you, charioteer,

§91

a pious man never strikes anyone engaged in a pious act *dharma-karme rata jane kabhu nā prahāre/ dhārmik*: this principle did not, however, stop Lakshman from killing Meghnād when he was defenceless and engaged in a pious *pūjā* to Agni! See I.1, Book VI, §413f. and Introduction, pp. lv–lvi.

§103

the mighty son of Nikashā i.e. Rāvan. See I.62.

To forgive this lament!—evil was the time that the two of you broke out in enmity! But who can break the strictures of Fate?
O great-armed one, the bewitching Fate that made wind and sea enemies, or the lion and the elephant,
Or Garuḍa and Vāsuki, has made Rām and Rāvan foes: who can blame them?'
Having won Rām's favour, Sāran returned swiftly to where the lord of the Rākshasas was sitting silently, his robes wet,
Alas, with tears of grief! Meanwhile Rām gave orders to his generals;
Armour was abandoned gladly; everyone took rest, each in his own tent.

§123

In the Asoka wood where Sitā sat, lonely as Kamalā, alas,
In the depths of the bottomless ocean, Saramā arrived—like Lakshmi
(Guardian-deity of the Rākshas race) in the guise of a Rākshasi bride. She sat down at Sitā's lotus-feet,
Touching them respectfully. Gently, Sitā asked:
'Tell me, moon-like one, why for two days there has been such wailing from the townsfolk?
Yesterday I heard with dread the noise of battle all day on the battle-field; the trees kept shaking, as if from an earthquake,

§103

Garuḍa and Vāsuki there are several myths which explain why Vishnu's vehicle Garuḍa (see I.218) and the snake-king Vāsuki (see I.33) are mortal enemies. See I.743 and II.337.

§123

Asoka wood see II.190. **lonely as Kamalā, alas,/ In the depths of the bottomless ocean** see I.472, 513. **Saramā** see Book IV, §67f. and the note to IV.67.

At the tramp of distant martial feet; I saw in the sky arrows like spikes of fire; at the end of the day,
The Rākshas army entered the city with shouts of victory; the Rākshas band played with a booming sound! Who won?
Who lost? Tell me quickly, Saramā!
My anxious heart refuses to be consoled! I do not know who I can ask here. If I ask the guards,
I get no answer. Hideous Trijaṭā—hear me,
Dear friend—with her blood-red eyes, and a razor-sharp sword in her hand—came last night to strike me down,
Blind with fury, horrible to look at as Chāmuṇḍā! The other guards stopped her:
Thus wretched though I am I survived, O lovely-haired Saramā! But my heart still quakes when I think of her!'

§147

Chaste Saramā spoke in sweetest tones: 'Luckily for you, O fortunate one,
Indrajit has been slain by force of arms! That is why Lankā is lamenting day and night! The Rākshas king has been powerless ever since!
Queen Mandodari is weeping; the Raksha womenfolk are distraught with mourning; the Raksha troops are dejected!
Through the power of your virtue, O lotus-eyed one, your brave brother-in-law Lakshman achieved in combat what the gods could not do:
Killed Meghnād, the vanquisher of Indra, invincible in the world!'

§123

Trijaṭā see V.409.

horrible to look at as Chāmuṇḍā see II.523.

§147

Indrajit i.e. Meghnād. See III.135 and I.1.

§157

Sweet-speaking Sitā replied: 'You alone in this city, O Raksha wife,
Bring words of comfort to me! Glorious is the leonine son of Sumitrā in the race of supreme heroes! Lucky was my mother-in-law Sumitrā to conceive such a son,
Dear friend! At last I see that God in his mercy has opened the door of my prison! Wicked Rāvan is Lankā's sole champion now!
We will see what happens—we will see what sorrow still lies in my destiny! But listen carefully!
The wailing is steadily increasing, my friend.' Saramā said melodiously,
'The Lord of the Rākshasas has made a pact with the Lord of the Rāghavas; he is taking his son to the shore of the sea to perform his cremation, my lady!
For seven days no one will take up hostile arms in the land of the Rākshasas—the jewel of men has promised this at Rāvan's request. Rām is an ocean of compassion,
Devi! It breaks my heart, sweet lady,
To think of the lovely demoness Pramilā: the beautiful Pramilā will abandon her body on the funeral pyre, in devotion to her husband;
She will go to heaven today to re-join her husband! When Madan, dear lady,
Was burnt to death by the fire of Siva's anger, did chaste Rati die too, along with her lord?'

§157

my mother-in-law Sumitrā *sumitrā śāśuṛī*: but she is only Sitā's mother-in-law by virtue of being the mother of Rām's half-brother Lakshman. See I.172. **Devi** see I.322. **When Madan . . . / Was burnt to death by the fire of Siva's anger** see I.33. **Rati** see II.265, 309.

§181

Saramā wept, distraught with sorrow, drenching herself with her tears.
Like kindness incarnate in the world, Sitā—always distressed by another's distress—
Tearfully addressed her friend: 'Unlucky was the time of my birth, O Rākshasi Saramā!
In any house I enter, my dear, I always extinguish the lamp of happiness—
Alas, image of misfortune that I am. God has given me a tragic destiny!
O blessed friend, see how my wonderful husband was exiled to the forest! And my wise brother-in-law Lakshman was exiled with him!
From grief for his son, my father-in-law expired! The city of Ayodhyā is dark now!
The royal throne is empty! Jaṭāyu died, from formidable armed opposition,
In striving to save my honour! But mark now, how my misfortune has brought about the death of Indrajit,
And all those other Raksha heroes, beyond count! And Pramilā will die,
Unparalleled in the world in her beauty! That such a flower should die, alas,
At the beginning of spring!' 'How can you say, lovely Sitā,'
Said Saramā, wiping tears from her eyes, 'that it is your fault?
Who was it who dragged you here, tore you like a golden creeper, robbing the tree you hugged?
Who brought the lotus of the Rāghav lake to this

§181

From grief for his son, my father-in-law expired see I.386 and II.173 for the death of Dasarath. **Jaṭāyu died** see IV.600.

Rākshas land? The King of Lankā is drowning through his own misdeeds! What more shall I say?'
Saramā wept with grief! Sitā, Rām's beloved,
Wept too in that Asoka forest, in pity for the Rākshasas, grieving at her enemies' grief!
§209
The western gate opened with a thunderous groan. Thousand of Rākshasas emerged; they had golden staffs in their hands,
With silken banners on them fluttering! They silently filed along both sides of the royal road! Then came the procession,
Headed by elephant-mounted drummers who filled the land with their pounding! Then came ranks of infantry on foot; then elephants and horses;
Then charioteers in chariots, subdued in their movement; then musicians playing mournfully!
For as far as could be seen, massed Rākshasas were heading solemnly towards the sea! Their brilliant golden armour dazzled the eye!
Their golden flag-staffs gleamed in the rays of the sun; in their headgear there were jewels;
On their belts, there were swords in scabbards; there were long spears in their hands;
Streams of tears flowed, alas, from their eyes!
§224
Martial Rākshasis (Pramilā's servants) came out,
Dressed for battle—awesome as Durgā, beautiful as Vidyādharis—
And Nrimunḍamālini on a black horse, wan-faced, alas,

§224
beautiful as Vidyādharis see III.378. **Nrimunḍamālini** see II.102.

Like the night deprived of the moon! Tears streamed unceasingly, drenching clothes,
Drenching horses, drenching the earth! Some women sobbed and wailed;
Some wept silently; some stared at the Raghu armies, with eyes fiery with anger,
Like a tigress (caught in a snare) beholding hunters nearby!
Alas, where were their smiles—bright as lightning?
Where were the arrows of their glances—which nothing can deflect in Kāma's battles? Pramilā's horse Vaḍabā came,
Flanked by guards, riderless, bereft of beauty as a stalk without a flower!
All around, attendants waved fly-whisks; other women tearfully accompanied them, walking not riding;
Sobbing filled the sky! Pramilā's armour shone on her horse's back—her sword,
Shield, quiver, bow and crown—
Adorned, ah! with priceless gems!
There was a jewel-studded girdle; and a gold-plated breast-plate; both seemed dulled—
The girdle at remembering, alas, Pramilā's slender waist!
The breast-plate at recalling her breasts that were peaked like mountains! Servants scattered parched rice and cowrie-shells, golden and other coins;
Singers sang plaintively; beating their gorgeous breasts, Rākshasis wept.

§251

Amidst the slow-moving chariots came Meghnād's noble

§224

Pramilā's horse Vaḍabā see III.115.

chariot—cloud-coloured, flashes of lightning in its wheels,
A rainbow-like banner flying from its crest; but it lacked beauty today, just as a framework for an image lacks beauty,
Alas, when its image is immersed and lost! The Rākshas charioteers howled,
Violently striking their breasts at times, senseless with grief! Adorning the chariot was a mighty bow,
A quiver, a shield, a sword,
A conch, discus, club and other weapons;
And a handsome breastplate; and a crown like the rays of the sun; and many more pieces of armour.
Singers were singing sadly of the grief of the Rākshasas! Some Rākshasas were scattering gold coins,
Like trees tossing in a fierce storm and scattering flowers! Water-carriers were sprinkling scented water to damp down the dust that was rising in dismay at the tramping feet. The chariot proceeded towards the sea-shore!

§268
In a golden palanquin, covered with flowers, the lovely Pramilā sat beside her husband's corpse—
Like Rati brought down to earth, to be with her dead husband Kāma! There was a dot of vermilion on her brow,
And a garland of flowers round her neck, and bracelets on her lotus-stalk-wrists: a Rākshas wife adorned with manifold adornments!
Fly-whisk-wavers sorrowfully waved lovely fly-whisks;

§268

Like Rati brought down to earth, to be with her dead husband Kāma i.e. after he was blasted by Siva's third eye. See I.33, and Book II, §309f.

attendants tearfully scattered flowers! Distraught with grief,
Raksha women sobbed unrestrainedly! Alas, where was the radiance that always lit up the moon of her face?
Where, alas, was that enchanting smile.
That perpetually played on her sweet lips, like sunbeams on *your* full lips, O lotus-clump?
Moon-like Pramilā sat with silent intensity—as if her soul had left her body to search for her husband in the place where he now dwelt; when a great tree withers,
The creeper withers too—the noble wife who chooses him in life or in death! In file after file,
Raksha charioteers followed, unsheathed swords in their hands; sunbeams brightly bounced off their swords;
The brilliance of their armour dazzled the eyes! All around, masters of the Vedas chanted the Vedas loudly;
The officiating priest carried the sacred fire and recited great mantras; Rākshas women carried various ornaments, clothes,
Sandal-wood, musk, pollen,
Saffron and flowers on golden platters; in golden pitchers there was holy Ganges water! Golden lamps shone all around!
Ḍhāk, ḍhol and other drums sounded noisily; there was clapping of hands,
And the beating of *mṛdaṅga* and gourds; and the din of conches and gongs; married Rākshasis ululated,

§268

Ḍhāk, ḍhol . . . mṛdaṅga the *ḍhāk* is a big drum hanging from the shoulder and beaten with two sticks and associated with Durgā-pujā (see I.483). The *ḍhol* is a similar drum from the Panjab, adopted for military use and more recently in Bhangra music. The *mṛdaṅga* is a smaller, tom-tom like drum.

Wet with tears; an auspicious sound on an inauspicious day, alas!

§300

Rāvan, King of the Rākshasas, emerged on foot,
Wearing white garments and a white shawl that was like the garland of *dhuturā*-flowers round the neck of Siva; his ministers were around him at a distance, subdued in demeanour.
The Rākshas king was silent, and his eyes were full of tears; his councillors were silent,
And all the chief Raksha guards. The citizens of Lankā followed tearfully behind—boys,
Women and the aged, emptying the city, which was dark,
Alas, now, as the houses of Gokul when Krishna is absent!
Wet with tears, everyone moved slowly towards the sea, filling the land with the sound of grieving!

§312

Rām said to Angad in gentle tones: 'Go with a thousand charioteers, great prince,
To the sea-shore, to show your sympathy to the Rākshasas. Go sensitively,
O hero! My heart is sorrowful at their grief! At a time like this I do not distinguish between friend and enemy,
Prince. Because the Rākshas king might be angered if he sees Lakshman—recalling what happened—
I am sending you, young king! But your father,

§300

garland of *dhuturā*-flowers Siva consumes a narcotic made from the datura (thorn-apple) plant.

dark,/ Alas, now, as the houses of Gokul when Krishna is absent see I.33 and Sources Notes, pp. 318–19, 331.

§312

Angad see I.218.

Vāli, crest-jewel of kings, got the better of Rāvan in battle;
So approach him, courteous sir, with humble courtesy.'

§323

Brave Angad proceeded to the sea-shore with a
thousand charioteers. The gods appeared in the sky—
Indra and his steed Airāvat,
Accompanied by his eternally youthful consort Sachi;
and his general Skanda (vanquisher of Tārak)
With his peacock banner, and Chitrarath in his
decorated chariot; and Pavan,
Ruler of the winds, on his deer; and Kritānta on his
massive buffalo;
And Kuber, lord of Alakā, in his flower-chariot;
And the moon came, spouse of the night and source of
calm nectar, dimmed by the sun's presence too;
And the smiling twin physicians of heaven came,
Asvini's sons; and many other gods.
Beautiful nymphs came, and Gandharvas, Apsarāses,

§312

your father,/ Vāli see I.218. Before he was overthrown by his younger brother Sugriv, King Vāli had humiliated Rāvan in battle.

§323

Indra and his steed Airāvat see III.378.

Sachi see II.14.

his general Skanda (vanquisher of Tārak) see I.689, II.491.

Chitrarath see II.527.

Pavan see I.218, 443.

Kritānta i.e. Yama. See VIII.100.

Kuber, lord of Alakā see I.62, 483.

flower-chariot i.e. the Pushpak. See IV.408.

the moon . . . source of calm nectar see II.337.

the smiling twin physicians of heaven . . . Asvini's sons i.e. the Asvin twins, sons of Samjñā (see I.417, VIII.113), who is also identified with Vaḍabā (see III.115).

Gandharvas, Apsarāses see I.375, II.14.

Kinnaras and Kinnaris. A heavenly orchestra played in the sky. Divine sages came—
Joyously—and many other beings, inhabitants of heaven.
§338
Arriving at the sea-shore, the Rākshasas quickly erected a fitting funeral pyre; porters brought logs of fragrant sandal-wood,
And quantities of ghee. Carefully washing the corpse in holy Ganges water, and dressing it in beautiful silk garments,
A group of Rākshasas placed it on the pyre. Rākshas priests solemnly recited mantras. Washing herself in the sacred water,
Chaste Pramilā took off her jewellery and gave it all away. Pranāming to her elders, and gently addressing her attendant demonesses,
Sweet-voiced Pramilā said: 'O friends, the *līlā* of my mortal life is ending at last today in this mortal world!
All of you return now to the land of the Daityas!
O Vāsanti, say all of this at the feet of my father!
And to my mother—' Alas, she broke off,
Tears streaming, lost for words. Vāsanti too burst into loud cries.
§355
Controlling her distress after a while, Pramilā said:

§323

Kinnaras and Kinnaris see VII.300. Kinnaris are female Kinnaras.

§338

Pranāming i.e. doing obeisance or *praṇām*. See VI.418. ***līlā*** play or sport, but in Indian tradition often used for the fluctuations of mortal existence, love, nature, etc. **land of the Daityas** i.e. Pramilā's parental land. M uses Daitya interchangeably with other words for demon or anti-god (see I.33, V.29, 91), and identifies the Rākshas Kālnemi as Pramilā's father (see III.413). **Vāsanti** see Book III, §17, and the notes to that paragraph.

'Tell my mother that God has written on my brow a fate that must be fulfilled at last!
I depart today with the one in whose hands my father and mother consigned me; what role does a wife have in the world without her husband? What more shall I say,
Dear friend? Do not forget me—this is my last plea to you all.'

§364

Ascending the pyre (as if on to a bed of flowers!) Pramilā sat joyfully at the feet of her husband,
With a wreath of flowers round her head. The Rākshas band played; priests loudly chanted the Vedas;
The Raksha women made an ululating sound; mixed with the sound of keening, it rose up into the sky!
Flowers rained down all around! Young Raksha girls laid various ornaments, clothes,
Sandal-paste, musk, pollen and vermilion on the pyre as was fitting;
Killing animals with sharp arrows, and smearing them with ghee, the Rākshasas placed them all around,
As they do round the foot of your altar on the great ninth day of your *pūjā*, O Durgā, in the homes of your Sākta devotees.

§377

Rāvan, in distress, moved forward and said:
'It was my hope, Meghnād, that I would finally close these two eyes of mine in your presence!

§364

Vedas see IV.175.

Killing animals . . . etc. See Introduction, pp. lxxxiii–lxxxiv for M's portrayal of the Rākshasas as devout (Saivite) Hindus. For Durgā-pujā, see I.483. Sāktas are Hindus who worship the mother-goddess, Siva's consort or *śakti*.

Resigning the burdens of rule on to you, son, I would make my great journey.
But Fate—how shall I understand her wiles?—has robbed me of that joy!
It was my hope, my child, that I would soothe my eyes by seeing you on the throne of the Rākshasas;
And my son's wife would be on your left, like Lakshmi in the form of guardian of the Raksha race! What vain hope!
Because of the sins of a previous life, I behold you today on this fell throne. The glorious sun of the Karburas is permanently eclipsed!
Did I worship Siva with such devotion, to deserve this? How shall I return—
Alas, who will tell me—how shall I return again to the empty palace of Lankā?
What deceiving consolation can I offer your mother, who will tell me? "Where is my son,
Where is my daughter-in-law?" Queeen Mandodari will ask. "To what joy have you left them,
Lord of the Rākshasas, on the sea-shore?" What shall I tell her then?
What, alas? O son,
O finest of warriors! Ever-victorious in battle! O Mother Lakshmi of the Rākshasas!
For what sin has harsh Fate written, on Rāvan's forehead, this torment?'

§377

The glorious sun of the Karburas i.e. Meghnād, the 'sun' of the Rākshasas. See Book I, §763, and notes to II.491. For Karburas, see I.33, IV.531. **O Mother Lakshmi of the Rākshasas** see I.472. **For what sin has harsh Fate written, on Rāvan's forhead, this torment?** See Introduction, pp. lv–lvi. *kapāl* is used in Bengali for both Fate and forehead. *āmār kapāle lekhā āche* means 'it is written on my forehead', i.e. it is my fate or destiny.

§401
On Mount Kailās Siva was disturbed! He shook the
locks on his head; the snakes there hissed horribly;
The fire on his brow crackled; Gangā amidst his hair was
turbulent, like a mountain-stream hurtling through a cave!
Mount Kailās trembled! The universe trembled with alarm;
Durgā nervously addressed Siva with her hands clasped:
§410
'Why are you angry, lord?—please tell me.
Through the edicts of Fate, Meghnād died in combat;
Rām is not at fault!
So if you wish unfairly to destroy him, first, my lord,
I beg you, blast me to ashes.' She clung to his feet.
§415
Affectionately raising chaste Durgā, Siva said: 'My heart
is wrenched,
O Daughter of the Mountain, with sorrow for the Rākshasas!
You know how much I love Nikashā's heroic son.
But at your request, O merciful one, I shall forgive noble
Rām and Lakshman.'
§420
Sorrowfully, the Trident-bearer commanded Agni:
'Purified by your touch,
O purifying one, bring quickly to this palace of goodness
the Rākshas couple, Meghnād and Pramilā!'

§401

Mount Kailās see I.33. **He shook the locks on his head** see II.87 for Siva's matted locks. **Gangā amidst his hair** see V.203.

§415

O Daughter of the Mountain i.e. the daughter of Nagarāj or Nagendra (Himavat, Himālaya). See II.287.

§420

the Trident-bearer i.e. Siva. See II.447. **Agni** see I.743, 751 and VI.7, 418.

§423
In the form of lightning, Agni rushed down to earth! The pyre suddenly flared up.
Everyone saw in amazement a chariot of fire; the vanquisher of Indra sat on a golden seat in that chariot, an image of the divine!
The lovely Pramilā sat to his left; the grace of eternal youth shone from her body; smiles of eternal joy played on her lips!
§430
The heavenly chariot took off swiftly into the sky; the assembled gods rained down flowers; the whole universe filled with shouts of joy!
§433
The Rākshasas put out the raging fire with pourings of milk. With extreme care they gathered up the ashes, and consigned them to the waves.
Dousing the cremation-ground with Ganges water, thousands of Raksha craftsmen quickly constructed, from golden bricks,
A memorial over the funeral pyre; its turrets soared high, piercing the sky!
§440
After bathing in soothing water, the Rākshasas now returned to golden Lankā, wet with tears—
Like Durgā, on the tenth day of her *pūjā*, when her image is immersed.
§443
Lankā, for seven days and nights, wept with sadness.

Here ends 'The Cremation Rites',
the ninth book of *Meghnādbadh kābya.*

§440
Like Durgā on the tenth day of her *pūjā* see I.483.

SOURCE NOTES

The following Source Notes are not, of course, the last word on Madhusudan's many sources and influences, but they will give an indication of his range. They are mostly based on my own reading of the epic poems, both Western and Indian, that he knew and sought to emulate. My references are to the following translations and editions:

Dante Alighieri, *The Divine Comedy*, translated with an Introduction, Notes, and Commentary by Mark Musa (Penguin Classics, 1984 [*Inferno*], 1985 [*Purgatory*], 1986 [*Paradise*])

Homer, *The Iliad*, translated with an Introduction by Martin Hammond (Penguin Classics, London, 1987)

Homer, *The Iliad*, translated by Alexander Pope, edited by Steven Shankman (Penguin Classics, London, 1996)

Homer, *The Odyssey*, translated by Walter Shewring, with an epilogue on translation; introduced by G. S. Kirk (The World's Classics, Oxford University Press, Oxford, 1980)

Kālidāsa, *The Birth of Kumāra*, translated by David Smith (The Clay Sanskrit Library, New York University Press and the JJC Foundation, 2005)

Kālidāsa, *The Loom of Time: A Selection of His Plays and Poems*, translated from the Sanskrit and Prakrit with an

Introduction by Chandra Rajan (Penguin Books India, New Delhi, 1989)

Krittibās, *Rāmāyaṇ*, edited by Harikrishna Mukhopadhyay, with an Introduction by Sunitikumar Chattopadhyay (Sahitya Samsad, Kolkata, 1957)

John Milton, *Paradise Lost*, edited with an Introduction and Notes by John Leonard (Penguin Classics, London, 2000)

The Mahabharata of Vyasa, condensed from Sanskrit and transcreated into English by P. Lal (Vikas Publishing House Pvt. Ltd., New Delhi, 1980)

The Ramayana of Valmiki, translated from the original Sanskrit by Makhan Lal Sen, a modernized version in English prose (Oriental Publishing Co., Kolkata, 1927; Munshiram Manoharlal Publishers, New Delhi, 1976, second revised edition 1978)

Torquato Tasso, *Jerusalem Delivered*, the Edward Fairfax translation [1600] newly introduced by Roberto Weiss (Centaur Press, London, 1962)

Torquato Tasso, *Jerusalem Delivered*, an English prose version translated and edited by Ralph Nash (Wayne University Press, Detroit, 1987)

Virgil, *The Aeneid*, translated and with an Introduction by David West (Penguin Classics, London, 1990, rev. ed. 2003)

I have also made use of other people's work on Madhusudan, and have gratefully given references after many of the Notes. These references are to the following books and articles, with pride of place given to Dinanath Sanyal's superb and copiously annotated Bengali edition of

Meghnādbadh kābya, without which my translation would have been totally impossible. The list includes some of my own published articles.

T. W. Clark, '*Meghnādbadhkāvya*, Canto VIII: *descensus averno*', *Bulletin of the School of Oriental and African Studies*, Vol. 30, No. 2 (1967), pp. 337–52

Jayanta Kumar Dasgupta, 'Western Influence on the Poetry of Madhusūdan Datta', *Bulletin of the School of Oriental and African Studies*, Vol. 7 (1933–35), pp. 117–31

Gargi Datta, *Madhusūdaner racanāy bhāratīya upādān* (Subarnarekha, Kolkata, 1989)

Julia Leslie, 'A Bird Bereaved: The Identity and Significance of Vālmīki's *krauñca*', *Journal of Indian Philosophy*, 26.5 (1998), pp. 455–87

Ghulam Murshid (ed.), *The Heart of a Rebel Poet: Letters of Michael Madhusudan Dutt* (Oxford University Press, New Delhi, 2004)

William Radice, 'Milton and Madhusudan', in G. R. Teneja and Vinod Sena (ed.), *Literature East and West: Essays presented to R. K. DasGupta* (Allied Publishers Ltd., New Delhi, 1995), pp. 177–194; also in David Arnold and Peter Robb (ed.), *Institutions and Ideologies: A South Asian Reader* (Centre of South Asian Studies, SOAS, 1993), pp. 104–19

William Radice, 'Xenophilia and Xenophobia: Michael Madhusudan Datta's *Meghnād-badh kābya*, in Rupert Snell and I. M. P. Raeside (ed.), *Classics of Modern South Asian Literature* (Harrassowitz Verlag, Wiesbaden, 1998), pp. 143–69

William Radice, 'Michael Madusudan Dutt (1824–1873): A Bengali Poet with Italian Connections', in Debraj Bhattacharya (ed.), *Of Matters Modern: The Experience of Modernity in Colonial and Post-colonial South Asia* (Seagull Books, Kolkata, 2008), pp. 149–72

William Radice, 'A Bengali Iliad: Michael Madhusudan Dutt's *Meghnādbadh Kāvya*' in Md. Mahbubar Rahman and Swarochish Sarker (ed.), *Prīti Kumār Mitra smārakgrantha/Pritikumar Mitra Commemorative Volume* (Institute of Bangladesh studies, University of Rajshahi, 2009), pp. 221–37

Alexander Riddiford, 'Homer's *Iliad* and the *Meghnādbadh* of Michael Madhusudan Datta', *Bulletin of the School of Oriental and African Studies,* Vol. 72, No. 2 (2009), pp. 335–56

Dinanath Sanyal (ed.), *Meghnād-badh kābya* (S. C. Sanyal & Co., Kolkata, 1917)

Clinton B. Seely, 'Rāma in the Nether World: Indian Sources of Inspiration', *Journal of the American Oriental Society*, Vol. 102, No. 3 (1982), pp. 467–76

Clinton B. Seely, 'Homeric Similes, Occidental and Oriental: Tasso, Milton, and Bengal's Michael Madhusudan Dutt', *Comparative Literature Studies*, Vol. 25, No. 1 (1988), pp. 35–56

Clinton B. Seely, 'The Raja's New Clothes: Redressing Rāvaṇa in *Meghnanādavadha Kāvya*', in Paula Richman (ed.), *Many Rāmāyaṇas: The Diversity of a Narrative Tradition in South Asia* (University of California Press, Berkeley and Los Angeles, 1991), pp. 137–155.

Clinton B. Seely, 'Who Does Your Dirty Work? NOT

Michael Madhusudan Datta's Hanuman', in Bhuiyan Iqbal (ed.), *Samāj o saṃskṛti, Ānisuzzāmāner sammāne prabandha-sambhār* (Mowla Brothers, Dhaka, 2007), pp. 391–408

Clinton B. Seely, 'Winds of Change: Michael Madhusudan Datta and *The Slaying of Meghanada*', in *Barisal and Beyond* (Chronicle Books, D.C. Publishers, New Delhi, 2008), pp. 106–17

Book I

As was well noted by Jayanta Kumar Dasgupta, the first scholar to write in English on Madhusudan's use of sources, 'While the Indian poets generally begin their works from the beginning of things, Madhusūdan follows the Western practice of suddenly plunging into the action of the poem. The first canto opens with the death of Vīrabāhu, one of the sons of Rāvaṇa, the Rākṣasa king of Lankā. The *Iliad* opens with the account of the pestilence in the Grecian camps and the wrath of Achilles over the ownership of a captive girl. The *Odyssey* begins with the descent of Athene in Ithaca after Odysseus has been enthralled for seven years in the island of Circe . . . .' (etc., Dasgupta, pp. 117–8)

§1
M's opening invocation, in which he calls on the goddess Bhārati (Sarasvati) to aid him in his great enterprise and also gives a prospect of the story that is about to unfold, immediately establishes his debt to the Western epic tradition. Cf. the invocations to the Muse at the beginning of the *Iliad*, the *Odyssey*, the *Aeneid*, and above all *Paradise*

Lost. 'Say, O ambrosia-speaking goddess' (*kaha, he debi amṛtabhāṣiṇi*) has a pivotal emphasis similar to 'Sing, Heav'nly Muse' (*Paradise Lost* I.6; see Radice 1995, p. 179, and Introduction, p. lxvif.). But note the artistry and originality with which M constructs his great beginning. It is comparable in tone and structure to Milton's, but by no means a copy.

Dante has an invocation to the Muses in Canto II of the *Inferno* (ll.7–9), not Canto I, but Canto I is comparable to M's invocation in that it prefigures the entire work that follows. He also has an invocation at the beginning of the *Purgatorio*, singling out Calliope, muse of heroic or epic poetry for special mention (*Purgatorio* I.7–12), and at the beginning of the *Paradiso*, where he invokes Apollo (ll. 13–27). See below, IV.1.

An invocation to a deity at the start of a poem is also normal in Indian tradition, but Dasgupta comments: 'While the general practice in Sanskrit and the older vernacular literatures of India is to begin a poem with a prayer to some god like Brahmā, Viṣṇu, or Śiva, Madhusūdan after the Western poets begins with a hymn to Sarasvatī, the Hindu goddess of learning. The Western practice is to offer invocations to the Muses.' (Dasgupta, p. 118)

Sanyal (p. 4) describes *Rākṣas-bharasā* ('the Rākshasas' hope') as 'a beautiful imitation of the Iliad's 'Hope of Troy'.

A version of the story of how Meghnād acquired the name 'Indrajit' can be found in the additional *Uttarākāṇḍa* that scholars agree was an addition to the original *Rāmāyaṇa* of Vālmiki:

> Ravana then arrived at Indraloka. Indra grew anxious at the news of Ravana's arrival and asked

the Adityas and the other gods to get ready to fight against Ravana.

Indra being greatly smitten with fear went to Vishnu for his advice as to how he could win victory over Ravana. Vishnu said that Ravana was invincible on account of Brahma's boon and so he could not accede to Indra's request to destroy Ravana. Vishnu assured Indra that he would kill Ravana afterwards, but not now. He advised Indra to fight against Ravana in the meantime.

Then all the gods gathered for fighting against Ravana, and a terrible battle commenced between the gods and the Rakshasas. Both were inexhaustible in battle.

Indra and his son Jayanta fought bravely along with the Vasus and the other gods. But Meghanada was more than a match for them. He smothered all the gods by his wonderful prowess.

Indra fought resolutely against Ravana, but in vain. Meghanada availed himself of the black art and made himself invisible. Indra became exhausted and Meghanada took him captive by his magic. Then the Rakshasas ceased from fighting, and Ravana and Meghanada repaired to Lanka with Indra as their prisoner.

After the defeat of Indra by Meghanada, all the gods headed by Brahma came to Lanka. Ravana was then seated in the throne-room surrounded by his sons and brothers.

Brahma said, 'My boy, Ravana! I have been much pleased with your son Meghanada, he has conquered heaven by his prowess. I have been really astonished by his valour and generosity. Meghanada will henceforth be known as Indrajit. He will be invincible in war; now release Indra, and tell me what you want from the gods for this release.'

Indrajit said, 'O Lord! Give me immortality as ransom for Indra's release.'

Brahma said, 'There is none immortal on earth; ask for some other boon.'

Indrajit said, 'O Lord, if I do not get immortality, then I ask for another boon for the release of Indra. When I shall worship fire with due rites, and shall set out for the conquest of my enemies, a chariot yoked with steeds will rise from the fire and none will be able to slay me so long as I shall be seated in that chariot; but I shall be destroyed, if I be engaged in fight before the completion of my worship with due rites. Everyone asks for immortality by virtue of *tapas*, but I wish to attain that by my valour.' Brahma said, 'My boy! You prayer will be granted.' Indra was then released and the gods went to heaven with Indra.

(*VR Uttarakāṇḍa* IX; Sen, pp. 583–4)

For the story of how Vālmiki acquired the metre of the *Rāmāyaṇa*, see Julia Leslie (1988). With a delightful combination of Indological and ornithological scholarship, she narrows down the identity of the bird that I have vaguely translated as 'heron' to the Indian Sarus Crane *(Grus antigone antigone)*.

'give you servant your foot's shade' uses an expression of obeisance (*pad-chāyā*) that occurs commonly in medieval Bengali literature, including the *Rāmāyaṇ* of Krittibās (Sanyal, p. 9).

§33
Rāvan's grief at the death of his son Virbāhu (who is not mentioned in Vālmiki's *Rāmāyaṇa*) is described in the medieval Bengali *Rāmāyaṇ* of Krittibās: 'Grief upon grief came to him then; the ten-faced king fell from his throne. Regaining consciousness the king wept profusely . . .' (*KR Laṅkākāṇḍa*, Mukhopadhyay, p. 335). As in *MBK*, the news is brought by a *bhagnadūt* (bringer of bad news).

Krittibās tells us that because of his devotion to Brahmā, Virbāhu received the boon of an elephant who would make him victorious in battle until that elephant was killed. He also says that as a devotee of Vishnu Virbāhu was confident that if killed by Vishnu's incarnation Rām he would go straight to Vishnu's heaven. But as Gargi Datta in her book on M's use of Indian sources says: 'Madhusudan only took from this story the account of Virbāhu's valour. He avoided Brahmā's boon and the matter of the elephant because it detracted from that valour. And his *bhakti* [piety] could not be present either—that was at odds with the poet's imagination. To Madhusudan, Rām is not an incarnation of Vishnu—he is a *dharmabhiru* [god-fearing] man merely . . .' (p. 84)

M is famed for his partiality to Rāvan and the Rākshasas, but it should never be forgotten that Rāvan in the *Rāmāyaṇa* is often a figure of nobility and splendour. In the *Āraṇyakāṇḍa*, for example, when his sister Surpanakhā arrives in his court with news of the terrible defeats that Rām has inflicted on the Rākshasas of Janasthān, 'she saw Ravan effulgent like a column of fire, seated on a golden throne raised on a golden dais and his counsellors sat in front of him, as the gods surround the throne of Indra. The great hero with gaping mouth was dreadful to look at like Death itself. He had ten heads, twenty arms, wide mouth and ample chest. He bore all the royal signs on his person, his hue was like the mild shine of blue gem (Lapis Lazuli), his teeth were white. He wore gold ear-rings on his ears and was clad in elegant robes.' (*Āraṇyakāṇḍa* XI; Sen, p. 185)

When Hanumān sees Rāvan for the first time, he effuses: 'O, how beautiful is this hero! What patience, what strength, what beauty and what auspicious marks does he possess! If he were not vicious, then he would be the protector of heaven, nay even of Indra. But his acts are cruel and ugly, this is why even the Gods and the Asuras are frightened by his sight. This hero being angry can reduce the earth into the sea.' (*Sundarakāṇḍa* XXXIV; Sen, p. 371)

Sanyal (p. 14) compares the simile of Rudra at the gate of the Pāṇḍav camp to a description in the medieval Bengali *Mahābhārat* of Kāsirām Dās.

§80

Maybe M had a simile from Homer in mind here: in *Iliad* XIII.389–91 the Trojan warrior (Hektor's nephew) Asios 'fell as an oak-tree falls of a poplar, or a tall pine which carpenters cut down in the mountains with fresh-whetted axes to make a ship's timber.' (Hammond, p. 210) In *Iliad* XIV.414–17, Hektor himself, hit by a stone hurled by Aias, crashes down like an oak-tree struck by a thunderbolt.

Cf. also Tasso in *Jerusalem Delivered* IX.39, where the crusader Latinus, after losing his five sons in battle, is himself slain by the Turkish sultan Soliman:

> On Appennine, like as a sturdy tree,
>   Against the winds that makes resistance stout,
> If with a storm it overturned be,
>   Falls down and breaks the trees and plants about;

So Latine fell . . .
(Fairfax/ Weiss p. 232)

Sanyal, however (p. 18), traces the *śālmalī*/ petal image to Kālidāsa's *Abhijñānaśākuntala* I.17:

The sage who would inure to harsh penance
this form ravishing in its artless beauty
is surely attempting to cut acacia wood
with the edge of a blue-lotus petal.
(Rajan, p. 176)

§142
See below, IV.46.

§156
Cf. similar descriptions in Virgil's *Aeneid*, such as the rising dust of Turnus's army approaching the Trojans in Book IX, especially as that particular description is preceded by an Indian reference: 'It was like the Ganges fed by the steady flow of its seven rivers and silently rising, or like the fertile waters of the Nile when it withdraws from the plains and settles back at last into its own channel. The Trojans saw this distant cloud of black dust suddenly gathering and the darkness rising on the plain . . .' (West, p. 188)

Tasso has the same image in *Jerusalem Delivered* III.10, where the approaching army of Crusaders is observed by the watchman on the walls of Turkish-occupied Jerusalem:

Then loud he cried, Oh, what a dust ariseth!
  Oh, how it shines with shields and targets clear!
Up, up to arms, for valiant heart despiseth
  The threat'ned storm of death, and danger near . . .
(Fairfax/ Weiss, p. 59)

§176

The pouncing lion-simile here is very Homeric. Cf. for example *Iliad* V.161–4, where Diomedes attacks Priam's sons Echemmon and Chromios: 'As a lion springs among cattle and breaks the neck of a heifer or a cow, as they graze in a coppice, so Tydeus' son sent these two hurling from their chariot, brutally, without a choice, and then stripped the armour from them: the horses he gave to his companions to drive back to the ships.' (Hammond, p. 71) There are at least nine other examples, and an equal number of 'lion in a snare' similes (as in II.550), corresponding to another Homeric subset. Thus 'the largest simile type in the *MBK* ("lion") corresponds to the largest simile type in the *Iliad*.' (Riddiford, p. 344, fn. 70) But often the lion becomes a tiger or elephant. See below, IV.46.

Of 'As when the sea quarrels tumultuously with the wind' (*sindhu yathā dvandvi bāyu saha/ nirghoṣe*), Seely writes: 'We see a nod to Virgil . . . with an allusion to conflict between wind and sea.' (Seely 2008, p. 111) See below, II.550.

Sanyal (p. 30) compares the messenger's proud boast at the end of his speech to Siward's question about his brave son at the end of Shakespeare's *Macbeth*:

Siward: Had he his hurts before?
Ross: Ay, on the front.
(*Macbeth* V.8.47–8)

§205

Cf. Carthage viewed from a hill-top in Book I of the *Aeneid*, though Lankā is already fully built, whereas Aeneas 'was amazed by the size of it where recently there had been nothing but shepherds' huts'. (West, p. 15)

But in his vision of 'captivating Lankā' M is more likely to have had Milton in mind, not only the 'delicious Paradise' of Eden itself, viewed enviously by Satan (*Paradise Lost* IV.130f), but Heaven itself, as viewed 'far off' by Satan on his journey from Hell to Eden: 'With opal tow'rs and battlements adorned/ Of living sapphire, once his native seat' (*Paradise Lost* II.1049–50). See also the description of Lankā in Book VI, §322f, as viewed by Lakshman and Vibhishan. (Radice 1995, pp. 180–1)

The beauty of Lankā is fulsomely described in the *Rāmāyaṇa*, so M is not being influenced here by his partiality for the Rākshasas. Hanumān is mightily impressed by the city when he first sees it:

> It was a highly beautiful city, girt by a golden wall, with lofty white mansions and yellow highways. Its gates were covered with creepers and adorned with streaming banners. The heavenly architect Viswakarma had built that city with great care.
>
> (*Sundarakāṇḍa* II; Sen, p. 314)

> It seemed to be the capital of the nether world guarded by the formidable Uragas or snakes, rather like Amaravati, the heavenly city, dotted with clouds charged with lightening and illumined with stars and other heavenly planets. Here and there streamers were streaming in the wind with a gentle murmuring noise. Its gates were made of gold and their thresholds were inlaid with rubies, gems and other precious stones. Its flights of stairs were wrought with gems. Everything was highly neat and clean.
>
> (Ibid., III; Sen, p. 316)

Rām too, after crossing the ocean, is bowled over, despite his anguish about Sitā:

> Then Ram seeing Lanka decked with flags began to think in a sorrowful mind. 'Alas! The gazelle-eyed Janaki is confined there like the star Rohini overshadowed by planets.' Then, heaving a deep sigh, Rama addressing Lakshmana said, "My boy! Just see this city of Lanka kissing the sky, as if the heavenly architect Viswakarma from his imagination has built this city upon the high hill. Seven-storied buildings white as the fleecy clouds stand everywhere in the city. Beautiful parks and gardens decorate the city. The birds are chirping in those beautiful gardens and the leaves of the trees with bees clinging to them are gently waving in the breeze, and the woods are echoing with the sweet notes of cuckoos.'
>
> (*Yuddhakāṇḍa* XV; Sen, p. 418)

§218

In the *Rāmāyaṇa*, Rāvana 'with [his ministers] Suka and Sarana ascended the lofty tops of his snow-white palace for reconnoitring the Vanara army. In front of him stood hills and forests and the wide expanse of the sea and its shore covered with the Vanara troops.' (*Yuddhakāṇḍa* XVII; Sen, p. 421) M hugely expands the poetic and emotional effect of this.

Gargi Datta (p. 89) points out that M takes his placing of Nila, Angad, Sugriv and Rām at the east, south, north and west gates of the walled city of Lankā from Krittibās, not Vālmiki. She also has interesting things to say about the importance of the walls and gates in M's conception of Lankā, how this was primarily influenced by the Greek city-state and the depiction of Troy in the *Iliad*, and how the west gate seems to acquire a special significance.

Ghaṭotkach is described as crushing enemies with his fall in the *Draunaparva* of Kāsirām Dās's *Mahābhārat*. The Ekāghni missile is also mentioned there. (Sanyal, pp. 38–9)

The source of the allusive simile at the end of this paragraph is the *Mahābhārata*. Seely (1988, pp. 45–6), mentions it as an example of the 'subversive similes' that M uses to attach positive and heroic associations to the Rākshasas. Because Ghaṭotkach fought on the Pāṇḍav side, Virbāhu and the Rākshasas are linked in the reader's mind to the heroic Pāṇḍavas, and Rām and his allies are therefore identified with the enemy—the Kauravas.

§386

Snake metaphors and similes in *MBK* serve a variety of purposes. Here Chitrāngada compares the 'mere human' Rām to a lowly snake who lashes back when attacked; in Book VI, Lakshman and Vibhishan, deceitfully entering Lankā to kill Meghnād, are compared to a snake, though Meghnād too is compared to 'a snake brought low'. See VI.309, 568.

Phal (fruit, result), as in *karmaphal* here or *prāktaner phal* in I.598—and at many other points in the epic such as II.425, has a role to play in the moral scheme of *MBK* comparable in significance, though different in meaning, to the forbidden fruit that Eve plucks and eats in Genesis and in *Paradise Lost*. See Radice 1995, pp. 182–4, and Introduction, p. liif.

§406

In the *Rāmāyaṇa*, Rāvan's boast that the world will lose either him or Rām comes after Lakshman is struck down, and before Rāvan's final battle with Rām: 'And verily I swear to you that you will find the earth either without Ravana or Rama.' (*Yuddhakāṇḍa* LXVIII; Sen, p. 528). The same idea can found in Krittibās: *āge laṅkā arāmā o abānara kari/ sugribere māriyā pāṭhāba yamapurī* ('Having first made Lankā Rāma-less or Vānara-less, I shall send Sugriv to Yama's city'). He says this during a conversation with his brother Kumbhakarna (*KR Laṅkākāṇḍa*; Mukhopadhyay, p. 286). Sanyal (p. 55) and Gargi Datta (p. 90) note both these parallels, and also a similar wordplay in a line in Kālidāsa's *Raghuvaṃśa*.

§417

Maybe M picked up the image of spears like 'sky-piercing *śāl*-trees' (*śālbṛkṣa abhrabhedī yathā*) from Tasso's *Jerusalem Delivered* XX.28–9, where the facing Christian and pagan armies are similarly described. The gold and jewels and banners are there too:

> Loose in the wind waved their ensigns light,
> Trembled the plumes that on their crests were set;
> Their arms, impresses, colours, gold, and stone,
> 'Gainst the sun-beams smil'd, flamed, sparkled, shone:
>
> Of dry-top'd oaks they seem'd two forests thick,
> So did each host with spears and pikes abound . . .
> (Fairfax/ Weiss, p. 516)

§443f

Vāruni, wife of the sea-god Varuna (though see Notes to I.443 for M's name for her), can be compared to Achilleus's mother Thetis in the *Iliad*. She is the daughter of Nereus, 'the old man of the sea', rather than his wife, but in her friendliness towards Lakshmi/ Kamalā, 'guardian goddess of the Rākshasas'—and thus by extension her sympathy for Rāvan and Meghnād—she is like Thetis when she rises 'from the sea like a mist' (Hammond, p. 12), comforts Achilleus in his grief at losing his concubine Briseïs to Agamemnon, and entreats Zeus to take his part against the rest of the Achaians.

Sanyal (p. 59) and Dasgupa (p. 119) note the Thetis connection, and also compare Vāruni to Sabrina, the presiding deity of the river Severn, who appears 'attended by water-Nymphes' at the end of Milton's *A Maske presented at Ludlow-Castle* ['Comus', 1637].

§443

Although Vāruni is wrong to think that the tumult overhead is a storm whipped up by 'the wind-lord' (*Vāyupati*, i.e. Pavan)—it is in fact caused by the emerging Rākhshas armies, 'the tramp of the warriors' feet'—her imaginings here are distinctly Virgilian. In *Aeneid* I, when Juno (who hates the Trojans) wants a storm to be whipped up to 'drive their fleet in all directions', she visits 'Aeolia, the home of the clouds, a place teeming with the raging winds of the south. Here Aeolus is king and here in a vast cavern he keeps in subjection the brawling winds and howling storms, chained and bridled in their prison.' (West, p. 4)

Although M's comment in his letter (see Notes, I.443) implies that he made up the name 'Vāruni', Gargi Datta (p. 103) points out that it occurs in Kālidāsa's play *Vikramorvaśīya*, which was itself a source for M's verse letter from Urvasi to Pururvā in his *Bīrāṅganā kābya* (where the name is also used).

§447
Descriptions of the emergence of the Rākshas army, such as here or in VII.158, can be compared to the famous 'catalogue of ships' in *Iliad* II.

§483
In the description here of Muralā rising from the sea like a flying fish, Gargi Datta (p. 90) finds an echo of Kālidāsa's *Meghadūta*:

> Your self intrinsically beautiful
> even in its shadow-form will enter Gambhīra's clear waters
> as into a tranquil pool of consciousness;
> do not therefore cavalierly dismiss
> her welcoming glances—those dazzling upward leaps
> of glittering white fishes bright as water-lilies.
> (*Meghadūta* 42; Rajan, p. 147)

For the description of Kamalā (Lakshmi), both Gargi Datta (ibid.) and Sanyal (p. 63) cite as a source some lines from the *Ādiparba* of the *Mahābhārat* of Kāsirām Dās, describing Lakshmi's emergence from the churning of the primeval ocean (see Notes to I.295, 513). They also compare the passage to M's description of Lakshmi in his poem *Tillottamāsambhab kābya*. Sanyal (ibid.) makes a further connection with a passage praising Lakshmi in the *Annadāmaṅgal* of Bhāratchandra Rāy.

§623
Seely (1988, p. 48) points out the positive effect of the comparison at the end of this paragraph between Meghnād and Krishna, the much-loved focus of Bengali Vaishnava devotion. His persuasive view that M used 'subversive

similes' from the stories of Krishna, Durgā and the *Mahābhārata* to counteract the negative and evil associations that Rāvan and the Rākshasas had acquired is developed further in his article of 1991.

Sanyal (p. 79) and Dasgupta (p. 119) compare Meghnād's pleasure-dome here with the palace and garden in Book XVI of Tasso's *Jerusalem Delivered*, in which the enchantress Armida imprisons the crusader hero Rinaldo. See Fairfax/ Weiss, p. 393f.

§678
Sanyal and Dasgupta also find an echo here of Rinaldo tearing himself away from Armida in *Jerusalem Delivered* XVI.34–5:

> His nice attire in scorn he rent and tore,
> For of his bondage vile that witness bore:
>
> That done, he hasted from the charmed fort . . .
> (Fairfax/ Weiss, p. 401; Sanyal, p. 82; Dasgupta, p. 119)

§689
For Pramilā's anxious farewell to Meghnād—here and also in Book V—see below, V.446, 588. Comparing the scene to Tasso (see above, §678), Dasgupta comments: 'But while in the Bengali poem the feelings are genuine, the enchantress in the Italian poem is sorry simply because her conquest is undone. A better comparison would be the grief of Andromache at the departure of Hector before his fight with Achilles.' (pp. 119–20)

The creeper and tree simile is used most beautifully by Tasso in *Jerusalem Delivered* XX.99. Edward and Gildippe, man and wife, fight alongside each other and are both killed by Soliman. First Gildippe is struck, and then Edward is felled too, unable to fight strongly with his right arm while holding his dying wife in his left:

> As the high elm (whom his dear vine hath twin'd
> Fast in her hundred arms and holds embrac'd)
> Bears down to earth his spouse and darling kind,
> If storm or cruel steel the tree down cast,
> And her full grapes to nought doth bruise and grind,
> Spoils his own leaves, faints, withers, dies at last;
> And seems to mourn and die, not for his own
> But for her death, with him that lies o'erthrown:
>
> So fell he mourning, mourning for the dame
> Whom life and death had made for ever his . . .
> (Fairfax/ Weiss, pp. 533–4)

We know that Tasso was among the poets that M was reading when he wrote *MBK*, because of references in his letters. For example:

> I am just now reading Tasso in the original,—an Italian gentleman having presented me with a copy. Oh! What luscious poetry. If God spares me for some years yet, I shall write a poem, a Romantic one in the *Ottava Rima* or stanzas of eight lines like his.
> (Calcutta, end of September 1860, to Raj Narạyan Basu; ibid., p. 153)

See also Introduction, pp. xvi–xvii.

§735
Note Rāvan's fears here, though they are much more muted and accepting than Priam's agony at Hektor's insistence on

entering the battle against Achilleus: 'Hektor, please, dear child, do not face this man alone, away from the others—so you do not go down under the son of Peleus and quickly meet your doom, you stubborn man, because he is stronger than you.' (*Iliad* XXII.138–41; Hammond, p. 352)

§763
Gargi Datta (p. 91) finds in the personification of Lankā in the court-singer's song of praise to Meghnād a parallel in a line in the Sanskrit play *Mahāvīracarita* by Bhavabhuti, in which after the death of Rāvan grief-stricken Lankā is similarly personified.

In connecting Meghnād with the sun—here and in II.491—M may have had at the back of his mind Satan's hatred of the sun, because it reminded him of his own former state:

> O thou that with surpassing glory crowned,
> Look'st from thy sole dominion like the God
> Of this new world; at whose sight all the stars
> Hide their diminished heads; to thee I call,
> But with no friendly voice, and add thy name
> O sun, to tell thee how I hate thy beams
> That bring to my remembrance from what state
> I fell, how glorious once above thy sphere . . .
> (*Paradise Lost* IV.33–39)

Later, Meghnād 'the sun of the Raksha race' will fall like Satan. See below, VI.642.

Book II

This is the book of *MBK* that is most directly modelled on Homer (see Radice 2009), and M stated as much in a letter to his friend Rajnarayan Basu. Enclosing a copy of Book II, he wrote at the beginning of September 1860: 'You must try and see what you can do with the enclosed. As a reader of the Homeric Epos, you will, no doubt, be reminded of the Fourteenth *Iliad*, and I am not ashamed to say that I have intentionally imitated it—Juno's visit to Jupiter on Mount Ida. I only hope I have given the Episode as thorough a Hindu air as possible.' (Murshid 2004, p. 144) In the *Iliad*, Zeus, king of the gods, favours the Trojans for most of the epic, because Thetis—one of his numerous lovers—has asked him to support her son Achilleus in his quarrel with Agamemnon, king of the Achaians. The quarrel begins the epic, in the tenth and last year of the Trojan war, and arises because Agamemnon has stolen Achilleus's concubine Briseïs from him, to compensate for having to give his own concubine Chryseïs back to her father Chryses, who is a priest of Apollo and has managed to get Apollo to visit a plague on the Achaians. Achilleus withdraws to his tent in a huff, which leaves the Greeks dangerously exposed to the Trojans and their supreme warrior Hektor. Zeus's wife Hera, however, sides with the Achaians, and this is a cause of dissension between her and her husband. In *Iliad* XIV she—to quote from the delightful summary that Alexander Pope supplies, as he does for all the books of his great translation—'forms a design to over-reach him; she sets off her charms with the utmost care, and (the more surely to enchant Him) obtains the magick girdle of Venus. She then applies herself to the God of Sleep, and with some difficulty, persuades him to seal the eyes of Jupiter (Zeus); this done, she goes to Mount Ida, where the God, at first sight, is ravished with her beauty, sinks in her embraces, and is laid asleep. Neptune (Poseidon) takes advantage of his slumber, and succours the Greeks.' As a result of Hera's deceit and seduction, for a while—while Zeus is asleep—the Achaians make headway against the Trojans, even though their greatest hero Achilleus is still sulking in his tent.

In Book II of *MBK*, Durgā (equivalent here to Hera) makes an equally seductive approach to her husband Siva (equivalent to Zeus), though for somewhat different reasons. Greek gods—including Zeus himself—seldom act morally. They are whimsical, constantly quarrelling amongst themselves, and generally favour one human being or another only according to whether they happen to feel flattered or not by their worship or neglect. Siva, in M's epic, is rather like a Greek god in that he sides with Rāvan simply because he has been an exceptionally loyal devotee—a devout Saivite, in fact. All the other gods take the side of 'Ram and his rabble', as M famously called them (Murshid 2004, p. 169), essentially for moral reasons—because Rāvan has sinned by abducting Sitā. (See Introduction, p. lii.) But first, Kamalā/ Lakshmi/ Ramā has to appeal to Indra (who has good cause to be afraid of Rāvan's son Meghnād because Meghnād once defeated him in battle: see above, pp. 306–8). Indra and his wife Sachi appeal to Durgā, and Durga has to bring round Siva. Moral arguments are not going to be enough, as he is immersed in *tapas* (ascetic meditation); so she enlists Kāma, the god of love.

As regards the way in which Siva arranges for the divine weapons that will eventually kill Meghnād to be handed by Māyā to Indra, by Indra to Chitrarath, and by Chitrarath to Rām, this—as Gargi Datta says (p. 72)—comes entirely from M's imagination. It has no source in the *Rāmāyaṇa*.

§1

In a letter to Rajnarayan Basu, M quotes four lines from this paragraph and comments:

By the bye, these lines will no doubt recall to your mind the lines,

And whisper whence they stole
Those balmie spoils—

of Milton, and the lines

Like the sweet south
That breathes upon a bank of violets
Stealing and giving odour—

(Murshid 2004, p. 174. M's quotations are from *Paradise Lost* IV.158–9 and *Twelfth Night* I.1. XX)

M uses the same image in V.258.

M originally had some different lines in mind for the opening of Book II. He quotes them in an earlier letter to Rajnarayan, and comments:

You will at once see whom I imitate:

Who of the gods impelled them to contend?
Latona's son and Jove's—
—Cowper's Homer's *Iliad*

Milton has imitated this—

Who first seduced them to that foul revolt?
The infernal serpent —Book I

(Murshid 2004, p. 125)

§126

Gargi Datta (p. 101) traces the Kailās/ Krishna's crown simile to Bengal's most celebrated Sanskrit poet Jayadeva, and to the Bhāgavata Purāna 10.3.9–10.

§168

This difference in attitude towards Rāvan, between Durgā and Siva, is comparable to the dissension between Zeus and Hera in their attitude to the Trojans, but it is nothing like as acrimonious, and as indicated above rests on a moral argument, which Durgā eventually wins. Hera, by contrast, hates the Trojans out of pique at the Judgement of Paris, the son of Priam and Hekabe, abductor of Helen, and thus the cause of the war between the Trojans and the Achaians. When asked to award the Golden Apple in a beauty contest between Aphrodite (Venus, goddess of love), Hera (Juno) and Athene (Minerva, the goddess of war), Paris gives it to Aphrodite. Hera therefore sides with the Achaians, and Aphrodite sides with the Trojans.

§287

In its sensuous allure, this passage can certainly be compared with Hera's decking of herself before her seduction of Zeus, though Durgā is assisted by Rati, whereas it is alone and 'behind closed doors' that Hera 'dressed herself in an ambrosial robe, which Athene had made for her in fine-napped cloth and embroidered it with many figures: she pinned it across her breast with golden clasps, and she fastened round her waist a belt hung with a hundred dangles . . .' (Hammond, p. 225)

M must also have been influenced by the dressing of Gauri/ Pārvati before her marriage to Siva in Kālidāsa's *Kumārasambhava* (see below, §309):

Like a vine with its flowers coming out,
like the night when the stars come out,
like a river with birds settling on it,

so she shone when her ornaments
were being put on her.
Gazing at herself resplendent
in the mirror's disk,
her long eyes stilled,
she became impatient
for Siva the Destroyer to come,
for women dress themselves
to be seen by their darlings.
(*Kumārasambhava*, Canto 7; Smith, p. 259)

The lovely simile at the end of the paragraph is evocative of feelings that M himself must have had when exiled from Bengal in Madras, 1848–56, or later in Europe, 1862–7. See below, VI.47.

§309
This and other references in *MBK* (e.g. in I.33) show that M was well acquainted with Kālidāsa's *Kumārasambhava* ('The Birth of Kumāra') which contains the famous story of how Madan (Kāma) tried to wake Siva out of his ascetic trance, and was burnt to ashes by a blast from Siva's third eye. However, M's account here of how Siva is eventually seduced and woken up by Durgā differs from Kālidāsa significantly, and mainly comes from his own invention and the influence of *Iliad* XIV, as mentioned above. In Kālidāsa's poem, Gauri/ Pārvati, after the failure of Kāma's attempt, breaks down Siva's resistance not through seductive allure but through feats of asceticism:

'From today, my stooping lady,
I am your slave,
purchased by your austerities.'

When Moon-crested Siva said this,
she at once cast off the weariness of her exertions,
for with the fruit
exhaustion turns into freshness.
(Ibid., Canto 5; Smith, p. 205)

Moreover, in *MBK* Siva and Durgā are already married, whereas in *Kumārasambhava*, Siva's defeat leads to his betrothal to Gauri, their grand marriage conducted by the Seven Sages and attended by all the gods, and the consummation that will give rise to Kumāra (Kārttikeya, god of war) who will destroy the demon Tārak.

Of Madan's upbringing by Māyāvati after he was reborn, Gargi Datta writes (p. 99): 'This story can be found in the *Harivaṃśa*, *Viṣṇuparvan*, ch. 104–8; in the Bhāgavata Purāna 10.55 (Birth of Pradyumna and the Killing of Sambar); and in ch. 200 of the Brahma Purāna . . . as well as Bhāratchandra's *Annadāmaṅgal.*'

§337
Cf. Hera's fear that if—as Zeus suggests—they make love *al fresco* on the peak of Mount Ida, 'where all is open to view', the other gods will see them and 'point us out'. She suggests going into the beautiful bedroom that her son Hephaistos has built for her, but Zeus replies: 'I shall wrap us in a golden cloud so think that not even Helios could see through it, and his light has the sharpest sight of all.' (Hammond, p. 229) Here it is Durgā who makes the golden cloud, but its effect is the same.

§367
Sanyal (p. 133) compares the ivory portals of Durgā's palace to the Gate of Ivory which is one of the two gates of sleep mentioned by Penelope at the end of *Odyssey* XIX

(Shewring, p. 241). They are also mentioned at the end of *Aeneid* VI: the Gate of Horn 'is an easy exit for true shades'; through the Gate of Ivory 'the powers of the underworld send false dreams up towards heavens'. Aeneas and the Sybil leave the underworld through the Gate of Ivory. (West, p. 140)

§400
In Kālidāsa's *Kumārasambhava*, Siva and Gauri/ Pārvati make love (as is implied here) on a mountainside, and spring suddenly breaks out:

> The Guru of the World revelled
> in the moon's pure white light
> on Kubéra's mountain, where,
> frightened by Rávana's roar,
> she tightly bound his neck in her arms.
>
> While he was taking his pleasure
> on the slopes of the Málaya mountain,
> the south wind, like a smooth-talking lover
> with filaments of cloves in his breath,
> shook the boughs of the sandal trees
> and wafted away his beloved's fatigue.
> (*Kumārasambhava*, Canto 8; Smith, p. 309)

§425
Note that Siva accepts here the argument that Rāvan is a sinner and that 'the wretch is sinking through his own misdeeds' (*nij karma-phale maje duṣṭamati*), but like Zeus in *Iliad* XIV he is essentially swayed by his wife's seductive beauty.

Seely (1982, p. 470), points out that Siva's support for

the Rākshasas can be easily sourced in the medieval Bengali tradition. In the *Mahābhārat* of Kāsirām Dās, Siva is referred to as 'Dānesvar' (Lord of the Dānavas), and in Krittibās's *Rāmāyaṇ* Siva says, 'My devotee, the ten-headed one,/ Stole away Sītā; now his death must be./ By your [Rāma's] arrows will his family perish;/ But he was truly a dear devotee of mine.' [Seely's translation]

For the significance of *phal* (fruit, result) in *MBK*, see above, I.386 and Introduction, pp. liif.

As regards the role of Māyā-devi in *MBK*, Gargi Datta (pp. 103–5) writes at some length about possible confusions with Durgā and Chaṇḍi, who are both sometimes given that name in Hindu mythology. But in the passage she quotes from Book V (§342) the goddess called 'Mahāmāyā' who speaks to Laskhman is clearly a deliberate conflation of Chaṇḍi and Māyā (see Notes, V.342); and as for Durgā and Māyā, M's plot in *MBK* makes them quite separate characters, as Gargi Datta herself concedes.

§467
Sanyal (p. 145) compares the unmoving manes of the horses to Kālidāsa's *Abhijñānaśākuntala* I.8:

The reins hanging slack,
the horses leap forward,
no, they glide over the track—
bodies out-stretched, ears flung back,
the tips of their plumes motionless . . .
(Rajan, p. 173)

§491
Sanyal (p. 150) finds in the 'lotus-hands' (*padma-kar*) of the Dawn a trace of Homer's recurrent 'rosy-fingered dawn'.

'Lotus-sun' (*pankaj-rabi*), however, he sources to the *Mahābhārat* of Kāsirām Dās, where Vyāsa, author of the epic, is described as *bhārat-pankaj-rabi* ('lotus-sun of India'). (p. 151)

§550
M may well have been inspired here by the storm in Book I of the *Aeneid* that Juno asks Aeolus to whip up. (Sanyal, p. 157; Dasgupta, p. 120) Is M's dramatic description here as necessary for his plot as Virgil's storm, which drives Aeneas and his surviving followers to the coast of Tyre (Libya) where he meets Queen Dido? On the face of it, not, but Seely has argued that the winds do intervene at particular points in *MBK* as 'agents of change', and this at a deeper level reflects the 'winds of change' sweeping through nineteenth century Bengal that produced a Western-influenced poet like M and whose effects he himself promoted through his literary innovations. See below, V.559, VI.216. (Seely 2008)

M's wind-imagery also recalls the changes in Nature wrought by the Fall in *Paradise Lost*:

> . . . now from the north
> Of Norumbega, and the Samoed shore
> Bursting their brazen dungeon, armed with ice
> And snow and hail and stormy gust and flaw,
> Boreas and Caecias and Argestes loud
> And Thrascias rend the woods and seas upturn . . .
> (*Paradise Lost* X.695–700)

For the simile of a lion breaking his chains, see above, I.176.

§576
Sanyal (p. 159) compares 'the scents of heaven' to 'A more than earthly fragrance shed' which he attributes to the *Iliad* but in fact can be found in the translation of Virgil's *Aeneid* by John Conington (1866), in the description of Venus after her exhortation to Aeneas (I.402f; Conington, twelfth impression, 1907, p. 19). (Riddiford, personal communication)

§597
Sanyal (p. 161) compares the epithet *deb-kul priya* ('loved by the gods') to 'favoured by the gods' in the *Iliad*, but in fact no mortal is favoured by all the gods in the Homeric tradition: the gods are partisan in human affairs. Sanyal may have been influenced by older translations of the *Iliad* in which the compound *diophilos* ('beloved of Zeus') was incorrectly rendered as 'beloved of the gods'. (Riddiford, ibid.)

Book III

Book III is very much 'Pramilā's book', and the character of Pramilā largely M's original creation, though sources for both her warlike and romantic qualities can be found in both Western and Indian sources.

§1
For Pramilā and Meghnād to be compared here with 'the women of Vraj' (including Rādhā herself) and Krishna is rightly mentioned by Seely (1988, p. 48; 1991, p. 144) as an example of the 'subversive similes' by which M gives the Rākshasas positive associations.

§47

Sanyal (p. 171) compares the lovely petals/ pearls/ tears image to 'Decking with liquid pearl the bladed grass' in Shakespeare's *A Midsummer Night's Dream* I.1.211.

§85

Gargi Datta argues (pp. 107–10) that Kāsirām Dās is a very exact source for Pramilā and her warlike companions. 'Roused by the noise of Arjun's god-given (*deb-datta*) conch,/ 'the war-like women (*bīrāṅganā*) merrily put on their battle-dress; / battle-drums thundered all around' (Kasirām Das, *Mahābhārat* III.87–9). She writes: 'Not just the name and the story, if one looks carefully one can see that the character of Kāsirām Das's Pramilā influenced the imaginative conception of Madhusudan's Pramilā too. For all the heroic sentiment (*bīr-ras)* he created in the pomp of Pramilā and her companions' preparations for battle, there is a mood of light playfulness (*smita kautuker bhāb*).' (p. 108) They are all too ready to give up arms for love, and Pramilā releases the sacrificial horse after extracting from Arjun an assurance that he will marry her when the sacrifice has been completed. 'The influence of this love-intoxicated band of women is clear in the boasting of Madhusudan's Pramilā and her companions. Heroic and erotic sentiment (*bīr-ras o kām-ras*) are thoroughly combined.' (p. 110)

§115

For Pramilā and her companions in warlike mode, M not only had the Amazons of Greek mythology as a general precedent but also the specific character of Camilla in *Aeneid* XI, who fights heroically with the Latin armies led by Turnus until she is killed by a spear thrown by the Etruscan Arruns (but guided by Apollo): 'There in the middle of all this bloodshed, exulting in it, was the Amazon Camilla with the quiver on her shoulder, and one side bared for battle. Sometimes the pliant spears came thick from her hand; sometimes, unwearied, she caught up her mighty double axe, and the golden bow and arrows of Diana rang on her shoulder.' (West, p. 256) Such passages might have blended in his imagination with Kāli, Durgā and the *Devī-māhātmya* (see Notes to V.113, p. 144).

Another source might have been the character of Clorinda in Tasso's *Jerusalem Delivered*:

> Against their foes Clorinda sallied out,
> And many a baron bold was by her side . . .
> (Fairfax/ Weiss, p. 60)

She fights on the Turkish side against the Crusaders led by Duke Godfrey of Bouillon, and wounds Godfrey in Book XI. In Book XII, Arestes, the aged eunuch who has brought her up, reveals that she was actually a Christian by birth, daughter of King Senapus of Ethopia and his queen. Arestes, a pagan, was bought as a slave by the king; his queen handed her over to Arestes when she was born fair-skinned—she feared that her husband would doubt the child's paternity. Arestes brought her up as a pagan, but she converts to the faith of her parents after receiving a mortal blow from the crusader-hero Tancred in Book XII.

There are plenty of warlike women in Spenser's *Faerie Queene*, which was influenced by Tasso as well as by Ariosto, but M does not seem to have used either Spenser or Ariosto as a source for *MBK*.

All in all, M's biographer Yogindranath Basu was right to say: 'Tilottomā, the heroine of Madhusudan's first poem, was formed bit by bit from various material ingredients.

The heroine of his second and greatest poem too was formed from the imagination of poets of various lands.' (quoted by Gargi Datta, p. 111) As well as the influences mentioned above, Bengali critics have included Byron's Maid of Saragossa, Pallas Athene in the *Iliad*, Padmini in *Padminī upākhyān* by M's contemporary Rangalal Bandyopadhyay (1827–1887), and Lakshmibai, The Rani of Jhansi (1828–1858), famous for her role in the Mutiny of 1857.

M's allusion to Vāḍaba at the end of the paragraph may have had an erotic charge, for at the end of Kālidāsa's *Kumārasambhava*, Siva's sexual appetite is described as 'unsated/ as is the submarine fire/ amid the ocean's waters' (Smith, p. 345).

§202

Sanyal (p. 190) sources Hanumān's description of Bhimā (Ugrachaṇḍā) to the *Sundarakāṇḍa* of Krittibās's *Rāmāyaṇ*: 'In front was the terrifying image of Ugrachaṇḍā/ skull in her left hand and sword in her right'.

§248

The striking simile of a ship here is reminiscent of one of M's best sonnets, *Sāgare tarī* ('Ship on the sea'), which I translated in 1976. Notice too the proud image of a snake at the end (see below, VI.568).

The Ship

I saw one night a ship on a strange sea,
Shaped like a huge nightfaring magic bird,
Her sails spread wide on air that slowly stirred
Their glimmering whiteness onward, steadily.
A string of lamps about the high cross-tree

Burned like a crown of gems of mingled hue,
Stupendous red and yellow, white and blue.
All round the frothing waves sang fulsomely,
Swelling as of to hymn her handsomeness,
Praising in joy her courage, form and might.
She swept her way, as when a path is cleared
Before a high-born maiden's proud progress.
Nobly she moved, spreading her path with light,
Just as a snake sheds glory, crest upreared.
(*Sāgare tarī*; Sonnet No. 77)

§294
For the Rākshasas as sorcerers, see below, V.490 (p. 349) and introductory comments on Book VI (p. 351).

§352
Sanyal (p. 204) compares Rām's 'fear' here to Arjun's reaction when he encounters Pramilā and her warlike companions in Kāsirām Das's *Mahābhārat* (see above, III.85). He argues that critics who have accused Rām of cowardice here have misunderstood that 'fear' implies wonder and amazement:

Weak women have become strong and taken up the bow:
How am I supposed to fight with them?
I am fearful at the sight—how shall I fight?
If defeated I will lose my reputation in the world.
(quoted by Sanyal, p. 204)

§364
Forest-fire similes in *MBK* (they can also be found in III.598, VI.361 and VII.610: see Riddiford, pp. 343–4)

can certainly be compared to similes in Homer such as *Iliad* II.455–8: 'As annihilating fire blazes through the deep forest on a mountain's peaks, and the glare can be seen from far off, so as they marched the gleam from the awesome bronze struck glinting through the air and reached the heavens.' (Hammond, p. 30)

§523
The comparison here between Pramilā and Chāmuṇḍā (i.e. Durgā) is—along with the Rākshas-Pāṇḍav and the Meghnād/ Pramilā-Krishna/ Rādhā links noticed elsewhere—among the 'subversive similes' analysed beautifully by Seely (1988). They combine to build up the grand, heroic and tragic character that M gives to the Rākshasas and especially to Meghnād and Pramilā.

Book IV

Book IV is mostly given over to Sitā's own account of her abduction, and is more closely based on the *Rāmāyaṇa* of Vālmiki—with some help from Krittibās—than any other book in *MBK*, which is no doubt why M begins with an invocation to Vālmiki. Nevertheless, Bengali critics have noticed subtle differences between M's Sitā and the Sitā of the *Rāmāyaṇa*. As Gargi Datta puts it, his main problem is that to follow the traditional account fully would mean highlighting Rāvan's sinfulness, 'yet Madhuṣudan's humanism has made him sympathetic towards Rāvan.' (p. 115) He gets round this problem by making Sitā's compassion extend even to those who have treated her so badly, and by making her blame her fate rather than Rāvan for what has happened.

M was aware that Book IV might be seen as something of a digression from the main action of his epic. He wrote to Rajnarayan Basu: 'I think I have constructed the poem on the most rigid principles and even a French critic would not find fault with me. Perhaps the episode of Sita's abduction (Fourth Book) should not have been admitted since it is scarcely connected with the main progress of the Fable. But would you willingly part with it? Many here look upon that Book as the best among the five [so far published], though Jotindra and his school call the Book III—Promilla's entry into the city—"The most magnificent".' (Murshid 2004, p. 166) But not only does the book fill in vital information about Rām's *casus belli* against Rāvan, it also follows a well established practice in the European (and Indian) epic tradition that earlier events are often dealt with in the form of a reminiscence. Cf. Raphael's account of Creation and the Fall of the Angels in Books V-VIII of *Paradise Lost*; or Aeneas's account to Dido in Book II of the *Aeneid* of the fall of Troy and his flight from the city leading his little son Ascanius by the hand and carrying his father Anchises on his back; or Odysseus's account of the Lotus-Eaters, Cyclops, Circe, etc. to King Alcinous of Phraeacia in Books IX-XII of the *Odyssey*. The device was also used by M's contemporary Richard Wagner in his epic music-dramas. (See Introduction, p. lxxvi.)

§1

M's second invocation here (see above, I.1) corresponds to Milton's invocations at the beginning of Books III and VI of *Paradise Lost*, to 'holy Light, offspring of Heav'n first born' and the muse of astronomy Urania respectively.

But in being addressed to 'master-poet Vālmiki ', author of the *Rāmāyaṇa*, M's invocation connects even more strongly with Milton's semi-invocation to the muse of his poetry: 'my celestial patroness, who deigns/ Her nightly visitation unimplored,/ And dictates to me slumb'ring, or inspires/ Easy my unpremeditated verse' (*Paradise Lost* IX.21–4).

In its exalted tone, the passage can also be compared to Dante's invocation to Apollo at the beginning of the *Paradiso*:

> O great Apollo, for this final task,
> make me a vessel worthy to receive
> your genius and the longed-for laurel crown.
>
> Thus far I have addressed my prayers to one
> peak of Parnassus; now I need them both
> to move into this heavenly arena.
>
> Enter my breast, breathe into me as high
> a strain as that which vanquished Marsyas
> the time you drew him from his body's sheath.
>
> O Power Divine, but lend me of yourself
> so much as will make clear at least the shadow
> of that high realm imprinted on my mind,
>
> and you shall see me at your chosen tree,
> crowning myself with those green leaves of which
> my theme and you yourself will make me worthy.
> (*Paradiso* I.13–27; Musa, pp. 1–2)

§46

M's tiger and elephant similes—which are quite frequent in *MBK*—can be regarded as 'orientalized' versions of Homer's 'lion' similes. Other examples can be found in

V.342 (tiger) and I.142 (elephant). There are at least 16 other examples. See Riddiford, p. 344. But he also frequently uses lion similes. See above, I.176.

However, the tigress/ doe simile comes straight from Vālmiki's *Rāmāyaṇa*:

> Thenceforth, Janaki being surrounded by the Rakshasis passed her days as a doe in the midst of tigresses, and was distressed like a deer caught in a trap and knew not a moment's respite. Grim-faced Rakshasis roared and intimidated her. She was overwhelmed with grief and fear and swooned in thinking of Rama and Lakshmana.
>
> (*Āraṇyakāṇḍa* XXV; Sen, p. 211)

Gargi Datta (p. 119) finds the influence of Kālidāsa in M's rich use of 'pathetic fallacy' here.

§67
'Sarama, the Rakshsasa lady, was a dear friend of Janaki.' (*VR Yuddhakāṇḍa* XXI; Sen, p. 429) There is a tradition that she was Vibhishan's husband, and M makes her explicitly so in *MBK*. This is not mentioned in the *Rāmāyaṇa* itself, but in the additional *Uttarakāṇḍa* we read: 'Then Dasagriva procured two brides for Kumbhakarna and Vibhishana—Vajrajwala, grand-daughter of Vairochana for Kumbhakarna, and Sarama, the virtuous daughter of the Gandharva king, Sailusha, for Vibhishana. Sarama was born on the bank of the Manasa Lake. Seeing the waters of the lake rising in the rains, the girl began to cry. Then her mother said, "*Saro mā vardhata*—Let not the lake rise." From that time the girl was named Sarama.' (Sen, p. 574 [adjusted])

§72f
Gargi Datta (p. 116) quotes Sitā's defence of Rāvan here—that she, not he, threw off her ornaments, so however villainous the rest of his behaviour Saramā is wrong to blame him for that—as an example of the subtlety with which M shifts some of the blame away from Rāvan, so as to preserve his heroic status.

§86
Vālmiki tells us that Sitā 'threw down her silken cloth of golden hue, her scarf and fine ornaments, thinking that they might inform Rama. But Ravana could not know anything of it on account of the speed of his flight.' (*Āraṇyakāṇḍa* XXIII; Sen, p. 207). But more of this is made by Krittibās. (Sanyal, p. 241)

§165
Similes of flood-waters, such as here or in VII.554 or VII.691, are certainly influenced by similar similes in Homer, e.g. *Iliad* V.87–91, where the Achaian warrior Diomedes sweeps over the plain 'like a river full in winter spate, which bursts the dykes in the speed of its current'. (Hammond, p. 69; see Riddiford, p. 343)

§175
Marrying creepers to trees is a famous trope in Kālidāsa's *Abhijñānaśākuntala*, and both Gargi Datta (p. 129) and Sanyal (p. 251) also find the influence of the *Uttararāmacarita* of Bhavabhuti in details such as the dancing in the woods with a hind.

§282f
M's Sitā here, in her panic, comes across better here than in the *Rāmāyaṇa* itself, where her anger against Lakshman

extends to a shocking accusation that he has designs on her:

> But Lakshmana thinking of Ram's directions was quite reluctant to go. At this, Janaki was beside herself with rage and said, 'You are not going to Ram's help even under these circumstances! You are his enemy in the guise of a friend. You wish for his death in order to secure me. It is clear to me that just for your lust for me you have refrained from going to your brother. You have not the least love for your brother, therefore you pray for his disaster.'
>
> (*Āraṇyakāṇḍa* XVII; Sen, pp. 197–8)

Also, by presenting the story as reminiscence, he can make Sitā herself acknowledge, 'I yelled at him in my madness'.

§290

Sanyal (p. 261) traces the allusion to Bhrigurām (Parasurām) to a line in Krittibās's *Rāmāyaṇ*, where Parasurām is described as singing Rām's praises.

He also (p. 262) compares 'A cruel tigress must have borne you and raised you in the jungle' to Dido's excoriation of Aeneas in *Aeneid* IV.365, quoting Dryden's translation of 1697:

> Not sprung from Noble Blood, nor Goddess-born,
> But hewn from hardened Entrails of a Rock;
> And rough *Hyrcanian* Tygers gave thee suck.
> (John Dryden, *Virgil's Aeneid*, IV.523–5)

§413

The fight between Rāvan and Jaṭāyu is very vividly described in the *Rāmāyaṇa* and the noble character of the bird-man-warrior is brought out more fully than in *MBK*. M doesn't seem to pick up on Jaṭāyu's immense age, which accounts for his wisdom, and also for his becoming tired so that Rāvan is able to cut his wings to pieces. He eventually dies in Rām's arms, telling him of Sitā's abduction but also offering him reassurance: 'The moment when Ravana carried away Sita is called *Vindya*. Whoever takes away anything (dishonestly) at this moment soon meets with his destruction like a fish devouring a hook, and the owner in no time gets back his lost property. But Ravana could not know this at that time. So don't be overwhelmed with grief for Sita. You will soon recover her.' (*VR Āraṇyakāṇḍa* XXXI; Sen, p. 221) See, however, below, VIII.611.

§464f

Sitā's dream of the future here—of the invasion of Lankā by Rām and his forces and her rescue from Rāvan—is comparable to the 'parade of Roman heroes', the vision of Rome's future triumph unfolded to Aeneas by the ghost of his father Anchises at the end of Book VI of the *Aeneid*. (Sanyal, p. 279; Dasgupta, p. 121)

Some of what she sees, however, is derived from Krittibās's *Rāmāyaṇ*: the soaring mountain, the five warriors, and the rivers running dry at the tramp of Rām's mighty army. (Gargi Datta, p. 124; Sanyal, p. 280)

§556

The *mandār*-flowers of Indian tradition may have blended in M's imagination with Milton's 'immortal amarant, a flow'r which once/ In Paradise, fast by the Tree of Life/ Began to bloom, but soon for man's offence/ To Heav'n removed where first it grew, there grows,/ And flow'rs aloft shading the Fount of Life . . .' (*Paradise Lost* III.353–7)

§595
Cf. 'When copper-eyed Jaṭayu, huge as a mountain, died, Rama broke forth in deep sorrow . . .' (*VR Āraṇyakāṇḍa* XXXI; Sen, p. 221)

§628
Gargi Datta (p. 119) cites Sitā's fatalistic self-blame here ('Unlucky was my birth . . .') as an example of how M absolves Ravān of some of the responsibility for her abduction, whereas in the traditional *Rāmāyaṇa* account he is wholly to blame. Sitā's sentiments come out even more explicitly in Book IX—see below, IX.181.

§676
M's portrayal of the friendship between Sitā and Saramā makes it clear that Saramā comes secretly and at considerable personal risk. This is not the case in Vālmiki's *Rāmāyaṇa*, where 'Saramā is engaged by Rāvan as a guard for Sitā'. (Sanyal, p. 239, 301)

Book V

The events in this book come mostly from M's own imagination, with some help from Tasso and Milton. They are not to be found in either Vālmiki or Krittibās.

§109f
The use here of 'the Goddess of Dreams' to convey a message, and the exact repetition of the message she has been told to impart, is very like (though not as sinister as) Zeus's use of an 'evil Dream' in *Iliad* II to go to Agamemnon and give him the false notion that immortals have now all turned against the Trojans and that it is therefore safe for the Achaians to attack them. (Hammond, pp. 19–20)

§113

Dasgupta (p. 122) compares 'Go alone to that wood, my dear' to 'Zeus's instruction conveyed by Iris to King Priam in the *Iliad*: "You must go alone, and no other Trojan with you . . ."' (*Iliad* XXIV.148; Hammond, p. 392). He also notes the parallel with *Iliad* II: 'This conception of Māyā is somewhat akin to Homer's description of Iris and to the dream of Agamemnon in the second book of the *Iliad* in which deluding Vision [Dream] stands near the Greek king in the guise of Nestor.' (Hammond, pp. 19–20)

§126f

Gargi Datta (p. 126–7) raises the question: why is Lakshman instructed to perform a *pūjā* to Chanḍi? She writes: 'Rāmchandra was a devotee of Pārvati [Durgā]—the poet has shown this in various ways. That Rāmchandra should receive an assurance from Pārvati before a life-or-death battle is appropriate and natural. Pārvati and Chanḍi are basically the same goddess. Rām and Lakshman want to summon up the Chanḍi who once came down to slay the [buffalo-]demon. Maybe in recollection of the Mārkanḍeya Purāna, the poet made a *pūjā* to Chanḍi a factor in the coming battle.' She goes on to mention an episode in Krittibās's *Rāmāyaṇ* in which Rām decides to make an offering of 108 blue lotuses to Chanḍi in order to achieve the destruction of Rāvan. He chooses an inauspicious time, and when the goddess hides one of the lotuses from him he offers to pluck out one of his own blue-lotus-like eyes to make up the lack. This may be why Lakshman picks some blue lotus to offer to Chanḍi when he reaches her temple in V.313.

Gargi Datta (p. 127) also points out that Chanḍi is an important deity in Bengal's *maṅgal-kābya* literature, in which worship of her brings great riches to Kālketu while neglect of her brings perils to Dhanapati. Danapati's son Srimanta saves his father by performing a *pūjā* to Chanḍi. The lotus-seated (*kamale kāminī*) Chanḍi of the *Caṇḍimaṅgal* was the subject of a sonnet by M, in which he writes of seeing her in a dream, praises Kabikankan Mukundarām Chakrabarti (author of the most famous *Caṇḍimaṅgal*), and ends:

You suffered sorrow in your life, O Brahmin:
Immersed in your song, who now does not worship you,
  O Chanḍi
Seated on a lotus on the lake of Bengal's heart?
(*Kamale kāminī*; Sonnet No.4)

§203
This is the Siva alluded to by M in I.33, in which Rāvan's door-keeper was compared to 'trident-bearing Rudra at the gate of the Pānḍav camp'. In the sixth chapter of the *Sauptik* ['Night-attack'] *parva* of the *Mahābhārata*, Asvatthāman, Kripa and Kritavarman approach the Pānḍava camp at night, where

Here they saw a giant horripilatory creature,
Guarding the entrance.
A bloody tiger skin round his loins dripped blood,
A black deer skin draped his upper body,
A large snake was his sacred thread;
His long arms brandished various weapons,
His mouth blazed, yawning and dreadful,
His face has thousands of eyes . . . .

When Asvatthāman's weapons fail to work against this monster, he prays to Siva, who appears in person, smiling, and saying: 'Krishna worshipped me often with truth, purity, penance and devotion in thought, word, and deed. There is none dearer to me than Krishna. Till now I have protected the Panchalas in battle. Now Time afflicts them—their lives have run out.' He infuses his *rudra-tej* into Asvatthāman, who then enters the camp 'accompanied by rakshasas and many invisible helpers', and ferociously slays Draupadi's five sons. (Lal, pp. 274–6)

§230
The phantom lion here is very like the Leopard, Lion and She-wolf that block Dante the Pilgrim's way in Canto I of the *Inferno*:

> . . . the figure of a lion loomed up before me,
>
> and he was coming straight toward me. It seemed,
> with head raised high, and furious with hunger—
> the air around him seemed to fear his presence.
> (*Inferno* I.45–8; Musa, pp. 68–9)

But whereas Lakshman is able to fend off the lion, Dante is driven by the three beasts back to the dark wood where he meets his guide Virgil, who tells him that they will remain there until a 'greyhound' comes to drive them back to hell. Another route must be taken, which Virgil will lead him along.

In Tasso's *Jerusalem Delivered* Book XV the warriors Charles and Ubaldo have to overcome a number of illusory monsters in order to rescue their fellow-crusader Rinaldo from enchanted captivity by the sorceress Armida. This may also have been a source for M (Lakshman is on his own here, but the two warriors in Tasso's passage remind one of Lakshman and Vibhishan in Book VI of *MBK*):

A little higher on the way they met
    A lion fierce, that hugely roar'd and cry'd;
His crest he reared high, and open set
    Of his broad gaping jaws the furnace wide;
His stern his back oft smote his rage to whet:
    But when the sacred staff he once espy'd,
A trembling fear through his bold heart was spread,
His native wrath was gone, and swift he fled.
(Fairfax/ Weiss, p. 385)

§258f
This passage seems directly reminiscent of the 'naked wantons' that Charles and Urbaldo have to contend with in Tasso's *Jerusalem Delivered* XV.57–66 (see above, §230):

Thus past they forward where the stream did make
An ample pond, a large and spacious lake:

There on a table was all dainty food
    That sea, that earth, or liquid air could give;
And in the crystal of the laughing flood
    They saw two naked virgins bathe and dive,
That sometimes toying, sometimes wrestling stood,
    Sometimes for speed and skill in swimming strive;
Now underneath they div'd, now rose above,
And 'ticing baits laid forth of lust and love . . .
(Fairfax/ Weiss, p. 387)

For the image of scents being stolen from the flowers by the breeze, see above, II.1.

§313
For the blue lotus, see above, V.126.

§342

For the tiger simile, see above, IV.46.

The heavenly breeze and Sarasvati's message from the sky at the end of this paragraph are comparable to the lovely conclusion to Dante's *Purgatorio* Canto XXIV:

> Soft as the early morning breeze of May,
> which heralds dawn, rich with the grass and flowers,
> spreading in waves their breathing fragrances,
>
> I felt a breeze strike soft upon my brow:
> I felt a wing caress it, I am sure,
> I sensed the sweetness of ambrosia.
>
> I heard the words: 'Blessed are those in whom
> grace shines so copiously that love of food
> does not arouse excessive appetite,
>
> but lets them hunger after righteousness.'
> (*Purgatorio* XXIV.145–53; Musa, p. 261)

§369

The 'bower of bliss' where Meghnād and Pramilā have been sleeping is comparable to Adam and Eve's 'blissful bower', beautifully described in *Paradise Lost* Book IV.689–719. Moreover, Meghnād's dawn-song to Pramilā here as they awake is very reminiscent of the opening of Book V of *Paradise Lost* where Adam wakes and leans over the still sleeping Eve with similar rapture. M may have picked up his bee simile from there:

> Awake
> My fairest, my espoused, my latest found,
> Heav'n's last best gift, my ever new delight,

Awake, the morning shines, and the fresh field
Calls us; we lose the prime, to mark how spring
Our tended plants, how blows the citron grove,
What drops the myrrh, and what the balmy reed,
How Nature paints her colours, how the bee
Sits on the bloom extracting liquid sweet.
(*Paradise Lost* V.17–25)

There is also a similar irony, because Meghnād and Pramilā 'are woken by the birdsong that celebrates Māyādevi's fatal instructions to Lakshman, while Adam and Eve's joy is overshadowed by their imminent Fall.' (Radice 1995, p. 189)

For the link at the end of this paragraph between Pramilā and the *gopīs*, see above, I.623 and III.1. and below, VI.599.

§446f
The long section here describing anxious farewells to Meghnād first by his mother, Mandodari, then by his wife Pramilā, is comparable in its emotional effect to Andromache's anxiety about her husband Hektor in *Iliad* VI, or the pleas of his mother Hekabe in *Iliad* XXII. Pramilā was equally anxious when Meghnād left her in I.689.

§490
Gargi Datta (p. 130) emphasizes what a reversal of the *Rāmāyaṇa* it is that Queen Mandodari should describe Rām as having 'magic [*māyābī*] powers', whereas traditionally the Rākshasas are regarded as 'sorcerers'. See below, Book VI, p. 354, and Introduction, p. lxxxiv. However, in III.294 Rām speaking to Vibhishan reacted

to Nrimuṇḍamālini with the traditional conception: 'Lankā is full of sorcery—/ A mesh of illusions; your elder brother Rāvan can change his shape at will.'

§504
Cf. Hektor to Andromache: 'But I would feel terrible shame before the men of Troy and the women of Troy with their trailing dresses, if like a coward I skulk away from the fighting. Nor is that what my own heart urges, because I have learnt always to be brave and fight in the forefront of the Trojans, winning great glory for my father and for myself.' (*Iliad* VI; Hammond, p. 102; Dasgupta, p. 122)

§541f
The beautiful imagery with which Pramilā's weeping is described here has been traced to Kālidāsa by Bengali critics (Gargi Datta, p. 131; Sanyal, p. 347).

§557
Meghnād is more reassuring here than Hektor, who has a much stronger sense of his impending doom when he bids farewell to Andromache in *Iliad* VI.

§558
The creeper and tree simile was also used when Meghnād leaves Pramilā at the end of Book I, and may owe something to Tasso. See above, I.689. But it also has a well-established Indian lineage. It is used, for example, by Vālmiki when he describes Tārā's grief over the dead body of her husband Vāli:

> At that time, Tara gazing upon the countenance of her dead husband, was plunged into an ocean of grief and fell upon the ground by embracing her lord,

as a tender creeper for its support twines round a broken tree.

(*Kiṣkindhyākāṇḍa* XVII; Sen, p. 260)

§599

For a loving, pleading message to be carried through the sky like this is an idea familiar in Sanskrit tradition from Kālidāsa's celebrated poem, *Meghadūta* ('The Cloud-Messenger'). In making the breeze itself, rather than a cloud propelled by a breeze, the message-bearer, M gives an active role to Pavan that is comparable to that of Aeolus in Virgil's *Aeneid*. (Seely 2008, p. 116; Dasgupta, p. 119)

For the comparison between Pramilā and the *gopīs*, see above, I.623 and III.1 and V.369.

Book VI

Book VI is the heart of *MBK* because it contains the murderous killing of Rāvan's son Meghnād that is M's chief subject—the fulcrum round which his entire epic revolves. For its dramatic and allegorical implications, see Introduction, p. lxxxif. and Radice (1998). This and Book VII—which deals with the immediate aftermath of the killing—are, as Gargi Datta rightly says in her study of M's Indian sources, based on the *Rāmāyaṇa* but with a number of highly significant differences. In both Vālmiki's *Rāmāyaṇa* and the medieval Bengali *Rāmāyaṇ* of Krittibās, Indrajit (Meghnād) attempts to demoralise Rām by conjuring up an illusory Jānaki (Sitā), to display from his chariot as Hanumān and his army of Vānaras (monkeys) advance into battle:

> Before others, Hanuman advanced towards Indrajit by plucking a mountain peak. On advancing,

> Hanuman saw Janaki on Indrajit's chariot, wearing a single braid of hair. Her face was lean with fasting, and her mind afflicted with sorrow. She was clad with a piece of dirty linen and her body was stained with dust. Hanuman took her to be Janaki and was greatly mortified at seeing her woes. He tried to divine Indrajit's motive. Then with the other Vanaras, Hanuman rushed towards Indrajit.
>
> Indrajit was dragging Sita by her hair, and then drew out his sword in the presence of all.
>
> The exquisitely beautiful magic Sita cried out, 'Alack! Rama, ah, alack, Rama!'
>
> (*VR Yuddhakāṇḍa* LVIII; Sen, p. 504)

Hanumān is appalled. As he rushes to attack Indrajit, Indrajit cuts the illusory Sitā into two pieces. The Vānaras start to fall back at this dreadful sight, but Hanumān urges them on. The massive stone he hurls at Indrajit misses the chariot but crushes many Rākshasas. Indrajit retaliates by killing many Vānaras. Hanumān tells them there is no point in fighting any more as Sitā is dead. He returns to Rām with this devastating news, and Rām collapses in despair. Lakshman vows to be revenged on Indrajit, but Rām's confidence is only revived when Vibhishan assures him that 'what Hanuman has said seems to be absurd like drying up the sea. I am fully aware of the evil intentions which Ravan bears towards Sita, and for that [his lust for her, which she has steadfastly resisted] he will never put her to death.' (Sen, p. 507). He explains the boon that Brahmā gave Indrajit (see above, I.1): that if he can complete a *yajña* (sacrifice) to Agni before going into battle, he will be invincible. 'His intention is to prevent the Vanaras from interfering with that sacrifice; therefore he has bewildered the Vanaras by producing this illusion. Let us now proceed with the army to Nikumbhila before he finishes the sacrifice.' (Ibid.)

All this can be found in the medieval Bengali *Rāmāyaṇ* of Krittibās, with some additional colourful touches. Vibhishan suggests that Hanumān be sent to confirm that Sitā is in the Asoka forest, closely guarded but alive and well. With his power to fly through the air, Hanumān does this in a trice (*KR Laṅkākāṇḍa*, Mukhopadhyay, p. 340). Rām dispatches Vibhishan, Lakshman and Hanumān to interrupt Indrajit's sacrifice. They proceed to the Nikumbhilā grove, backed up by the army of *Kapis* (Vānaras), who easily defeat the Rākshasas who are guarding the gates of Lankā. When Hanumān sees Indrajit in the process of performing the sacrifice, he leaps on to the *yajñakuṇḍa* (sacrificial fire-pit), puts out the flames, and fills it with his own urine—just about the most desecrating and insulting thing he can do. (For further details, see Seely 2007, though his article is based on a different edition of *KR*.) As in *VR*, the battle that then ensues between Lakshman (advised and assisted by Vibhishan and Hanumān, and backed up by the Vānaras) and Indrajit (supported by an army of Rākshasas) is quite complicated. When the going gets tough for the Vānaras, Jāmbuvān's army of Bāllukas (bears) lends them support. At one point, the horses of Indrajit's chariot are slain, and he is reduced to fighting on foot. But using his magic powers of invisibility he disappears from the battlefield and comes back in another chariot. Eventually, Lakshman slays Indrajit by firing a special *Brahmāstra* weapon. Indrajit's head rolls on the ground in two pieces, and the Vānaras play football and hockey with them. There is huge jubilation—among the gods in heaven too—at Indrajit's death.

M's treatment is very different. The need to kill Meghnād before he completes the sacrifice to Agni is there, but there is no illusory Sitā, and Meghnād is not a 'sorcerer' (as in Vālmiki and Krittibās) but a Kshatriya hero who can only rely on his own strength and bravery. Magic powers, if they are present at all, are transferred to the assistance that Māyā-devi gives to Lakshman and Vibhishan, making them invisible so that they can evade the Rākshas guards. (See Gargi Datta, p. 73.) There are no supporting armies. To kill Meghnād when he is unarmed and alone—and even has to resort to hurling the *pūjā*-vessels at Lakshman in self-defence—is a *kauśal,* a 'trick' (see Notes, I.1 and V.29). The unfairness of it is comparable to Achilleus's brutal slaying of Hector in the *Iliad*, which does him no credit, as it is achieved through deception in battle by Pallas Athene, and is followed by the dragging of his corpse round the walls of Troy and the burning alive of twelve Trojan heroes on Hector's funeral pyre. (See Radice 2009, p. 235.)

Dasgupta (p. 124) suggests that 'Madhusūdan might have had in mind Shakespeare's Achilles, in *Troilus and Cressida*, striking the unarmed Hector':

Hector: Now is my day's work done; I'll take good breath:
Rest, sword; thou hast thy fill of blood and death.
Puts off his helmet and lays his sword aside.
Enter Achilles *and Myrmidons.*
Achilles: Look, Hector, how the sun begins to set;
How ugly night comes breathing at his heels:
Even with the vail and darking of the sun,
To close the day up, Hector's life is done.
Hector: I am unarm'd; forgo this vantage, Greek.

Achilles: Strike, fellows, strike! This is the man I seek.
Hector falls. (V.9.3–10)

Troilus and Cressida has never been a popular play, but it is possible that under Captain D. L Richardson's inspiring influence at Hindu College (see Introduction, p. xlvf.) M read it, and might have learnt from the way Shakespeare cuts the Greek and Trojan heroes down to size. But the cynicism of Shakespeare's treatment is absent from *MBK*.

§47
M wrote in a despairing letter to Ishwarchandra Vidayasagar, Versailles, 18 June 1864: 'I hope I shall not have to cry out with Ram in my poem of Meghnada, *brithā, he jaladhi, āmi bā̃dhinu tomāre!* ['Vainly, O ocean, did I bind you with stone!' Murshid 2004, p. 207]. See Introduction, p. liii. The lines are very reminiscent of Krittibās's *Rāmāyaṇ* (*Laṅkākāṇḍa*, Mukhopadhyay, p. 340): *yata pariśrama saba halo akāraṇe / brithā kena karilāma sāgar bandhane* ('All labour has been to no purpose. Why did I bind the sea in vain?').

M would have appreciated the references Dante makes in *The Divine Comedy* to his own exile from Florence. In *Paradiso* XVII, his great-grandfather Cacciaguida, who he first encounters in *Paradiso* XV as a star-like light falling from the right arm of the cross of Christ, prophesies:

> You shall be forced to leave behind those things
> you love most dearly, and this is the first
> arrow the bow of your exile will shoot.
> And you will know how salty is the taste
> of others' bread, how hard the road that takes
> you down and up the stairs of others' homes.

But what will weigh you down the most will be
the despicable, senseless company
whom you shall have to bear in that sad vale;

and all ungrateful, all completely mad
and vicious, they shall turn on you, but soon
their cheeks, not yours, will have to blush from shame.
(*Paradiso* XVII.55–66; Musa, p. 204. See Radice 2008, p. 00.)

See above, II.287, for M's famous simile of an exile hearing the music of his native land.

Rām's faint-heartedness is similar in tone to the fears that Dante expresses to Virgil in Canto II of the *Inferno*, especially given that later in *MBK* Rām will enter the underworld 'like another *Aeneas*' (see below, Book VIII):

'But why am I to go? Who allows me to?
I am not Aeneas, I am not Paul,
neither I nor any man would think me worthy;

and so, if I should undertake the journey,
I fear it might turn out an act of folly—
you are wise, you see more than my words express.'
(*Inferno* II.31–6; Musa, p. 80)

At the end of the paragraph, 'lured by false hope'—*bhuli āśār chalane*—strikes a strong echo with the first line of M's famous confessional poem *Ātma-bilāp*, which begins *āśār chalane bhuli*. The phrase was used by Ghulam Murshid for the title of his Bengali biography of M (1995, rev. 1997). See below, IX.377, Introduction, p. xxiv, and pp. cxv–cxvi for a complete translation of *Ātma-bilāp*.

§84
Sanyal (p. 362) compares Lakshmi's prophecy to the Witches 'All hail, Macbeth, that shalt be King hereafter!' in Shakespeare's *Macbeth* I.3.50.

§143
Dhumrāksha and Kesari are named as Vānara [monkey] generals in Krittibās's *Rāmāyaṇ*. (Sanyal, p. 366)

§158
The snake and the peacock fighting in the sky recall portents such as the two serpents who emerge from the sea in Book II of the *Aeneid* and terrifyingly seize and kill the two young sons of the priest Laocoon (West, p. 31). The Trojans think this is a punishment for his fears that the wooden horse made by the Greeks is a trick: they have been persuaded by the lying Greek Sinon that it is an offering to Minerva, though in fact Laocoon is right. M may also have been thinking of the simile in *Aeneid* XI of an eagle fighting a snake in the sky, used by Virgil to describe the fight between Venulus and the Etruscan Tarchon, in the war between the Latins and the Trojans (allied with the Etruscans): 'just as when a tawny eagle has seized a snake and flown up into the sky, winding its talons round it and digging in its claws; meanwhile the wounded serpent writhes in sinuous coils, its scales stiff and rough, and hisses as it reaches up with its head . . .' (West, p. 259)

Cf. also the portent that the Trojans see in *Iliad* XII.200–3, which Poulydamas interprets in very negative terms, much to Hektor's fury: 'A bird-omen had appeared to them as they stood eager to cross, a soaring eagle which skirted the front of the army from right to left, holding in its talons a monstrous blood-red snake, alive and still struggling . . . (Hammond, p. 193)

§216
Another example here of what Seely has described as the 'winds of change' running through *MBK*, whose primary source he finds in Virgil. 'They affect the outcome of the narrative. They, in fact, dictate the outcome of the narrative.' (Seely 2008, pp. 112–13)

§309
The snake metaphor here is surely reminiscent of Satan in *Paradise Lost*, who enters Eden in the guise of a serpent. The *kauśal* ('trick') by which they are entering Lankā so that Lakshman can kill Meghnād is comparable (though very different in character) to Satan's deception of Eve. There are further snake references in §429, 491 and 568, though in the last instance Meghnād is himself compared to 'a snake brought low by the power of a mighty *mantra*'. (Radice 1995, p. 181)

§316
The connection with Durgā herself here (*bhīmākṛti*) is also noted by Seely (1988, p. 50) as part of the link that M makes between the Rākshasas and the Saivite/Sākta tradition in Bengal. It is also appropriate because Rāvan in *MBK* is a staunch devotee of Siva.

§322f
For the description of Lankā here, see above, I.205.

M took Chikshur and the names of other Rākshasas mentioned in VII.158 not from Vālmiki or Krittibās but from the Mārkanḍeya Purāna. (Sanyal, p. 381, and see Notes to IV.113)

§413
Dasgupta (p. 122–3) writes: 'In the sixth canto, Lakṣhmaṇa

and Bibhīṣhaṇa enter the chamber of sacrifice where Indrajit is worshipping. They go unseen, guarded by Māyā. In the *Iliad*, Priam goes to the Greek camp attended by Hermes and unseen to other eyes (Bk. xiv, "Great Priam entered, unperceived by all") . . . . Bibhīṣhaṇa and Lakṣhmaṇa are hidden in a mist like Aeneas conveyed by Venus in a cloud to Carthage (Bk. I). In the *Odyssey*, Pallas Athene surrounds Odysseus with a mist to enable him to enter invisible the palace of King Alcinous (Bk. vii). Again, in the *Iliad*, Paris is "from the field conveyed wrapt in a misty cloud" (Bk. iii).'

§429
For the cobra simile, see above, §309.

§485
In making the death of his hero the product of a dastardly trick, M could not have been unaware of the way in which the Trojans are defeated by the Greeks by the trick of the Wooden Horse, as described by Aeneas in Book II of Virgil's *Aeneid*.

§491
To compare Meghnād—here and also in §592—with Arjun's son Abhimanyu in the *Mahābhārata* is another example of 'subversive similes' M uses to give the demonic Rākshasas heroic and tragic associations. See Seely (1988), p. 46.

Gargi Datta makes a similar point: 'In this description the poet's sympathy for Meghnād is expressed—in comparisons with Mirhir [Earth] . . ., Garuḍa . . ., or Mahadeva [Siva] his greatness is firmly established. On the other hand the poet repeatedly compares Lakshman to Kali, Rāhu, a snake, a tiger, a lion, etc.' (p. 68)

For the snake metaphor, see above, §309.

§520f
The verbal confrontation here between Meghnād and Vibhishan here is similar in tone—and also in some of its words and phrases—to Indrajit's scandalized berating of his uncle Vibhishan in Krittibās's *Rāmāyaṇ* (*Laṅkākāṇḍa*, Mukhopadhyay, p. 342). Similar sentiments can be found in Vālmiki's *Rāmāyaṇa*. Compare Meghnād's appeal to the Sāstras in §579 with *VR Yuddhakāṇḍa* LXI (Sen, p. 511): 'If a stranger be accomplished, and one's own people be without any accomplishments whatsoever, still a stranger is always a stranger and one's own people always continue to be one's own.' Gargi Datta lists a number of lines where M's 'almost literal following of Kaviguru Vālmiki can be seen'. (p. 69)

§568
For the snake simile, see above, §309. Snakes of course can be glorious in Hindu tradition (see above, III.248), though Milton's 'serpent subtlest beast of all the field' (*Paradise Lost* IX.86) has his lofty grandeur too until God curses him after the Fall so that 'Upon thy belly grovelling thou shalt go,/ And dust shalt eat all the days of thy life.' (*Paradise Lost* X.177–8) And contrary to the usual Christian tradition, Tasso has a noble image of a snake in *Jerusalem Delivered* VII.71 that M would have appreciated. Raymond, Earl of Toulouse, is getting on in years, but when flushed with heroic enthusiasm

> New vigour blushed through those looks of his,
>   It seem'd he now resum'd his youthful days:
> Like to a snake whose slough new changed is
>   That shines like gold against the sunny rays . . .
> (Fairfax/ Weiss, p. 182)

§579
Meghnād's famous words to his uncle here were used as an epigraph in Chapter VII of Romesh Chunder Dutt's historical novel, *Mahārāṣṭra jīban prabhāt* (1878), which glorifies the rise of Maratha power. An analogy is implied between Vibhishan's treachery and Raja Yasvant Singh, the Rajput traitor who served the interests of the Emperor Aurangzeb by fighting against the Marathas. See Indira Chowdhury, *The Frail Hero and Virile History: Gender and the Politics of Culture in Colonial Bengal* (Oxford University Press, Delhi, 1998), pp. 56–7.

§592
The simile of the mother driving away mosquitoes from her sleeping son seems to have been taken directly from *Iliad* 4.130–133, where Athene protects Menelaos from an arrow: 'She brushed it just a little from the flesh it sought—like when a mother brushes a fly from her child, as he lies sweetly sleeping . . .' (Hammond, p. 56). See Sanyal, p. 405, Dasgupta, p. 124, Gargi Datta, p. 70 and Riddiford, p. 342.

§621
The catastrophic, cosmic effects of Meghnād's death here are comparable to Eve's plucking and eating of the apple in *Paradise Lost*, though Milton, to express the power and horror of her Fall, uses dramatic brevity both here and when Adam follows suit:

> Earth felt the wound, and Nature from her seat
> Sighing through all her works gave signs of woe,
> That all was lost . . . .
> (*Paradise Lost* IX.782–4)

Earth trembled from her entrails, as again
In pangs, and Nature gave a second groan;
Sky loured, and muttering thunder, some sad drops
Wept at completing of the mortal sin
Original . . .
(Ibid., IX.1000–4)

For the comparison with Krishna and the effect of his departure on 'the children of Vraj', see above, I.623, III.1 and V.369.

§642

In comparing Meghnād's death to the setting of the 'lotus-sun' (prefigured in II.491), M may have recalled Satan's sun-like glory before he fell from heaven. See above, I.763.

A more direct source would have been Vālmiki: 'As the rays of the sun vanish, when the sun is set, so all the Rakshasas made themselves scarce after the fall of Indrajit. Indrajit was lying on the battlefield like the sun deprived of its light or like an extinguished flame.' (*VR Yuddhakāṇḍa* LXII; Sen, p. 516) Gargi Datta (p. 71) notes this connection, but also points out that in the *Rāmāyaṇa* Indrajit dies in the evening, whereas in *MBK* he dies at dawn.

In the *Rāmāyaṇa*, fallen sun-imagery is also used when Rāvan himself is killed. Vibhishan grieves over the body of his brother with the words: 'Alas! (By your fall) it seems the sun has fallen on the ground; the moon is sunk in darkness; the fire is extinct; and the cause of popular religion is gone for ever.' (Ibid., LXXIII; Sen, p. 539)

Gargi Datta says about M's treatment of Meghnād's death: 'In his analysis of the mind of the helpless, weaponless, proud hero the modern poet [M] shows an amazing power in which his modern way of imagining is revealed. This quality is not present in Vālmiki or Krittibās.' (p. 70)

Riddiford (p. 346) compares Meghnād's prophecy that his death will be avenged by his father, Rāvan to the prophecy of the dying Patroklos at the end of *Iliad* XVI that 'already now death and strong fate are standing close beside you, to bring you down at the hands of Achilleus' (Hammond, p. 274). He also compares this to Matthew Arnold's *Sohrab and Rustum*, in which 'the transformation of the relationship between comrades to one between father and son is very distinctive'. He makes this point as part of a general argument that M must have read Arnold's poem of 1853 when he was in Madras, and could have been influenced by Arnold's attempt to 'miniaturise and "orientalise" the *Iliad*' (p. 351).

§671f

Vibhishan's grief-stricken reaction to his nephew's death—even though he has played a part in it—is a huge addition of depth and psychological realism by M to the death of Indrajit in the *Rāmāyaṇa*. In both Vālmiki and Krittibās there is general *ānanda* ('joy') in which Vibhishan himself joins in: 'Then Vibhishana, Hanuman and Jambuvan began to praise Lakshmana for the death of Indrajit and greeted him repeatedly in joy. The Vanaras began to roar in delight and began to brandish their tails. Every one was speaking of Lakshmana's victory, and many of them embraced one another in joy and began to talk of Lakshmana's victory, and about Lakshmana's valour. The gods too were immensely delighted at that heroic feat of Lakshmana, a dear friend of theirs.' (*VR Yuddhakāṇḍa* LXIII; Sen, p. 517)

§694
To associate Lakshman and Vibhishan with Asvatthāman is particularly 'subversive', as his murder of Draupadi's five sons was cruel and dastardly. In fact he thinks he has slain the five Pāṇḍavas themselves, and runs to boast to his dying uncle Duryodhan about it.

Seely (1988, p. 47; 1991, p. 146), cites M's use of the *Mahābhārata* here as one of the three 'substrata stories' (the others being of Krishna and Durgā) that subvert the reader's response to the triumph of Lakshman and Rām.

Book VII

Although in his treatment of the aftermath of Meghnād's death, M does not depart so radically from the *Rāmāyaṇa* as he does in Book VI, there are some significant differences. In *MBK*, the news of Meghnād's death is communicated to Rāvan by Siva's envoy Virbhadra 'disguised as a Raksha messenger' (§118). In *VR*, it is his ministers who tell him (Sen, p. 518), and in *KR* the ministers nervously decide to send a *bhagnadūt*, a 'messenger of bad news'. In all three versions, Rāvan is at first struck dumb with grief (see below, IX.377) then roused to fury and revenge: M makes this a direct infusion of *rudra-tej* (Siva's anger) through the agency of Virbhadra, who is then replaced by a vision of Siva himself. But M does not show Rāvan roused to the murder of Sitā herself. In *VR*, he is dissuaded from doing so by his counsellor Suparsva; in *KR* it is Queen Mandodari (Meghnād's mother), who stops him, asking him how he can dare to add to his sins by killing a woman. Mandodari is grief-stricken in all three texts, but in *MBK* she appears only briefly (§329) after Rāvan has called up his armies, whereas in *KR* she has a passage of *bilāp* (lament) straight after Rāvan himself receives the news, and in *KR* she has a much longer lamentation after Rāvan himself has been slain by Rām (*Yuddhakāṇḍa* LXXIV; Sen, pp. 541–4). In both these passages of lament, she blames her husband for bringing destruction on himself by abducting Sitā in the first place. Once the battle starts—the only battle in *MBK*—the main difference between M and his Indian precursors is that the gods are much more actively involved. Alerted by Kamalā, who fears for Lakshman's safety, Indra joins in with his armies on the side of Rām ('I do not fear Rāvan,/ Now that his son . . . is no more!' §294). Earth (Mahi/ Vasudhā), fearing Siva's destructive powers, appeals to Vishnu, who agrees to save the universe 'by restraining the power of the gods; but Indra will not be able to save Lakshman; Siva is mightily pained by the grief of the Rākshasas.' (§472). In the battle, Rāvan fights with Indra himself (§616f). He is unable, however, to save Lakshman (§736). Durgā then appeals to Siva 'to save Lakshman's corpse' (§744), which will permit the eventual revival of Lakshman between Books VIII and IX. In depicting the active engagement of the gods in this way, M follows the Homeric model (though with some moral differences—see Introduction, p. lii).

Gargi Datta points out (p. 82) that whereas Lakshman's behaviour in Book VI can be described as cowardly, in Book VII he fights against Rāvan bravely, and in this respect M follows the *Rāmāyaṇa*, where Lakshman is 'a great hero'.

§121f

In his powerful projections of Rāvan's grief and fury at the death of his son Meghnād—here and in Book IX (see below,

IX.377)—and his earlier grief at Virbāhu's death (I.62f), M must certainly have learnt from passages in the *Aeneid* such as Priam's grief and rage at the killing of his son Polites by Pyrrus in Book II (West, p. 40), or Mezentius's grief when Aeneas kills his son Lausus in Book X (West, pp. 234–5).

§158
For the emerging Rākshas armies, see above, I.447, and for the Rākshas generals mentioned, see VI.322.

§178
Seely (1988, p. 50) notes this passage as an example of the Saivite/ Sākta associations that M gives the Rākshasas. See above, III.523 and VI.316.

Gargi Datta (pp. 78–9) sees here the direct influence of the description of Chanḍi and her armies in the Mārkanḍeya Purāna (see Notes, IV.113), with the names too of the Rākshasas in the previous paragraph (§158) found there but not in the *Rāmāyaṇa*. The link shows M's wish to glorify the Rākshasas.

§300f
The involvement of Indra's entire divine army in the ensuing battle is comparable to the involvement of the Olympian gods in the battle between the Trojans and Achaians in Books XX-XXI of the *Iliad*. The difference is that Zeus asks the gods to take sides, and they fight against each other as well as in support of their chosen side. In *MBK* the gods are stacked up on Rām's side against the Rākshasas. However, because of the dastardly killing of Meghnād in Book VI, Siva's basic sympathy for his loyal devotee Rāvan revives to the extent of supplying him with the *rudra-tej* he needs to slay Lakshman in revenge for Meghnād's death.

§440
For the Virgilian dust-clouds here and in §526, see above, I.156. For the simile of an army advancing like waves on a beach, cf. *Iliad* IV.422–8: 'As when the sea's swell hurls on a booming shore, wave after wave at the west wind's stirring: first it rears in the open water, then breaks in loud roaring on the land's edge, and round the head-rocks it rises arching into crests, and flings spits of salt foam. So then, rank after rank, the Danaan battalions moved in ceaseless advance to war.' (Hammond, p. 63) But notice how, as nearly always in his similes, M is much more concise than Homer.

Indian sources can also be found for this description. Sanyal (pp. 455–6) and Gargi Datta (p. 75) compare it to the armies of Rām's ancestor Raghu mustering in Kālidāsa's *Raghuvaṃśa*, Canto IV, and in the battle scenes in the *Rāmāyaṇa* the sky is often covered by clouds of dust. In the fight between Rām and his forces and the Rākshasas led by Akampan, 'Dust raised by the trampling of the warriors covered the sky. Nobody could discern his friend or foe.' (*Yuddhakāṇḍa* XXXVI; Sen, p. 454)

§472
Vishnu's admission of his limitation here in response to Earth's appeal shows that Siva in *MBK* is definitely 'Mahādeva'—the greatest of all the gods, with a final say in the affairs of gods, men and demons comparable to Zeus's supremacy in the *Iliad*.

§506
In the *Rāmāyaṇa* Indra loans his chariot to Rām, but that happens at the beginning of Rām's final battle with Rāvan, after (not before) Lakshman has been felled and revived:

> At that time, the denizens of heaven seeing Rama standing on the ground and Ravana seated on a chariot talked among themselves saying such a contest was unequal since one was on the ground and the other was on the car. At these words Indra, king of the gods, said to Matali, 'Take this chariot soon to Rama and tell him that the king of the gods has sent down this chariot for you. O charioteer! go down on the earth and accomplish this noble deed.'
> (*VR Yuddhakāṇḍa* LXIX; Sen, p. 530)

§554
See above, IV.165.

§587
Siva's *mahārudra-tej* here can be compared with fire instilled into Diomedes by Athene, goddess of war, in *Iliad* V.4–8: 'She set untiring fire blazing from his helmet and shield . . . . Such was the fire she made burn from his head and shoulders, and she spurred him into the eye of the battle, where the fighters swarmed the thickest.' (Hammond, p. 67) The way Durgā intervenes here to protect Skanda, is of course very like the way the Homeric gods intervene to protect or weaken the heroes they favour or despise.

§676
The pun on Tārā's name can also be found in the *Rāmāyaṇa*: 'Then Hanuman, the chief of the Vanara hosts, seeing Tara, like a star fallen on the ground from the sky, gently said . . .' (*Kiṣkindhyākāṇḍa* XVI; Sen, p. 258)

§691
See above, IV.165.

§762
For the Rākshas-Durgā link, see above III.523, VI.316 and VII.178.

Book VIII

Rām's descent, guided by Māyā, to *pret-deś* ('the land of ghosts') to meet his father Dasarath is the section of *MBK* that has been most intensively studied for sources and influences, notably by Clark (1967) and Seely (1982). Since no such journey is found in the *Rāmāyaṇas* of either Vālmiki or Krittibās (though there is some Indian precedent for it in the *Gautamī-māhātma* of the Brahma Purāna—see Seely, 1982, p. 470), M was clearly heavily indebted to Virgil (who may himself have been influenced by Odysseus's descent to Hades in *Odyssey* XI), Dante and Milton and the English Bible, and explicitly stated as much in a letter to Rajnarayan Basu: 'Mr Ram is to be conducted through Hell to his father, Dasaratha, like another *Aeneas*.' (Murshid 2004, p. 160) But despite this Western influence, M's vision of the underworld (a conflation of Naraka, Pātāla and Pitri-loka in Hindu cosmology, according to Clark) is also derived, Seely argues, from the medieval Bengali *Mahābhārat* of Kāsirām Dās.

The reason for Rām's journey is stated in §100, and is a complete departure from the traditional *Rāmāyaṇa* story. In both Vālmiki and Krittibās, Rām consults his physician Sushena after Lakshman's apparent death at the hands of Rāvan. Earlier (*VR Yuddhakāṇḍa* LXIII; Sen, p.

517), Sushena has cured Lakshman of severe wounds acquired in his fight with Indrajit by hiving him a medicine to smell. This time, Sushena sends Hanumān to the Himalayas to bring back four special herbs from the Gandhamādan mountain (the name means 'intoxicating with fragrance'). Unable to find the specific herbs there, Hanumān carries the whole mountain back to Sushena, who finds the herbs, crushes them, and gives them to Lakshman to inhale. Lakshman is instantly cured completely (*VR Yuddhakāṇḍa* LXVIII; Sen, p. 529). In M's version, Durgā, alarmed at Rām's grief, appeals to her husband Siva, who tells her to send Māyā to guide Rām down into 'Kritānta [Yama]'s city', where 'His father,/ King Dasarath, will tell him how his brother will come back to life again.' This Dasarath duly does at the end of Book VIII (§759). Hanumān's role in fetching the herbs is not described, and Rāvan's minister Sāran seems to think that Mount Gandhamādan came by itself. See Notes to IX.18.

§1–7

The beautiful linkage here between night, stars and fires on the battlefield is like the end of *Iliad* VIII: 'So all night long they sat on the avenues of battle, with high thoughts on their minds: and their fires burned in their numbers. As when stars show brilliant in the sky round the shining moon . . . . So many were the Trojans' fires . . .' (Hammond, pp. 131–2). The Trojan fires are lit at Hektor's command so that supper can be cooked, and they are kept alight as watch-fires to prevent the Achaians fleeing in their ships under cover of night. It is not so clear here what the fires are for, so M has probably brought them in for poetic effect.

§18f
Rām's grief over the body of his brother can certainly be compared with the treatment of the same scene by Vālmiki and Krittibās, but the differences are greater than the similarities. M may have some words and phrases from his sources in mind—cf. 'Rise up, I say..' echoing Krittibās's *uṭha re lakṣmaṇa bhāi* ('Rise, O brother Lakshman . . .'), or 'What shall I say, when your mother asks . . .' being similar to 'What shall I say to mother Sumitrā . . .' in Vālmiki—but he has clearly internalized, imagined and re-expressed the scene in his own unique manner. See *KR Laṅkākāṇḍa* (Mukhopadyay, pp. 351–2) and *VR Yuddhakāṇḍa* LXVIII (Sen, pp. 528–9).

§49
Cf. Rām's faint-heartedness here with Agamemnon's despair at the beginning of *Iliad* IX, which follows Hektor's Zeus-supported triumph in battle and the lyrical end to Book VIII mentioned above: 'Come then, let us all do as I say—let us away with our ships to our dear native land. We shall never now take the broad streets of Troy.' (Hammond, p. 133)

However, as Seely (1982, p. 469) rightly says, Rām's grief and despair over the body of Lakshman 'is nothing new', for it can also be found in both Vālmiki and Krittibās.

§100
In *Aeneid* VI, Aeneas is guided down to the underworld by the Sybil of Cumae, and to authorize his passage is told by her to pluck a branch from a golden tree and carry it as a gift to Pluto's wife Proserpina (West, p. 119). Siva's *triśūl* here is equivalent to Aeneas's Golden Bough, and 'like a pillar of flame' (*agni-stambha-sama*) has echoes of the

nineteenth century Bengali translation of the Bible, where the phrase occurs twice, in Exodus xiii, verses 21 and 22. (Clark, p. 340)

At the beginning of Dante's *Purgatorio*, Cato of Utica permits Dante and Virgil to start the ascent of Mount Purgatory when it has been explained to him that Dante is not a fugitive from Hell, but a living man. As a symbol of the removal of all stains from Hell, Cato tells Virgil to tie a reed round Dante's waist. This can be compared with the Golden Bough not only as a kind of passport, but because when Virgil pulls the reed from the ground a second plant immediately springs up to replace it—in the same way that when the Golden Bough is plucked 'another comes to take its place' (West, p. 119). See Musa, pp. 2–5 and his Notes on p. 15. The *triśūl* that Māyā carries for Rām has a similar kind of miraculous aura and power.

§134

Seely (1982, p. 471) sources the tunnel that Māyā makes to the *Kiṣkindhyākāṇḍa* of Krittibās's *Rāmāyaṇ*, where 'Hanumān and his fellow monkeys, while searching the south of India for Sītā, happen upon a tunnel already in existence'; and also the *Laṅkākāṇḍa* of the same work, where 'a second descent to *pātāla* is made by Hanumān . . . to search out and rescue both Rāma and Lakṣmaṇa, who had been spirited away by Mahīrāvaṇ, Rāvaṇa's son'. However, Seely stresses (ibid.) that in *MBK* it is not actually to Pātāla (one of the three worlds that make up the universe, the others being earth and heaven) that Rām and Māyā descend, but to 'the land of ghosts' (*pret-deś*, *pret-purī*).

Māyā's instructions to Rām can be compared to Circe's instructions to Odysseus in Homer's *Odyssey*. Succumbing to his persuasions that she should let him and his companions go, she also keeps her promise that she would advise him how to get back home to Ithaca: 'Son of Laertes, subtle Odysseus, if it is in spite of yourselves that you all stay in my palace still, then you must stay here no longer. But another path must be travelled first; you must visit the house of dread Persephone and of Hades, and there take counsel from the spirit of Theban Teiresias. The blind seer's thought is wakeful still, for to him alone, even after death, Persephone has accorded wisdom; the other dead are but flitting shadows.' (*Odyssey* X.488–95; Shewring, p. 125)

§158

Cf. 'They walked in the darkness of that lonely night with shadows all about them, through the empty halls of Dis and his desolate kingdom, as men walk in a wood by the sinister light of a fitful moon when Jupiter has buried the sky in shade and black night has robbed all things of their colour.' (*Aeneid* VI.268–72; West, p. 122) However, if one reads on one agrees with Clark: 'The general impression remains that there is more light and colour in Rāma's underworld than in that of Aeneas, which by contrast is grey and misty.' (Clark, p. 341)

§162

The Vaitarani river here matches the river Acheron that circles hell in Dante's *Inferno*. Equally, it is 'Acheron, the river of Tartarus' in Virgil's underworld: 'a vast quagmire of boiling whirlpools which belches sand and slime into Cocytus, and these are the rivers and waters guarded by the terrible Charon in his filthy rags.' (West, p. 123) The milk-pan simile is, in Clark's words, 'a homely, original addition' (Clark, p. 341). Virgil seems to conflate Acheron and the Styx, whereas in Dante's geography of the underworld, the Styx is a separate river, second of the nine rivers of hell, and has a separate boatman, Phlegyas (see *Inferno* VIII.13–30; Musa, p. 139). But all the rivers are connected. *Inferno* XIV.94–119 describes how the Acheron, the Styx and the Phlegethon have their source in Crete, and all end up in Cocytus, the pool at the bottom of hell. (Musa, pp. 199–100, 202)

§175f
The 'bridge of desires' (*kāmarūpī setu*) by which the virtuous spirits cross the Vaitarani, with the sinners forced by 'Death's henchmen' (*Yamadūt*) to swim across, is M's innovation. In Virgil's account, Charon takes some across in his boat, while 'others he pushes away far back from the sandy shore.' (West, p. 123) He also agrees to take Aeneas and the Sybil across, after the Sybil has shown him the Golden Bough (West, p. 126). In Dante's *Inferno,* Charon refuses Dante and Virgil passage, as he recognizes Dante as a living man and not a damned soul (*Inferno* III.70–99; Musa pp. 91–2).

The gold of the bridge and its disappearing nature can be compared to the golden bridge that Rinaldo encounters in the enchanted wood in Book XVIII of Tasso's *Jerusalem Delivered*:

> The knight some way sought out the flood to pass,
>   And, as he sought, a wond'rous bridge appear'd,
> A bridge of gold, a huge and weighty mass,
>   Of arches great of that rich metal rear'd:
> When through that golden way he enter'd was,
>   Down fell the bridge, swelled the stream, and wear'd

The work away, nor sign left where it stood,
And of a river calm became a flood.

He turn'd, amaz'd to see it troubled so,
    Like sudden brooks increas'd with molten snow;
The billows fierce that tossed to and fro,
    The whirlpools suck'd down to their bosoms low . . .
(Fairfax/ Weiss, p. 448)

§185

M's division of the spirits into good and bad follows Christian tradition (blended with the Hindu conception of *dharma*: see Introduction, pp. liv–lv). In *Aeneid* VI, Charon discriminates between those who have been buried and the unburied who 'wander for a hundred years, fluttering round those shores until they are at last allowed to return to the pools they have so longed for.' (West, p. 124)

In mentioning the north, west and east gates here, and later in §262 the south gate that leads to eighty-four *kuṇḍa* (lakes or circles of hell), M followed the *Śānti parba* of Kāsirām Dās's *Mahābhārat*, where Yama's city is described. This is when Yudhishṭhira, on advice from Vyāsa himself, seeks counsel after the carnage of the battle of Kurukshetra from Bhishma, who fought on the Kaurava side and now lies dying on the battlefield. *Yamapurī* (Yama's city) is included in Bhishma's reflections on life and death. This connection with Kāsirām Dās was first noted by Clark, but is analysed in much more detail by Seely (1982, pp. 471–476). M's description is more elaborate than in Kāsirām Dās's epic, but some details are taken directly from it, for example the brutal role here of 'Death's henchman [or henchmen]' (*Yamadūt*):

Before the southern gate flows the Vaitarani Rover
Which scalds a sinner's body by its very touch.
With blows from clubs, Yama's henchmen bash in heads
Of all those sinners as they swim across it.
(Seely's translation, 1982, p. 473)

§213

Here M borrows directly from the famous lines that begin Book III of Dante's *Inferno*—the inscription above the gate of hell:

I AM THE WAY INTO THE DOLEFUL CITY,
I AM THE WAY INTO ETERNAL GRIEF,
I AM THE WAY TO A FORSAKEN RACE.

JUSTICE IT WAS THAT MOVED MY GREAT CREATOR;
DIVINE OMNIPOTENCE CREATED ME,
AND HIGHEST WISDOM JOINED WITH PRIMAL LOVE.

BEFORE ME NOTHING BUT ETERNAL THINGS
WERE MADE, AND I SHALL LAST ETERNALLY.
ABANDON EVERY HOPE, ALL YOU WHO ENTER.
(*Inferno* III.1–9; Musa, p. 89)

§221f

M clearly revels in his description of all these personified horrors at the gate of Hell, whereas Virgil gives a briefer list, and places them earlier on in the journey, at the beginning of the road that leads to Acheron: 'before the entrance hall of Orcus, in the very throat of hell, Grief and Revenge have made their beds and Old Age lives there in despair, with white-faced Diseases and Fear and Hunger, corrupter of men, and squalid Poverty, things dreadful to look upon, and Death and Drudgery besides . . .' (West, pp. 122–3)

As well as Virgil, Dante and Milton, M's western sources for his vision of the underworld may also include Book IV of Tasso's *Jerusalem Delivered*, which tells of how

> Satan his fiends and sprites assembleth all
>   And sends them forth to work the Christians' woe . . .
> (Fairfax/ Weiss, argument to Book IV, p. 78)

M's raving Drunkenness (*pramattatva*) or howling *Insanity* (*unmattatā*) has a touch of the monsters described by Tasso:

> There were Sileno's foul and loathsome rout,
>   There Sphinxes, Centaurs, there were Gorgons fell,
> There howling Scyllas yawling round about,
>   There serpents hiss, there seven-mouthed Hydras yell . . .
> (Fairfax/ Weiss, p. 80)

This section of Tasso's epic was itself a source for Milton, though not a major one. See Nash, Introduction, pp. xxi-xxii.

§262
The eighty-four lakes are found in Kāsirām Dās. See above, §185.

§308
Clark finds echoes in the imagery here of Dante and Virgil, but Seely (1982, p. 474) writes: 'However, no reaching to

European sources is necessary, for the echoes here are of Kāśirāmadāsa. The Bengali *Mahābhārata*'s nether world, across the Vaitaraṇī, reveals a comparable scene.' He goes on to find precise verbal echoes, noting that 'Dutt has transferred the "diamond" hardness (*vajra*) of the insects (*kiṭa* and *pokā*) onto the talons (*vajra*[diamond]-*nakhā* [taloned]) of flesh-eating birds.'

§313

In 'righteousness shields them with impenetrable armour' (*abhedya kabace dharma ābaren tāre*) Clark finds an echo of 'the metaphors of the armour of God used by St Paul in Ephesians vi' (Clark, p. 345).

§352

Virgil was fond of bees, wrote about them in his fourth *Georgic*, and has several bee-similes in the *Aeneid*. M here may have picked up the simile in *Aeneid* VI, ll.705–6, describing souls round the river Lethe whose waters they must drink before being born again in new bodies: 'Around it fluttered numberless races and tribes of men, like bees in a meadow on a clear summer day, settling on all the many-coloured flowers and crowding round the gleaming white lilies while the whole plain is loud with their buzzing.' (West, p. 134)

There are also bee similes in Homer, e.g. *Iliad* II.67–90 (Hammond, p. 21), and Milton followed his great predecessors with his simile of the fallen angels swarming round Satan's new palace of Pandemonium like 'bees in springtime' clustering round a hive (*Paradise Lost*, I. 767–775).

The surprise of the ghosts here on seeing a living man has parallels in Dante, e.g. when the shades on Mount

Purgatory observe with astonishment Dante's conversation with his old friend Forese Donati:

> Talking did not slow down our walk, nor did
> walking our talk: conversing, on we sped
> like ships enjoying favourable winds.
>
> And all those shade, looking like things twice dead,
> absorbed the miracle through caved-in eyes:
> this was a living man which they beheld!
> (*Purgatorio* XXIV.1–6; Musa, p. 257)

§375

To compare ghosts with dry autumn leaves is a common trope in the Western epic tradition. Clark compares the image to the leaves being driven away 'like ghosts' in Shelley's 'Ode to the West Wind' (Clark, p. 122), but since M clearly wrote Book VIII of *MBK* with *Aeneid* VI closely to hand, he may also have picked up Virgil's description of the ghosts crowding round Charon's boat, 'as many as are the leaves that fall in the forest at the first chill of autumn' (*Aeneid* VI.309–10; West, p. 123).

The image can also be found in Dante, derived no doubt from Virgil:

> As in autumn when the leaves begin to fall,
> One after the other (until the branch
> Is witness to the spoils spread on the ground),
>
> So did the evil seed of Adam's Fall
> Drop from that shore to the boat . . .
> (*Inferno* III.112–6; Musa, p. 93)

Milton, however, uses it for the fallen angels rather than the ghosts of the departed:

. . . he [Satan] stood and called
His legions, angel forms, who lay entranced
Thick as autumnal leaves that strow the brooks
In Vallambrosa, where th'Etrurian shades
High overarched embow'r . . .
(*Paradise Lost* I.300–4)

§414

The hissing snakes hanging down the back of the 'female envoy of Death' (*Kṛtānta-dūtī*) recall Virgil's 'raving Discord with blood-soaked ribbons binding her viperous hair' (*Aeneid* VI.280–1; Clark, p. 347).

§431f

The emphasis on lust here shows how deeply M had absorbed the effects of the Fall in Christian tradition. See Introduction, pp. lviii–lix. In *Paradise Lost*, lust is the first thing that Adam and Eve feel after they have both eaten the apple. Instead of the 'Divinity within them breeding wings' that they expect,

. . . that false fruit
Far other operation first displayed,
Carnal desire inflaming; he on Eve
Began to cast lascivious eyes, she him
As wantonly repaid; in lust they burn:
Till Adam thus gan Eve to dalliance move.
(*Paradise Lost* IX.1011–5)

Cf. also the 'bevy of fair women' in the Tents of Wickedness that the archangel Michael later shows to Adam:

. . . richly gay
In gems and wanton dress; to the harp they sung
Soft amorous ditties, and in dance came on:

The men though grave, eyed them, and let their eyes
Rove without rein, till in the amorous net
Fast caught, they liked, and each his liking chose . . .
(*Paradise Lost* XI.582–7)

§465
The violence of the imagery here has parallels in Dante's *Inferno*: e.g. the dogs who rip apart the profligates Lano of Siena and Giacomo da Sant' Andrea:

Behind these two the wood was overrun
by packs of black bitches ravenous and ready,
like hunting dogs just broken from their chains;

they sank their fangs in that poor wretch who hid,
they ripped him open piece by piece, and then
ran off with mouthfuls of his wretched limbs.
(*Inferno* XIII.124–9; Musa, p. 190)

§477
M's lurid vision of 'the reward of these sinners in hell' is certainly very Christian, in the tradition of Dante's *Inferno* and Milton's *Paradise Lost*. In one of his sonnets written during his sojourn in Europe, *Paralok* ('Afterlife') he came out with similarly uncompromising sentiments. See Radice 1995, pp. 183–4, and Introduction, p. li for a translation of this sonnet.

§500
Seely (1982, p. 475) notes that this description is an expansion of four lines in Kāsirām Dās's *Mahābhārat*:

The eastern gate presents a feast for the eyes,
Yogurt, milk, and morsels, and a pleasant lake.
All womenfolk who perish with their spouses

Go with their husbands through the eastern gate.
(Seely's translation, 1982, p. 475)

§522

The presence of ice and snow here as well as fire is reminiscent of Dante's *Inferno*. Compare the description of the frozen lake Cocytus in the deepest pit of hell, in whose ice the shades of Traitors are immobilized like frogs—an image that M may have picked up with his own 'immense lake' and 'gigantic frogs':

At that I turned around and saw before me
a lake of ice stretching beneath my feet,
more like a sheet of glass than frozen water.

In the depths of Austria's wintertime, the Danube
never in all its course showed ice so thick,
nor did the Don beneath its frigid sky,

as this crust here; for if Mount Tambernic
or Pietrapana would crash down upon it,
not even at its edges would a crack creak.

The way the frogs (in the season when the harvest
will often haunt the dreams of the peasant girl)
sit croaking with their muzzles out of water,

so these frigid, livid shades were stuck in ice
up to where a person's shame appears;
their teeth clicked notes like storks' beaks snapping shut.

And each one kept his face bowed towards the ice:
the mouth bore testimony to the cold,
the eyes, to sadness welling in the heart.
(*Inferno* XXXII.22–39; Musa, p. 363)

§546

The 'field' (*kṣetra*) that Rām sees in front of him owes a lot in tone and imagery to Virgil's beautiful description of the Elysian fields: 'Here a broader sky clothes the plains in glowing light, and the spirits have their own sun and their own stars. Some take exercise on grassy wrestling grounds and hold athletic contests and wrestling bouts on the golden sand . . .' (West, p. 133)

Seely (1982, p. 475) notes that Māyā's words here can be sourced to Kāsirām Dās's lines: 'Those warriors who fell in face to face warfare/ Enter by the western gate the home of Yama' and 'And those who fell in face to face combat/ . . . They all travel through this northern gate'. [Seely's translation] He further notes that 'in face to face [open] combat' (*sammukh-saṃgrame*) is picked up by M not only again at the beginning of the next paragraph, §582 (*sammukh-samare*) but also in the celebrated opening of his epic: *sammukh-samare paṛi, bīr-cūṛāmaṇi / bīrbāhu* (I.1–2). He comments: 'Both the initial lines and the ones in canto 8 anticipate the final episode, Meghanāda's funeral. With but a few words, Dutt unifies his entire narrative. And those unifying words are drawn from the Bengali *Mahābhārata*.' He acknowledges, however, that M's treatment of the 'warriors' section' is much more detailed and heroic than Kāsirām Dās's.

§598

The exclusion here of souls whose funeral rites (*śrāddha*) have not yet been performed parallels the exclusion of unburied souls in Virgil's eschatology (Dasgupta, p. 127; Clark, p. 349; and see above, §185).

§611f

In the *Āraṇyakāṇḍa* of the *Rāmāyaṇa*, after being received by the sage Agastya, Rām meets Jaṭāyu for the first time:

> On his way Ram saw a formidable bird of very huge size, and thinking it to be a monster he questioned, 'Who art thou?'
>
> Thereupon the bird replied with a sweet voice, 'My boy! I am a friend of your father.'
>
> (*Āraṇyakāṇḍa* III; Sen, p. 168)

Jaṭāyu then gives Rām a full account of his lineage, after which he 'embraced him in delight and bowed to him in respect and heard from him the tales of friendship between his father and the bird.' (Ibid., p. 169) When Jaṭāyu dies after being mortally wounded by Rāvan in his attempt to save Sitā, Rām lights his funeral pyre with words that account for his presence here among the greatest of dead heroes:

> 'O fatherly Jatayu, may you attain that high region that is reached by the heroes who are not afraid of entering the field of battle, that is attained by the giver of lands, by the performers of sacrifices and by those who keep sacred fire always alive in the family. Ah, hero, I am myself setting fire to the pyre, may you attain excellent regions hereafter.'
>
> Saying this, Rama placed Jatayu on the funeral pyre as one would do to his kinsman.
>
> (*Āraṇyakāṇḍa* XXXI; Sen, pp. 221–2)

For Rām to address Jaṭāyu here as 'uncle' (*tāt*) is a mark of his respect for his father's friend.

§661
Seely (1982, p. 476) comments: 'The Bengali *Mahābhārata*'s nether world has a section for divine sages (*deva-ṛṣi*) and holy men (*sannyāsī*, *deva-dvija*). In two passages, it is past the northern gate where they dwell.' M has them 'at the western gate' (*paścim duyāre*).

§686f
Clark writes of this section: 'The luscious beauty of the land they now approached and the jewelled magnificence of its buildings may owe something to St. John's vision of the New Jerusalem [in the Book of Revelation].' (Clark, pp. 349–50)

Dilip was famous for his height: Sanyal (p. 543) quotes a line from Kālidāsa's *Raghuvaṃśa* that also mentions it.

§722
Clark continues: 'Daśaratha's worship seems more reminiscent of a Christian saint making intercessions in heaven than of a Hindu soul awaiting rebirth in *pitṛi-loka*.' (Clark, p. 350)

§742
Rām's moving encounter with his father here closely follows Aeneas's encounter with Anchises: 'When he saw Aeneas coming towards him over the grass, he stretched out both hands in eager welcome, with the tears streaming down both his cheeks, and these were the words that broke from his mouth: "You have come at last," he cried. "I knew your devotion would prevail over all the rigour of the journey and bring you to your father. Am I to be allowed to look upon your face, my son, to hear the voice I know so well

and answer it with my own?' (*Aeneid* VI.684–9; West, p. 134). 'Verbal similarities again are obvious.' (Clark, p. 351)

§759
'I am swimming now in a shoreless sea, father' (*akūl sāgare bhāse dās, tāt, ebe*) echoes *Aeneid* VI.692–3: 'I understand how many lands you have travelled and how many seas you have sailed to come to me here' (West, p. 134; Clark, p. 351)

§759f
Dasarath's instructions for the future now, telling Rām where to find and how to procure the herb that will bring Lakshman back to life, are equivalent to Anchises's grand foretelling of the future of Rome, 'the glory that lies in store for the descendants of Dardanus, for the men of Italian stock who will be our descendants, bright spirits that will inherit our name . . .' (West, p. 136) M took the herb and its application from the traditional *Rāmāyaṇa* story, but for the instructions to come from Dasarath himself is his own innovation.

§795
The restriction of Rām's journey to the underworld to one night was attributed by Clark (p. 351) to the influence of Dante and *Hamlet*, 'where the royal ghost dared not disregard the passage of night.' However Seely (1982, p. 468, 469) points out that Krittibās's *Rāmāyaṇ* 'also stipulates a one-night time restriction in the narrative: Hanumān must resort to holding the sun in his armpit so that it does not rise'. In both Vālmiki and Krittibās the time is filled with an account of Hanumān's fetching of the herbs that will revive Lakshman, with more detail on

this in Krittibās than in Vālmiki. M leaves these details out (see IX.18 and my note on this paragraph, p. 282), and instead interrupts the story with Rām and Māyā's journey.

§800

Here we have M's most heart-rending and haunting adoption from Virgil: Rām's inability to 'touch a shade' exactly follows Aeneas's attempt to embrace Anchises: '"Give me your right hand, father. Give it to me. Do not avoid my embrace." As he spoke these words his cheeks were washed with tears and three times he tried to put his arms around his father's neck. Three times the phantom melted in his hands, as weightless as the wind, as light as flight of sleep.' (West, p. 134) This is not the only place in the *Aeneid* where this poignant idea occurs. In Book II, after Aeneas loses his wife Creusa in his flight from the burning ruins of Troy, he encounters her phantom. She tells him not to grieve for her but to follow his destiny and look after their son: 'Three times I tried to put my arms around her neck. Three times her phantom melted in my arms, as weightless as the wind, as light as the flight of sleep. ' (West, p. 47)

Virgil may have got the idea from Homer. Cf. *Iliad* XXIII.97–101, where the ghost of the dead Patroklus appears to Achilleus in a dream: '"But stand closer to me now: let us embrace each other, if only for a short while, and have our pleasure in the sorrow of tears." So speaking Achilleus reached out with his arms, but could grasp nothing. The ghost vanished away under the earth like smoke, squeaking.' (Hammond, p. 367) The same idea (with 'three times', as in the *Aeneid*) can be found in the *Odyssey*, when Odysseus descends to Hades and meets the ghost of his mother: '. . . my mind was full, and I longed to embrace my dead mother's ghost; three times did I spring forward to her, for the will to clasp her was strong in me; three times she vanished from my arms, like a fleeting shadow, a fleeting dream. Each time keen anguish went through my heart, and my words came forth in rapid flight . . .' (*Odyssey* XI.204–9; Shewring, p. 132)

Book IX

M completes his epic with a book that has no direct source in either Indian or Western tradition. Indrajit's cremation is not described in the *Rāmāyaṇa*, though Rāvan's is, and M has taken some details and something of its tone from that. He has also taken elements from the funeral of Hektor in the *Iliad*, but everything in the book is re-imagined and re-created in a highly original way. As Gargi Datta says (p. 151), 'With its combination of the Indian tradition of suttee [Pramilā's self-immolation on her husband's funeral pyre] and the military funeral rites of the Greeks, the book presents a novel picture indeed.'

§18
The revival of Lakshman through the magic properties of a herb can be compared with the curing of the mortally wounded Aeneas with 'a dittany herb' that—in *Aeneid* XII (West, pp. 275–6)—Venus invisibly brings down from Mount Ida in Crete to add to the medicines that Iapyx is vainly applying—though M certainly didn't need this as a direct source. See above, introductory comments on Book VIII, p. 366.

§28
The seven-day truce is comparable to the nine days of mourning for Hektor, plus two further days for the burial

and funeral feast, that Priam asks of Hektor in *Iliad* XXIV. However, it is Rāvan's minister Sāran who conveys this request to Rām, whereas in the *Iliad*—in one of the most moving passages in all literature—it is the aged King Priam himself who goes to Achilleus.

§70

Sāran's safe passage here has precedents in the western epic tradition. In Tasso's *Jeruslem Delivered* VI.17, for example, a pagan herald is graciously received by Duke Godfrey:

> And when the man before the presence came
> Of princely Godfrey and his captains bold;—
> My Lord, quoth he, may I withouten blame
> Before your grace my message brave unfold?—
> Thou may'st, he answer'd, we approve the same,
> Withouten fear be thine ambassage told . . .
> (Fairfax/ Weiss, p. 137)

§181

Gargi Datta (p. 117) cites this moving passage as an example of the way in which M's shifts some of the moral blame away from Rāvan and the Rākshasas. (See above, IV.628.) Sitā blames herself—'God has given me a tragic destiny'—for the whole catalogue of misfortunes, including the death of Indrajit and the widowhood of Pramilā. Such is her nobility of character that she is able to 'grieve at her enemies' grief'. This capacity is not absent from the Sitā of Vālmiki's *Rāmāyaṇa.* (After Rāvan has been slain, she is sympathetic towards the Rākshasas who guard her, and is described as 'always sorry for the distressed'. Sen, p. 547.) However, Gargi Datta goes on: 'But in the *Rāmāyaṇa* there is no mention of Sitā hearing the news of Indrajit's death; Indrajit is not given so much prominence in the *Rāmāyaṇa*—he is just one among Lankā's many heroes. Sitā is only told about Rāvan's death. After Indrajit's death Rāvan sets off to attack Sitā with his sword. That is what is described in the *Rāmāyaṇa*.' (p. 118)

§209
The funeral procession here has something of the solemn grandeur of the heavenly pageant in Canto XXIX of Dante's *Purgatorio*:

> I saw the slender flames as they advanced,
> leaving the air behind them color-streaked—
> so many streaming pennants overhead!
>
> And thus the sky became a painted flow
> of seven bands of light, all the same shades
> as Delia's cincture or Apollo's bow.
>
> These bands extended farther back than eyes
> could see and all together, I would say,
> they measured, side by side, a good ten strides.
>
> And under that magnificence of Heaven
> came four-and-twenty elders, two by two,
> all of them wearing crowns of fleur-de-lis.
> (*Purgatorio* XXIX.73–84; Musa, p. 311)

But a more direct source must be Rāvan's own funeral procession in the *Rāmāyaṇa*:

> Then, the Rakshas Brahmanas with tearful eyes dressed Ravana with a piece of red silken cloth and placed his body on a golden bier. The bards began

to sing Ravana's praise aloud along with the trumpets' notes; and all raised the bier decorated with flowers and flags and proceeded towards the south. Vibhishana proceeded at the head and the priests followed with fire deposited in vessels. Ladies of the palace followed crying in quick paces. But in faltering gait, on account of the want of the habit of walking.

(*Yuddhakāṇḍa* LXXV; Sen, pp. 544–5)

§251f

Cf. the description in Tasso's *Jerusalem Delivered* of the funeral of Dudon, leader of the group of Crusaders known as the Adventurers. He is killed in Book III by the Circassian warrior Argantes:

Beside the hearse a fruitful palm-tree grows,
  Ennobled since by this great funeral,
Where Dudon's corpse they softly laid in ground;
  The priests sung hymns, the soldiers wept around.
Among the boughs they here and there bestow
  Ensigns and arms, as witness of his praise . . .
(Fairfax/ Weiss, p. 75)

Seely (1991, pp. 147–9) cites the immersion image here, with its associations with Durgā-pujā, as an example of the way in which the reader's responses to *MBK* are complicated by allusions to the stories of Krishna, Durgā and the *Mahābhārata*. See also below, IX.440.

§268

Pramilā's quiet dignity here is very different from Andromache's wild distress at the death of Hektor in *Iliad*

XXII, but the unrestrained sobbing of the 'Raksha women' is like that of the women of Troy who accompany Andromache in her lament. Compare too Tārā's grief at the cremation of her husband Vāli in the *Rāmāyaṇa*. Both she and the other Vānara women weep unrestrainedly. (*Kiṣkindhyākāṇḍa* XX; Sen, p. p. 265–6)

§300
Rāvan's attire maintains his connection with Siva, though his devotion to Siva has not in the end been rewarded. (Gargi Datta, p. 151). In many ways this is the Rāvan as described by Vibhishan in his eulogy at Rāvan's funeral in the *Rāmāyaṇa*—not a malevolent demon but a noble and pious hero whose greatness is acknowledged by Rām himself (see Introduction, p. xcv) in a classic example of *de mortuis nil nisi bonum*:

> Then Vibhishana said with a sorrowful heart, 'Rama! thou hast slain today him whom even the gods could not conquer before. This hero had granted more than what was asked of him, he supported his dependants and friends most liberally; he enjoyed everything that was precious or delicious. He contributed to the prosperity of his friends and to the destruction of his enemies. He was well-versed in the Vedas and Vedangas, a great Yogi and was chief amongst the performers of the Angihotra sacrifice and other rites. Now, if you permit me I may perform his funeral rites.'
>
> Rama was deeply sorry at these words of Vibhishana and with a sad heart said, 'Enmity ends with death. Our end as been gained, now perform

his funeral rites. Know that Ravana was dear to me as he was to you.'

(*Yuddhakāṇḍa* LXXIII; Sen, p. 540)

For the effect of the comparison with Krishna's absence from Gokul, see above, I.623 and III.1, V.369 and VI.621.

§364

It is interesting to compare Pramilā's *satī* with Dido's bitter and grief-stricken suicide at the end of Book IV of the *Aeneid*, after Aeneas has deserted her. In both deaths there is a funeral pyre, with Dido's pretext for building hers her desire to burn Aeneas's armour and other relics, together with their marriage bed and with an effigy of Aeneas on it. Pramilā's motivation and mood as she mounts the pyre are utterly different from Dido's, and the M's sources for the nobility of her *satī* are to be found in Indian, not Western tradition, though there is a contemporary parallel in Brünnhilde's self-immolation at end of Wagner's *Götterdämmerung* (1874) or Isolde's *Liebestod* at the end of *Tristan und Isolde* (1859). See Introduction, p. lxxvi.

§377

Rāvan's great lament (*bilāp*) here over the body of his son can be compared with Mezentius's grief at the death of son Lausus in *Aeneid* X—especially as Mezentius is a brutal Etruscan tyrant who has been overthrown by his people and is being harboured by Aeneas's chief Latin enemy, Turnus (hence the Etruscan king Evander's willingness to side with the invading Trojans). Rāvan, as the king of the demonic Rākshasas and the abductor of Sitā, is similarly brutal and monstrous, yet M shows him to be capable of deep, human feeling. Virgil shows similar insight into Mezentius's feelings, with the difference that he is also penitent—aware of his past crimes in a way that Rāvan is not: 'Was I so besotted with the pleasure of living that I allowed my own son to take my place under my enemy's sword? Is the father to be saved by the wounds of the son? Have you died so that I might live? Now for the first time is death bitter to me! Now for the first time does a wound go deep. And I have ever stained your name, my son, by my crimes . . .' (West, p. 235) One can also look to the lament of Evander at the death of his son Pallas in *Aeneid* XI (West, pp. 242–3).

In the *Iliad*, a possible influence on M here can be found in Achilleus's grief at the death of Patroklus (*Iliad* XIX). As regards Rāvan's determination to blame Fate rather than himself, cf. Agamemnon in *Iliad* XIX.87–92, where he attributes his quarrel with Achilleus to 'Zeus and Fate and Erynis that walks in darkness: they put a cruel blindness in my mind at the assembly on that day when by my own act I took away his prize from Achilleus. But what could I do? It is god who brings all things to their end. This blindness is Ate, eldest daughter of Zeus, the accursed goddess who blinds all men . . . .' (Hammond, p. 313)

In *Paradise Lost* we can find an analogy in Satan's despair at the prospect of Eden at the beginning of Book IV:

All hope excluded thus, behold instead
Of us outcast, exiled, his new delight,
Mankind created, and for him this world.
So farewell hope, and with hope farewell fear,
Farewell remorse: all good to me is lost . . .
(*Paradise Lost* IV.105–90)

Rāvan too is bidding farewell to hope, but whereas Satan in bidding farewell to remorse as well indicates that he does feel some remorse, Rāvan, as a Rākshas, has no conception that he has done anything wrong. See Introduction, p. lv.

Some readers, however, will feel no need to go to Western sources, for, as Gargi Datta (pp. 153–4) points out, in tone and style Rāvan's speech is very similar to his lament at the death of Indrajit in the *Rāmāyaṇa*. She comments: 'In the language of this lament there is no ornament, and M's language too is not lit up with elaborate imagery. The language is as simple as sobs of heart-rending grief, and the sentences are short and touching to the heart.'

> Ravana at once fell unconscious at this cruel news of his son's death. When he regained his sense, he became overwhelmed with grief. His mind became restless. Ravana then began to lament in grief, 'Alas, my boy! you conquered Indra, but how could you be slain by Lakshmana's arrows? O foremost of heroes! what to speak of Lakshmana, in your wrath you could pierce even Death himself with arrows, and could crush the peaks of the Mandara into atoms. When you die, Yama, the god of death appears to be powerful to me. Who dies in the service of his master, repairs to heaven; this is the way with the great warriors on earth. Surely you have repaired to heaven. This day the Suras and Asuras will sleep in peace, seeing Indrajit thus slain. Without Indrajit my eyes appear to have lost their vision. Today in my harem I shall hear the cries of the Rakshasa women like that of the cow-elephants in the

> mountain cave. Alas, my boy! whither hast thou gone, leaving the throne, Lanka, Rakshasas, your wife and myself? O hero! you were to perform my funeral rite, whereas I shall have to perform that of yours! Alas, Rama, Lakshmana, Sugriva and others are still alive; whither hast thou gone without removing those thorns in our sides?'
>
> (*Yuddhakāṇḍa* LXIV; Sen, p. 518)

Whatever these various literary sources and analogues, M had an emotional source much nearer to hand: his own famous autobiographical poem, *Ātma-bilāp* ('Self-lament', 1861), which begins: 'Dazed by the tricks of hope, what, I wonder, what fruits have I gained?' See pp. cxv–cxvi, and Introduction, p. xxiv.

§415
Note that Siva in *MBK* retains his sympathy for Meghnād, Rāvan and the Rākshasas right to the end, even though he has (ever since Book II.425) accepted the inevitability of their punishment. Cf. Zeus's abiding sympathy for Hektor in *Iliad* XX.168–72, where he accepts the inevitability of Achilleus's slaughter of Hektor—and gives Athene a free hand—but with heaviness in his heart: '"Oh, I love this man who is being pursued round the wall under the gaze of my eyes. My heart is saddened for Hektor, who has burned the thigh-bones of many oxen to me on the peaks of valleyed Ida, and again on the city's height."' (Hammond, p. 355)

§440
Seely (1991, p. 148) emphasizes the importance of the Durgā-pujā simile here, as part of his argument that 'Dutt's

epic poem tells not one tale but four tales simultaneously, with the three subordinate stories—three of the most prominent tales in Bengali Hinduism—running counter and subtly undermining the dominant Rāma story.' (Ibid., p. 138)

INDEX

This index is limited to the characters and plot of *Meghnādbadh kābya*. It does not include places (except Lankā), or names mentioned only in similes and allusions or in the Notes, Source Notes and Introduction. Sanskrit spellings are given in brackets where they differ from the transliteration used in the translation.

MĀTALI
brings Indra's chariot II.109
supplies Indra with a new chariot VII.631

MĀYĀ
receives Indra in her temple II.475
gives Indra the weapons that will defeat Meghnād II.491
tells him to give the weapons to Lakshman II.491
promises to protect Lakshman II.491
arrives at Indra's palace V.29
tells Indra that she will guide Lakshman so that he can kill Meghnād V.61
leaves Indra and Sachi V.91
emerges from heaven and calls Svapna-devi V.109
tells Svapna-devi to go to Lakshman in the guise of his mother Sumitrā to tell him to go to the Chanḍi-temple V.113
speaks to Lakshman in the Chanḍi-temple V.342
tells Lakshman how she will make him invisible so that he can enter the Nikumbhilā grove and kill Meghnād V.342
enters Lakshmi's temple dressed as a Rākshas wife VI.246
asks Lakshmi to withdraw her protection from the Rākshasas so that Lakshman can kill Meghnād VI.251
ascends the city wall with Lakshmi to watch Lakshman and Vibhishan advancing VI.288
allows Lakshman and Vibhishan to enter the Nikumbhilā temple invisibly VI.413
deflects the *pūjā*-equipment that Meghnād hurls at Lakshman
speeds towards Lankā carrying a trident VIII.113
tells Rām she will take him to Yamapuri to meet Dasarath VIII.134
leads Rām through a tunnel to underworld VIII.158
explains what the bridge over the Vaitarani river signifies VIII.185
wards off Yama's envoy with her trident VIII.199
explains the significance of the burning lake VIII.313